SCIENTIFIC BASIS OF
DRUG DEPENDENCE

BIOLOGICAL COUNCIL
THE CO-ORDINATING COMMITTEE FOR SYMPOSIA
ON DRUG ACTION

SCIENTIFIC BASIS OF DRUG DEPENDENCE

A Symposium

Edited by
HANNAH STEINBERG
Reader in Psychopharmacology
University College London

With illustrations

J. & A. CHURCHILL LTD.
104 Gloucester Place, London
1969

Standard Book Number
7000 1394 6

© J. & A. Churchill Ltd. 1969

All Rights Reserved. No part of this publication may be reproduced, stored in a retrieval system, or transmitted, in any form or by any means, electronic, mechanical, photocopying, recording or otherwise, without the prior permission of the copyright owner.

Printed in Great Britain at the Pitman Press, Bath

PREFACE

Drug taking and drug dependence are complex, controversial and apparently increasing. This symposium shows how scientists of many disciplines are tackling many interesting and urgent problems. It ranges from the by no means straightforward matter of definitions and general principles of approach to laboratory experiments and clinical and social factors. Opiates, the traditional drugs of dependence, have been joined by barbiturates, amphetamines, cocaine, cannabis and others, and also by alcohol, the traditional socially accepted drug. These drugs differ greatly in their pharmacological properties, and we are still a long way from knowing how far these properties are responsible for dependence and how far explanations must be sought elsewhere. Nevertheless, as the title of the symposium implies, there is already enough evidence to suggest a scientific basis. A good deal of this evidence is set out and discussed here.

The symposium was organized by a committee consisting of P. H. Connell, G. Edwards, C. R. B. Joyce, E. Marley, H. McIlwain (*chairman*), J. L. Mongar, W. D. M. Paton, A. V. S. de Reuck, H. Steinberg (*hon. secretary*), G. I. M. Swyer and C. W. M. Wilson, and was sponsored by the British Pharmacological Society, the Association of Medical Advisers in the Pharmaceutical Industry, the Biochemical Society, the British Medical Association, the British Neuropathological Society, the British Psycho-analytical Society, the British Psychological Society, the British Society for Cell Biology, the Chemical Society, the Experimental Psychology Society, the Laboratory Animals Centre, the Pharmaceutical Society of Great Britain, the Physiological Society, the Royal Institute of Chemistry, the Royal Medico-Psychological Association, the Royal Society of Medicine, the Society for Drug

Research and the Society for the Study of Addiction. It was held in the Edward Lewis Theatre of the Middlesex Hospital Medical School, London, in April 1968, and some 450 people attended. The committee are grateful to the Medical School for facilities, to the Wellcome Trust for a generous grant and to the Ciba Foundation for hospitality for overseas visitors.

I thank Miss G. Blunt and Mrs. L. Exton for help with organizing the symposium, Miss M. Lindley for her editorial assistance and Mr. A. S. Knightley of J. & A. Churchill Ltd, for his co-operation in the business of book production.

H.S.

CONTENTS

Session I: **Definitions and Approaches**
Chairman: W. D. M. PATON

	PAGE
Chairman's Introduction	3
Introduction: Definitions and Perspectives: *Aubrey Lewis*	5
Psychological Functions of Drug Use: *Isidor Chein*	13
A Pharmacological Approach to Drug Dependence and Drug Tolerance: *W. D. M. Paton*	31
Humoral Transmitters, Supersensitivity, Receptors and Dependence: *H. O. J. Collier*	49
Withdrawal Phenomena as Manifestations of Disuse Supersensitivity: *Seth Sharpless* and *Jerome Jaffe*	67
Is there a Relationship between Protein Synthesis and Tolerance to Analgesic Drugs? *B. M. Cox* and *M. Ginsburg*	77
DISCUSSION: *Dean, Graham, Chein, McLean, Kosterlitz, Collier, Neal, Paton, Brown* and *Steinberg*	86

Session II: **Pharmacology and Biochemistry**
Chairman: H. MCILWAIN

Chairman's Introduction	95
The Relationship of the Disposition and Metabolism of Morphine in the CNS to Tolerance: *S. J. Mulé*	97
Tolerance to Barbiturates by Increased Breakdown: *H. Remmer*	111

	PAGE
Distribution and Metabolism in Man of Some Narcotic Analgesics and Some 'Amphetamines': *A. H. Beckett*	129
Development of New Potent Analgesics: *Paul A. J. Janssen*	149
Search for Addiction in a New Analgesic: *J. Madinaveitia*	155
DISCUSSION: *McLean, Mulé, Remmer, Beckett, Ginsburg, Collier, Madinaveitia, Lister, Lewis, Paton, Kumar, Richter, Neal, McIlwain* and *Janssen*	165

Session III: Laboratory Studies of Animal and Human Behaviour

Chairman: HANNAH STEINBERG

Chairman's Introduction	175
Drug Self-Administration and Conditioning: *Travis Thompson* and *Roy Pickens*	177
Psychogenic Dependence in Monkeys: *Gerald A. Deneau*	199
How Rats Can Become Dependent on Morphine in the Course of Relieving Another Need: *R. Kumar, Hannah Steinberg* and *I. P. Stolerman*	209
An Analysis of the Mechanisms Involved in the Taste for Drink: *C. W. M. Wilson*	221
APPENDIX: Cannabis and Alcohol: Is there a Scientific Basis for Comparison?	237
Addictive Drugs Cause Suppression of Paradoxical Sleep with Withdrawal Rebound: *Ian Oswald, J. I. Evans* and *S. A. Lewis*	243
An Experimental Approach to the Examination of Drinking Patterns of Alcoholics: *Nancy K. Mello, Jack H. Mendelson* and *H. Brian McNamee*	259
Quantitative Estimates of Dependence on the Symbolic Function of Drugs: *C. R. B. Joyce*	271

DISCUSSION: *Hinde, Thompson, Deneau, Kumar, Malleson, Pickersgill, McNamee, Rosenthal, Collier, Joyce* and *Paton* 280

Session IV: **Social and Clinical Factors**
Chairman: SIR DENIS HILL

Chairman's Introduction 286

Drug Dependence in Great Britain: A Challenge to the Practice of Medicine: *P. H. Connell* . . . 291

The Natural History of Drug Dependence: Some Comparative Observations on United Kingdom and United States Subjects: *J. H. Willis* . . . 301

The Assessment of Heroin Usage in a Provincial Community: *J. Zacune, G. Stimson, A. Ogborne, M. Mitcheson* and *A. Kosviner* 323

Observations on Heroin Abuse by Young People in Crawley New Town: *R. de Alarcon, N. H. Rathod* and *I. G. Thomson* 331

The Natural History of Urban Narcotic Drug Addiction—Some Determinants: *George E. Vaillant* . . . 341

Stabilized Addiction and Normal Drinking in Recovered Alcohol Addicts: *D. L. Davies* 363

Non-Dependent Drug Use: Some Psychological Aspects: *Beryl A. Geber* 375

    Appendix 1: Drug use grid 388

    Appendix 2: Use of amphetamines . . . 390

The Phoenix House Therapeutic Community: An Overview: *Mitchell S. Rosenthal* 395

DISCUSSION: *Oswald, Vaillant, Hill, de Alarcon, Zacune, Willis, Neal, Rosenthal, Mullin, Connell, Richter* and *Wartburg* 409

PARTICIPANTS

List of chairmen (C), speakers and their co-authors, and participants in the discussions.

The affiliations and addresses are those current at the time of the Symposium.

A. H. BECKETT	Department of Pharmacy, Chelsea College of Science and Technology, London, S.W.3.
D. A. BROWN	Pharmacology Department, St. Bartholomew's Hospital Medical College, London, E.C.1.
I. CHEIN	Research Center for Human Relations, New York University, 21 Washington Place, New York, N.Y. U.S.A.
H. O. J. COLLIER	Department of Pharmacological Research, Parke-Davis & Co., Hounslow, Middlesex.
P. H. CONNELL	Institute of Psychiatry, Maudsley Hospital, Denmark Hill, London, S.E.5.
B. M. COX	Department of Pharmacology, Chelsea College of Science and Technology, London, S.W.3.

PARTICIPANTS

D. L. DAVIES   Maudsley Hospital,
                   Denmark Hill, London, S.E.5.

R. de ALARCON   Graylingwell Hospital,
                   Chichester, Sussex.

A. C. R. DEAN   Physical Chemistry Laboratory,
                   University of Oxford,
                   South Parks Road, Oxford.

G. A. DENEAU   Kettering-Meyer Laboratories,
                   Southern Research Institute,
                   2000 Ninth Avenue South,
                   Birmingham 5,
                   Alabama, U.S.A.

J. I. EVANS   University Department of Psychiatry,
                   Royal Edinburgh Hospital,
                   Edinburgh 10.

BERYL A. GEBER   Department of Psychology,
                   London School of Economics and
                   Political Science,
                   Houghton Street, London, W.C.2.

M. GINSBURG   Department of Pharmacology,
                   Chelsea College of Science and Technology, London, S.W.3.

J. D. P. GRAHAM   Department of Pharmacology,
                   Institute of Preventive Medicine,
                   The Parade, Cardiff.

PARTICIPANTS

Sir Denis Hill (C)	Institute of Psychiatry, Maudsley Hospital, Denmark Hill, London, S.E.5.
R. A. Hinde	Sub-Department of Animal Behaviour, Department of Zoology, University of Cambridge, High Street, Madingley, Cambridge
J. Joffe	Albert Einstein College of Medicine, Department of Pharmacology, Yeshiva University, Eastchester Road and Morris Park Avenue, Bronx, N.Y. 10461, U.S.A.
P. A. J. Janssen	Research Laboratoria, Janssen Pharmaceutica, Beerse, Belgium.
C. R. B. Joyce	Department of Pharmacology and Therapeutics, London Hospital Medical College, Turner Street, London, E.1.
H. W. Kosterlitz	Physiology Department, University of Aberdeen, Marischal College, Aberdeen, AB9 1AS.
A. Kosviner	Addiction Unit, Maudsley Hospital, Denmark Hill, London, S.E.5.
R. Kumar	Department of Pharmacology, University College London, Gower Street, London, W.C.1.

Sir AUBREY LEWIS	Institute of Psychiatry, Maudsley Hospital, Denmark Hill, London, S.E.5.
S. A. LEWIS	University Department of Psychiatry, Royal Edinburgh Hospital, Edinburgh 10.
R. E. LISTER	Arthur D. Little, Ltd., Inveresk Gate, Musselburgh, Midlothian, Scotland.
H. McILWAIN (C)	Department of Biochemistry, Institute of Psychiatry, Maudsley Hospital, Denmark Hill, London, S.E.5.
A. E. M. McLEAN	Department of Experimental Pathology, University College Hospital Medical School, University Street, London, W.C.1.
H. B. McNAMEE	Department of Psychiatry, University of Dundee, Dundee, Scotland.
J. MADINAVEITIA	Pharmaceutical Division, ICI Ltd., Alderley Edge, Macclesfield, Cheshire.
N. MALLESON	Student Health Service, University of London, 2 Woburn Square, London, W.C.1.
NANCY K. MELLO	National Center for Prevention and Control of Alcoholism, National Institute of Mental Health, Chevy Chase, Maryland, U.S.A.

PARTICIPANTS

J. H. Mendelson	National Center for Prevention and Control of Alcoholism, National Institute of Mental Health, Chevy Chase, Maryland, U.S.A.
M. Mitcheson	Addiction Research Unit, Maudsley Hospital, Denmark Hill, London, S.E.5.
S. J. Mulé	Addiction Research Center, National Institute of Mental Health, P.O. Box 2000, Lexington, Kentucky 40501, U.S.A.
P. Mullin	Department of Psychological Medicine, Southern General Hospital, Glasgow, S.W.1.
M. J. Neal	Department of Pharmacology, University of Cambridge, Downing Street, Cambridge.
A. Ogborne	Addiction Research Unit, Maudsley Hospital, Denmark Hill, London. S.E.5.
I. Oswald	University Department of Psychiatry, Royal Edinburgh Hospital, Edinburgh 10.
W. D. M. Paton (C)	Department of Pharmacology, University of Oxford, South Parks Road, Oxford.
R. Pickens	Department of Psychiatry and Neurology, University of Minnesota, Minneapolis, Minnesota, U.S.A.

PARTICIPANTS

MARY PICKERSGILL	Department of Psychology, Bedford College, Regent's Park, London, N.W.1.
N. H. RATHOD	Graylingwell Hospital, Chichester, Sussex.
H. REMMER	Institute of Toxicology, University of Tübingen, Germany.
D. RICHTER	Medical Research Council, Neuropsychiatric Research Unit, Woodmansterne Road, Carshalton, Surrey.
M. S. ROSENTHAL	Addiction Services Agency, Human Resources Administration, 250 Broadway, New York, N.Y., 10007, U.S.A.
S. K. SHARPLESS	Albert Einstein College of Medicine, Department of Pharmacology, Yeshiva University, Eastchester Road and Morris Park Avenue, Bronx, N.Y., 10461, U.S.A.
HANNAH STEINBERG (C)	Department of Pharmacology, University College London, Gower Street, London, W.C.1.
I. P. STOLERMAN	Department of Pharmacology, University College London, Gower Street, London, W.C.1.

T. Thompson	Department of Psychiatry and Neurology, University of Minnesota, Minneapolis, Minnesota, U.S.A.
I. G. Thomson	Graylingwell Hospital, Chichester, Sussex.
G. E. Vaillant	Department of Psychiatry, Tufts University School of Medicine, Boston, Mass. 0211, U.S.A.
W. P. von Wartburg	Roche Laboratories, Basel, Switzerland.
J. H. Willis	York Clinic, Guy's Hospital, London, S.E.1.
C. W. M. Wilson	Department of Pharmacology, University of Dublin, Trinity College, Dublin 2.
J. Zacune	Addiction Research Unit, Maudsley Hospital, Denmark Hill, London, S.E.5.

Session I

DEFINITIONS AND APPROACHES

Chairman: W. D. M. PATON

CHAIRMAN'S INTRODUCTION

OPENING the first session, I suggested as a working definition the following: that drug dependence arises when, as a result of giving a drug, forces—physiological, biochemical, social or environmental—are set up which predispose to continued drug use. It must be confessed that, both in this definition, and in the planning of the session, considerable prominence was given to the role played by physiological and biochemical mechanisms, with the withdrawal syndrome particularly in mind. Yet one of the most important outcomes of the whole symposium has been the evidence, both in animals and man, that strong dependence can arise even though there is little or no evidence of the classical withdrawal syndrome when administration of a drug ceases. Thus, although in four of the papers several interesting approaches to the withdrawal syndrome are surveyed, the central issue of drug dependence has shifted elsewhere and seems to lie in the nature of the primary 'reward' which the drug provides.

By a second, analogous shift of emphasis, the opiates are losing their too dominant position in scientific investigation, and the relevance of drugs such as cocaine, the amphetamines and the barbiturates, with different pharmacology yet equally capable of inducing dependence, is being recognized. This in turn brings the suspicion that any unitary theory of drug dependence, if it is to cover so diverse a range of drugs, is for the time being likely to be either misleading or too vague for usefulness.

Finally, when one turns to the psychological and social factors predisposing to dependence, a third re-orientation is called for, arising from the recognition that these factors differ widely in different countries, varying not only with cultural differences, but with quite simple differences in formulation and accessibility of illicit drugs. Enough is already known to make it clear that drug-dependence in the U.K. has its own characteristics and must be studied in its own right, and that prediction from experience in other countries cannot be relied on.

So far as an understanding of drug dependence itself is concerned, therefore, one looks first to a combination of experimental animal psychology and neurophysiology to define the neurological mechanisms involved in 'reward', and to social psychology to define the reinforcing factors of the environment. But the analysis of the pharmacological actions of particular drugs, of tolerance and of the withdrawal syndromes (perhaps discriminated more delicately, and individually characterized for each drug) remains important. Knowledge of detailed mechanisms of synaptic action may well prove essential when an understanding of the neurological processes involved in reward has been obtained, and control of these processes is attempted; and it is already obvious that withdrawal symptoms can be a useful diagnostic tool, and are likely to remain so until methods for determination of opiates in tissues are much improved. The investigator interested in dependence as it occurs in practice will, however, need to be mentally nimble. In a short time we have had to learn to take intravenous amphetamines as seriously as the opiates; and there is no reason to suppose that synthetic or natural chemistry may not have further shocks in store.

INTRODUCTION: DEFINITIONS AND PERSPECTIVES

AUBREY LEWIS

Institute of Psychiatry, Maudsley Hospital, London

SINCE this symposium is about drug dependence, it is perhaps useful to consider at the outset the meaning of the term and its recent historical background. Semantic niceties are often unwelcome in scientific discussion, but some weighty and authoritative committees have thought it very important to get the right words for this condition or, as one might call it, this form of servitude.

The term which it superseded was 'drug addiction', itself recent. The Departmental Committee on Morphine and Heroin addiction, which reported in 1926, defined an addict as "a person who, not requiring the continued use of a drug for the relief of the symptoms of organic disease, has acquired, as a result of repeated administration, an overpowering desire for its continuance, and in whom withdrawal of the drug leads to definite symptoms of mental or physical distress or disorder". Here, the person is defined, not the condition and, strictly interpreted, it would seem that those who develop an overmastering craving for, say, morphine which they are being given for the relief of pain due to organic disease, are excluded from among the addicts. A less narrow but more colourful definition, put forward in 1935, was that "addiction is a state of bondage to a masterful drug, usually, but not always, of the narcotic class, and is manifested by craving, tolerance, intense discomfort of a specialized type on withdrawal of the drug, and tendency to relapse".

When the World Health Organization tackled the problem

some fifteen years ago, they ruled that a distinction must be drawn between addiction and habituation, and that "only the expressions drug addiction and addiction-producing drugs should be used in documentation with respect to substances brought under, or to be brought under, international control". In a gloss on this, they boldly asserted that "there are some drugs, notably morphine ... whose specific pharmacological action, under individual conditions of time and dose, will always produce compulsive craving, dependence and addiction in any individual ... Sooner or later there must come a time when the use of the drug cannot be interrupted without significant disturbance, always psychic (psychological) and sometimes physical. Such drugs ... must be rigidly controlled". They go on to declare that "there are other drugs which never produce compulsive craving, yet their pharmacological action is found desirable to some individuals to the point that they readily form a habit ... They do not need rigid control. There are some drugs whose pharmacological action is intermediate in kind and degree between the two groups ..." In that first pronouncement by the World Health Organization, dependence was referred to loosely in passing, without emphasis.

Five years later (1957), a World Health Organization report dealt with the matter more summarily. Declaring that there are many and widely divergent views on what constitutes an addiction; and that the point at which drug use becomes drug addiction depends to quite an extent on the orientation of the observer, they define an addict as "a person who habitually and compulsively uses any narcotic drug so as directly to endanger his own or others' health, safety, or welfare". In this definition, the emphasis had been shifted to underline a social implication—the harm an addict may do to others. As a rule this is not included among the characteristics of addiction, though it is the main reason for interfering with the addict's freedom of action.

In 1961 an Interdepartmental Committee, of which Lord

Brain was Chairman, defined drug addiction as a state of periodic or chronic intoxication produced by the repeated consumption of a drug and showing five specified characteristics, one of which was "a psychological and physical dependence on the effects of the drug"; whereas drug habituation included among its characteristics "some degree of psychological dependence on the effect of the drug, but absence of physical dependence and hence of an abstinence syndrome".

Meanwhile the World Health Organization Expert Committee had been having second thoughts. They noted that their effort to differentiate addiction from habituation had not proved workable; and they proposed, in 1964, to use only one term, 'drug dependence', which could be applied to drug abuse generally. This is the dispensation under which we now live and hold symposia.

The Expert Committee emphasized that the description of drug dependence as a state is a concept for clarification and not, in any sense, a specific definition. They recognized five types of dependence, respectively related to morphine, barbiturate, cocaine, amphetamine and cannabis. They added that "alcohol is outside the terms of reference of the Committee, but is nevertheless an agent that can admittedly cause psychic and physical dependence". Psychological dependence was characteristic of all of the five types enumerated, but physical dependence, they recognized, occurred only in the morphine-like and barbiturate-like types (and, of course, alcohol).

Physical dependence is more fully described in the report as "requiring the presence of the drug for maintenance of homeostasis and resulting in a definite, characteristic and self-limited abstinence syndrome when the drug is withdrawn". In psychic dependence (1965) "there is a feeling of satisfaction, and a psychic drive that require periodic or continuous administration of the drug to produce pleasure or to avoid discomfort".

The criterion, therefore, of physical dependence on a drug

was taken to be the development of a withdrawal syndrome—an objective criterion; and the criterion of psychological dependence was taken to be a desire or need to take the drug, together with subjective appreciation of its effects. The characteristics of psychological dependence can, therefore, only be inferred from the statements and behaviour of the affected person; they may be heavily influenced by his candour, veracity and general psychological state and by the prevailing social outlook.

Physical dependence, for a given individual and a given dose pattern, usually takes an invariable form. Psychological dependence can vary according to the internal state of the individual and his circumstances at the time. No doubt craving is a real experience, but it is very hard to measure and state its limits.

In 1965 four experts who have played a prominent part in the study of narcotic drugs, prepared a statement on behalf of the World Health Organization. They emphasized that physical and psychological dependence on a particular drug may both develop, but that psychological dependence "can and does develop, especially with stimulant-type drugs, without any evidence of physical dependence and, therefore, without an abstinence syndrome developing after drug withdrawal". They also pointed out, less convincingly, that "physical dependence too can be induced without notable psychic dependence". Psychic dependence, according to them, is related to pharmacological action but is more particularly a manifestation of the individual's reaction to the effects of the specific drug—a nice distinction, somewhat hard to sustain.

It seems reasonable to conclude that once the abstinence syndrome has been adequately described for a particular category of drugs, it can be confidently applied, and is serviceable: but that the stated indicators of psychological dependence are too woolly to enable the term to be used with precision and uniformity. A hypochondriac, for example, may regularly take large quantities of salicylate for the relief, say, of headache, declaring that he has a desire and a need to take it and that he "has subjective appreciation of its effects". It therefore conforms to the requirement specified for a drug which can produce psychological dependence. If this be conceded, it can be extended to apply to any drug which a hysteric may habitually take, or an obsessional feel compelled to have recourse to in order to relieve tension. Indeed, it goes further, and must be applied in the case of, for example, psychogenic polydipsia—a disorder easily mistaken for diabetes insipidus—in which the hysterical or obsessional patient, though physically healthy, has to consume very large quantities of water—water which we must then, I suppose, regard as a drug of dependence.

However, as I said at the outset, semantic issues are not in high favour when scientific problems are under discussion and it is well to agree that, for the time being anyhow, the terms and definitions promulgated by the World Health Organization are reasonable working tools. The important thing, at this stage of our ignorance, is not precise definition but the study of detailed issues, such as this symposium is concerned with. At the same time, the needs of the epidemiologist must be recognized. Assessment and comparison of the amount of drug misuse in given countries or regions is hampered if there is confusion about the significance of the governing terms. This handicap has a damaging effect on psycho-social research in particular. Because psycho-social issues bulk so large in the study of drugs, an exact meaning of psychological dependence needs to be devised and agreed upon.

It is informative to compare the situation as it is today with the situation that prevailed at the beginning of the century. Now the drugs which are mainly causing concern are grouped in six types—according to their similarity to morphine, barbiturate, alcohol, cocaine, cannabis and amphetamine; some would add LSD and khat. Sixty or seventy years ago, the list embraced four of these, viz. morphia, alcohol, cannabis and cocaine, and, in addition, chloroform, ether, chloral, sulphonal, phenacetin, tobacco (as a stimulant and intoxicant), and tea and coffee. Alcohol and morphine, then as now, were given major consideration.

At that time, the principle of classification was not dependence but toxic effect on the central nervous system. Hence the inclusion of tea and coffee, then credited with more severe damage than was justified. Tobacco was included because it produced, in some people, "a peculiar psychological state in which hallucinations of sight and hearing obtain, and in which the patient passes through psychical waves of excitation and depression". The results of excessive coffee are painted in alarming colours: "the sufferer is tremulous and loses his self-command; he is subject to fits of agitation and depression. He has a haggard appearance ... As with other such agents, a renewed dose of the poison gives temporary relief, but at the cost of future misery". Tea is no better: "Tea has appeared to us to be especially efficient in producing nightmares with ... hallucinations which may be alarming in their intensity. Another peculiar quality of tea is to produce a strange and extreme degree of physical depression. An hour or two after breakfast at which tea has been taken ... a grievous sinking ... may seize upon a sufferer, so that to speak is an effort ... The speech may become weak and vague ... By miseries such as these, the best years of life may be spoilt".

I quote these passages not to amuse you (though that would be a proper aim after the tedious disquisition on terminology), but to point to the likelihood that some of the statements now made about canabis and other drugs much in the public eye, may seem to our successors overwrought. These drugs are, in some cases, suffused with a certain glamour (LSD is a good example), and, in other cases, violently reprobated on emotional rather than objective grounds. This is a recurring feature of the drug landscape. The writers I have just been quoting about tea and coffee were among the most eminent of their day—Clifford Allbutt, the Regius Professor at Cambridge, and W. E. Dixon, whose standing as a pharmacologist is well known. They were the mouthpieces of enlightened opinion, and the problems that troubled them have a bearing on some of our own uncertainties. Thus, while fully aware of the miseries and harm entailed by the misuse of opium, they looked abroad and then at home, and wrote "opium is used, rightly or wrongly, in many oriental countries, not as an idle or a vicious indulgence, but as a reasonable aid in the work of life. A patient of one of us took a grain of opium in a pill every morning and every evening of the last fifteen years of a long, laborious and distinguished career. A man of great force of character, concerned in affairs of weight and of national importance, and of stainless character, he persisted in this habit, as being one which gave him no conscious gratification or diversion, but which toned and strengthened him for his deliberations and engagements ... The habit had arisen on the not improper advice of a physican who found him liable to intermittent ... glycosuria. The opium was continued, however, not on this account but for its own sake."

So rare and atypical an observation has no place as a guide to policy or treatment. It does, however, serve as a reminder that although we classify the dependent drugs according to a small number of types, there is immense individual variation in their pharmacological, and even more in their psychological and social, effects: and perhaps also that we may sometimes be too ready to adopt the prevalent distinctions between what are thought to be very harmful and what are thought to be comparatively innocuous drugs. The gradations of danger between consuming tea and coffee at one end of the scale and injecting heroin intravenously at the other, may not be permanently those which we now assign to particular drugs, and on which legislative action may be based. Amphetamine, for instance, and barbiturate move up the scale; cannabis moves down: and although alcohol retains its high place as a potentially ruinous poison, its abuse is not visited with the dire legal penalties held over the head of less damaging substances.

PSYCHOLOGICAL FUNCTIONS OF DRUG USE

Isidor Chein

Research Center for Human Relations, New York University

WHEN a chemical agent is involved in human misbehaviour, many of us tend to become preoccupied with the chemical and overlook the misbehaving human. Thus, there are still many who regard the problem of obesity in the relatively simplistic terms of an imbalance between caloric intake and caloric output. To correct the condition, they tamper with the furnace, throw in some chemicals to improve the efficiency of combustion, or prescribe a dietary regimen to bring the caloric intake into line with the output. When the treatment fails, they throw up their hands in disgust, adopt a self-righteous stance, and accuse the patient of wilful self-indulgence and characterological defects. They have little patience with or understanding for the possibilities that (1) misbehaviours of food intake or the most manifest consequences of such misbehaviours may have a bearing on the total psychological economy of the patient and (2) the issue of caloric balance may, as such, call for little attention in either understanding or correcting the misbehaviour.

The analogy to misbehaviours involving non-alimentary chemicals, if less than perfect, ought nevertheless to be clear. When a person habitually misbehaves with respect to the intake of drugs, attention tends to be focused on the chemical and not on the person. It is assumed that the effect of the chemical as such is the most relevant and perhaps the only relevant factor explaining the misbehaviour. One may, for instance, assume that the effect is universally overwhelmingly attractive so that individual personalities are irrelevant.

misbehaviour; and (3) those associated with meanings of drugs and drug misbehaviour which are not subsumed under the first two classes.

In the case of functions associated with psychopharmacological properties of drugs we must distinguish between the direct psychic effects and the meanings with which these effects are invested; functions that depend on these meanings are class (3) and not class (1) functions. Thus, if I read the data correctly, the direct effect of a drug like LSD is no different when it leads to an experience of nightmarish terror than when it leads to one of mystical revelation. In both cases, the direct psychopharmacological effect seems to be one of profound distortion of sensory and perceptual processes. Such distortion must indeed be terrifying to one who has not at least temporarily relinquished his normal this-worldly base of operations and concerns. Terror is the normal reaction to the sudden loss of moorings, to finding oneself in an unstructured situation in which sensori-perceptual data become totally unreliable as cues to conduct. Mystical experience, by contrast, requires a total self-absorption in the experience of the moment, a total divorce from any other concerns; and the greater the novelty of the experience in these conditions, the greater the feeling of exposure to mystical revelation. In either condition, a weaving pattern of light (the primary drug effect) may be interpreted as a writhing serpent. With normal concerns intact, the serpent may represent a threat to one's security; in successful absorption with immediate experience there can be no threat and the serpent may represent the mandala, one of the prime if not very profound secrets of the universe, and what a revelation it is to discover that a circle need not after all close in on itself! To assure the mystical experience rather than the nightmare, however, requires careful staging especially for the relatively naive subject and the build-up of the mood of absorption in immediate experience.

Let me illustrate some functions associated with direct psychopharmacological effects of drugs. A young man is going out with his girl. There is a demand character in this situation that the young man should surrender some of his normal reserve; but the latter may serve defensive functions so that the situation is frightening. Or the young man may suffer from certain inhibitions that are dysfunctional in this situation. Or the prospective relation with the girl may be a drab and pallid imitation of what he yearns for in his romantic dreams. Consider, now, what three drugs—heroin, alcohol, and marijuana—have to offer him. In appropriate doses, heroin offers him detachment from his troubles, a separation of the observing and active self from the self that is immersed in the activities of the world; it affords him a position of immunity, an observer's post where he cannot be touched while he maintains the illusion of engagement with his girl. Alcohol offers some lessening of inhibitions, some danger of the emergence of impulses—e.g. homosexual or hostile—which he cannot control, no security against the demands of intimacy, and perhaps enough clouding of consciousness so that he does not apprehend the terrors of his situation too clearly. Marijuana offers the promise of dressing a drab affair with an exotic aura that stems mainly from distortion of the sense of subjective time. All three drugs are interchangeable to the degree that they mask or mitigate our young man's ineptitude; but none would be relevant were there not the need to mitigate the ineptitude in the first place, and one would be more functional than another depending on the source of ineptitude or difficulty that most needs mitigating.

Obviously, too, there are kinds of needs that are not entailed in the rather trivial example I have just cited. Alcohol is hardly appropriate when one's problem is the management of aggression—unless, that is, one drinks oneself into oblivion, and oblivion is an acceptable way out. Nor is marijuana very useful if it is the drabness of one's total existence that requires masking. Similarly, if inordinate ambition has led a physician to overextend his practice and prevents the retraction of the practice to manageable limits, an opiate is the drug of choice in making the resulting tension tolerable. Alcohol not only interferes more markedly with the efficiency of performance but is more readily detected by one's patients. Moreover, the detachment from one's activities and condition which is the characteristic primary effect of opiates in suitable doses actually facilitates this type of medical practice. The use of one's career as an instrumentality of one's ambition rather than as a mode of self-expression is protected by alienation from the activities involved; otherwise, there is the danger of becoming engaged (in the existentialist sense of the term) with these activities and the engagement may demand a change in the pattern of their conduct. Detachment is, of course, a mode of alienation.

The particular psychopharmacological effects of any particular drug are irrelevant to the second class of functions of drug use. Associated with the use of drugs are the activities of procuring the drug, preparations for administration, and so on. Some of these activities or the entire process may lend themselves to the fulfilment of certain functions.

For example, it is a fairly commonplace observation that many confirmed cigarette smokers are unable to enjoy smoking while blindfolded. Apparently, these individuals find the sight of the smoke or the glowing coal produced by their own smoking activities to be a necessary condition of smoking satisfaction. It is difficult to explain this phenomenon in terms of the biochemical exchange that goes on in cigarette smoking, and it would seem that we must seek elsewhere for an explanation. In my own case, I am confident that the symbolism of smoke and fire has some bearing on the matter. Without going into details and with some oversimplification, it seems to me that the sight of the smoke affords me assurance of my competence;* and I smoke most

* The distinction may not be a very meaningful one to most readers, but I feel impelled to add that I am not referring to competence in carrying through any particular task, but to competence and potency as a quality of my 'self', of my essential 'being'.

heavily when I stand most in need of such reassurance. I am thus asserting that one of the functions of the act of smoking is to afford, in Freudian primary process terms, reassurance with regard to personal competence.

There is another common function of the activity of smoking that does not involve any special symbolism at all. It is related to a requirement of non-automatized complexly integrated behaviours. In the carrying out of such behaviours, it is necessary to suppress responses to divergent behavioural instigations, attending to irrelevant intrabodily and external stimuli or to how rather than what one is doing, reverting to incompleted activities that have been temporarily deferred, and so on. To the extent that these divergent activities are not successfully suppressed, the whole structure of behaviour is threatened with falling apart. The more challenging the central task and the more taxing it is, the more serious the threat; the very difficulty of carrying on itself generates divergent activities. The suppression of divergent action tendencies poses some difficulties, however. Impulses have been set off in the nervous system which cannot be simply willed out of existence and which can only travel in the direction of motor outlets. These impulses, quasi-random in character, require some management. If one can set up some relatively routinized activities that demand only minimal attention for such quasi-random energy inputs to channel into, routinized activities that can be carried on in most circumstances and that can increase or decrease depending on the ebb and flow of such inputs, the management problem is greatly simplified; a safety-valve will have been introduced into the organismic economy. Moreover, the minimal attentional requirements for the pursuit of these routinized activities inhibit attention to other irrelevancies, but are hardly likely to lead to encounters with instigators to other divergent activities. In other words, these routinized activities serve as an innocuous channel for wandering attention. Now, it will be obvious that smoking—the extraction of a cigarette, its manipulation, the lighting up, the puffing and further handling of the cigarette, the very contemplation of the smoke, the quashing of the cigarette, the extraction of a new cigarette—that this activity, or its variants in pipe or cigar smoking, serve most admirably the function of harnessing the otherwise uncoordinated psychomotor irradiation associated with carrying on complex behaviour in difficult circumstances. In radically different circumstances, but for the same reasons—namely that it facilitates the handling of quasi-random stimulus input and minimizes the entanglements of wandering attention—smoking facilitates relaxed contemplation and reverie. The pace and style of smoking activity is, however, appropriately toned down.

I doubt that many smokers would offer an explanation of their smoking that would exactly parallel my preceding account, but few habituated smokers would, I think, deny its consistency with their smoking patterns. At any rate, I do not pretend to have exhausted the functions of smoking in this account.* My sole concern has been to illustrate a function for taking drugs that inheres in the activity rather than in the consequences of the biochemical interaction that is involved.

The high prevalence of so-called addiction to heroin in major metropolitan areas of the United States along with the low levels of actual intake and the virtual disappearance of severe withdrawal reactions† argue strongly for the relatively minor role

* Nor have I dealt with the issue of how non-smokers cope with the same problem. There may well be other and perhaps less conspicuous forms of routine activity that meet the same specifications—e.g. ubiquitous appropriateness, subjectness to acceleration and deceleration, offering an innocuous channel for wandering attention, etc. We must not foreclose the possibility, however, that habitual smokers are more likely than non-smokers to engage in activities that challenge their integrative capacity and hence are in greater need of something to fulfil the described function. On the one hand, this possibility is consistent with other differences that have been noted between smokers and non-smokers—e.g. the tendency of smokers to 'live harder'. On the other hand, it is possible that chronic reliance on smoking has prevented smokers from developing their capacities to function smoothly on the integrative-demand levels at which they normally operate—thereby generating a vicious circle.

† The large number of deaths from overdoses of heroin (in New York City

of the psychopharmacological functions of heroin use in these areas. To be sure, there are substantial numbers of addicts who periodically discontinue use (with the unconscious connivance of the police and enforcement authorities) in order to overcome the developed tolerance and to be able to get the psychopharmacological effects. To these individuals the revolving door pattern that characterizes the life of the chronic heroin user is itself functional for the continuance of the addiction. There are also some who are able to confine their use to periods of personal crisis, with sufficiently long intermissions for the developed tolerance to wear off. Most chronic users, however, go on for inordinately long periods even as they complain of the lack of effect and, in many instances, wonder why they do it. In these cases, one needs to look for the non-psychopharmacological functions.

Perhaps, of course, they are hoping for miracles, a return to halcyon days when drugs could be relied on to function as one wants them to. Perhaps, too, they get just enough reinforcement for this hope from such involuntary and unplanned-for interruptions as do occur for sufficiently long periods to undo the achieved tolerance levels. Actually, the mechanism involved is similar to that involved in the self-medication indulged in by many people. An enormous amount of aspirin, for instance, must be consumed in order to avert headaches that have not yet developed but are only anticipated; and the non-development of the headaches confirms the efficacy of the aspirin.

Indeed, if we examine the self-medication patterns of many

---

alone, informal information from Board of Health sources indicates that they were running about three hundred per year before 1967 and are estimated to be occurring at about four hundred per year since then) may seem to contradict these statements. The explanation is, however, a simple one. Apart from rumours of deliberately planted '*hot* shots' to eliminate addicts who have become dangerous to the traffickers, it is a certainty that the preparation of the product for use is not quality-controlled. The process of mixing relatively pure heroin with adulterants is not carried out with great care or competence. Consequently there are individual packets that may carry quite high concentrations which are lethal to users who have not been able to build up appropriate tolerance levels. The high death rates attest to the normally low dosages.

individuals, we can discover a more fundamental mechanism at work. These individuals will go on taking medications that they expect to be ineffective, and if they are hoping for miracles the hopes must be profoundly unconscious. What these people are doing is to refuse to admit their utter impotence and helplessness. As long as one can do something towards improving one's condition, no matter how ineffective that something may be, one is not overwhelmed by feelings of impotence. To be able to go on fighting the decrees of fate, no matter how ineffectively, proves one's autonomy and autonomy is antithetical to helplessness.

So the heroin addict may go on taking pharmacologically ineffective doses of heroin while hoping for a miracle and as a way of denying his helplessness. The degradation and punishment that one encounters as an addict is, however, a high price to pay for a hoped-for miracle and there are less painful and more dignified ways of denying one's helplessness. One needs to seek for other functions of this mode of life to make it intelligible that there are people who cling to it; and, as I see the typical urban addict, one has not far to seek.

From his earliest days, the addict has been accorded the treatment due to a *thing*, not to a person, a being whose needs and feelings are to be respected. Through his family, he has been callously relegated to the indignities of existence in a slum. Within the bosom of his family, he has been an instrumentality of the whims and requirements of other household members. In the rough and tumble of the street, he has been subject to the bullying of older and stronger boys and to the manipulations of those cleverer than he. At school, he has been regarded as ineducable and hence principally as a problem whose conduct must be controlled and kept in line. To the police, he has been a potential law breaker and hence someone to be pushed around. To the local shopkeepers, he has been a potential trouble maker and hence someone to be shooed away. Even when he was given something good, it was given reluctantly and in a manner that declared, "This is so you should behave better. Don't get the idea that you are entitled to it as a human being". To all this, his addiction permits an answer. "*You* are a storekeeper. *You* are a teacher. *You* are a letter carrier. *You* are a cop. *You* are a parent, a man, a woman, a citizen, a voter, a landlord, a housewife. *Me*, I'm a *junkie*. A junkie is a *person*, not a *thing*. *Me*, I'm a person." Through his addiction he acquires a socially validated human identity, a despised identity, but an identity nonetheless.

From almost his earliest days, the addict has been an outcast. In countless ways he has been told he does not belong. As a member of a despised racial or ethnic group, society has told him that he is beneath contempt. In his household, he was made to feel that he was underfoot and in the way. If he learned anything at school, it was not the pratings of democracy but that there is no place for persons like himself, that to find a place he must become something other than what he is. To this, too, his addiction offers an answer. Through his addiction, he finds a place in a subsociety where he is unequivocally accepted as a peer. It is a subsociety which does not demand interpersonal skills, a capacity for give and take, mutual trust, intimate sharing—all qualities of which he was systematically deprived throughout his developmental years. It is, in brief, a subsociety in which he can feel comfortable. But to find a society in which one is fully accepted and in which one feels comfortable is to find a society in which one belongs.

From almost his earliest days, the addict has been systematically educated and trained into incompetence. Unlike others, therefore, he could not find a vocation, a career, a meaningful, sustained activity around which he could, so to say, wrap his life. The addiction, however, offers an answer to even this problem of emptiness. The life of an addict constitutes a vocation—hustling, raising funds, assuring a connection and the maintenance of supply, outmanoeuvering the police, performing the rituals of preparing and of taking the drug—a vocation around which the addict can build a reasonably full life.

It is interesting, too, that when he slips and is caught in the toils of the law, these functions continue to be served in the total absence of the drug. As an institutional inmate, he has a socially validated identity, is a member of a subsociety in which he can feel that he belongs, and he still has his calling, changed in content to be sure, in accordance with his changed circumstances, but a calling that offers a stream of activity at which he rather quickly becomes reasonably competent—not the formal institutional activities, but the informal activities of managing his institutional milieu. He is learning the ropes that lead to special favours and other advantages, serving as initiator and guide to new inmates, manoeuvering for position and status, and preparing for the resumption of his old life when he leaves the institution, making new connections, being brought up to date on new developments in the extra-institutional phase of his vocation, and so on.

The life of an addict can thus serve a humanizing function, by offering an identity, a place in society where one belongs, and a vocation around which to build one's life. The humanizing function may also be carried on in a less elaborate form. If Edwin Schur's account of the addicts who stay within the framework of the medical treatment system in Great Britain is correct, for example, these are essentially inadequate and lonely people who are unable to reach out effectively in human communion. That is, they suffer, literally and figuratively, from a severe impairment of a distinctively human attribute. Their initial use of narcotics may well have been to ease the pain of their loneliness. On the maintenance doses that they receive, however, the psychic effects of the drug must soon be wiped out. Why, then, do they stay in treatment? My hypothesis is that they continue as addicts and in treatment because this offers them a bridge into a genuinely human relationship. In the person of the physician, they have found someone who accepts them for what they are, who is concerned about their welfare, to whom they can unburden themselves of some of their despair, and who proves that he cares by offering them the stuff in which they have convinced themselves their lives are rooted. In this relationship, they can feel that they have become more human.

It may be noted that, in my examples of the activity-controlling functions of smoking and the humanizing functions of heroin addiction, there are no special meanings of the drug or of the pattern of drug involvement which have led to the drug use. The third class of functions to which I have referred involves special meanings of a drug or its use that play a role in instigating the use. Two of my earlier examples belong to this third class—the function of smoking involving the symbolism of smoke and fire and the taking of medications as a means of denying helplessness. Smoking as a symbol of masculinity and the taking up of smoking by an adolescent male as a means of convincing himself or others of his masculinity would be a more commonplace example.

There are at least three special meanings associated with drugs that play important roles on the contemporary drug scene. The first involves illegality and disreputability which confer on certain acts a hostility-expressing function. When an act is condemned by social definition then, by that very fact, it acquires a meaning that makes it eligible as a means of expressing hostility and contempt for and defiance of the respectable elements of society or particular representatives of it such as one's parents. This is the basic condition of what has been described as the versatility of delinquent subcultures. The particular act through which such hostility is expressed is not in itself of great importance; whether, on any given occasion, one performs one or another is determined in large measure by opportunity. Drug misbehaviour is one of many ways of misbehaving, but it is precisely as misbehaviour that it becomes attractive when one is looking for ways of expressing hatred, contempt, defiance. In terms of this function, the particular drug that is used makes little difference and it is equally well served by drugs that may have diametrically opposed pharmacological effects—alcohol, barbiturates, amphetamines, opiates, cannabis, psychedelics, the vapours of glue or carbon tetrachloride, and remarkable combinations may all be used by the same person from time to time, depending on what happens to be available.

The second special meaning involves a status-conferring function. Certain actions and experiences may be highly valued by a person's important reference groups. Through such valuations, these actions and experiences acquire a meaning that makes them eligible as means of achieving status, respect, admiration, recognition. An act of derring-do is perhaps easily carried out when the occasion arises and one may even be able to bring about the occasion; but experience is unfortunately not always at one's command even though the occasion seems appropriate. When the experience fails, it becomes all the more important to convince oneself and others that the experience has indeed occurred. Many a jazz or an opera buff, an art connoisseur, a devotee of esoteric literary cults, is, I suspect, a pretender; many a glorious sexual experience is a sorry imitation. The language has been acquired, and one speaks it with fervour. Fervent speech may deceive the outsider, but it does not produce the experience. It is necessary, however, to deceive oneself as well. In this area, it is not easy to accept oneself as an impostor. Fraud is tolerable and indeed may be experienced as a source of pride when practiced on persons whom one devalues; and the success of the fraud will itself lead to the devaluation of the defrauded. At stake in the present context, however, is the esteem of one's important reference groups; to deceive them consciously demands that they be devalued and, unless they can be replaced by new reference groups in which case the whole effort is a waste, the success of the deceit is a gateway to alienation. The fervour is, therefore, as much for one's own benefit as it is to persuade others.

Now, drug misbehaviour enters the arena of status achievement both through the avenue of practice and the avenue of experience. Of the former, little need be said. Drug taking, like the baiting of police, may prove one's bravery or that one is a regular guy; one may engage in the practice with no other gratification involved. On the level of experience, however, the matter is more complicated. Drug-induced experience has been highly valued on grounds that range from personal ecstasy to religious revelation, from peaceful serenity to passionate turbulent intoxication, from self-understanding to universal insight.

Whatever the experience attributed to any particular drug, there is a high valuation placed by many honoured sources in most civilized societies on the virtues of mind stretching through rich and diversified experience *per se*. We have been urged to invest in opening ourselves to music, art, literature of the most varied sorts, to travel and immerse ourselves in the cultures of other societies, to range back in history to the beginnings of recorded time, to explore religious values and beliefs in which we have not been raised. We have been taught to expect that not everything we taste will be good, but that we ought to taste nonetheless. To be sure we have also been subject to the propaganda of constraint, to taboos and prohibitions—but these have typically been explicitly rooted in fears that premature encounters with certain ideas might lead us to bad conduct and the boundaries of legitimate experience are accordingly circumscribed in specific directions. The virtue of range and depth of experience, however, has tended not to be challenged.

Along come drugs with highly touted virtues, offering extraordinary experiences. Inevitably, there will be those who respond. What happens when the promised experience does not eventuate, when the user is not transported out of this world, when the great insights do not emerge, when he feels no closer to God? In some circles, he can declare: "The emperor has no clothes!" and that is the end of the matter. In other circles, the failure is assumed to be in himself; and it is assumed to be correctible. After all, can you expect to appreciate surrealism when suddenly exposed to it for the first time? You must master it in order to be able to experience it. Can you, raised in a culture that mixes Aristotelianism and Thomism with technology and the values of the market place, be expected to comprehend the pearls of Zen wisdom? You must submit to its discipline to experience its values. So with drugs. In the meantime, you join the crowd and scream of the beauties of the emperor's clothes, relying on your own fervour to convince yourself that the emperor is really not naked or that the tailor was, after all, a sublime artist to have exposed the beauties of that magnificent body.

In the enterprise of self-deception there is one relevant psycho-pharmacological effect of most of the drugs that are likely to be used. Intoxication diminishes self-criticism, and dulled self-criticism facilitates self-deception. Thus, Oliver Wendell Holmes, coming out of ether anaesthesia but still subject to its effects, could experience the great insight that would solve all problems of philosophy. He had no investment in the revelatory powers of ether, however, and could later realize that the revealed truth which he had written down—"The odor of turpentine pervades throughout"—still leaves one or two problems of philosophy to be solved. Suppose, though, that Holmes had the investment and that he had not recorded his insight. He could then go around with the feeling that he had been made privy to one of the great secrets of the universe and that, deep in his unconscious, he was still custodian of the great truth.

My point is not that great truths and products of great beauty cannot emerge out of abstracted, cloudy, drowsy states. My point is simply that many a drug user has an investment in believing that they do emerge in drugged states, that these users are not in a condition to evaluate the experience while drugged, and that they treasure the recollection of having had the great experience rather than the recollection of the experience itself when they are in a state in which they are capable of evaluating it. My point is, further, that the self-deception which so commonly occurs in these conditions is typically in the service of a status-gaining function.

The third and last special meaning of drug taking which I shall consider is tied up with the function of bringing about a better world. There are important segments among contemporary youth who are disillusioned with respect to the integrity and wisdom of the adult world that runs their lives. The disillusionment stems from many sources that feed into a common stream: it is up to the youth to change the world and the youth can do this by exercising the power of civil disobedience. Many believe—as, incidentally, I myself do—that policies bearing on drug use are hypocritical, irrational, sadistic, politically motivated, and an infringement on civil liberties. In the context of civil disobedience, participation in the use of drugs has acquired the meaning of striking a blow for a better, saner, more just world. I have argued with some of these young people that they are putting marijuana on a par with issues of war and peace, with the rectification of injustices to maltreated minority groups, and with the elimination of poverty. Some have argued in response and in all of the innocence of youth that any known corruption that is tolerated corrupts the whole. They therefore felt themselves to be morally obligated to participate in drug use. Right or wrong, this is a long way indeed from chemistry.

Summary

I have been trying to generate some perspective as to why people misbehave with drugs. In my own innocence, I believe that understanding a problem has some bearing on dealing with it rationally.

REFERENCES

Chein, I., Gerard, D. L., Lee, R. S. & Rosenfeld, E. (1964). *The Road to H: Narcotics, Delinquency and Social Policy*. New York: Basic Books. (London: Tavistock Publications, with the order of the title and subtitle reversed.)

Chein, I. (1965). The use of narcotics as a personal and social problem. *Narcotics*, pp. 103–117. Ed. by Wilner, D. & Kassebaum, G. G. New York: McGraw-Hill.

Chein, I. (1966). Psychological, social and epidemiological factors in drug addiction. *Rehabilitating the Narcotic Addict*. Washington, D.C.: U.S. Government Printing Office. Vocational Rehabilitation Administration, U.S. Department of Health, Education and Welfare.

Schur, Edwin M. (1962). *Narcotic Addiction in Britain and America*. Bloomington: Indiana University Press.

A PHARMACOLOGICAL APPROACH TO DRUG DEPENDENCE AND DRUG TOLERANCE

W. D. M. PATON

Department of Pharmacology, University of Oxford

FACED with the variety of drugs capable of inducing dependence, a pharmacologist must, to begin with, narrow the field. Accordingly I should like to discuss chiefly the opiates, and to explore what answers can be given to the questions: What do they *do*? and What account can one give of their action and of the mechanisms by which they induce tolerance and abstinence syndromes?

From previous work (reviewed by Seevers & Deneau, 1963), two main approaches emerge. The first is that the opiates have, in principle, two actions, one responsible both for the analgesia and depressant phenomena, the other for a set of stimulant effects. It could thus be suggested that with continued administration of the drug the stimulant action would tend to reduce the analgesic or depressant effect; that as the dose was increased, this antagonism would become more and more obvious, thus giving the appearance of tolerance; and finally that if the drug was withdrawn, the stimulant effects could outlast the depressant action and give rise to the abstinence syndrome. The second main approach, formulated explicitly by Himmelsbach, is an example of Le Chatelier's principle, whereby the action of the drug brings into play counteractions restoring the organism to its original state. In the present instance, a central depression would evoke a compensating excitation, which would gradually produce tolerance, and, when the drug was withdrawn, an over-action, before the compensating mechanisms in turn disappeared in the absence of the force which brought them into play. At this strategic level, there has recently been a considerable clarification. Dr. Deneau made the simple experiment of giving monkeys a course of morphine sufficient to produce the abstinence syndrome, but in one group of monkeys so exposed he added the antagonist laevallorphan. Since these antagonists are poor antagonists of the stimulant phenomena, the abstinence syndrome should (on the dual action theory) be little affected; but on the Himmelsbach approach, where the abstinence syndrome depends on the primary action, and will therefore be sensitive to laevallorphan, then the abstinence syndrome should be reduced in parallel with the reduction of the primary effect of the drug. The result was unequivocally in support of the latter view. The investigator can therefore, I think, allow himself to concentrate on the primary action of morphine, even when it is tolerance and dependence, rather than (say) analgesia, with which he is concerned. But, of course, the theory says nothing about the nature of the primary action, nor of the countervailing response to which it gives rise.

The effect of opiates on transmitter release

For a closer approach, it seems reasonable to assume that the action of opiates is on nerve cells. We need to consider, therefore, interference (either by excitation or depression) with the activity of the nerve terminals; with the mechanisms of transmitter release; with transmitter action on the postsynaptic membrane, with transmitter disposal; and with propagation of excitation from the postsynaptic chemoceptive surface to the postsynaptic soma and axon. At all these points other drugs can be named which have a more or less specific action. From the evidence available, albeit largely from experiments on the autonomic nervous system, the best provisional answer seems to be that the opiates simply reduce release of transmitter at nerve endings. The resting output of acetylcholine by strips of guinea-pig intestine is reduced by morphine, although choline synthesis is not depressed (Schaumann, 1956; 1957). Further, also with guinea-pig ileum, the twitches evoked by brief shocks, which are due to excitation of the cholinergic postganglionic nerves of Auerbach's plexus activating the smooth muscle, are depressed by opiates, although the response of smooth muscle to directly applied acetylcholine is unchanged (Paton, 1956; 1957). If some procedure abolishes the effect of nerve stimulation although direct application of transmitter to the postsynaptic element is unaffected, it is strong evidence that transmitter output is in some way being interfered with. This was confirmed by direct measurement of acetylcholine output by eserinized preparations. (The same results have been obtained with the strips of longitudinal muscle mentioned below (Figure 1).) At about the same time Trendelenburg (1957), using the cat's nictitating membrane *in vivo*, showed that morphine reduced the response to postganglionic stimulation, but not to injected catecholamine. The problem of output of sympathin is still technically elusive and direct demonstration of reduction of output by opiates has not been achieved. There are many reasons why it is much harder to collect the released sympathin than it is to collect released acetylcholine. Finally J. W. Thompson (1960, cited by Cairnie *et al.*, 1961), using his isolated innervated nictitating membrane preparation, which contains effectively only sympathetic nerves, smooth muscle and some connective tissue, showed again that morphine reduced the response to nerve excitation but not to added noradrenaline. And Cairnie *et al.* (1961) have produced additional evidence on other sympathetically innervated systems supporting the same interpretation.

Although the results with the cholinergic system of the intestine were the most complete, they were also in one respect ambiguous, since some of the acetylcholine might conceivably have come, say, from the mucous membrane and not be of nervous origin. Although this would be an interesting action of

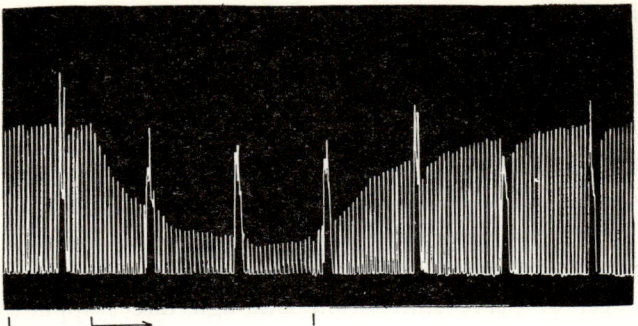
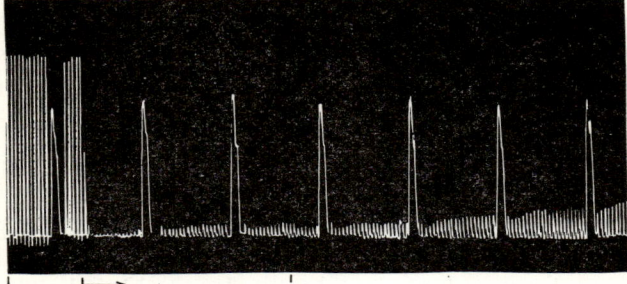
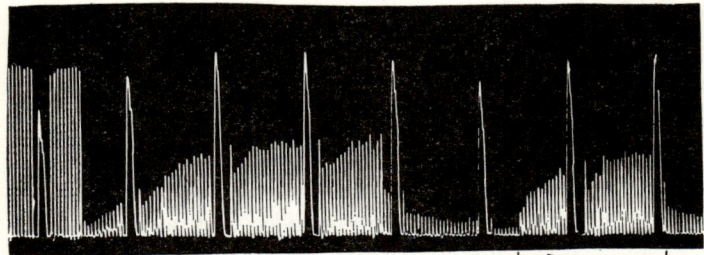

FIG. 1. Longitudinal strip of guinea-pig ileum in 10 ml bath of Krebs solution bubbled with 95% O_2/5% CO_2 at 37°C, field stimulated with maximal shocks lasting 1 msec at 6/min. Every 4 min, ACh (0.2 μg) injected and washed out after 20 sec, with replacement of morphine if necessary; the stimulus was sometimes intermitted during the action of ACh.

Morphine sulphate in a dose of 0.1 μg/ml (upper panel) and 10 μg/ml (middle panel) depress the twitch without affecting the response to ACh. A dose of 100 μg/ml yields a depression followed by recovery, during which ACh is slightly potentiated; withdrawal of morphine is followed by a greater reduction of the twitch, surmountable by re-applying morphine.

morphine, it could hardly be regarded as very relevant to its central action. But this point has now been cleared up with Dr. Aboo Zar (Paton & Zar, 1968), in experiments which showed that it was possible to obtain strips of the longitudinal muscle of the guinea-pig ileum either fully innervated, partially innervated (Figure 2), or fully denervated. With such strips we could show that all the acetylcholine released comes exclusively from

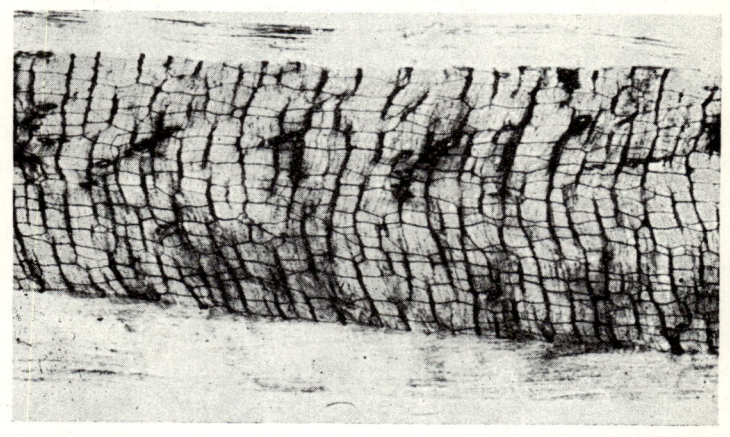

FIG. 2. Photomicrograph of longitudinal muscle strip, showing the plexus and regions at the edge of the strip plexus-free and containing only smooth muscle (from Paton & Zar, 1968 by courtesy of the *Journal of Physiology*).

the nerve plexus. The action of the opiates on the release of acetylcholine from these strips is, therefore, an action on the nervous tissue. Perhaps I should add that the local anaesthetic effect of morphine is trivial, so that some more specific mechanism of action must be sought.

One may question whether the nerve network of the intestine is worth considering, even momentarily, as an analogue of the central nervous structures involved in morphine action. But one may answer, first, that it is a true nerve network capable of quite complicated (and still unsolved) integrated behaviour. Second, the concentrations of morphine required for action are somewhat lower than might be expected assuming that an ordinary therapeutic dose of morphine is dissolved in the extracellular fluid. Third, and perhaps more significant than these comparisons of doses (which could easily vary with species), is the fact that if you compare opiates, the potency ratios on the intestine and in man run remarkably close (cf. Paton, 1956; Martin, 1966). The biggest range is between fentanyl on the one hand, which I find to be active in a concentration of 1 ng/ml on the intestine, and codeine on the other; both in man and on the intestine they yield a potency ratio of about 500. Finally, although this is a rather complicated question to discuss in full, it can be shown that, just as in man, so on the gut nalorphine is both an agonist, i.e. it produces morphine-like actions, and also an antagonist to morphine (Gyang & Kosterlitz, 1966).

One may notice, in addition, that other drugs inducing dependence, such as noradrenaline and adrenaline, amphetamine and cocaine, also reduce transmitter output. In a study of the general anaesthetics Speden (1965) showed that chloroform and halothane, among others, can reduce transmitter output. It is known that barbiturates and methylpentynol (Oblivon) reduce the output of acetylcholine, in this case from the perfused superior cervical ganglion. One has thus a fairly general situation, that a good many of these drugs share at least one primary action, that of interfering with the release of the transmitter mediating the synaptic action. Finally, Beleslin & Polak (1965) showed that the output of acetylcholine into the fluid perfusing the cerebral ventricle is depressed by morphine. I am sure that this is again a depression of neurogenic acetylcholine release, although there is some uncertainty as to the exact origin of the acetylcholine (probably the caudate nucleus, and perhaps other structures). All this evidence shows, I think, that there is a good *prima facie* case that many of the drugs inducing dependence, and the opiates in particular, specifically depress transmitter release. It also suggests that the nerve network of the gut provides an *in vitro* preparation which might be helpful for analysing the mechanism of action of these drugs in more depth.

The consequences of depression of transmitter release

If we take as a working hypothesis, that the opiates in their action on the brain depress transmitter release, as they do at peripheral autonomic sites, could we expect the phenomena of tolerance and of withdrawal? Certainly Himmelsbach's view assumes that depression of synaptic transmission would give rise to some reaction which tended to overcome that depression, and hence, when the depressant influence was removed, to exaggerated synaptic activity. It is rather striking that the signs of abstinence include many autonomic responses involving an unusual simultaneous activation both of cholinergic and adrenergic elements (Table 1). But if it is viewed simply as a reaction to

Table 1

Abstinence Syndrome

Central	Skeletal	Sympathetic	Parasympathetic
Apprehension	Pain in limbs	Hyperpyrexia	Perspiration
Restlessness	Muscle rigidity	Hyperglycaemia	Rhinorrhoea
Sleepiness	Muscle weakness	Pallor	Lacrimation
Quarrelling	Muscle tremor	Pilo-erection	Salivation
Insomnia	Abnormal postures	Increase in urinary catecholamines	Hyperacidity
Strabismus	Yawning		Diarrhoea
Vomiting			Abdominal cramps
			Miosis
			Cough

impairment of release both of acetylcholine and of noradrenaline, such a pattern is to be expected.

But, to go deeper, one must enquire as to the nature of these compensating reactions. The nature of the primary action, depression of transmitter release, opens the way to at least two approaches. The first is the suggestion (Paton, 1963) that if as a result of morphine application acetylcholine is dammed back within the terminal axone, then as a result its axonal concentration should rise. In due course it might rise sufficiently for that fraction of it released by nerve impulse to become again effective. Thus even though morphine may reduce the fractional release by the impulse, the corresponding reduction of volley output could be overcome by the rising internal concentration, and 'tolerance' would appear. A corollary of course is that if morphine is withdrawn, and after it has been eliminated from the tissue, an exaggerated release of transmitter could occur, giving rise to withdrawal symptoms. This process of transmitter retention one could call the 'surfeit' theory. The second proposal is that of a development of denervation supersensitivity, which Dr. Collier and Dr. Sharpless discuss (this volume, pp. 49 and 67), and which flows from the demonstration, primarily by Professor Emmelin that supersensitivity will follow pharmacological denervation as well as anatomical denervation.

I should like simply to make four points about the 'transmitter surfeit' approach. First (Figure 3) one finds with the intestine preparation that tolerance to morphine-like substances comes on over a period of hours (Paton, 1957; Gyang & Kosterlitz, 1968); and similar results have been described in whole animals. Nalorphine is the most rapidly accommodating drug I know, with a very considerable recovery from its depressant action within four hours; but most opiates seem to behave more like those of Figure 3, requiring for large reduction of their effect a period of six to eight hours. Although slow for the experimenter, this is a rather rapid time-course to be accounted for by denervation supersensitivity. The magnitude of depression of transmitter output (60–80%) would be large enough to produce supersensitivity, judging from Emmelin's data (reviewed 1961; 1965), but it seems that a period of days is required for this supersensitivity to develop. Transmitter accumulation could, however, develop

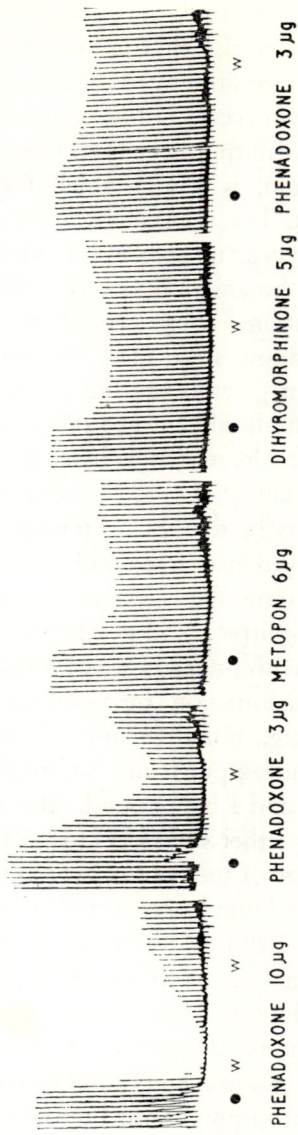

FIG. 3. Comparison of various opiates on the twitch of the guinea-pig ileum, stimulated coaxially at 6/min, showing the diminishing effect of phenadoxone, 3 μg. Time intervals between successive tests are respectively 50, 37, 32 and 22 min. (From Paton, 1957, by courtesy of *British Journal of Pharmacology*).

much more rapidly. Second, if transmitter is accumulating in the nerve endings, a rise in transmitter content should be demonstrable. We have attempted this on the intestinal strip, but no significant rise in acetylcholine content could be detected. However, the volley output, even at morphine-sensitive frequencies of stimulation, is a very small fraction of the total acetylcholine content, less than 1/2000. A calculation of the amount one could expect to accumulate yields an amount too small to detect. If the fraction of acetylcholine immediately involved in acetylcholine release could be isolated, it might be a different proposition, since there is evidence that this may vary, at least transiently, with the rate of acetylcholine output (MacIntosh, 1963). It should be noted, however, that there is evidence that both after having morphine, and during anaesthesia the acetylcholine content of the brain rises (citations by Beleslin & Polak, 1965). It may be that the proportion between the transmitter actually involved in release and the total transmitter in the tissue is more favourable in brain tissue. Third, even if accumulation of transmitter could not be shown by direct assay, it might be possible, with preparations of intestine, to show some sort of rebound phenomenon on withdrawal of an opiate. With a different drug, noradrenaline, which, like morphine, depresses acetylcholine output from Auerbach's plexus, this can be done, as Dr. Vizi and I have found. But with drugs such as morphine, which are rather slowly removed from the tissue, the gradual drift in the size of the control twitch makes it impossible to be sure that such rebound occurs with the procedures I have used so far. Finally, I should like to draw the analogy with a different area of drug action, that of the hypotensive drugs bretylium, guanethidine and reserpine. All three drugs can be made to have a comparable effect in reducing sympathetic transmission; but it is only bretylium whose action is simply to reduce transmitter output; both the other drugs deplete the endings of their amine content (Muscholl, 1965). It is interesting that it is bretylium that has almost lost its therapeutic usefulness because of the tolerance it induces. In contrast, guanethidine and reserpine, whatever difficulties there may be in their therapeutic use, do not fail because of developing tolerance. This is just the result, of course, which would be expected on the 'surfeit' hypothesis.

There is too little direct evidence to justify analysing further the differences between the 'surfeit' and the 'supersensitivity' hypotheses. The two approaches need not be mutually exclusive; it might even be possible that early tolerance is due to transmitter accumulation, and that this leads on to a further phase of tolerance as supersensitivity takes over.

The role of partial agonism

It might be argued, however, that neither of these theories is correct; instead the drugs concerned might possess both agonist and antagonist activity, i.e. the opiates as a class might be 'partial agonists' (Gyang & Kosterlitz, 1966). This approach would suggest that tolerance to a drug like morphine arises because it is capable of antagonizing both its own action and that of similar drugs, and that with continued administration this antagonistic power becomes more and more prominent. It would follow, I think, that development of tolerance should be more striking with nalorphine than with morphine, and still more striking with drugs such as cyclazocine or pentazocine; this does not square with the evidence. Further, the rate of development of tolerance seems to be much too slow. Even with nalorphine, tolerance takes several hours to appear, yet it is a very familiar finding in the pharmacology of nalorphine, both experimental and human, that the antagonism to morphine which it produces can be exerted in minutes. An equally rapid antagonism by nalorphine to the action of morphine can be shown *in vitro* on the twitch of the guinea-pig ileum strip (Figure 4). If then the antagonism exerted by the drug can reach its full magnitude in a few minutes, it seems unlikely that this antagonism can account for a process developing slowly over a period of many hours or days. Consequently, while it seems both correct and illuminating

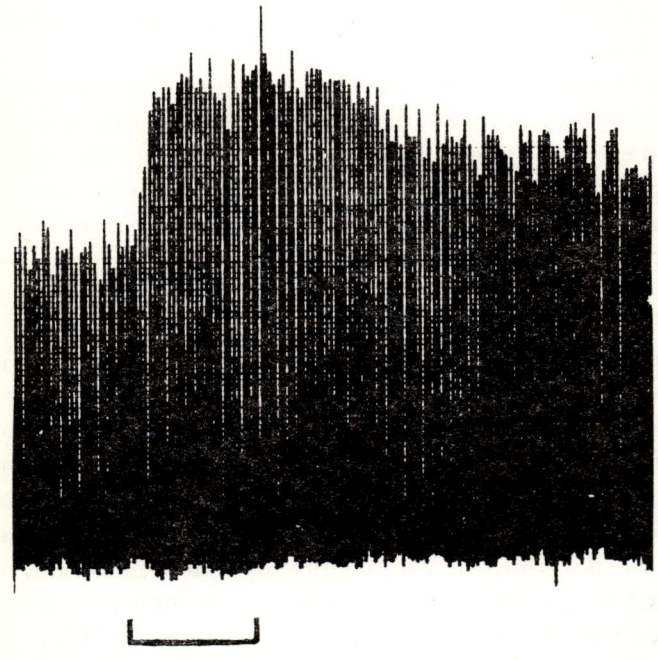

Fig. 4. Longitudinal strip mounted and stimulated as in Fig. 1, in the presence of 10 μg/ml morphine applied 25 min previously. During period marked by bar, 5 μg/ml nalorphine was present.

to classify the opiates as partial agonists with varying proportions of antagonistic power, it cannot be viewed as an explanation of the phenomenon of tolerance.

Morphine self-reversal

There is one other phenomenon to which I must allude, described in an earlier paper (Paton, 1957): namely that if a large dose of morphine is added in the presence of a small dose, the twitch of the intestine is not further depressed but may be enhanced, and that if the morphine is then withdrawn, the twitch is profoundly depressed and is then restored to normal levels by re-applying the large dose of morphine. At the time, I thought the initial small dose of morphine was necessary in some way to condition the preparation. But this is not the case. With a sufficiently large dose of morphine there may be almost no depression of the twitch, the effect being the same whether the dose is applied directly or preceded by a series of lower doses. Morphine, in its effect on the nerve plexus of the intestinal strip, thus has a curious dose-response curve (Figures 1 and 5); its depressant action is detectable at around 10 ng/ml (13 nM), reaches a maximum at around 10 μg/ml (13 μM), and then becomes more transient, so that at 1 mg/ml (1·3mM) the depression may be quite fleeting or even absent. This particular self-induced tolerance can, therefore, develop very quickly indeed. But it is also short-lived. Figure 5 shows a test of the sensitivity to morphine of the strip, in its state of depressed response shortly after withdrawing a large dose of morphine; the response to a small test dose of morphine represents a roughly normal sensitivity, and it cannot at this point be regarded as tolerant. These are phenomena for which I know no pharmacological analogy, and suspect that they are peculiar to the opiates. If so, and if they occur centrally as well, they could obviously contribute very readily to the syndrome of tolerance, and would suggest that tolerance should develop much more rapidly as the higher doses were reached, in a manner specific to the opiates.

The role of the safety factor in synaptic transmission

My last point is simply to comment on the question of how drugs such as the opiates, which depress transmitter release, can have selectivity of action. Thus far, the effects of such drugs might be expected to resemble those of a general anaesthetic.

One cause of specificity is that the receptors with which the opiates interact are chemically specialized and are probably localized at particular sites. But a more general factor may also contribute. It is clear from work with peripheral synapses, such as the ganglion and the neuromuscular junction, that they

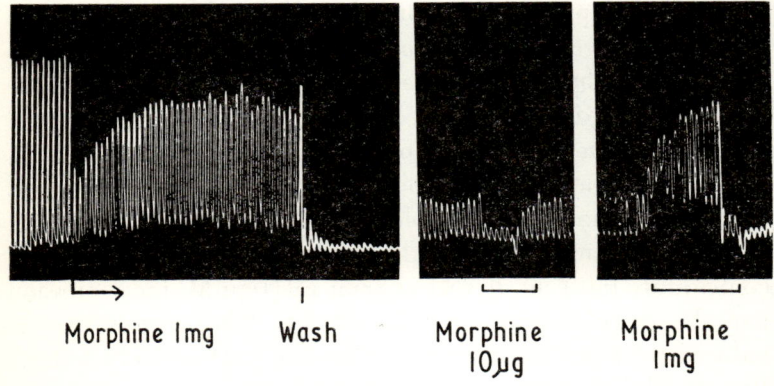

Fig. 5. Longitudinal strip mounted and stimulated as in Fig. 1. Left hand panel, addition and withdrawal of morphine (100 μg/ml); middle panel, 15 min later, test of sensitivity to 1 μg/ml morphine; right hand panel, 7 min later partial restoration of twitch by re-applying 100 μg/ml morphine.

operate with a considerable margin of reserve, the so-called 'safety factor'. Transmitter output or action needs to be attenuated three to five-fold before synaptic block can be displayed at reasonably slow rates of stimulation (cf. Paton & Waud, 1967). If then there are in the central nervous system synapses, even using the same transmitter, but with varying safety factors, then those whose safety factor is least will be most sensitive to any drug interfering with transmitter output. Another consequence of this principle is that if a drug has only a limited maximal depressant action (nalorphine is probably an example), then it will only be able to show its effect on those synapses where a depression of output by that limited amount will overcome the safety factors concerned.

Conclusions

(1) The action of opiates, and of a number of other drugs producing dependence, on peripheral autonomic structures is to reduce output of the synaptic transmitters concerned.

(2) If this action is reflected in the central nervous system, then the process of tolerance and the withdrawal syndrome could follow from at least two mechanisms: (*a*) the damming back of transmitter within the nerve terminals, leading to transmitter 'surfeit'; (*b*) the development of supersensitivity of the post-synaptic structures as a result of a pharmacological denervation. It is suggested that transmitter surfeit might account for the earlier stage of tolerance, supersensitivity for the later, and withdrawal symptoms be attributable to each according to the duration of the exposure.

(3) Although one can recognize agonist and antagonist activities in varying proportions in different opiates, i.e. they are 'partial agonists', the antagonist element cannot be regarded as an adequate explanation of their ability to produce tolerance.

(4) On the intestine preparation, opiates such as morphine seem to have in addition some special capacity to reverse their action as the concentration of opiate rises. This may be an additional element in the exceptionally rapid development of tolerance to opiates.

(5) If a drug depresses transmitter release, then the pattern of its central nervous action will depend not only on the incidence of specific receptors for the drug, but on the distribution of synaptic safety factors in different regions of the brain.

(6) The 'surfeit' hypothesis suggests at least one practical approach; if it is at least in part correct, then it should be possible to attenuate both tolerance and intensity of withdrawal symptoms

by finding a drug or a procedure which will prevent the accumulation of transmitter during the period when its release is inhibited.

REFERENCES

Beleslin, D. & Polak, R. L. (1965). Depression by morphine and chloralose of acetylcholine release from the cat's brain. *J. Physiol.*, **177**, 411–419.

Cairnie, A. B., Kosterlitz, H. W. & Taylor, D. W. (1961). Effect of morphine on some sympathetically innervated effectors. *Brit. J. Pharmac. Chemother.*, **17**, 539–551.

Emmelin, N. (1961). Supersensitivity following 'pharmacological denervation'. *Pharmac. Rev.*, **1**, 17–37.

Emmelin, N. (1965). Action of transmitters on the responsiveness of effector cells. *Experientia*, **21**, 57–112.

Gyang, E. A. & Kosterlitz, H. W. (1966). Agonist and antagonist actions of morphine-like drugs on the guinea-pig isolated ileum. *Brit. J. Pharmac. Chemother.*, **27**, 514–527.

MacIntosh, F. C. (1963). Synthesis and storage of acetylcholine in nervous tissue. *Canad. J. Biochem. Physiol.*, **41**, 2555–2571.

Martin, W. R. (1966). Assessment of the dependence-producing potentiality of narcotic analgesics. *Clinical Pharmacology*, Vol. I, Ch. 9. London: Pergamon Press.

Muscholl, E. (1965). Drugs interfering with the storage and release of adrenergic transmitters. *Pharmacology of Cholinergic and Adrenergic Transmission. Proc. Second Int. Pharmacological Meeting*, **3**, 291–302.

Paton, W. D. M. (1956). The responses of, and release of acetylcholine by guinea-pig small intestine in response to coaxial electrical stimulation. *Abstr. Twentieth Int. Physiol. Cong.*, Bruxelles, pp. 708–709.

Paton, W. D. M. (1957). The action of morphine and related substances on contraction and on acetylcholine output of coaxially stimulated guinea-pig ileum. *Brit. J. Pharmac. Chemother.*, **11**, 119–127.

Paton, W. D. M. (1963). Cholinergic transmission and acetylcholine output. *Canad. J. Biochem. Physiol.*, **41**, 2637–2653.

Paton, W. D. M. & Waud, D. R. (1967). The margin of safety of neuromuscular transmission. *J. Physiol.*, **191**, 59–90.

Paton, W. D. M. & Zar, M. A. (1968). The origin of the acetylcholine released from guinea-pig intestine and longitudinal muscle strips. *J. Physiol.*, **194**, 13–33.

Schaumann, W. (1956). Influence of atropine and morphine on the liberation of acetylcholine from the guinea-pig's intestine. *Nature, Lond.*, **178**, 1121–1122.

Schaumann, W. (1957). Inhibition by morphine of the release of acetylcholine from the intestine of the guinea-pig. *Brit. J. Pharmac. Chemother.*, **12**, 115–119.

Seevers, M. H. & Deneau, G. A. (1963). Physiological aspects of tolerance and physical dependence. *Physiological Pharmacology* Vol. I, pp. 564–640. New York & London: Academic Press.

Speden, R. N. (1965). Effect of some volatile anaesthetics on the transmurally stimulated guinea-pig ileum. *Brit. J. Pharmac. Chemother.*, **25**, 104–118.

Trendelenburg, U. (1957). The action of morphine on the superior cervical ganglion and on the nictitating membrane of the cat. *Brit. J. Pharmac. Chemother.*, **12**, 79–85.

HUMORAL TRANSMITTERS, SUPERSENSITIVITY, RECEPTORS AND DEPENDENCE

H. O. J. COLLIER

Department of Pharmacological Research, Parke-Davis & Company, Hounslow, Middlesex

CAN a single mechanism be envisaged that explains the genesis of psychic and of physical dependence and of the type of tolerance associated with dependence? In trying to answer this question, I want to describe a biological model that represents the genesis of these states and to suggest how concepts of endogenous transmitter substances and drug-receptor interaction can be applied to the working of the model and to the processes it represents. Whereas I hope to be able to draw something that looks like a picture, I know that, even if I succeed, it can only be a rough sketch, partly because the area in view is so vast and partly because the opinion expressed is based upon published evidence, and lacks the detail of experiments designed to test its truth.

A basic requirement of theories of drug dependence of the type proposed here is that a drug inducing dependence interacts with an endogenous humoral transmitter that excites or inhibits a nerve cell. Such a transmitter substance is supposed to be the normal product of a nerve cell and its release at a sufficient rate from that cell is supposed to excite or inhibit an adjoining nerve cell. A drug inducing dependence may be supposed to interact with a natural transmitter by increasing or decreasing the rate of release or by blocking or facilitating the access of transmitter to the cell that it affects. Thus, in a relationship between three cells, one producing an excitatory transmitter, one producing an inhibitory transmitter and the third responding to either, a drug may conceivably interact with a transmitter in one, or more, of eight ways: by (1) depressing or (2) inducing release of excitatory transmitter; (3) depressing or (4) inducing release of inhibitory transmitter; blocking access of (5) excitatory or (6) inhibitory transmitter to the responding cell; or facilitating access of (7) excitatory or (8) inhibitory transmitter to that cell. Some of the mechanisms by which such interactions between drugs and humoral transmitters may perhaps lead to drug dependence are discussed below.

An all-purpose model

Supersensitivity induced by drugs

A model proposed for physical dependence and associated tolerance is what Emmelin (1961) called 'the supersensitivity of pharmacological denervation'. Sharpless & Halpern (1962) suggested that this effect might underlie the convulsions resulting from withdrawal of barbiturates after the induction of physical dependence. This model has been developed for barbiturates by Sharpless & Jaffe (1963; Jaffe & Sharpless, 1965). It was suggested independently, in 1961 by Grumbach (Jaffe, 1965) and later by myself (Collier, 1966) to account for physical dependence and accompanying tolerance towards morphine.

In the supersensitivity of pharmacological denervation, repeated treatment with a drug blocking excitation of an effector organ sensitizes that organ, just as surgical denervation does (Emmelin, 1961). The salivary gland, for example, can be made supersensitive to adrenaline by blockade of its acetylcholine receptors with atropine (Emmelin & Müren, 1951, 1952) or its nerve supply with the ganglion blocker, chlorisondamine (Emmelin, 1959). Skeletal muscle can be made supersensitive to acetylcholine by preventing the release of this transmitter with botulinum toxin (Thesleff, 1960). Vascular and splenic smooth muscle, the nictitating membrane and the radial muscle of the iris can be made supersensitive to catecholamines by depleting their normal noradrenaline supply with reserpine (Burn & Rand, 1958 *a* & *b*; 1959). Supersensitivity begins to develop after a few days of drug treatment and reaches a maximum within about two weeks. It declines to normal during the week after withdrawal.

Supersensitivity may develop towards endogenous substances other than the normal transmitter. For example, Alonso-de-Florida, del Castillo, Gonzalez & Sanchez (1965) found that surgically denervated guinea-pig diaphragm became supersensitive not only to acetylcholine, but also to bradykinin, histamine and 5-hydroxytryptamine. Cannon & Rosenblueth (1949) cite other examples. Fleming (1966) has reported that pharmacological denervation also can engender non-specific sensitivity. After treatment of guinea-pigs for several days with chlorisondamine, isolated pieces of ileum were more than normally responsive to histamine, 5-hydroxytryptamine and potassium, as well as to acetylcholine.

The examples of the supersensitivity of pharmacological denervation that I have been able to find in the literature apply to the blockade by drugs of excitatory processes. That drugs could also give rise to supersensitivity towards inhibition seems likely, because cutting the inhibitory nerve supply of the smooth muscles of bronchioles, intestine, uterus or blood vessels can induce this type of supersensitivity (Cannon & Rosenblueth, 1949). Experimental proof that drugs can induce supersensitivity towards inhibition would be worth getting.

The converse of supersensitization by a blockading drug has also been described. Emmelin & Müren (1952) found that sialagogic drugs, such as pilocarpine and adrenaline, reduced the sensitivity of salivary glands, previously made supersensitive with atropine or by denervation. This process, however, did not reduce sensitivity below normal levels.

Most of the work on supersensitivity has been done with peripheral organs; but Sharpless & Halpern (1962) showed that a comparable process can also occur in the central nervous system. They found that, in the isolated cerebral cortex of the cat, supersensitivity emerged in two to three weeks after surgical denervation. Poschel & Ninteman (1966) have obtained evidence that treatment with α-methyltyrosine induces a supersensitivity to methamphetamine of the hypothalamic 'reward' system of the rat.

Physical dependence

The supersensitivity of pharmacological denervation offers a flexible model of physical dependence, the character of which might be expected to vary with the circumstances of the blockade and of the central nervous structures and mediators involved. If a drug blocks a normal excitatory transmitter supplying a nerve cell of the brain, that cell may be expected to become supersensitive. Such supersensitivity should cause tolerance to the drug, since less transmitter would be needed to elicit a response. If the blockade occurs at or near the responding cell itself, so that little transmitter from elsewhere can reach it, supersensitivity and hence tolerance should be great. On lifting the blockade by withdrawing the drug, the normal amount of transmitter is likely to elicit more than normal excitation, when it again reaches the sensitized cell. Access of the transmitter would then reduce the sensitivity of the cell to its ordinary level. Such a pattern of physical dependence is seen with opiates, where tolerance of central origin and withdrawal effects are severe.

If a drug cuts off the supply of normal excitatory transmitter to a nerve cell at a point more distant from the cell than its surface, and the cell thus remains accessible to leakage of transmitter (or of another excitatory substance) from the neighbourhood, less supersensitivity and hence less tolerance to the drug would be expected to develop. Such an arrangement might provide a model of the development of tolerance and physical dependence towards barbiturates.

The fact that morphine has many interactions with humoral mediators may help to bring these speculations closer to reality. In 1954, Vogt showed that morphine liberates noradrenaline from the cat's brain and, in 1962, Türker & Akcasu showed that it liberates 5-hydroxytryptamine from the same organ. In 1957, Paton and Schaumann independently reported that morphine lessens the amount of acetylcholine liberated by guinea-pig ileum. Morphine was later shown to exert a comparable effect in the cat's brain (Beleslin & Polak, 1965; Beleslin, Polak & Sproull, 1965). Again, Gaddum and Picarelli (1957) distinguished, in the ileum, receptors for 5-hydroxytryptamine blocked by morphine from those blocked by lysergide.

The fact that the effects of opiate withdrawal in the dog and rat closely resemble those of injecting 5-hydroxytryptophan led me to propose a few years ago that one way in which morphine might induce dependence would be by occupation of 5-hydroxytryptamine receptors on appropriate brain cells (Collier, 1966). If this proposal is to be maintained, in the face of the conclusion that tolerance to and dependence on morphine, nalorphine and cyclazocine develop only in respect of their agonist and not their antagonist activity (Jasinski, Martin & Haertzen, 1967; Martin, 1968), the assumption seems needed that morphine antagonism depends on receptors different from those of morphine agonism, and their interaction is allosteric. The alternative mechanism of morphine dependence, previously proposed and further discussed above, that morphine cuts off the supply of excitatory transmitter and thus induces supersensitivity on a deprived nerve cell, does not encounter such a difficulty.

Psychic dependence

If the psychic effects of a drug arise in a comparable way to its physical effects, although they are expressed in different forms and observed by different means, then the supersensitivity of pharmacological denervation should provide a basic model of psychic as well as of physical dependence on drugs. For this, the model must apply to centres of the brain concerned with psychic events and responding to psychoactive drugs.

With the exception of the changes in sleep pattern observed by Oswald & Thacore (1963) after withdrawal of amphetamine, physical abstinence effects are seen only after treatment with drugs that mainly depress the central nervous system, such as morphine, ethanol and barbiturates. Psychic dependence, however, can occur towards either stimulant or depressant drugs. The model therefore needs a two-way adaptor, to accommodate psychic dependence.

This requirement may be met by the two systems of the brain postulated to explain the phenomena of self-stimulation with implanted electrodes in experimental animals (Olds, 1962). One of these systems is concerned with reward and the other with punishment. The reward system has been sited mainly in the medial forebrain bundle and the punishment system in the periventricular fibres (Stein, 1964). To integrate the two systems, cross-inhibition between them has been proposed (Olds, 1962). Stimulation of the posterior amygdala with electrodes implanted in the human brain has shown that comparable systems for euphoria and dysphoria may be assumed for man as well as for the self-stimulating rat (King, 1961).

Since the reward and punishment systems are supposed to be cross-inhibited, activation of the reward or depression of the punishment system would be expected to have comparable results. These would include a lessening of drives, accompanied by a sense of gratification and the reinforcement of the behaviour leading to these effects. Fifteen years ago, Wikler (1953) drew attention to the great reduction of drives during morphine dependence. A survey of the mental effects of drugs inducing psychic dependence leads me to conclude that the lessening of hunger, sex, fear or other drives is a common property of all these drugs.

The linked reward (euphoria) and punishment (dysphoria)

systems—or 'eudystat' as M. H. Seevers (1967, personal communication) has called them—provide a mechanism for operant conditioning, which is today seen as the main factor in the genesis of psychic dependence (Nichols, 1963; Weeks & Collins, 1964; G. A. Deneau, T. Yanagita & M. H. Seevers, 1965, personal communication; Nichols & Hsiao, 1967; Pickens & Harris, 1968). The eudystat can also be used to explain psychic withdrawal effects, to which addicted persons bear witness, by gearing it to the basic model of the supersensitivity of pharmacological denervation.

This composite model can be applied either to mainly depressant or to mainly stimulant drugs that induce psychic dependence. We might suppose, on the one hand, that depressant drugs act by blocking excitation of the punishment system. This supposition is supported by the findings of Geller & Seifter (1960, 1962) that meprobamate and barbiturates strongly attentuate punishment discrimination in trained rats. Supersensitivity of the blockaded punishment system would then follow, the resulting dependence having psychic aspects, for the system itself involves psychic events.

Stimulant drugs inducing dependence, such as cocaine and amphetamine, might be supposed, on the other hand, to block inhibition of the reward system. This supposition is consistent with the finding of Stein (1964) that amphetamine lowers the threshold of excitation of the reward system. With continued drug blockade, supersensitivity of the reward system to inhibition might be expected. Such supersensitivity would lead to tolerance during treatment, and to a rebound effect on withdrawal, in the shape of excessive inhibition of the reward system. The resulting dependence would again have a heavy psychic component, because the reward system also involves psychic events.

That mainly stimulant drugs inducing psychic dependence, such as cocaine, amphetamine and nicotine, interact with adrenaline or noradrenaline (Burn & Tainter, 1931; Cannon &

Rosenblueth, 1949; Emmelin & Müren, 1951; Burn & Rand, 1958a & b, 1959) lends some support to these ideas.

As with physical dependence, the particular site at which a drug blocks the transmitter supply of a brain cell might determine whether or not tolerance is prominent alongside psychic dependence. Some drugs, such as cocaine and cannabis, are said to induce psychic dependence without tolerance; but there seems to be a possibility that psychic tolerance exists as an entity distinct from physical tolerance, as some of the features of cocaine addiction suggest. Cocaine is well known not to induce physical tolerance; yet a man or monkey addicted to this drug tends to increase the dose and thus to poison himself (Jaffe, 1965; M. H. Seevers, 1967, personal communication). Such a tendency would be explicable if cocaine induces psychic tolerance without its physical counterpart. Experiments would be worth doing to determine whether psychic tolerance really happens.

The existence of drugs that affect the eudystat, but do not induce psychic dependence, raises a difficulty. The phenothiazine tranquillizers, which are non-addictive central depressant drugs, have been shown to raise the threshold of self-stimulation (Olds, 1962) and to increase punishment discrimination (Geller & Seifter, 1960) in the rat. If the phenothiazines act by increasing inhibition of the reward system, no inducement towards repeating the dose would be expected.

At first sight, reserpine might seem even more difficult to understand, since it induces sensitivity of pharmacological denervation in several peripheral structures (Burn & Rand, 1958a & b, 1959) and is also psychoactive, although it does not induce psychic dependence. The difficulty does not seem great, however, when we reflect that reserpine tends to be dysphoric and even gives rise to melancholia in some people. That nalorphine induces physical but not psychic dependence (Martin, 1967; M. H. Seevers, 1967, personal communication) is also understandable in the light of its dysphoric properties.

Certain central stimulant drugs, such as monoamine oxidase inhibitors, are also not incriminated as inducing psychic dependence. Perhaps the long latencies between taking the drug and the onset of its effect, and between withdrawing the drug and the disappearance of this effect, account for lack of withdrawal dysphoria and of drug seeking behaviour.

Receptor mechanisms

There is a comfortable feeling among pharmacologists that when drug actions have been stated in terms of receptors we understand these actions. This feeling seems to date at least from the time of Ehrlich, who called people pig-headed who did not accept his ideas about receptors, which he once described as 'special catching claws or traps of the protoplasm' (Marquardt, 1949).

To translate into terms of receptors the model of the supersensitivity of pharmacological denervation and its interpretation through humoral transmitter blockade, three assumptions may be made. First, that an increase in the number of receptors heightens and a decrease lowers response; second, that depriving a cell of humoral transmitter increases the number of receptors for transmitter on the cell; and third, that subsequent exposure of the cell to transmitter reduces the number of receptors (Collier, 1965a & b, 1966).

According to these assumptions, pharmacological blockade of an endogenous humoral transmitter in the brain should induce further receptors for transmitter on the appropriate brain cells. An increase in receptor number should in turn permit a stronger response to such transmitter as passes the blockade, with accompanying tolerance. If the receptor blockaded lies on the responding cell, tolerance should differ quantitatively from that occurring when the blockade is at a distance from this cell, which remains accessible to the leakage of transmitter from unblockaded sources.

After drug withdrawal, transmitter should become more accessible to more receptors, with consequent abstinence effects. On continued exposure to normal amounts of transmitter, the number of receptors should decline and abstinence effects subside. If some of the additional receptors are left, this might explain any persistent after-effects of the drug (Cochin & Kornetsky, 1964).

Number of receptors and intensity of response

Suppose that a certain number of transmitter molecules (insufficient to elicit a maximal response) in a certain volume of solution reversibly interacts with a number of pharmacological receptors on the surface of a cell with which that solution is in contact. Suppose also that each transmitter-receptor interaction yields a quantum of response. If the concentration of transmitter remains unaltered, a reduction in the number of accessible receptors (as by antagonist occupancy) will lead to a lessened total response, because the probability of encounter is lessened. Conversely, if the number of receptors is increased, the response will be heightened. These considerations would apply either in rate theory (Paton, 1961) or in occupation theory of drug-receptor interaction.

Drug-induced changes in the number of receptors

That drugs can lessen the accessible number of receptors, either by occupancy or by destruction, is a commonplace of receptor theory. The concept that deprivation of humoral transmitter can lead to an increase in the number of its receptors is rarer, but it has occasionally been proposed. Thus, Axelsson & Thesleff (1959), by releasing acetylcholine iontophoretically from the tip of a micropipette, showed that, after denervating a striated muscle, sensitivity to this transmitter spread out from the motor end-plate over the general surface of the whole muscle fibre until, after one or two weeks, sensitivity everywhere equalled that hitherto restricted to motor end-plates. Pharmacological denervation with botulinum toxin induced, in about the same period, a similar change in sensitivity to acetylcholine applied by micropipette (Thesleff, 1960). These effects were conceived as a spread of acetylcholine receptors over the surface of the muscle fibre.

Pharmacological and silent receptors

A further distinction may also be made. That is between 'pharmacological' and 'silent' receptors. Gaddum (1961) used the term 'pharmacological receptor' for any receptor that interacts with a drug molecule to give a pharmacological response. All other receptors may provisionally be termed 'silent', whether their interaction with a drug leads to its storage or to its removal from the body, either by excretion or destruction. Thus, the receptors for 5-hydroxytryptamine in blood platelets and for acetylcholine on cholinesterases are both silent. The concept of silent receptors may help to explain some types of tolerance, especially where this occurs without dependence. In the genesis of dependence, I have only supposed pharmacological receptors to be involved.

There are several examples of drugs inducing silent receptors. One is the ability of many drugs to increase the available amount of an enzyme that destroys them (Remmer, 1965). Another example comes from immunology. We owe to Ehrlich (1900) the conclusion that small molecules of ordinary drugs do not induce circulating antibody. This is still true within limits, and it applies for example to the free molecules of peptide hormones such as gastrin and angiotensin. If, however, before these peptides are injected they are adsorbed onto the surface of microparticles of polyacrylate (Berglund, 1965; Stremple, Abramoff, Van Oss, Wilson & Ellison, 1967) or carbon (Boyd, Landon & Peart, 1967), they do induce formation of specific antibodies, circulating in the blood.

Mechanisms of receptor increase

The mechanism by which receptors might increase in number in response to drug treatment is unknown, but there is evidence suggesting that protein synthesis is involved. Thus, the development of tolerance to morphine in the mouse and rat is inhibited by actinomycin D (Cohen, Keats, Krivoy & Ungar, 1965), by puromycin (Smith, Karmin & Gavitt, 1966) and by 8-azaguanine (Spoerlein & Scrafani, 1967). Moreover, there is a latency of about two days before tolerance towards a single large dose of morphine appears in the rat (Spoerlein & Scrafani, 1967). The long persistence of traces of tolerance induced by morphine is consistent with some synthetic event underlying the development of tolerance. The question whether actinomycin D or like-acting drugs inhibit the onset of dependence also would be worth looking into.

Pursuing such observations, Ungar & Cohen (1966) have claimed that brain extracts, from rats made tolerant to morphine, induce morphine tolerance in mice. If this claim is confirmed, in spite of the failure of Tirri (1967) to do so, it would seem to point to a parallel between morphine tolerance and infective drug-resistance in bacteria. In the experiments of Ungar & Cohen, however, morphine tolerance was induced in mice by cell-free dialysates of rat brain, whereas, in bacteria, cell-to-cell contact has so far been needed for the transfer of drug-resistance (Watanabe, 1963).

The effectiveness of interaction between transmitter and its receptors may sometimes increase quite quickly. For example, cocaine rapidly raises sensitivity to noradrenaline. Nakatsu & Reiffenstein (1968) have given evidence that this effect, in the isolated rat vas deferens, can be interpreted as an increased receptor utilization. The rapid effectiveness of cocaine suggests that other ways of increasing receptor numbers than by chemical synthesis should also be envisaged. Such mechanisms might include the re-arrangement of end-groups on receptors already present, the activation of inactive receptors or the protection of active ones from inactivation by endogenous processes.

The foregoing adopts the concept of M. H. Seevers (1967, personal communication) that psychic dependence arises in association with the balance of the linked reward-punishment systems of Olds (1962). A drug inducing psychic dependence is supposed to change this balance by blockade of a transmitter inhibiting the reward or exciting the punishment system. From this blockade, a supersensitivity of pharmacological denervation is expected, leading to tolerance and withdrawal effects that could be purely psychic. The possible role in psychic dependence on cocaine of another type of supersensitivity towards transmitter is worth considering.

Cocaine induces a supersensitivity to noradrenaline and some other sympathomimetic amines that is faster in onset than that of denervation and does not depend on deprivation of neurohumoral transmitter (Trendelenburg, 1959, 1963). If noradrenaline or other amine potentiated by cocaine were the transmitter that excites the reward or inhibits the punishment system, such a supersensitivity should tip towards reward the balance of the reward-punishment relationship and induce dependence by operant conditioning. In as much as the sensitization was direct, tolerance or withdrawal effects would be expected only to the extent that a deprivation of transmitter arose through feed-back. Dependence should also develop faster through a direct sensitization of this kind than through deprivation of transmitter.

These considerations raise three questions. First, has dependence on cocaine the characteristics to be expected from a direct effect on the reward-punishment system? Second, do other psychoactive drugs, such as methylphenidate, inducing a comparable sensitivity in effector organs (Maxwell, 1965; Maxwell, Wastila & Eckhardt, 1966), give rise to a dependence similar to that of cocaine? Third, do other drugs that induce a dependence like that of cocaine sensitize effector organs to noradrenaline?

The view has been advanced (Reiffenstein, 1968; Nakatsu & Reiffenstein, 1968) that supersensitivity towards cocaine arises through an increase in the efficiency of the interaction between noradrenaline and its receptors. In rate-theory (Paton, 1961) this effect might be visualized as an increased ability of the receptor to release or to destroy the noradrenaline molecule after the two have interacted. In occupation-theory this would represent an increased 'efficacy' (Stephenson, 1956) or 'intrinsic activity' (Ariens, 1966) or noradrenaline.

An improved efficiency of interaction between transmitter and receptor offers an alternative to the mechanism I have proposed to account for dependence (and accompanying tolerance) in which the number of pharmacological receptors for a neurohumoral transmitter substance increases on an appropriate nerve cell. Where dependence is accompanied by tolerance, either of these receptor changes might be supposed to arise through deprivation of natural neurohumoral transmitter.

Summary

There are two distinct theories of dependence embodied in what I have said. One is that the supersensitivity of pharmacological denervation provides a model of how dependence happens. This model can be applied not only to physical dependence, but also to psychic dependence, by gearing the model to the two-way adaptor of the linked reward and punishment systems of the brain. The other theory accounts for dependence in terms of drug-induced change in the number of receptors for endogenous humoral transmitter.

The two theories are complementary and they may be neatly fitted together, if we suppose that an increase in the number of receptors for transmitter underlies the supersensitivity of pharmacological denervation; although we should beware of neatness in explanations of biological phenomena. Thus, there are the complications that supersensitivity may extend to endogenous substances other than the blockaded transmitter and that drugs might increase the effective number of receptors by other means than blockade of humoral transmitter.

It can be concluded that the model of the supersensitivity of pharmacological denervation and the theory of drug-induced increase in receptors for endogenous mediator each offer the possibility of accounting for drug dependence, with or without accompanying tolerance, and that the two theories fit well together. Fortunately, both suggest further experiments.

REFERENCES

Alonso-de-Florida, F., del Castillo, J., Gonzalez, C. C. & Sanchez, V. (1965). The anaphylactic reaction of denervated skeletal muscle in the guinea-pig. *Science*, **147**, 1155–1156.

Ariens, E. J. (1966). Receptor theory and structure-action relationships. *Advances in Drug Research*, **3**, 235–285.

Axelsson, J. & Thesleff, S. (1959). A study of supersensitivity in denervated mammalian skeletal muscle. *J. Physiol. Lond.*, **147**, 178–193.

Beleslin, D. & Polak, R. L. (1965). Depression by morphine and chloralose of acetylcholine release from the cat's brain. *J. Physiol. Lond.*, **177**, 411–419.

Beleslin, D., Polak, R. L. & Sproull, D. H. (1965). The release of acetylcholine into the cerebral subarachnoid space of anaesthetized cats. *J. Physiol. Lond.*, **177**, 420–428.

Berglund, G. (1965). Preparation of an antiserum to an antigen of low molecular weight. *Nature, Lond.*, **206**, 523–524.

Boyd, G. W., Landon, J. & Peart, W. S. (1967). Radiommunoassay for determining plasma-levels of angiotensin II in man. *Lancet*, ii, 1002–1005.

Burn, J. H. & Rand, M. J. (1958a). Noradrenaline in artery walls and its dispersal by reserpine. *Brit. med. J.*, **1**, 903–908.

Burn, J. H. & Rand, M. J. (1958b). The action of sympathomimetic amines in animals treated with reserpine. *J. Physiol. Lond.*, **144**, 314–336.

Burn, J. H. & Rand, M. J. (1959). The cause of the supersensitivity of smooth muscle to noradrenaline after sympathetic degeneration. *J. Physiol. Lond.*, **147**, 135–143.

Burn, J. H. & Tainter, M. L. (1931). An analysis of the effect of cocaine on the actions of adrenaline and tyramine. *J. Physiol. Lond.*, **71**, 169–193.

Cannon, W. B. & Rosenblueth, A. (1949). *The supersensitivity of denervated structures*, pp. 47–57, 66–69, New York: Macmillan.

Cochin, J. & Kornetsky, C. (1964). Development and loss of tolerance to morphine in the rat after single and multiple injections. *J. Pharmac. exp. Ther.*, **145**, 1–10.

Cohen, M., Keats, A. S., Krivoy, W. & Ungar, G. (1965). Effect of actinomycin D on morphine tolerance. *Proc. Soc. exp. Biol. Med.*, **119**, 381-384.
Collier, H. O. J. (1965a). A general theory of the genesis of drug dependence by induction of receptors. *Nature, Lond.*, **205**, 181-182.
Collier, H. O. J. (1965b). In *Hashish: its chemistry and pharmacology*. Ed. by Wolstenholme, G. E. W. & Knight, J. p. 83-87. London: Churchill.
Collier, H. O. J. (1966). Tolerance, physical dependence and receptors. *Advances in Drug Research*, **3**, 171-188.
Ehrlich, P. (1900). On immunity with special reference to cell life. *Proc. roy. Soc.*, **66**, 424-448.
Emmelin, N. (1959). Supersensitivity due to prolonged administration of ganglion-blocking compounds. *Brit. J. Pharmac. Chemother.*, **14**, 229-233.
Emmelin, N. (1961) Supersensitivity following 'pharmacological denervation'. *Pharmac. Rev.*, **13**, 17-37.
Emmelin, N. & Müren, A. (1951). Sensitization of the submaxillary gland to chemical stimuli. *Acta physiol. scand.*, **24**, 103-107.
Emmelin, N. & Müren, A. (1952). The sensitivity of submaxillary glands to chemical agents studied in cats under various conditions over long periods. *Acta physiol. scand.*, **26**, 221-231.
Fleming, W. W. (1966). Nonspecific supersensitivity of the guinea-pig ileum produced by chronic ganglion blockade. *The Pharmacologist*, **8**, 193.
Gaddum, J. H. (1961). In *Enzymes and Drug Action*, Ed. by Mongar, J. L. & de Reuck, A. S. V. p. 441. London: Churchill.
Gaddum, J. H. & Picarelli, Z. P. (1957). Two kinds of tryptamine receptor. *Brit. J. Pharmac. Chemother.*, **12**, 323-328.
Geller, I. & Seifter, J. (1960). The effects of meprobamate, barbiturates, d-amphetamine and promazine on experimentally induced conflict in the rat. *Psychopharmacologia, Berlin.* **1**, 482-492.
Geller, I. & Seifter, J. (1962). The effects of mono-urethans, di-urethans and barbiturates on a punishment discrimination. *J. Pharmac. exp. Ther.*, **136**, 284-288.
Jaffe, J. H. (1965). Drug addiction and drug abuse. In *The Pharmacological Basis of Therapeutics*, Ed. by Goodman, L. S. & Gilman, A. 3rd ed. pp. 285-311. London: Collier-Macmillan.
Jaffe, J. H. & Sharpless, S. K. (1965). The rapid development of physical dependence on barbiturates. *J. Pharmac. exp. Ther.*, **150**, 140-145.
Jasinski, D. R., Martin, W. R. & Haertzen, C. A. (1967). The human pharmacology and abuse potential of N-allylnoroxymorphone (naloxone). *J. Pharmac. exp. Ther.*, **157**, 420-426.
King, H. E. (1961). Psychological effects of excitation in the limbic system. In *Electrical Stimulation of the Brain*, Ed. by Sheer, D. E. pp. 477-486. Austin: University of Texas Press.
Marquardt, M. (1949). *Paul Ehrlich*, pp. 79, 151. London: Heinemann.
Martin, W. R. (1967). Opioid antagonists. *Pharmac. Rev.*, **19**, 463-521.

Martin, W. R. (1968). A homeostatic and redundancy theory of tolerance to and dependence on narcotic analgesics. In *The Addictive States*, pp. 206–225. Williams & Wilkins, Baltimore.

Maxwell, R. A. (1965). Concerning the mechanism of action of methylphenidate on the responses of rabbit vascular tissue to norepinephrine. *J. Pharmac. exp. Ther.*, **147**, 289–297.

Maxwell, R. A., Wastila, W. B. & Eckhardt, S. B. (1966). Some factors determining the response of rabbit aortic strips to dl-norepinephrine-7-H^3 hydrochloride and the influence of cocaine, guanethidine and methylphenidate on these factors. *J. Pharmac. exp. Ther.*, **151**, 253–261.

Nakatsu, K. & Reiffenstein, R. J. (1968). Increased receptor utilization: mechanism of cocaine potentiation. *Nature, Lond.*, **217**, 1276–1277.

Nichols, J. R. (1963). A procedure which produces sustained opiate-directed behaviour (morphine addiction) in the rat. *Psychological Reports*, **13**, 895–904.

Nichols, J. R. & Hsiao, S. (1967). Addiction liability of albino rats: breeding for quantitative differences in morphine dependence. *Science*, **157**, 561–563.

Olds, J. (1962). Hypothalamic substrates of reward. *Physiol. Rev.*, **42**, 554–604.

Oswald, I. & Thacore, V. R. (1963). Amphetamine and phenmetrazine addiction. Physiological abnormalities in the abstinence syndrome. *Brit. med. J.*, ii, 427–431.

Paton, W. D. M. (1957). The action of morphine and related substances on contraction and on acetylcholine output of the coaxially stimulated guinea-pig ileum. *Brit. J. Pharmac. Chemother.*, **12**, 119–127.

Paton, W. D. M. (1961). A theory of drug action based on the rate of drug receptor combination. *Proc. roy. Soc. B.*, **154**, 21–69.

Pickens, R. & Harris, W. C. (1968). Self-administration of d-amphetamine by rats. *Psychopharmacologia, Berlin*, **12**, 158–163.

Poschel, B. P. H. & Ninteman, F. W. (1966). Hypothalamic self-stimulation: its suppression by blockade of norepinephrine biosynthesis and reinstatement by blockade of norepinephrine biosynthesis and reinstatement by methamphetamine. *Life Sciences*, **5**, 11–16.

Reiffenstein, R. J. (1968). Effects of cocaine on the rate of contraction to noradrenaline in the cat spleen strip: mode of action of cocaine. *Brit. J. Pharmac. Chemother.*, **32**, 519–597.

Remmer, H. (1965). Drug-induced formation of smooth endoplasmic reticulum and of drug metabolizing enzymes. *Proceedings of the European Society for the Study of Drug Toxicity*, **4**, 57–76.

Schaumann, W. (1957). Inhibition by morphine of the release of acetylcholine from the intestine of the guinea-pig. *Brit. J. Pharmac. Chemother.*, **12**, 115–118.

Sharpless, S. K. & Halpern, L. N. (1962). The electrical excitability of chronically isolated cortex studied by means of permanently implanted electrodes. *Electroenceph. clin. Neurophysiol.*, **14**, 244–255.

Sharpless, S. K. & Jaffe, J. H. (1963). The electrical activity of neuronally isolated cortex during barbiturate withdrawal. *The Pharmacologist*, **5,** 250.

Smith, A. A., Karmin, M. & Gavitt, J. (1966). Blocking effect of puromycin, ethanol and chloroform on the development of tolerance to an opiate. *Biochem. Pharmac.*, **15,** 1877–1879.

Spoerlein, M. T. & Scrafani, J. (1967). Effects of time and 8-azaquanine on the development of morphine tolerance. *Life Sciences*, **6,** 1549–1564.

Stein, L. (1964). Amphetamine and neural reward mechanism. In *Animal Behaviour and Drug Action*, Ed. by Steinberg, H., de Reuck, A. V. S. & Knight, J. pp. 91–118. London: Churchill.

Stephenson, R. P. (1956). A modification of receptor theory. *Brit. J. Pharmac. Chemother.*, **11,** 379–393.

Stremple, J. F., Abramoff, P., van Oss, C. J., Wilson, S. D. & Ellison, E. H. (1967) Antibodies to synthetic human gastrin 1. *Lancet*, **ii,** 1180–1182.

Thesleff, S. (1960). Supersensitivity of skeletal muscle produced by botulinum toxin. *J. Physiol. Lond.*, **151,** 598–607.

Tirri, R. (1967). Transfer of induced tolerance to morphine and promazine by brain homogenate. *Experientia*, **23,** 278

Trendelenburg, U. (1959). The supersensitivity caused by cocaine. *J. Pharmac. exp. Ther.*, **125,** 55–65.

Trendelenburg, U. (1963). Supersensitivity and subsensitivity to sympathomimetic amines. *Pharmac. Rev.*, **15,** 225–276.

Türker, K. & Akcasu, A. (1962). Effect of morphine on 5-HT of cat's brain. *New Istanbul Contrib. clin. sci.*, **5,** 89–97.

Ungar, G. & Cohen, M. (1966). Induction of morphine tolerance by material extracted from brain of tolerant animals. *Int. J. Neuropharmacol.*, **5,** 183–192.

Vogt, M. (1954). The concentration of sympathin in different parts of the central nervous system under normal conditions and after administration of drugs. *J. Physiol. London.*, **123,** 451–481.

Watanabe, T. (1963). Infective heredity of multiple drug resistance in bacteria. *Bact. Rev.*, **27,** 87–115.

Weeks, J. R. & Collins, R. J. (1964). Factors affecting voluntary morphine intake in self-maintained addicted rats. *Psychopharmacologia, Berlin*, **6,** 267–279.

Wikler, A. (1953). Opiate addiction. pp. 54–60. Springfield, Illinois: Thomas.

WITHDRAWAL PHENOMENA AS MANIFESTATIONS OF DISUSE SUPERSENSITIVITY

SETH SHARPLESS AND JEROME JAFFE

Albert Einstein College of Medicine, New York and The University of Chicago

WHEN a tissue is exposed to an exotic chemical environment there are likely to be significant changes in the metabolism of the surviving cells. If these changes impair the capacity of the cells to function in the old environment, and if time is required for their reversal, sudden withdrawal of the exotic compound may expose the altered state and disrupt the normal functioning of the cell. It is appropriate to refer to such a condition as physical dependence. Any system endowed with multiple chemical regulatory mechanisms is likely to become dependent in this sense on *some* chemical agents and fail to become dependent on others.

This is a satisfactory but trivial account of the concept of dependence. It does not explain the unique potency of narcotic and hypnotic substances in producing dependence, and it does not account for the fact that physical dependence on such compounds is manifested chiefly by changes in nerve cells rather than in other tissues. In considering these problems, we have been led to a theory relating the development of dependence to the *disuse* of certain neural circuits (Sharpless and Halpern, 1962; Jaffe and Sharpless, 1963, 1965, 1966; Sharpless and Jaffe, 1966). According to the 'disuse hypothesis', dependence on narcotic and hypnotic compounds is secondary to the normal therapeutic action of the drugs—a decrease in the activity of certain central nervous pathways. It is the decreased activity *per se* and not the drug that produces the change, and any agent that depresses activity in the same pathways, regardless of how this is achieved, ought to induce similar changes, which would be manifested in characteristic abstinence phenomena if input were abruptly restored to the altered pathways.

This hypothesis has much in common with the 'homeostatic theory' of Himmelsbach (1943) and especially with the more recent 'homeostatic and redundancy theory' of Martin (1966). Such theories at least have the virtue of making the phenomena of physical dependence comprehensible in a biological framework. Opiates and barbiturates could hardly have constituted a threat to survival in the environment of our evolutionary ancestors, but there are other agents that might have acted similarly to reduce activity in central nervous pathways: injury, disease, bizarre environments involving privation of some specific sensory input, exposure to gases or vapours with narcotic potency, and the ingestion of poisonous plants or animals. Certainly, an organism that developed a mechanism for coping with the chronic reduction of activity in vital nervous pathways, no matter how produced, would have had a distinct evolutionary advantage. Such a mechanism might operate to bring about a gradual increase in the efficacy of excitatory synapses during periods of reduced impulse traffic. It would be purchased cheaply: at the cost merely of developing a tendency to over-react for a while when input is first restored to the previously disused pathways.

Disuse supersensitivity in autonomic neuroeffector junctions

There is ample evidence that changes of this kind occur in specific junctions in the central and peripheral nervous systems. These changes have been studied most extensively in autonomic effector junctions in connection with the phenomena of 'denervation supersensitivity'. In elaborating the analogy between denervation supersensitivity and withdrawal phenomena, it should be remembered that the term 'denervation supersensitivity' is itself poorly defined and is used for several quite distinct phenomena. For example, we know that at least two factors are involved in the supersensitivity of autonomic effector organs deprived of their adrenergic nerve supply. The first of these is a loss of a catecholamine uptake mechanism in the nerve ending (Hertting, Axelrod & Whitby, 1961; Kirpekar, Cervoni & Furchgott, 1962). The type of supersensitivity resulting from this develops abruptly when the nerve ending degenerates. There is a second type of supersensitivity that develops very slowly, over a period of several weeks. This slowly developing kind of supersensitivity appears in both adrenergic and cholinergic neuroeffector junctions, and it has been called 'disuse supersensitivity' because it seems to be produced by any agent that blocks the flow of impulses down the motor pathway.

Our concept of disuse supersensitivity is based chiefly on the studies of Emmelin and his associates on the salivary gland (1961), and on those of Trendelenburg and his associates on the nictitating membrane and sweat gland (1963). Extrapolating somewhat from the work of these and other investigators, disuse supersensitivity in autonomic effector organs seems to have the following characteristics. (1) Although it probably begins to develop as soon as input is decreased, disuse supersensitivity approaches a maximum slowly, about two-thirds of the total increment in sensitivity occurring in two weeks. (2) It is produced by any agent that blocks the flow of impulses down the motor pathway. (3) It is reversible. When input is restored, the supersensitivity gradually subsides, and in autonomic effector organs it can be prevented from developing if the effector organ is directly activated by means of exogenous sympathomimetic or parasympathomimetic drugs. (4) In contrast to the supersensitivity produced by impairment of the uptake mechanism in adrenergic nerve endings, *disuse* supersensitivity is relatively unspecific. Thus, the effector organ becomes sensitized to *both* acetylcholine and noradrenaline when it is deprived of *either* adrenergic or cholinergic input.

This last feature of disuse supersensitivity—its lack of chemical specificity—implies that the change cannot be attributed to the proliferation of a specific cholinotropic (cholinergic) or adrenotropic (adrenergic) receptor; it suggests, rather, that disuse is affecting the coupling between receptor occupation and activation of the secretory or contractile mechanism (Sharpless, 1964).

Disuse supersensitivity in neurones

Contrary to the earlier observations of Cannon and Rosenblueth (1936), it now seems that denervated sympathetic ganglion cells do not respond to smaller concentrations of acetylcholine than normal cells. This was shown by Volle and Koelle (1961), who recorded electrical activity of postganglionic axons, and more recently by D. A. Brown (1966), who recorded the electrical activity of chronically denervated ganglion cells *in vitro*. In neurones, however, the receptive part of the cell is separated from the reaction mechanism, the neurosecretory apparatus, by an all-or-none conducting system. It is entirely possible that the neurosecretory apparatus is affected by disuse in such a way that more transmitter is liberated per nerve impulse from the disused nerve ending. It has been shown by Brown, Davies and Ferry (1961), for example, that the splenic nerve liberates more sympathin per impulse after a period of disuse. The possible roles of increased transmitter liberation and receptor proliferation in the development of physical dependence has been discussed by Collier (1966).

It may be inappropriate to include increased transmitter release under the term 'supersensitivity', although in a synaptic network, an increase in the capacity of prejunctional elements to liberate transmitter would not easily be distinguished from an increased sensitivity of postjunctional elements. Furthermore, such a change might result from an alteration in the mechanism coupling depolarization of the nerve terminal to activation of the neurosecretory mechanism, and in this respect, the effect of disuse on neurones might be similar to the effects of disuse on smooth muscle and gland cells, for in the latter, as we have suggested, there is reason to believe that it is the coupling mechanism rather than a specific receptor that is altered by disuse.

There is now fairly convincing evidence that some form of disuse potentiation (involving either an increase in the potency of the disused presynaptic element or an increase in the sensitivity of the postsynaptic element) occurs in the central nervous system. Something akin to disuse supersensitivity may have been demonstrated even in monosynaptic spinal pathways. Thus, tenotomy, an operation that would be expected to relieve the tension on stretch receptors in the muscle and in this way to reduce the activity of Ia afferent fibres from the tenotomized muscle, results in a gradual increase in the number of neurones that can be discharged through a single synapse by stimulating the disused afferent fibres (Beranek and Hnik, 1959; Kozak and Westerman, 1961).

In our laboratory, Friedman and Jaffe (1966) have taken advantage of the existence of a group of cholinoceptive cells in the anterior hypothalamus, which are involved in temperature regulation. When cholinomimetic drugs are injected locally (Lomax and Jenden, 1966), or when centrally acting cholinomimetic drugs are administered systemically, the activation of these neurones produces a fall in body temperature in some species, including mice. The receptors are evidently of the muscarine-sensitive type, for they can be activated by pilocarpine and other muscarine-like agents, and the action can be blocked by atropine and scopolamine. It is not blocked by single systemic doses of methscopolamine (Friedman and Jaffe, 1966; Friedman, 1968).

This is a convenient system with which to carry out experiments analogous to those performed by Emmelin and his colleagues, with the important difference that the elements to be rendered supersensitive are cholinoceptive cells in the central nervous system rather than peripheral gland cells. Friedman and Jaffe have been able to show, in a carefully controlled and frequently replicated experiment, that the central cholinoceptive elements do become supersensitive after prolonged treatment with scopolamine. The time course of the development and decay of supersensitivity is about the same as that observed in the salivary gland. If scopolamine is withdrawn after five days of daily treatment (200 mg/kg/day, orally) the hypothermic response to pilocarpine increases as scopolamine is metabolized, attaining a maximum much greater than the normal response in about twenty-four hours; it then begins to subside as input is restored, coming back to the control level in about seventy-two hours. With a longer period of chronic scopolamine treatment, the supersensitivity to pilocarpine reaches a higher level and lasts for a longer time after withdrawal. The supersensitivity is not affected by the presence of a peripheral cholinergic blockade established by methscopolamine.

Experiments on surgically isolated cerebral cortex

According to the disuse hypothesis, the presence of the drug is not directly responsible for the development of the latent hyperexcitability that characterizes physical dependence. Because the direct cause is disuse or reduced activity, the presence of the drug should not be necessary; any other agent that reduces activity in the same pathways ought to have similar effects.

It is possible to isolate an area of cerebral cortex in the cat by subpial undercutting and circumsection (Burns, 1950). The cortical neurones are thus cut off from external neuronal input; only the blood supply remains substantially intact. An epileptiform discharge can be elicited in such a slab of cortex by repetitive electrical stimulation, and this discharge is practically identical with that which can be elicited in intact cortex. Gradually, however, over a period of weeks, the isolated slab becomes more susceptible to epileptiform activity in the sense that the threshold for the electrically induced afterdischarge falls and the duration of the afterdischarge increases to many times the initial value (Echlin and McDonald, 1954; Grafstein and Sastry, 1957; Sharpless and Halpern, 1962).

Many changes occur in chronically isolated cortex: the largest neurones undergo retrograde degeneration and may disappear entirely; there are falls in the acetylcholinesterase and choline acetylase levels (Echlin and Battista, 1962; Hebb, Krnjević & Silver, 1963); in kittens, there may be a prolific growth of axon collaterals (Purpura, 1961). We do not know whether any of these changes plays a significant role in the increased susceptibility to paroxysmal activity. A report by Rutledge, Ranck, & Duncan (1967) suggests that *disuse* may be the critical factor. These investigators *exercised* the isolated cortical slab by subjecting it to daily, subconvulsive electrical stimulation; in this way, they were able to prevent the development of an increased susceptibility to epileptiform activity.

Because seizures are a conspicuous feature of the barbiturate withdrawal syndrome, we have undertaken several experiments to determine whether the cerebral cortex changes during chronic barbiturate intoxication in a manner similar to the consequences of surgical isolation (Sharpless & Jaffe, 1966). Cats were subjected to long periods of barbiturate intoxication by intravenous administration of an anaesthetizing dose of pentobarbital several times a day. The animal was allowed to emerge from anaesthesia for eight hours every night, when it was fed, cleaned and exercised. After the animal had clearly become dependent, as judged by susceptibility to pentylenetetrazol-induced seizures during a trial withdrawal period, the brain stem was sectioned (creating a *cerveau isolé* preparation), and the barbiturate was withdrawn. A day later, a slab of cortex was isolated in the usual manner and tested for susceptibility to electrically induced convulsive activity.

We were thus able to study a freshly isolated slab of cortex in an unanaesthetized, *cerveau isolé* preparation, physically dependent on barbiturates and undergoing withdrawal. The results were disappointing. In only a few cases were the isolated slabs of cortex more susceptible to electrically induced epileptiform activity than normal cortex. Even in these cases the change was negligible by comparison with that produced by surgical isolation. Thus, the degree of barbiturate intoxication that we were able to achieve was not sufficient to reproduce the effects of surgical isolation at the cortical level; however, this degree of intoxication *was* adequate to produce a marked change in some subcortical structure, as indicated by the great sensitivity of the animals to a convulsant drug. We do not regard this experiment as a satisfactory test of the disuse hypothesis. We know that sleep, and presumably moderate barbiturate intoxication, can alter greatly the pattern of cortical activity, while decreasing only slightly the total quantity of unit firing in association cortex (Evarts, 1961; Yamamoto & Schaeppi, 1961). To test the disuse hypothesis, we would have to maintain a level of barbiturate intoxication that would truly depress cortical unit activity. Alternatively, the subcortical structures primarily affected by the barbiturate (the arousal mechanism?) would have to be deprived of input by surgical means. Neither experiment seems feasible at present.

Use-hypertrophy in redundant pathways—Martin's theory

Martin (1966) has suggested an alternative to the disuse hypothesis. Both theories share a common assumption: physical dependence represents an adaptation of nervous tissue to the altered pattern of nervous activity produced by the drug, rather than to the presence of the drug entity itself. In Martin's theory, as a result of the drug-induced depression in a specific nervous pathway, recurrent and surround inhibition is diminished, and parallel or 'redundant' pathways (which are not themselves depressed by the drug) are disinhibited. The net effect is that the redundant pathways are exercised more than usual and tend to hypertrophy. When the drug is withdrawn, the sum of the activities of the previously depressed pathway and the hypertrophied redundant pathways produces an exaggerated response.

The two theories are directly opposed with respect to the effects of use on excitatory junctions. Intuitively, Martin's approach may be somewhat more attractive, for it appeals to traditional associationistic theories of learning and familiar analogies (e.g. hypertrophy of a muscle by exercise). A direct, experimental test of the two theories does not seem possible by any available techniques, and it may be asked whether there are any important differences in the practical consequences of the two approaches. There does seem to be a difference in emphasis. Thus, Martin's approach focuses attention on persistent effects of dependence, which may last for some months (Sloan & Eisenman, 1966). These effects are not easily explained by our disuse hypothesis without additional assumptions. On the other hand, the rapid regression of classical withdrawal symptoms must also be explained, and we have already noted that the time course of development and decay of classical withdrawal phenomena is quite similar to that of disuse supersensitivity in peripheral junctions (Jaffe & Sharpless, 1965).

It is possible of course, that both processes occur, disuse supersensitivity in some pathways and use-hypertrophy in others, and that they follow different time courses. In that case, both processes might be activated by the radical change in the pattern of nervous activity produced by a potent central nervous depressant.

Acknowledgements: This work was supported by U.S. Public Health Service Grants NB-02583, NB-06656, MH-11,540, MH-12,621 and Career Development Awards NB-15,296 and MH-25,383.

REFERENCES

Beránek, R. & Hník, P. (1959). *Science*, **130**, 981.
Brown, D. A. (1966). *Brit. J. Pharmac.*, **26**, 511.
Brown, G. L., Davies, B. N. & Ferry, C. B. (1961). *J. Physiol.*, **159**, 365.
Burns, B. D. (1950). *J. Physiol.*, **111**, 50.
Cannon, W. & Rosenblueth, A. (1963). *Amer. J. Physiol.*, **116**, 408.
Collier, H. O. J. (1966). In *Advances in Drug Research*, **3**, p. 171, Ed. by Harper, N. J. & Simmonds, A. B. New York: Academic Press.
Echlin, F. & Battista, A. (1962). *Trans. Amer. Neurol. Ass.*, **87**, 190.
Echlin, F. & McDonald, J. (1954). *Trans. Amer. Neurol. Ass.*, **79**, 75.
Emmelin, N. (1961). *Pharmac. Rev.*, **13**, 16.
Evarts, E. V. (1961). In *The Nature of Sleep*, Ciba Foundation Symposium, p. 171. Ed. by Wolstenholme, G. E. W. & O'Connor, M. London: Churchill.
Friedman, M. (1968). Supersensitivity to Pilocarpine in a Central Thermoregulatory System. Ph.D. dissertation. Albert Einstein College of Medicine, New York.
Friedman, M. & Jaffe, J. (1966). *Pharmacologist*, **8**, 199.
Grafstein, B. & Sastry, P. (1957). *Electroencephal. Clin. Neurophysiol.*, **9**, 723.
Hebb, C. O., Krnjević, K. & Silver, A. (1963). *Nature, Lond.*, **198**, 692.
Hertting, G., Axelrod, J. & Whitby, L. (1961). *J. Pharmac. exp. Therap.*, **134**, 146.
Himmelsbach, C. K. (1943). *Fed. Proc.*, **2**, 201.
Jaffe, J. & Sharpless, S. K. (1963). *Pharmacologist*, **5**, 249.
Jaffe, J. & Sharpless, S. K. (1965). *J. Pharmac. exp. Therap.*, **150**, 140.
Jaffe, J. & Sharpless, S. K. (1966). *Res. Publ. Ass. Res. Nerv. Ment. Dis.*, **46**, 226.
Kirpekar, S., Cervoni, P. & Furchgott, R. (1962). *J. Pharmac. exp. Therap.*, **135**, 180.
Kozak, W. & Westerman, R. A. (1961). *Nature*, **189**, 753.
Lomax, P. & Jenden, D. (1966). *Int. J. Neuropharm.*, **5**, 353.
Martin, W. R. (1966). *Res. Publ. Ass. Res. Nerv. Ment. Dis.*, **46**, 206.
Purpura, D. (1961). *Ann. N.Y. Acad. Sci.*, **94**, 605.
Rutledge, L. T., Ranck, J. B. Jr. & Duncan, J. A. (1967). *Electroencephal. Clin. Neurophysiol.*, **23**, 256.
Sharpless, S. K. (1964). *Ann. Rev. Physiol.*, **26**, 357.
Sharpless, S. K. & Halpern, L. (1962). *Electroencephal. Clin. Neurophysiol.*, **14**, 244.
Sharpless, S. K. & Jaffe, J. (1966). *J. Pharmac. exp. Therap.*, **151**, 321.
Sloan, J. & Eisenman, A. J. (1966). *Res. Publ. Ass. Rec. Nerv. Ment. Dis.*, **46**, 96.
Trendelenburg, U. (1963). *Pharmac. Rev.*, **15**, 225.
Volle, R. & Koelle, G. (1961). *J. Pharmac. exp. Therap.*, **133**, 223.
Yamamoto, S. & Schaeppi, U. (1961). *Electroencephal. Clin. Neurophysiol.*, **13**, 248.

IS THERE A RELATIONSHIP BETWEEN PROTEIN SYNTHESIS AND TOLERANCE TO ANALGESIC DRUGS?

B. M. Cox and M. Ginsburg

*Department of Pharmacology, Chelsea College of Science and Technology
University of London*

This paper is concerned only with the narcotic analgesic drugs and with the phenomenon of tolerance to these drugs, applying the definition that tolerance is the capacity to withstand an effect of a drug acquired by exposure to the same drug. It is usually stated that physical dependence on morphine is always associated with tolerance, and we suppose that is justification enough for the question of tolerance to be discussed at this symposium.

Our purpose is to examine the proposition that the change in cellular constitution and biochemistry underlying the development of tolerance to morphine and similar drugs is to be found in the genetic control of protein synthesis. Although this idea has been expressed many times, the first experimental evidence for it was given in 1965 by Cohen, Keats, Krivoy & Ungar, when they reported that actinomycin D prevented the development of tolerance to morphine in rats and mice. Actinomycin D is an inhibitor of RNA polymerase and it would be quite fair to doubt whether experiments, in which such a drug was given to animals over periods of weeks and in doses large enough to kill some of them, can be interpreted meaningfully.

One way to get around this criticism is to study the effect of actinomycin D on acute tolerance to morphine in experiments which need involve no more than a few hours of exposure to the protein synthesis inhibitor. Acute tolerance to the analgesic effect of morphine can be induced in conscious rats given continuous intravenous infusion of the drug at rates of between 5 and 10 mg/kg/hr. At first analgesia increases to a plateau but after about 200 minutes of infusion, responsiveness to the painful stimulus gradually returns, and when the infusion has been in progress for six hours or more the stimulus required to evoke a

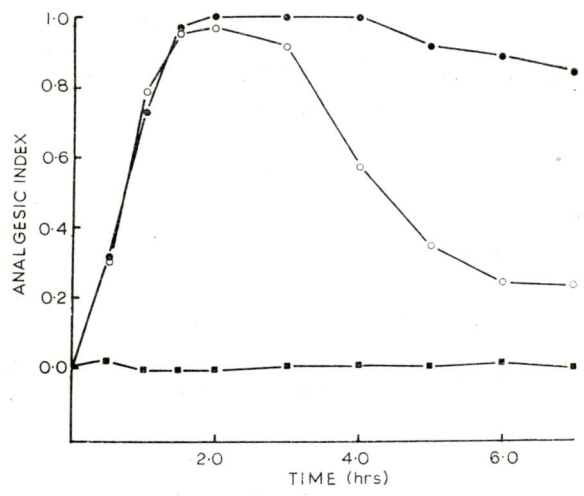

FIG. 1. Analgesia in rats during infusion of morphine, 7·5 mg/kg/hr ○; morphine, 7·5 mg/kg/hr + actinomycin D, 10 μg/kg/hr ●; and actinomycin D, 10 μg/kg/hr ■. The test was based on the responsiveness of rats to a painful pressure stimulus applied to the tail; see Cox, Ginsburg and Osman (1968) for details.

response is not much more severe than before the infusion of the analgesic was started (Figure 1). When the infusion contains actinomycin D (10 μg/kg/hr) as well as morphine, the onset of analgesia is unchanged but the restoration of responsiveness to pain between the second and seventh hours of infusion is absent. Similar experiments have been carried out in which infusion of heroin, pethidine and etorphine were given to rats. With each of these drugs in appropriate doses, the analgesia declines after 2–4 hr of infusion and the acute tolerance produced in this way is prevented when actinomycin D is added to the infusion.

The effect of actinomycin does not seem to be one of simple potentiation of the analgesia because a difference between the actinomycin treated and control rats is apparent only after a degree of tolerance has developed. There is no change in the time course of the onset or the maximum level of analgesia, even if the actinomycin is infused for two hours before administration of the analgesic is started. When morphine infusions are given

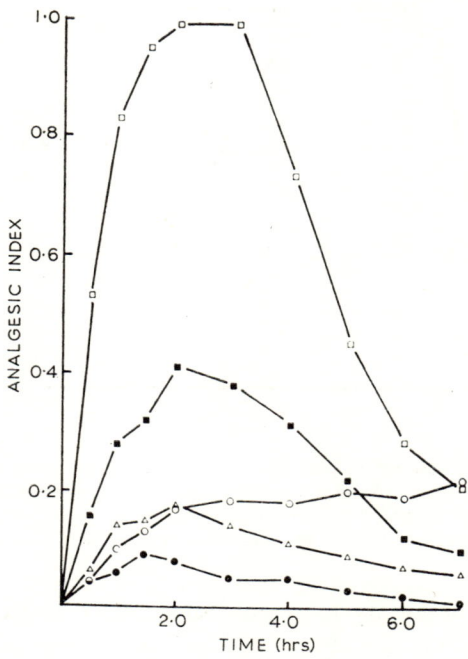

FIG. 2. Development of tolerance to morphine in rats given infusions of morphine (7·5 mg/kg/hr) for seven hours on each of four successive days. □, day 1 morphine only; ●, day 2 morphine only; △, day 3 morphine only; ■, day 4 morphine only; ○, day 4 morphine + actinomycin, 10 μg/kg/hr.

for seven hour periods on successive days, the tolerance developed on one day is carried forward to the next, and during each day as the infusion of morphine proceeds the degree of tolerance increases. Addition of actinomycin D to the infusion prevents the decline in analgesia during the later hours of infusion but does not reverse the pre-existing tolerance (Figure 2).

These results suggest that the prevention of morphine tolerance by actinomycin D is not due to modification or inhibition of a normal process but is due to prevention of some change brought about by the analgesic drug. Also, as an inhibitor of RNA

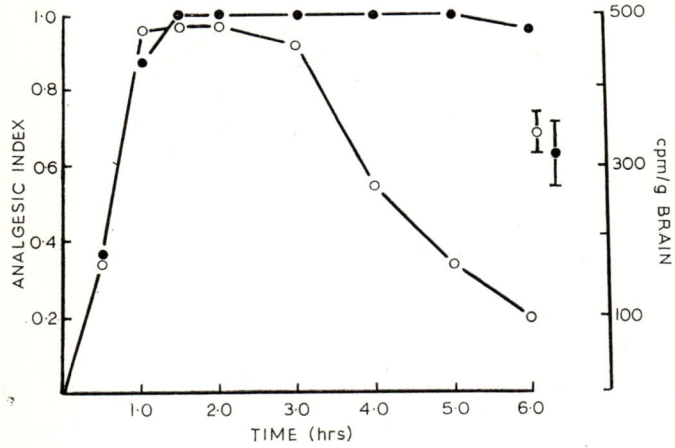

FIG. 3. Radioactivity in ethylene dichloride fraction from brain after 6 hr intravenous infusion of rats with ^{3}H-dihydromorphine (2·5 mg/kg/hr) with and without actinomycin D (20 μg/kg/hr). ○, ^{3}H-dihydromorphine alone; ●, ^{3}H-dihydromorphine + actinomycin.

polymerase, actinomycin would not affect protein synthesis directed by RNA already formed and would not, in these short-term experiments, cause gross depletion of proteins normally present in the cell, such as enzymes important for metabolism of analgesics. In fact, we have performed experiments which show that demethylation of pethidine by liver microsome fraction is not impaired in preparations from actinomycin treated rats. In other experiments (Figure 3) we have shown that in rats given infusions of dihydromorphine labelled with tritium, the amounts of radioactivity extractable from the brain, with ethylene dichloride, does not depend on whether tolerance is allowed to develop or whether it is prevented by simultaneous administration of actinomycin.

Nevertheless, the site of action of actinomycin seems to be in the brain. Actinomycin given intracerebrally is effective in doses much lower than required intravenously (Figure 4). A measure of the degree of tolerance developing during infusion of

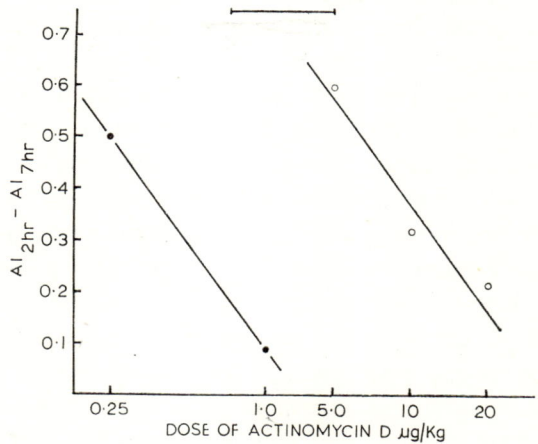

FIG. 4. Comparison of intracerebral and intravenous administration of actinomycin D in preventing tolerance to morphine. The actinomycin D was given as a single injection at the start of a seven hour intravenous infusion of morphine (7·5 mg/kg/hr). The ordinate gives the difference in the analgesic index measured after two and seven hours of infusion. ▬▬▬, no actinomycin; ●——●, intracerebral actinomycin; ○——○, intravenous actinomycin.

morphine is given by the difference in analgesic indices at the second and seventh hour of infusion. Figure 4 shows the difference plotted against dose of actinomycin given intravenously or intracerebrally, as a single injection at the start of the morphine infusion. The dose ratio, intravenous: interacerebral, is about 10:1.

If it is valid to assume that the effect of actinomycin is, in fact, due to inhibition of protein synthesis then one would conclude that the acquisition of tolerance is associated with, and in some way due to the induction of the synthesis of a unique RNA and protein. Evidence supporting this assumption has been obtained in experiments in which other inhibitors of protein synthesis have been tested for the capacity to prevent morphine tolerance (Table 1). With the single exception of chloramphenicol which is known to be more effective in bacterial systems, it could be shown that all the drugs tested prevented acute tolerance to the analgesic effect of intravenously infused morphine. Treatment with 6-mercaptopurine and with 5-fluorouracil was usually ineffective unless the drug was given by a series of intracerebral injections starting one or two days before the morphine infusion. Cycloheximide, like actinomycin D, was effective when added to the morphine infusion and was more potent when given intracerebrally. Puromycin was tested by the intracerebral route only. All these drugs inhibit protein synthesis, acting at different stages of the transcription of the genetic code and the assembly of amino acids in peptide chains. It seems reasonable, therefore, to conclude that the inhibition of protein synthesis is causally related to the prevention of morphine tolerance and that morphine tolerance is generated by an induced alteration of protein synthesis in the brain.

The questions that we might now ask ourselves are—how does morphine affect the direction of protein synthesis and how does the altered protein synthesis result in diminished susceptibility to the analgesic effect of morphine? One interesting proposal of Ungar and Cohen (1966) that bears on the second question is that the brain of morphine-tolerant animals contains a substance which, when injected into non-tolerant animals, confers morphine

Table 1

Prevention of acute tolerance to morphine by substances that inhibit protein synthesis in various ways

		Probable modes of action	Route of administration	Inhibition of tolerance development
Drugs affecting transcription	Actinomycin D	Inhibition of RNA polymerase by binding to DNA[a]	IV IC	++ ++++
	6-Mercaptopurine	? Inhibition of purine synthesis ? Incorporation into nucleic acid[b]	SC + IV SC IC	(+) (+) +++
	5-Fluorouracil	Inhibition of ribosome formation[c]	IV IC	0 +
	Chloramphenicol	Inhibition of (bacterial) ribosome formation[d]	IV Oral + IV	0 0
Drugs affecting assembly	Puromycin	Inhibition of binding of amino acids; antagonism of tRNA[e]	IC	++++
	Cycloheximide	Inhibition of movement of ribosomes along mRNA[f] strands	IV IC	++ ++++

a Hamilton, Fuller & Reich, 1963; Goldberg & Reich, 1964.
b Carter, 1959; Salser, Hutchinson & Balis, 1960; Handschumacher & Welch, 1960.
c Iwabuchi, Otaka, Kono & Osawa, 1966; Hignett, 1966; Hills & Horowitz, 1960.
d Rendi & Ochoa, 1962; Hahn & Wolfe, 1962.
e Yarmolinsky & de la Haba, 1959; Nathans, 1964.
f Wettstein, Noll & Penman, 1964; Colombo, Felicetti & Baglioni, 1965.

tolerance upon them. Their evidence suggests that the 'tolerance factor' is a relatively small molecule, possibly a polypeptide with about six amino acid residues. So far we have been unsuccessful in attempts to repeat the observations of Cohen and Ungar. In our experiments, mice have been injected with extracts prepared in various ways from brains of normal rats and rats with a high degree of tolerance to morphine; the tests for the analgesic effect of morphine given to the recipient mice were so arranged that the observer did not know whether an individual mouse had received the extract from normal or tolerant rat brain. We should be reluctant to rule out the possibility of a tolerance factor on the basis of these experiments and the fault may be in the inadequacy of our technique, though where it fails is not clear to us.

Figure 5 represents an attempt at drawing up a scheme to show various ways in which tolerance to morphine might develop via

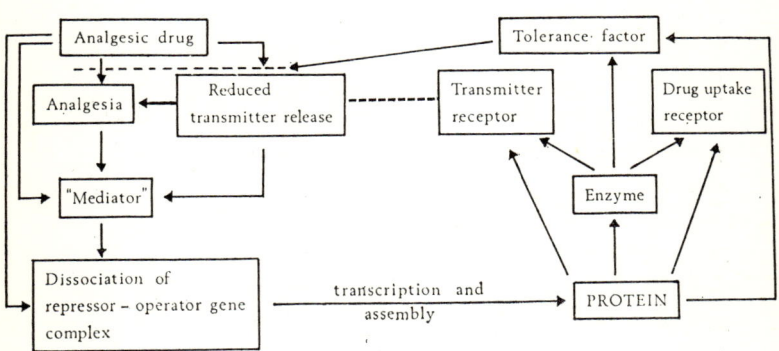

FIG. 5. A scheme showing some of the possible pathways for the development of tolerance to morphine, by a mechanism that involves induction of protein synthesis.

a pathway that involves a change in the direction of protein synthesis. It is, of course, highly speculative and almost every arrow deserves to be accompanied by a question mark. There are dangers in making assumptions about the molecular mechanism of induction of protein synthesis in animals because many of the concepts of the Jacob-Monod model depend on observations made in micro-organisms. In fact, Greengard (1967) has stated recently that "there is no justification at present to equate enzyme induction in animals with 'derepression' or with 'stimulation of RNA synthesis'". We regard this scheme as sufficiently speculative to allow us to ignore Greengard's warning, and in it we propose that the analgesic drug affects protein synthesis through derepression of an operator gene that controls the synthesis of a protein capable of modifying the analgesic response. As an alternative to morphine itself being the derepressor, one must consider the possibility that dissociation of the hypothetical repressor-gene complex could be brought about indirectly. A secondarily released effector (such as a local hormone or a metabolic product) which may or may not be incidental to the analgesic effect, could be involved.

The right-hand side summarizes possible roles for the protein, some of which are mentioned by Drs. Collier and Sharpless (this volume, pp. 49–66 and 67–76). The protein could be involved in the formation of drug uptake receptor, receptor for neurotransmission or a transmissible tolerance factor.

Finally, Sharpless (1964) has suggested that denervation supersensitivity is brought about by hyperexcitability of the receptor membrane due to the absence of a stabilizing protein of which the synthesis is induced by transmitter released during normal neuronal activity. If denervation supersensitivity and tolerance to narcotic analgesics are truly analogous this hypothesis should be modified because it involves repression rather than induction of protein synthesis. However, it might be that the protein induced during the development of tolerance binds or inactivates a membrane stabilizing substance.

Acknowledgements: We are indebted to Mr. O. H. Osman and Mr. A. Parker-Rhodes for their valuable contributions to this work and our thanks are due to Dr. Mushett of the Merck Sharp and Dohme Research Laboratories and to Mr. Dobbs of Reckitt and Sons Ltd. for their generosity in supplying actinomycin D (Dactinomycin) and tritiated dihydromorphine, respectively.

REFERENCES

Carter, C. E. (1959). *Biochem. Pharmac.*, **2**, 105–111.
Cohen, M. J., Keats, A. S., Krivoy, W. & Ungar, G. (1965). *Proc. Soc. exp. Biol. Med.*, **119**, 381–384.
Colombo, B., Felicetti, L. & Baglioni, C. (1965). *Biochem. biophys. Res. Commun.*, **18**, 389–395.
Cox, B. M., Ginsburg, M. & Osman, O. H. (1968). *Brit. J. Pharmac. Chemother.* In the press.
Goldberg, I. H., Reich, E. (1964). *Fed. Proc.*, **23**, 958–964.
Greengard, O. (1967). *Adv. Enzyme Res.*, **5**, 397–405.
Hahn, F. E. & Wolfe, A. D. (1962). *Biochem. biophys. Res. Commun.*, **6**, 464–468.
Handschumacher, R. E. & Welch, A. D. (1960). In *The Nucleic Acids*, Vol. III, Ed. by Chargaft, E., & Davidson, J. N. London: Academic Press.
Hignett, R. C. (1966). *Biochim. Biophys. Acta*, **114**, 559–564.
Hills, D. C. & Horowitz, J. (1966). *Biochemistry*, N.Y., **5**, 1625–1632.
Iwabuchi, M., Otaka, G., Kono, M. & Osawa, S. (1966). *Biochim. Biophys. Acta*, **114**, 83–94.
Nathans, D. (1964). *Fed. Proc.*, **23**, 984–989.
Rendi, R. & Ochoa, S. (1962). *J. biol. Chem.*, **237**, 3711–3713.
Salser, J. S., Hutchinson, D. J. & Balis, M. E. (1960). *J. biol. Chem.*, **235**, 429–432.
Sharpless, S. K. (1964). *A. Rev. Physiol.*, **26**, 357.
Ungar, G. & Cohen, M. (1966). *Int. J. Neuropharmac.*, **5**, 183–192.
Wettstein, F. O., Noll, H. & Penman, S. (1964). *Biochim. Biophys. Acta*, **87**, 525–527.
Yarmolinsky, M. B. & de la Haba, G. L. (1959). *Proc. nat. Acad. Sci.*, **45**, 1721.

DISCUSSION

Dean: First I should like to describe briefly some observations on the action of barbitone on bacterial cells, for they have a bearing on the general theme on this symposium. The more or less specific inhibition of enzyme systems is often one of the primary actions of antibacterial agents, and clearly the cells could become resistant by the development of more of the enzyme. Indeed, kinetic theories of drug resistance have been formulated on this basis (Dean & Hinshelwood, 1966). Goldstein (1965) has also pointed out how the system *Escherichia coli*-barbitone might be used as a model for studying the effects of prolonged drug administration such as the development of tolerance, addiction and the withdrawal syndrome. The situation at the end of one subculture in the presence of barbitone was considered to be analogous to the state of tolerance in animals, and the expansion of the enzyme system converting L-alanine to pyruvate was demonstrated. If the drug was suddenly removed an excess of enzyme would be present, so that the particular action would proceed at an accelerated rate, and this, it was suggested, might be analogous to the withdrawal syndrome in animals.

We have investigated the effect of barbitone on the glucose dehydrogenase activity of cells of *Aerobacter aerogenes* (Dean & Moss, 1967). This enzyme system was chosen because it is involved in the primary attack on the carbon substrate in a salts-glucose medium and because it has been known for some time that barbiturates inhibit dehydrogenases in brain tissue (Davies & Quastel, 1932). Barbitone reduced the glucose dehydrogenase activity of resting cells. After growth during one subculture in a barbitone medium the activity of this enzyme was higher than in the control, and was higher still after a subsequent subculture in a drug-free medium. Re-addition of the drug at this stage would obviously counteract this 'withdrawal effect'.

Barbitone had other actions on the cells. It induced a lag before growth began and when growth began it did so at a reduced rate, and the higher the concentration the greater the effect. The mean size was also higher throughout the first subculture than in the control, indicating an inhibition of division relative to the growth of the cells. In our conditions one subculture corresponds to about five to six generations of growth, which in terms of bacterial cells adjusting to a changed environment is a relatively short time. Subculture in drug-medium was therefore continued, and during this process the lag rapidly disappeared and the growth rate improved up to a limit. This 'training' was easily lost on subculture in the drug-free medium and was considered to be a relatively unstable physiological adaptation involving most of the cells in the population, for as far as lag and growth rate were concerned, a return to the original state before exposure to the drug had occurred. Although the high glucose dehydrogenase activity observed on the first exposure fell on continued subculture in the presence of the drug, it remained higher than normal and increased again on growth in the drug-free medium at any stage of the 'training' process. What is important to this discussion here is that this effect was of a more permanent nature than those described earlier. For example after about 150 generations of growth in the presence of the drug followed by about 400 generations of growth in its absence, the glucose dehydrogenase activity of the cells was still higher than normal. The inhibition of division was equally persistent. Although, as pointed out earlier, 'withdrawal symptoms' could be removed by the re-addition of the drug, at no stage during the 'training' process could the cells be said to be dependent on the drug for growth, for not only was growth possible but it proceeded at a more rapid rate in the absence of the drug than in its presence. The picture which emerges, therefore, from these experiments is one in which a relatively unstable physiological adaptation of the cells to the action of barbitone is accompanied by changes of a much more permanent nature. The relevance to experiments with animals of the patterns of behaviour observed in rapidly growing bacterial cells is an open question, but elsewhere in this session (this volume, pp. 31–37, 51, and 71) we have had examples of elegant experiments having all the attributes of physiological adaptations. I wonder, however, if more permanent effects are not also involved and should like to open the discussion by posing the general question as to how far recovery from addiction to drugs is ever complete.

REFERENCES

Davies, D. R. & Quastel, J. H. (1932). Dehydrogenations by brain tissue. The effect of narcotics. *Biochem. J.*, **26**, 1672–1684.

Dean, A. C. R. & Hinshelwood, C. (1966). *Growth, Function and Regulation in Bacterial Cells.* Oxford: Clarendon Press.

Dean, A. C. R. & Moss, D. A. (1967). The action of barbitone on *Aerobacter (Klebsiella) aerogenes. Brit. J. Pharmac. Chemother.*, **29**, 89–98.

Goldstein, D. B. (1965). Effects of barbital on amino acid metabolism in *Escherichia coli. Mol. Pharmac.*, **1**, 31–46.

Graham: I should like to ask Dr. Chein to comment on a proposition which has been put to me, namely that the pharmacological action of a drug involved in drug dependence is less important than the other factors (which I will collectively term 'psychological') in the initiation, development and continuance in the individual and in the epidemiology of drug dependence.

Chein: Basically, I believe that the relative roles of pharmacological and psychological factors in drug dependence vary with the particular class of cases. Thus, I have little doubt that the pharmacological effects of narcotics are major factors involved in addiction amongst physicians in the United States. The pharmacological effects seem to be of relatively little importance among the addicts of the American urban slums.

McLean: (1) Surely Dr. Chein cannot use absence of withdrawal symptoms as a criterion for absence of pharmacological effect. Most of us have a pharmacological effect from alcohol, but I hope we would not show withdrawal symptoms. (2) The inner weaknesses which he postulates that lead people to become drug users seem to have no predictive value because one could, *post-hoc*, find such in any man.

Chein: (1) The question at issue is concerned with the role of pharmacological effect in *addictive* use. My argument is that given apparently addictive use of a drug which produces dependency and tolerance, the absence of withdrawal symptoms indicates that the drug is not being taken with sufficient frequency and/or dosage level to produce dependence. By the same token, however, the relatively low dosage must have its effects overcome by tolerance. The addictive use, therefore, cannot be explained by the pharmacological effect.

(2) Granted that certain information can have no predictive value, it does not follow that it can have no scientific value. As Michael Scriven has pointed out, the theory of evolution has no predictive value; it does not follow that it has no scientific value. In general, however, the argument implied by the question fails to distinguish between necessary and sufficient conditions. Given that one knows only that some necessary condition obtains, this information is of little value in making predictions. It is useful in negative predictions to know that a necessary condition does not obtain, and it is useful in positive predictions to know that it, and other relevant conditions, do

obtain. Actually, I do not postulate that certain inner weaknesses are necessary conditions of addiction. What I do say is that given these conditions, and other favourable conditions, it is more likely that a person will succumb than if these conditions do not obtain. Thus, for instance, I think that in New York City, for a white youth, on the average, to experiment with heroin calls for a greater degree of personal disturbance than would be true for a Negro youth. The social environment of Negro youth is so much more conducive to such experimentation than the social environment of white youth.

Kosterlitz: I should like to comment on one of the questions raised in Professor Paton's paper. He asked whether the development of tolerance to narcotic analgesic drugs is likely to be related to the fact that these drugs are all partial agonists. I do not think that such a relationship exists; Gyang and I found that self-antagonism or tachyphylaxis is demonstrable within minutes after first exposure of the guinea-pig ileum to a narcotic agonist, e.g. morphine, or a narcotic antagonist, e.g. nalorphine, whereas the appearance of tolerance is measured in terms of hours. Moreover, Martin and his colleagues at Lexington have recently shown that the development of physical dependence requires the presence of agonist activity, since the pure antagonist, naloxone, is ineffective in this respect.

Collier: Martin (1967) has also argued, from the biphasic dose-response curves of agonist-antagonist mixtures, that "there are two analgesic receptors, one where morphine acts as agonist and nalorphine as a competitive antagonist and the other where morphine is inactive and nalorphine is an agonist" (Martin, 1967, p. 508). This hypothesis, coupled with the conclusion to which Dr. Kosterlitz refers, that tolerance to and dependence on morphine, nalorphine and cyclazocine result only from their agonist activity, cannot easily be reconciled with any theory that physical dependence on morphine arises through its direct blockade of receptors for a transmitter substance on a nerve cell. An alternative explanation of the biphasic dose-response curves of narcotic agonist-antagonist mixtures, however, may avoid this difficulty. This alternative is the assumption that separate receptors exist for agonist and antagonist actions and that the number of agonist receptors that must be affected to give maximal analgesia depends on the number of antagonist receptors affected. With this arrangement, the interaction between, say, morphine and nalorphine, leading to the surmountable antagonism described by several authors, would occur at a common point in the pathways leading from agonist and antagonist receptors.

REFERENCES

Martin, W. R. (1967). Opioid antagonists. *Pharmac. Rev.*, **19**, 464–521.

Neal: Professor Paton has told us about the correlation of narcotic analgesic activity and the inhibitory action of these drugs on coaxially stimulated guinea-pig ileum. I should like to ask him if a similar correlation exists in the case of general anaesthetics.

Also, I wonder if he has tried using ileum from morphine dependent guinea-pigs to see whether, in fact, tolerance is produced in peripheral systems.

Paton: (1) There is, of course, a well-known general correlation; anaesthetics depress all excitable structures on which they have been tested at roughly similar concentrations. There are, however, detailed differences (Speden, 1965) in their proportionate action on transmitter output and on effector cell response. In another respect, the correlation between action on ileum and central action is poor: some substances, notably hexafluoroethyl ether, are actually convulsant, and some anaesthetics, e.g. chloroform and hexafluoro-benzene, are stimulant to smooth muscle (Speden & Rang, 1964), but Rang found that these two 'stimulant' actions correlate very poorly.

(2) I have not tested ileum strips from morphine-dependent animals.

REFERENCES

Speden, R. M. (1965). *Brit. J. Pharmac.*, **25**, 104–118.
Speden, R. M. & Rang, H. P. (1964). *Brit. J. Pharmac.*, **22**, 356–365.

Brown: To amplify a point raised by Dr. Sharpless: denervation does not appear to increase the sensitivity of the superior cervical ganglion in the sense of producing "receptor-spread". In certain circumstances an increased response to acetylcholine can be detected after preganglionic denervation, but this is probably a consequence of the loss of acetylcholinesterase (which is located principally presynaptically at this site), for there is no enhancement of the action of cholinesterase-resistant stimulant compounds. Of course, this may be an exceptional case. On the other hand, for good anatomical reasons, it is the only neural site—as opposed to effector organ—at which the effects of denervation have been studied directly. It would be helpful to have more detailed information on the effects of denervation on specific central neurones.

Dr. Sharpless also raised the possibility that denervation may increase the amount of transmitter released by the next neurone in the chain after excitation. It does not seem likely that there is a substantial change in the amount of transmitter released from the postganglionic nerves from the superior cervical ganglion after preganglionic denervation. In some experiments I assessed the response of the ganglion to stimulants by recording the contraction of the nictitating membrane. After correcting for the decentralization supersensitivity of the membrane to the postganglionic transmitter (noradrenaline), the apparent sensitivity of the denervated ganglion to carbachol so determined was not greatly different from that obtained by recording ganglionic responses directly. There is however undoubtedly room for more direct investigation of this possibility.

Steinberg: Dr. Dean (p. 88), in discussing bacterial adaptation to barbiturates, wondered how far changes induced by drugs of dependence were permanent and whether complete recovery ever occurred. My colleagues and I (Rushton, Steinberg & Tomkiewicz, 1968) have recently found long-term effects in behavioural experiments with amphetamine-barbiturate mixtures. A single injection of a mixture greatly stimulated the spontaneous activity of rats in an unfamiliar environment; when the rats were re-tested in the same environment, as long as three months later, stimulant effects could still be detected.

REFERENCE

Rushton, R., Steinberg, H., & Tomkiewicz, M. (1968). *Nature, Lond.*, **220**, 885–889.

Session II

PHARMACOLOGY AND BIOCHEMISTRY

Chairman: H. McIlwain

CHAIRMAN'S INTRODUCTION

PURSUING now the subject of drug dependence to biochemical pharmacology we have the opportunity of extending one of the themes of the last session: namely, the connection of protein synthesis in the brain with the development of tolerance.

The first extension is to different organs: as tolerance to some drugs is based on renal or hepatic mechanisms, do these depend on, for example, enzyme adaptation? The second extension is to different substances: can protein or ribonucleic acid changes be recognized in an animal's reaction to barbiturates or to amphetamine? The third extension is to different aspects of cerebral functioning. Drug dependence as a behavioural and social phenomenon involves relationships between animal and environment, as well as between animal and drug. Do, therefore, the behavioural changes of drug dependence also involve specific changes in ribonucleic acid or protein synthesis? If they do involve such changes, then there will be similarities in the basic mechanisms of the development of tolerance and dependence. Although these two reactions of an animal to a given substance are distinct, they frequently coincide for members of some chemical series and this coincidence would be explained. Further—and this is relevant to the final two contributions in this session—the search for non-addicting analgesics might be replaced or assisted by one for agents which differentially affect different types of cerebral protein synthesis.

THE RELATIONSHIP OF THE DISPOSITION AND METABOLISM OF MORPHINE IN THE CNS TO TOLERANCE

S. J. MULÉ

*National Institute of Mental Health Addiction Research Center,
Lexington, Kentucky*

THE development of tolerance to the pharmacological effects of narcotic analgesics is well known (Eddy, 1955; Seevers & Woods, 1953). The mechanism responsible for the attenuated action of these drugs, however, is unknown. Several possible explanations for the phenomena of tolerance have been suggested and include: (1) altered disposition and metabolism; (2) prevention of access of the drug to the site of action; (3) cellular adaptation based on biochemical changes within neuronal cells; (4) progressive receptor occupation, ultimately resulting in receptor saturation.

During the past few years a concentrated effort to obtain experimental data concerning the altered disposition and metabolism postulate has been made (Mulé & Woods, 1962; Mulé *et al.*, 1962; Mulé, 1965; Mulé *et al.*, 1967). This report, therefore, is primarily concerned with the results of these studies as they relate to tolerance development with morphine.

Methods

The preparation of the ^{14}C and ^{3}H-labelled morphine, estimation of morphine in biological materials, biological and chemical procedures, chromatographic techniques, subcellular fractionation, chemical and enzymatic assays, were as reported by Mulé and Woods (1962); Mulé *et al.* (1962); Mulé (1965) and Mulé *et al.* (1967).

Results

Single N-^{14}C-methyl labelled morphine injections in nontolerant and tolerant dogs

The levels of free morphine in various areas of the cerebral cortex grey and white matter were significantly lower in the tolerant dogs as compared with the nontolerant dogs at 35 min, 4 and 8 hr after drug. At 8 hr the mean cortical grey matter levels of morphine in the tolerant animals were 52% lower than the corresponding level in nontolerant dogs ($P < 0.01$). Cortical white matter levels in nontolerant and tolerant dogs increased similarly for 4 hr. After 4 hr the levels in the tolerant animals decreased, whereas the levels in the nontolerant animals were relatively constant up to 8 hr. At 8 hr the white matter levels of free morphine in the tolerant dogs were 40% lower than in the nontolerant dog.

The mean cerebellar levels of free labelled morphine (grey and white matter) were lower in the tolerant dogs as compared with the nontolerant dogs at comparable time intervals.

At each time interval in selected subcortical areas of the CNS the levels of free labelled morphine in the CNS tissues of tolerant dogs were lower than in the nontolerant dog. The predominantly cellular areas of the CNS (i.e. caudate nucleus, dorsal thalamus, hypothalamus) contained the highest levels of free morphine in both non-tolerant and tolerant dogs. Subcortical regions of the CNS which consist primarily of myelinated nerve fibre bundles (olfactory tracts, pons, cerebral penduncles) showed lower concentrations of morphine than predominantly cellular subcortical areas. The levels of free morphine in the spinal cord of tolerant dogs were lower than in the nontolerant dog.

Plasma and cerebrospinal fluid (CSF) levels of free labelled morphine were determined at various time intervals. Maximum levels of free morphine were observed 15 min after drug in both nontolerant and tolerant dogs (450 ng/ml) in the plasma. The concentrations fell to half of the maximum level at about 1 hr. At 2 hr after drug the levels of morphine in the tolerant dogs were below the levels in the nontolerant dog and remained lower for altogether 8 hr. The concentration of free morphine in nontolerant and tolerant dogs at 8 hr was 18 and 4 ng/ml, respectively.

CSF levels of free morphine were also maximal at 35 min after drug (100 ng/ml). The CSF levels in the tolerant dogs were lower than the nontolerant levels at 4 and 8 hr. The biological half-life values in the CSF of nontolerant and tolerant dogs were 6·5 hr and 3 hr, respectively.

Consecutive N-^{14}C-methyl labelled morphine injections in nontolerant and tolerant dogs

The mean cerebral cortical grey matter levels of free morphine at 35 min in nontolerant and tolerant dogs were not statistically different ($P > 0.05$). Four and 8 hr after drug the mean cerebral cortical grey levels of morphine in tolerant dogs were significantly lower ($P < 0/01$) than in the nontolerant dogs. Mean cerebral cortical white matter concentrations of free morphine were significantly higher ($P < 0.01$) in tolerant dogs at 35 min and significantly lower 8 hr ($P < 0.01$) after drug.

The mean cerebellar grey matter concentrations of free morphine were similar at 35 min and 4 hr in the nontolerant and tolerant dog. However, the 8 hr levels were lower in the tolerant dogs. The levels of drug were higher at 35 min in the cerebellar white matter and lower at 4 hr and 8 hr in the tolerant animals as compared with the nontolerant data.

The distribution of free labelled morphine in selected subcortical tissues following consecutive injections of labelled drug was also determined. The apparent maximum levels of free morphine occurred 35 min after drug in both nontolerant and tolerant dogs. The levels of free morphine in tolerant dogs appeared to be higher at 35 min, about the same at 4 hr and were lower at 8 hr, in comparison with levels at corresponding times in the nontolerant dogs. Again it seems that the predominantly cellular tissue contained higher levels of the drug in both the nontolerant and tolerant dogs, in comparison with the myelinated nerve fibre regions of the CNS in these dogs.

Following consecutive subcutaneous injections of 2 mg/kg of labelled morphine maximal concentrations of free morphine were observed in the plasma at 15 and 30 min (450 ng/ml) in both nontolerant and tolerant dogs. At 8 hr the concentration of free morphine was about 14 ng/ml in both groups. Conjugated morphine peaked at 40 to 60 min (900–1200 ng/ml) for the nontolerant and tolerant dogs. At 8 hr the levels of conjugated morphine were 123 and 170 ng/ml in the tolerant and nontolerant dogs, respectively. In general the levels of free drug were equal in both groups, but conjugated morphine was considerably lower in the tolerant dogs as compared with the nontolerant dogs.

Maximum levels of free morphine were obtained in the cerebrospinal fluid of nontolerant dogs (95 ng/ml) and tolerant dogs (158 ng/ml) 35 min after drug. Subsequently, the levels of drug declined rapidly in both groups and at 8 hr were almost identical. Biological half-life values were 3·8 hr and 3 hr for nontolerant and tolerant animals, respectively.

Effect of nalorphine on the CNS levels of labelled morphine in nontolerant dogs

A pronounced increase (25–42%) in the mean cortical and cerebellar levels of morphine occurred in the nalorphine-antagonized dogs as compared with the morphine control dogs.

The increase in the levels of morphine was apparently greater in cortical and cerebellar white matter than in grey matter of the nalorphine-antagonized animals.

Data were also obtained on the effect of nalorphine upon free labelled morphine in subcortical tissues and biological fluids. The morphine levels of the nalorphine-antagonized animals were elevated in comparison with the control animals. The subcortical areas which demonstrated the largest percentage increase over controls were cervical spinal cord, dorsal thalamus and cerebral peduncles. The mean percentage increase in the morphine levels of the CNS areas analysed was $25 \pm 3\%$ (S.E.) as compared with control values.

The mean plasma and cerebrospinal fluid levels of free labelled morphine in the nalorphine-antagonized dogs at the time of sacrifice were 34 and 14% higher, respectively, than the morphine controls.

The simultaneous injection of both morphine and nalorphine or pretreatment of the nontolerant dogs with unlabelled nalorphine (Mulé et al., 1962) resulted in an increase or no change in the CNS levels of ^{14}C-labelled morphine as compared with controls.

Effect of nalorphine on the distribution of labelled morphine in the CNS and other tissues of the tolerant dog

The mean cerebral and cerebellar cortex grey and white matter levels of free morphine were significantly lower in the nalorphine-antagonized dogs as compared with the control animals at 65 min after drug. The mean percentage decrease at 65 min was 42 and 45% in the cerebral cortex and 50–56% in the cerebellar cortex. No statistically significant change was observed at 165 and 275 min in the cerebrum and cerebellum.

The levels of free morphine were lower in the subcortical tissues and fluids in the nalorphine-antagonized animals as compared with control values at 65 min. The percentage decrease for all the areas ranged between 24 and 50%. At 165 min after drug the values in the two groups were quite similar and at 275 min the levels of free morphine in the antagonized dogs were lower than controls. Nalorphine did not appear to have a significant effect on morphine in a specific area of the CNS or a preferential effect upon grey or white matter.

The plasma levels of free morphine in the nalorphine-antagonized dogs were essentially lower than control values at each time. Maximal levels of conjugated morphine were observed about 60 min after drug in both control and nalorphine-antagonized dogs. About 65 min after drug the levels of morphine in the control animals dropped below the values in the antagonized animals and remained lower for altogether 120 min. However at 180 and 275 min the values in both groups were quite similar.

The CSF levels of free drug were lower in the antagonized animals as compared with control values at 65 and 275 min and similar at 165 min after drug administration.

It is also interesting that nalorphine quite effectively caused a reduction in the levels of morphine at each time interval in the heart, lung, liver and kidney. The percentage decrease ranged from 5 to 73% with the predominant effect occurring at 65 and 275 min after the injection of labelled morphine.

Chromatographic studies of CNS extracts and urine of nontolerant, tolerant and nalorphine-antagonized dogs

Paper chromatographic studies of the extracts of the brain and urine were performed as described by Mulé et al. (1962) and Mulé (1965). These studies provided no evidence for the existence of an N-^{14}C-methyl labelled metabolite of morphine either in the CNS or urine of nontolerant, tolerant or nalorphine-antagonized dogs.

Intracellular localization of ^{3}H-morphine in the brain of nontolerant and tolerant guinea-pigs

In the primary fractions the largest percentage of the drug appeared in the microsomal supernatant ($68 \pm 4\%$), with values of $10 \pm 3\%$ in the crude nuclear fraction, 14 ± 1 in the crude mitochondrial fraction and $6 \pm 1\%$ in the microsomal fraction. Purification of the crude nuclear fraction revealed that only $2 \pm 0.3\%$ of the drug was associated with the nuclei (N_2). The data on the subfractions of the crude mitochondria showed that the largest percentage of the drug appeared in fraction A ($3 \pm 0.4\%$) and that 1% or less of the administered ^{3}H-morphine was found in the nerve endings or free mitochondrial fractions. Following osmotic stock of the crude mitochondria $4 \pm 2\%$ of the drug was found in swollen mitochondria (M_1), $1 \pm 0.6\%$ in synaptic vesicles (M_2) and $8 \pm 3\%$ with the mitochondrial supernatant fraction (M_3).

Calculating the data on the basis of pmoles per protein per fraction revealed high values only for the microsomal supernatant (10 ± 3) and the mitochondrial (M_3) supernatant (8 ± 5). All other values ranged between 0.1 and 2.3 pmole/mg protein.

The percentage distribution of ^{3}H-morphine in the brain intracellular fractions from tolerant guinea-pigs as well as the pmoles of H^3-morphine/mg of protein in each fraction were not statistically different from those observed for the nontolerant animals.

Intracellular localization of ^{3}H-morphine in the liver of nontolerant and tolerant guinea-pigs

The microsomal supernatant fraction of the liver had the largest percentage concentration ($52 \pm 7\%$) of ^{3}H-morphine, followed by the crude nuclei ($25 \pm 5\%$) and approximately the same values were found for the mitochondrial ($10 \pm 1\%$) and microsomal-1 ($11 \pm 2\%$) fractions. The lower percentage values for microsomal-2 in comparison with microsomal-1 were due to the loss of microsomes at the centrifugation speed of 10,000 x g in the preparation of microsomal-2 fraction. Very little difference was observed between the rough ($3 \pm 1\%$) and smooth ($4 \pm 4\%$) microsomal fractions. After purification of the crude nuclear fraction only $3 \pm 2\%$ of the morphine was associated with the purified nuclei.

The picomoles of ^{3}H-morphine/mg of protein in the liver subcellular fraction were high for the supernatant, mitochondrial and purified nuclear fraction. The pmoles/mg of protein for the microsomal fraction (1, 2, rough and smooth) were quite similar. Morphine, therefore, was not specifically associated with the ribosomes of the endoplasmic reticulum.

In the tolerant guinea-pig subcellular fractions the values obtained either as a percentage of the homogenate or as pmoles/mg of protein were not significantly different from those observed with the intracellular fractions from the nontolerant guinea-pigs.

Nalorphine administered to the nontolerant or tolerant guinea-pig did not alter the intracellular localization of ^{3}H-morphine in either brain or liver.

Discussion

These studies were initiated to obtain optimal information about the relationship of the physiological disposition of morphine in the CNS and the phenomenon of tolerance.

To compare the disposition of labelled morphine in the CNS, the drug was administered as a single injection and by consecutive injections to nontolerant and tolerant dogs. The data obtained following a single injection represent both uptake and total free morphine in the nontolerant dog, but only uptake in the tolerant dog. A comparison between consecutively injected animals represents the best manner in which the CNS distribution of labelled morphine and its relationship to the phenomenon of tolerance may be correlated. In this case the major consistent significant difference between nontolerant and tolerant dogs was that the levels of labelled morphine were lower in the CNS of tolerant dogs 8 hr after drug. This indicated an apparently faster rate of egression of free morphine from the CNS of these animals.

It is interesting to note the considerably higher levels of morphine in grey matter as compared with white matter in either the nontolerant or tolerant dog at the early time intervals. However, at later times the levels of morphine in white matter were the same as the grey or were higher. Apparently morphine penetrates into and egresses from grey matter at a faster rate than occurs in white matter. It seems likely that the difference in penetration and egression may be related to the multiple membranes of the laminated myelin sheaths found in white matter as well as the greater vascular density of grey matter (Dunning and Wolfe, 1937) and exceedingly faster circulation rate in comparison with white matter (Landau et al., 1955).

Estimations of the percentage of the dose administered to the consecutively injected tolerant dogs and the singly injected nontolerant dogs in the CNS at the time of maximum concentration were 0.11–0.13% and 0.07–0.1%, respectively.

The antagonism experiments with nontolerant dogs were difficult to understand completely, since administration of morphine before nalorphine resulted in a significant increase in the CNS levels of morphine; but simultaneous injection of both drugs or pretreatment with nalorphine resulted in an increase or no change in CNS levels of morphine. However, regardless of the sequence of injections nalorphine effectively antagonized the CNS pharmacological effects of morphine in the nontolerant dogs. Therefore, there was a poor correlation between the quantities of free morphine present in the CNS of the nalorphine-antagonized animals and the decreased CNS pharmacological activity of morphine. It is conceivable that nalorphine displaces morphine from CNS receptor sites, or occupies these sites if administered before morphine, but cannot prevent morphine from gaining access to the CNS or displace it from the CNS. Equally plausible is the fact that nalorphine may simply interfere with biochemical mechanisms which are involved in narcotic drug action, even though equal or higher levels of morphine are present in the CNS.

In the morphine tolerant dogs nalorphine effectively reduced or caused no statistically significant change in the CNS of labelled morphine. Therefore, the effect of nalorphine on the physiological disposition of morphine appears to be different in the tolerant and nontolerant animal. The question arises as to whether the mechanism of antagonism differs in the tolerant and nontolerant state or whether the biochemical and physiological changes induced by morphine are of sufficient magnitude to be reflected in altered disposition of the drug, yet do not reflect receptor occupation or activity.

The intensity of the 'abstinence syndrome' was greatest at the early time interval after nalorphine in the tolerant dogs, but signs of abstinence were still evident 275 min after drug. The quantity of morphine in the CNS at this time appeared to be sufficient to maintain the physically dependent animal.

However, it is conceivable that the reduced levels of morphine in the nalorphine-antagonized dogs may represent the morphine that was associated with the pharmacologically active receptor sites. The lack of a statistically significant change in drug levels at 165 and 275 min may simply reflect the rapid excretion of nalorphine from the CNS (Hug & Woods, 1963), in comparison with the slow decline with morphine (Mulé & Woods, 1962), thus allowing reoccupation of some of the active sites by morphine. Certainly the reduction of the abstinence syndrome with time and the higher levels of labelled morphine at 165 and 275 min in comparison with the 65 min level of drug in the antagonized dog support these ideas.

Chromatographic studies did not provide evidence for an N-C^{14}-methyl labelled metabolite of morphine in the CNS of nontolerant, tolerant or nalorphine-antagonized dogs. This certainly indicates that a metabolite of morphine is not involved in the process of tolerance development in the dog.

The intracellular disposition of ^3H-morphine in nontolerant guinea-pigs was primarily localized in the microsomal supernatant fractions of brain (68%) and liver (52%). The drug was not significantly bound (2% or less) to soluble proteins in these fractions or to molecules with a molecular weight greater than 12,000 (compounds with a molecular weight greater than 12,000 would be retained by the dialyzer tubing). This indicates that morphine was present in high concentrations and primarily free within the cell cytoplasm.

From 10 to 25% of the drug was found in the crude nuclear fractions of brain and liver. Purified nuclei contained 2-3%. About 14% of the morphine was localized in the mitochondrial fraction of the brain. Following submitochondrial fractionation about 7% of the total morphine was found. Three per cent was located in the myelin fragments with 1% or less associated with the nerve endings and the free mitochondria. Therefore, 50% of the drug was not bound and a remarkably small quantity of drug was bound to cholinergic and noncholinergic nerve ending particles. Following hyposomatic shock of crude mitochondria about 1% was found with the M_2 fraction (synaptic vesicles). Thus very little morphine was attached to the synaptic vesicles which are the morphological storage units for acetylcholine within brain nerve endings.

The percentage of morphine in the microsomal fractions of the brain (6%) and liver (11%) was relatively small. The absence of a real difference between the levels of morphine in the rough and smooth microsomes of the liver indicated the lack of an affinity for the ribosomes.

The intracellular localization of ^{3}H-morphine in the brain and liver of tolerant guinea-pigs was not different from the results obtained with nontolerant guinea-pigs. These results suggest that tolerance is not associated with altered disposition of the narcotic drug.

No difference in the intracellular disposition of morphine was observed following the administration of nalorphine to nontolerant and tolerant guinea-pigs. Nalorphine, therefore, does not appear to displace morphine from intracellular binding sites of either brain or liver. Thus, these studies have apparently not provided further information concerning the subcellular site of action of nalorphine.

Summary

(1) Concentrations of free N-^{14}C-methyl labelled morphine after a single injection were lower in the CNS of tolerant dogs in comparison with nontolerant dogs at various time intervals.

(2) The levels of free morphine in the CNS of tolerant dogs following consecutive 2 mg/kg subcutaneous injections as compared with consecutively injected nontolerant dogs were higher at 35 min, similar at 4 hr and much lower at 8 hr.

(3) Generally, cerebral cortical grey matter contained the highest concentrations of free morphine in both nontolerant and tolerant dogs. Cerebral cortical and cerebellar white matter levels of morphine were lower than grey at early time intervals and about the same or higher at later time intervals.

(4) The administration of labelled morphine before non-labelled nalorphine in nontolerant dogs resulted in a significant increase in the CNS levels of morphine. Simultaneous injection of both drugs or pretreatment with nalorphine resulted in an increase or no change in the CNS levels of morphine as compared with control values.

(5) The administration of morphine (2 mg/kg) to tolerant dogs followed in 35 min by nonlabelled nalorphine (2 mg/kg) resulted in a statistically significant decrease (42–56%) in CNS levels of morphine at 65 min and no real change at either 165 or 275 min following the labelled drug.

(6) Chromatographic studies of the CNS extracts of nontolerant, tolerant and nalorphine-antagonized dogs provided no evidence for the existence of an N-^{14}C-methyl labelled metabolite of morphine.

(7) ^3H-Morphine was primarily localized in the microsomal supernatant fractions of the brain (68%) and liver (52%) of nontolerant and tolerant guinea-pigs.

(8) Neither tolerance development to morphine nor antagonism by nalorphine altered the intracellular localization of ^3H-morphine.

(9) It is concluded that neither distribution nor metabolism of morphine provides any further insight into the mechanism of tolerance development and that tolerance to the narcotic drugs is probably related to changes in the biochemistry of the cellular environment.

REFERENCES

Dunning, H. S. & Wolfe, H. G. (1937). The relative vascularity of various parts of the central and peripheral nervous system of the cat and its relationship to function. *J. Comp. Neurol.*, **67**, 433–450.

Eddy, N. D. (1955). The phenomena of tolerance. *Origins of Resistance to Toxic Agents*, Sevay, M. G., Reid, R. D. & Reynolds, O. E. 223–243. New York: Academic Press.

Hug, C. C. & Woods, L. A. (1963). Tritium-labeled nalorphine: its CNS distribution and biological fate in dogs. *J. Pharmac. exp. Ther.*, **142**, 248–256.

Landau, W. M., Freygang, W. H., Roland, L. P., Sokoloff, L. & Kety, S. S. (1955). The local circulation of the living brain; valves in the unanesthetized and anesthetized cat. *Trans. Am. Neurolog. Assoc. 80th Ann. Meeting*, 125–129.

Mulé, S. J. & Woods, L. A. (1962). Distribution of N-C^{14}-methyl labeled morphine 1. In central nervous system of nontolerant and tolerant dogs. *J. Pharmac. exp. Ther.*, **136**, 232–241.

Mulé, S. J., Woods, L. A. & Mellett, L. B. (1962). Distribution of IV-C^{14}-methyl labeled morphine II. Effect of nalorphine in the central nervous system of nontolerant dogs and observations on metabolism. *J. Pharmac. exp. Ther.*, **136**, 248–249.

Mulé, S. J. (1965). Distribution of N-C^{14}-methyl labeled morphine III. Effect of nalorphine in the central nervous system and other tissues of tolerant dogs. *J. Pharmac. exp. Ther.*, **148**, 393–398.

Mulé, S. J., Redman, C. M. & Flesher, J. W. (1967). Intracellular disposition of H^3-morphine in the brain and liver of nontolerant and tolerant guinea pigs. *J. Pharmac. exp. Ther.*, **157**, 459–471.

Seevers, M. H. & Woods, L. A. (1953). The phenomena of tolerance. *Am. J. Med.*, **14**, 546–557.

TOLERANCE TO BARBITURATES BY INCREASED BREAKDOWN

H. Remmer

Institute of Toxicology, University of Tubingen

Drug tolerance can be regarded as a type of adaptation of cell or organism to an alien chemical environment. It is due either to diminished response by the cell or to accelerated breakdown of the drug. The sensitivity of receptors in the central nervous system is known to decrease after repeated administration of such drugs as narcotics, analgesics, anaesthetics and hypnotics. Because we know nothing about the receptors it is almost impossible to elucidate the altered biochemical reaction in the cells.

It has often been suggested, but not proved, that the organism exposed to unphysiological chemical substances becomes adapted to metabolize these compounds faster. I should like to recall experiments carried out by Faust (1900) who claimed that accelerated breakdown is the cause of tolerance to morphine. Similarly, Pringsheim (1908) believed that the alcoholic is able to metabolize alcohol faster. But these results could never be confirmed.

Tolerance resulting from breakdown of drug

I wish to discuss here tolerance resulting from an increased oxidation of drugs to less effective or inactive metabolites, and to explain why it is advisable, even necessary, to differentiate barbiturate tolerance caused by a decreased response of the central nervous system from that caused by increased breakdown in the liver. The following experiments can be cited (Remmer, 1959).

(1) A dog received a daily dose of hexobarbitone for 5 days. Blood samples were collected at the times indicated for 3–4 hr, and the concentration of hexobarbitone in the blood was determined (Fig. 1a). The rate of decline of the level of hexobarbitone increased between the first and third anaesthetic dose. The fifth

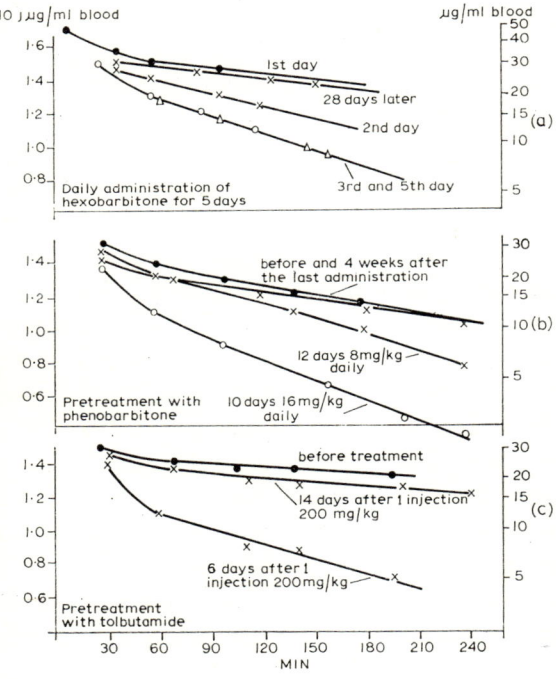

FIG. 1. Decrease in the concentration of hexobarbitone (30 mg/kg I.V.) in the blood of dogs pretreated with hexobarbitone (30 mg/kg I.V.), phenobarbitone and tolbutamide.

dose of hexobarbitone caused no further change. Twenty-eight days later the injection was repeated, and the decline of the level of barbiturate corresponded very closely to that observed on the first day.

The time needed for a 50 per cent fall of the level of hexobarbitone decreased from 180 min. on the first day to 70 min. on the third and following days. The dogs began to walk around without ataxia 80 min. after the injection on the first day and 40 min. after the injection on the third day—at the time when the concentration of hexobarbitone in the blood reached about 27 μg/ml.

(2) Four rabbits were made tolerant with one subcutaneous dose of 60 mg/kg of pentobarbitone daily for 3 days. On the fourth day this group and another untreated group of four rabbits received one intravenous injection of 60 mg/kg of pentobarbitone (Table 1). The duration of anaesthesia was taken as the time

Table 1

Accelerated breakdown as a cause of tolerance to pentobarbitone

Rabbits	Duration of anaesthesia		Pentobarbitone level in blood (μg/ml.)		Percentage decrease/hr
	I	II	I	II	
4 untreated	67 ± 4	109 ± 10	9·9 ± 1·4	6·5 ± 0·9	41 ± 1·5
4 treated	30 ± 7	46 ± 12	7·9 ± 0·6	5·2 ± 0·2	79 ± 5

Rabbits pretreated for 3 days with one injection of 60 mg/kg pentobarbitone s.c. daily and tested on the fourth day after receiving 60 mg/kg of pentobarbitone: I, gaining of righting reflex; II, running without ataxia.

from injection to waking (I) and to running around without ataxia (II). Every 20–30 min. blood was collected for measurement of the concentration of pentobarbitone. Pretreatment with pentobarbitone shortened the period of anaesthesia considerably, but these tolerant rabbits did not have higher concentrations of pentobarbitone in the blood after anaesthesia, which would be expected if there was a decrease in the sensitivity of receptor sites in the central nervous system. The opposite seems to be the case; the amount of drug in the tolerant animals is slightly but significantly lower.

(3) The same results were obtained when rats or mice were used instead of dogs or rabbits, if they were treated with short acting barbiturates (Remmer, 1963). These experiments provided the best evidence that the only reason for the shortened anaesthesia is an increased elimination of short acting barbiturates from the blood. Such an accelerated elimination should be regarded as a completely unspecific type of adaptation, which can be induced by many compounds; not only by those barbiturates which are used for measuring their rate of elimination, but also by the long acting barbitone and phenobarbitone which can speed up the elimination of short acting barbiturates (Fig. 1b; Remmer & Siegert, 1964). Surprisingly, tolbutamide (Fig. 1c), a hyperglycaemic agent which has no resemblance to barbiturates, and numerous other compounds, which will be mentioned later, have the same effect, and are able to shorten the time of anaesthesia produced by short acting barbiturates (Fig. 1c; Remmer, Siegert & Merker, 1964; Remmer, 1962).

Oxidation of drugs

Bush, Butler and Dickison (1953) have shown that hexobarbitone is not excreted unchanged. It loses its hypnotic action by oxidation to ineffective metabolites. We must therefore assume that the faster elimination is a result of a higher rate of oxidation. To test this hypothesis, I have carried out *in vitro* and *in vivo* experiments with rats. I used phenobarbitone; glutethimide, another powerful hypnotic; nikethamide, a stimulant of the central nervous system; tolbutamide, a hypoglycaemic agent, and ethanol as inducing drugs. Ethanol produces the required effect if administered in large doses for 2 or 3 weeks.

These compounds differ chemically and in their pharmacological action, but they all induce tolerance to barbiturates. This can be demonstrated by determining how long an animal sleeps after being given hexobarbitone or Eunarcon (Na-N-methyl-5 isopropyl-5-(2′ bromallyl)barbiturate), another short acting barbiturate, which is also converted to an oxidized metabolite. Brodie and Axelrod and their co-workers showed that enzymes of the so-called endoplasmic reticulum in the cells of the liver are

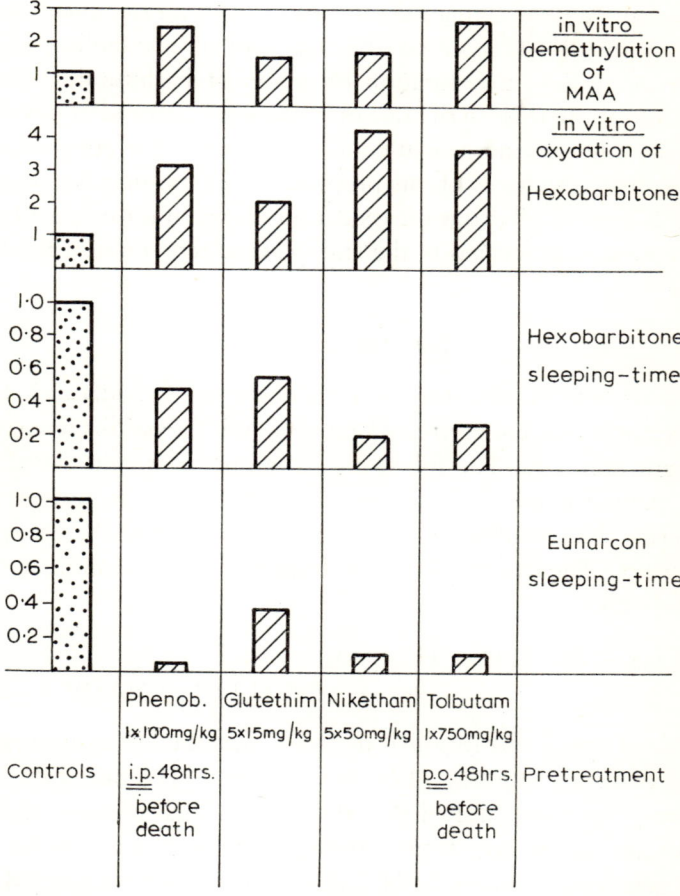

FIG. 2. Rate of oxidation of monomethylaminoantipyrine (MAA) and hexobarbitone incubated with liver supernatant, and sleeping times after I.P. injection of two short acting barbiturates compared using untreated and pretreated rats (Brodie et al., 1958); values of controls = 1·0.

responsible for the oxidation of drugs (Brodie, Gillette & La Du, 1958; Axelrod, 1960). Using their methods I have found that the small structures, prepared from the liver* of rats sleeping for much shorter times after being given barbiturates, were able to oxidize hexobarbitone more quickly (Fig. 2). A close correlation between rates of oxidation *in vitro* and sleeping times can be demonstrated. This shows that the rate of metabolism in the liver determines the duration of action of barbiturates. There was also an increase in the rate of oxidation if, instead of hexobarbitone, aminopyrine was used as the substrate for enzymes prepared from the livers of rats pretreated with barbiturates (Fig. 2). This is true for all drugs the oxidation of which is catalysed by an enzyme system located in the endoplasmic reticulum of the liver cells.

Induction of enzymes

What is the reason for the increased rate of oxidation? Is an activator formed in pretreated animals, or is the oxidizing enzyme system induced? The following experimental results show that an enzyme is induced. First of all, however, it is necessary to describe the reactions and the enzymes involved in the oxidation of drugs. The hydroxylation of drugs and steroids can be written as follows:

$$A\text{-}CH_3 + NADPH + H^+ + O_2 \longrightarrow A\text{-}CH_2OH + NADP^+ + H_2O$$

Axelrod (1960) and Brodie *et al.* (1958) found that the hydroxylation of drugs requires TPN and oxygen. Hayaishi (1964) and Mason (1957) established that the oxygen incorporated into the substrate originated from atmospheric oxygen. The second oxygen atom oxidizes TPNH. For this type of reaction Mason introduced the term "mixed function oxidase".

---

* The biochemist calls these structures microsomes after isolating them from the liver cells.

Estabrook et al. (1963) recognized that the oxygen-activating enzyme is a specific cytochrome, closely related to haemoglobin, called cytochrome-P_{450} or CO-cytochrome. For oxygen uptake this cytochrome has to be reduced by an electron transport system consisting of an FAD-containing flavoprotein and another component, as yet unknown, through which the electron transfer takes place from TPNH to the iron of cytochrome-P_{450}. Carbon monoxide inhibits the uptake of oxygen by competing for a binding site on the iron atom (Fig. 3).

Cytochrome-P_{450} is apparently the first enzyme which increases after induction with phenobarbitone and the drugs

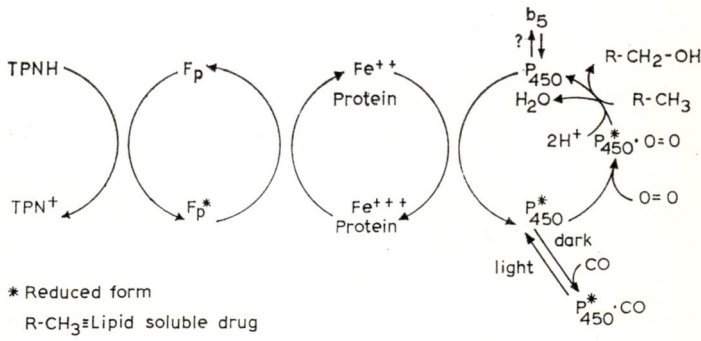

Fig. 3. Schematic representation of the pathway of electron transport for reduction of cytochrome-P_{450}, and the activation of oxygen for hydroxylation reactions (Remmer et al., 1968). The non-haem-iron protein (Fe-protein) has been detected in adrenal mitochondria with cytochrome-P_{450} for hydroxylation of steroids (Estabrook et al., 1963).

mentioned. The magnitude of induction depends on the dose administered, the duration of treatment and the state of nutrition.

The time course of induction provides further evidence for the involvement of cytochrome-P_{450} in drug hydroxylation. The rise and fall of cytochrome-P_{450} after an injection of phenobarbitone corresponds very closely to the rate of oxidation of

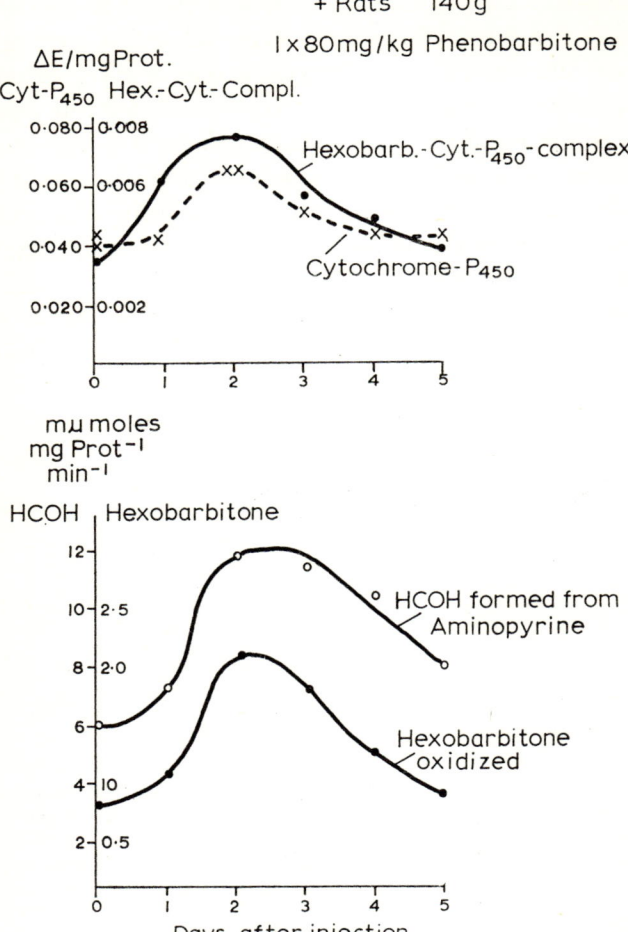

FIG. 4. Time course of induction after a single dose of phenobarbitone (80 mg/kg). The upper part shows the rise and fall of cytochrome-P_{450} and the complex formed after addition of excess hexobarbitone (Remmer et al., 1968) to microsomes prepared from rat livers 1–5 days after injection of phenobarbitone. The lower part shows the course of the oxidation of aminopyrine and hexobarbitone by the same microsomal preparations.

hexobarbitone and aminopyrine (Fig. 4). The induction of cytochrome-P_{450} lasts only four to five days after one dose of phenobarbitone. But after repeated administration it lasts three weeks in rabbits and from four to twelve weeks in dogs. This indicates that the increase in cytochrome-P_{450} outlasts the elimination of the inducing agent by several weeks.

The induction of cytochrome-P_{450} precedes considerable changes in the liver cells. After repeated doses of phenobarbitone, or of several other lipid-soluble drugs, the weight of the liver increases. This is a typical hypertrophy of the liver (Kunz et al., 1966). At the same time the activities of numerous microsomal and some cytoplasmic and mitochondrial enzymes, for example esterases, reductases and conjugases (Remmer & Merker, 1963a) increased as well as of cytochrome-P_{450}. Several microsomal enzymes, however, which have nothing to do with the breakdown of drugs, such as glucose-6-phosphatase, nucleosidase and ATPase, are activated only slightly or not at all (Fig. 5).

Cytoplasmic enzymes, such as UDP-glucose-dehydrogenase (Touster et al., 1962), some transaminases (Greim, unpublished), conjugases (Schellhas et al., 1965) and several others are also induced (Orrenius & Ernster, 1967). There is a greater increase in the activities of the enzymes in the microsomes from the smooth membranes of the endoplasmic reticulum than in those from rough membranes (Remmer & Merker, 1963a; Fouts, 1961). Chemical determinations showed that there is a two-fold rise in the protein and lipid content of the smooth membrane fraction (Fig. 5 and Remmer & Merker, 1963a). The results of pharmacological and biochemical experiments can be confirmed morphologically; electron microscopy has shown that there is an augmentation of smooth membranes with no change in the appearance of other cell structures (Remmer & Merker, 1963b; Orrenius et al., 1965).

The mechanism for increasing enzymes and membranes remains unexplained. All the changes occurring in the cell can be seen as part of an unspecific adaptation enabling the organism to discard an excess of foreign lipid-soluble compounds. Oxidation

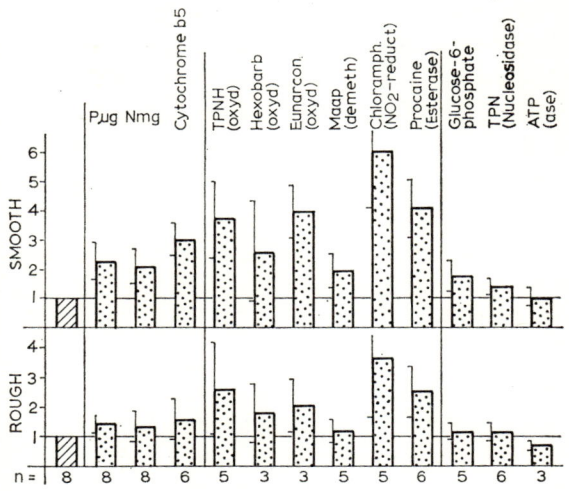

FIG. 5. The phosphorus, nitrogen and cytochrome-b_5 content of the smooth and rough membrane microsome fractions obtained from 1g of rabbit liver, and the activity of several enzymes in the rough and smooth membrane fractions of 1g of liver after pretreatment with 8 × 50 mg of phenobarbitone. 1, Values for enzyme activities from microsomes of untreated rabbits (▨).

makes them more soluble in water so that they can be excreted through the kidneys.

Cross tolerance

Having represented tolerance as a type of unspecific adaptation due to increased oxidation in the liver I should like to discuss very briefly examples of cross tolerance. Not all drugs which are hydroxylated in the liver have inducing properties. Almost all alkaloids and several other compounds listed in Table 2 fail to induce the enzymes (Remmer, 1964). This is also true of morphine and pethidine. Tolerance to these drugs and related analgesics is never due to increased breakdown (Remmer, 1962).

Inducing drugs such as barbiturates, however, can stimulate the oxidation of pethidine. The principal pathway of pethidine metabolism includes an oxidative demethylation. Consequently any induction by barbiturates or other inducing agents speeds breakdown to ineffective or less effective (Fig. 6) metabolites of

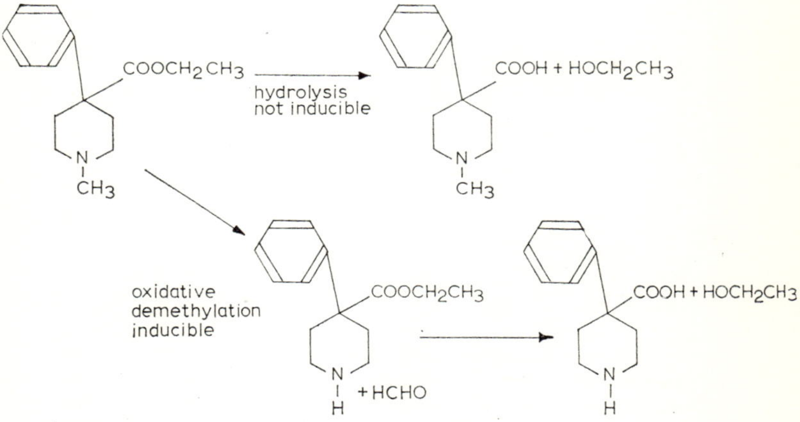

FIG. 6. Metabolism of pethidine. The oxidative demethylation to norpethidine is the principal route of breakdown. It is the only step which is inducible in experiments with rats (Remmer & Alsleben, 1958; Alsleben, 1963).

pethidine (Remmer & Alsleben, 1958). This is the reason why rats treated with phenobarbitone become more tolerant to pethidine. The graph in Fig. 7 shows the number of rats not responding to electrical stimulation of the tail after injection of pethidine. The maximum analgesic effect was achieved after thirty minutes. Nearly all rats failed to respond. The broken line in the graph represents the response of rats receiving the same dose of pethidine but which have been pretreated with phenobarbitone. Only

60% of the rats responded to the electrical stimulation because pethidine is metabolized faster, and therefore loses nearly 50% of its analgesic effect.

These results indicate that a person taking phenobarbitone should

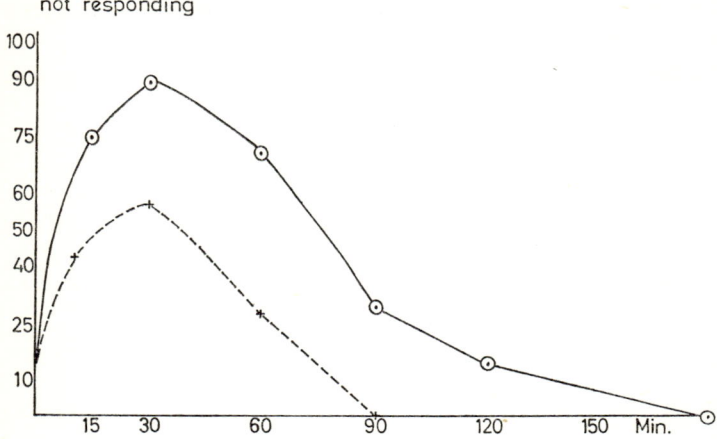

FIG. 7. Loss of responsiveness to electrical stimulation of the tail in male rats treated with a single injection of pethidine (50 mg/kg s.c.). After 30 min. 90% of the rats did not react (O). Pretreatment with phenobarbitone (100 mg/kg every other day for 4 weeks) reduced and shortened the effect of pethidine (+).

become tolerant to pethidine, but he will not become tolerant to a higher dose of morphine. This is chiefly metabolized by conjugation with *glucuronic* acid, a pathway which is not activated (Table 2 and Gross & Thompson, 1940). Thus, inducing agents such as phenobarbitone produce cross tolerance to pethidine but not to morphine.

Role of the central nervous system

Tolerance to analgesics which has nothing to do with an increased breakdown brings me back to the other form of tolerance which is characterized by diminished responses of the receptors in the central nervous system. Despite many efforts, the reason for the tremendous tolerance to morphine which can develop

Table 2

Cross tolerance by increased breakdown

Drug-hydroxylating enzymes in the liver	*Drugs becoming less active or inactive*
induced by	by hydroxylating enzymes
barbiturates	all hypnotics (except barbitone)
glutethimide	,, sedatives (except ethanol)
nikethamide	,, antiepileptics
tolbutamide	,, phenothiazines
phenylbutazone	,, tranquillizers
antihistaminics	dicoumarol
ethanol	pethidine etc.
several insecticides etc.	
not induced by	by conjugating enzymes
morphine	morphine
pethidine	salicylates etc.
nicotine	
atropine	by dehydrogenase
caffeine etc.	ethanol

in animals and man is not yet known. I think that it is impossible to elucidate altered reactions in the cells of the ganglia while the biochemical basis of the so-called receptor site is unknown.

A similar problem arises with any attempt to explain tolerance to barbiturates by decreased responses of the central nervous system. Butler *et al.* (1954) were the first to show the huge accumulation of the long acting phenobarbitone. Only 10–20% of this barbiturate is eliminated from the body daily. The concentration rises from day to day until the amount of drug eliminated equals the intake (Fig. 8) and reaches a level in the blood and brain which is five to ten times higher than after the first administration. If this high concentration of phenobarbitone were present after one application, as a result of the five to ten-fold increase in dose, it would produce a dangerous and severe hypnotic effect. Physicians observe, however, that, in spite of a slow, but

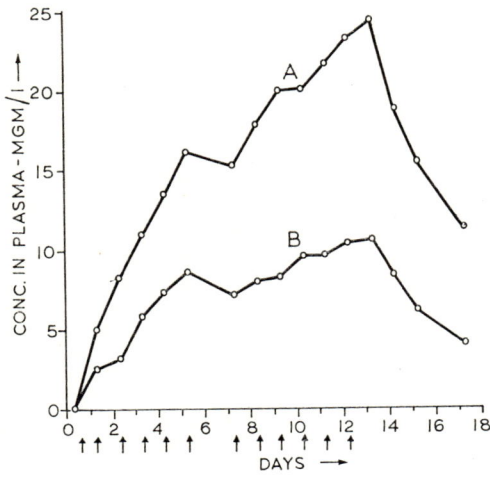

FIG. 8. Accumulation of phenobarbitone in the plasma of two patients receiving 4 mg/kg (0·27 g., A) and 2 mg/kg (0·125 g., B) daily. The accumulation in patient A was not completed when the treatment ended (arrows). The figure is derived from Butler, Mahafee, & Waddell (1965).

five to ten-fold, increase in phenobarbitone, the hypnotic effect does not increase much; it may even diminish if the central nervous system becomes adapted. So tolerance to the long acting phenobarbitone is chiefly due to a decrease of the response of the central nervous system. Increased breakdown of phenobarbitone plays a minor role. In the case of barbitone which is oxidized to a very small extent (10%, Goldschmidt & Weber, 1957) and is dependent on the kidney for elimination, increased metabolism is not a cause of tolerance (Table 3).

It seems to me that the central nervous system adapts by counteracting the hypnotic effect, using inherent physiological mechanisms, which are able to overcome sedative or hypnotic

Table 3

Tolerance to Barbiturates

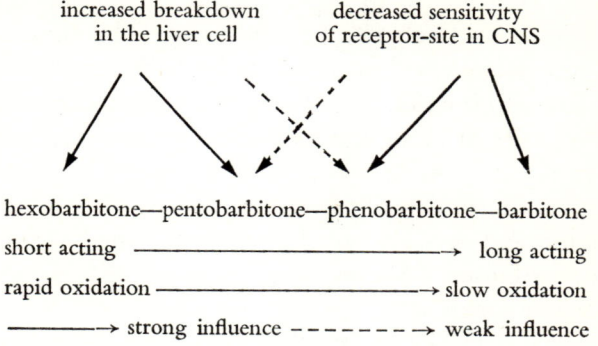

hexobarbitone—pentobarbitone—phenobarbitone—barbitone

short acting ──────────────────→ long acting

rapid oxidation ──────────────→ slow oxidation

────→ strong influence − − − − − −→ weak influence

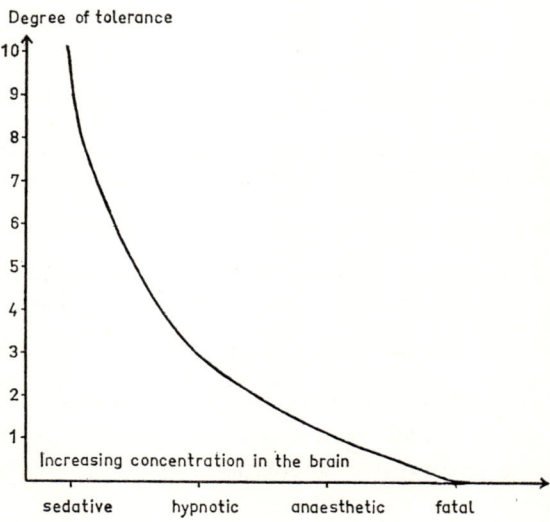

FIG. 9. The smaller the dose of a hypnotic the easier the adaptation. Pretreated rats tolerant to a hypnotic or anaesthetic dose did not tolerate a fatal dose. This is not like morphine tolerance, in which the LD_{50} is much increased.

effects of long acting barbiturates more easily than the anaesthetic action. Administering anaesthetic doses of phenobarbitone or barbitone daily to rats, I observed a very weak tolerance. If animals are pretreated with larger doses of barbiturates the LD_{50} does not increase (Gruber & Keyser, 1949). This indicates that they do not tolerate a dose which is fatal for animals not pretreated with barbiturates. The much easier adaptation of animals to smaller doses of barbiturates can be expressed in the scheme shown in Fig. 9. On the other hand enhanced breakdown by oxidation is the principal reason for tolerance to short acting barbiturates, as I was able to demonstrate with hexobarbitone and pentobarbitone. A diminished response by the receptors plays a minor role.

Finally, I should like to list (Table 4) several different characteristics of tolerance to barbiturates due to increased breakdown,

Table 4

Tolerance to barbiturates

By increased oxidation in the liver	By decreased sensitivity of receptors in the CNS
(1) Completely unspecific, can be evoked by all inducing agents	(1) More or less specific, can be evoked only by barbiturates and hypnotics
(2) Starts after 12–48 hr	(2) Starts immediately (acute tolerance)
(3) Stays after disappearance of the drug from the body for one to several weeks	(3) Stays so long as the drug is effective in the body
(4) Intensified if dose increases	(4) Diminished if dose increases

and to a diminished sensitivity of the receptors in the central nervous system, which would make it possible to distinguish between these two types of adaptation.

Summary

Barbiturates and many other drugs induce their own oxidative breakdown in the endoplasmic reticulum. The induction of these enzymes is the first step in an adaptation of the liver cells, which enables them to accelerate the conversion of lipid-soluble foreign compounds to more water-soluble metabolites and to excrete them faster from the cells into the blood stream. This is the chief reason for the shorter lasting action and diminished effect of barbiturates and other hypnotics during tolerance.

REFERENCES

Alsleben, B. (1963). Inaugural dissertation, Frei Universität Berlin.
Axelrod, J. (1960). *Arch. exp. Pathol. Pharmak.*, **238**, 24.
Brodie, B. B., Gillette, J. R. & La Du, B. N. (1958). *Ann. Rev. Biochem.*, **27**, 427.
Bush, M. T., Butler, T. C. & Dickison, H. L. (1953). *J. Pharmac. exp. Therap.*, **108**, 104.
Butler, T. C., Mahaffee, C. & Waddell, W. J. (1954). *J. Pharmac. exp. Therap.*, **111**, 425.
Estabrook, R. W., Cooper, D. Y. & Rosenthal, O. (1963). *Biochem. Z.*, **338**, 741.
Faust, E. S. (1900). *Arch. exp. Pathol. Pharmak.*, **44**, 217.
Fouts, J. R. (1961). *Biochem. Biophys. Res. Commun.*, **6**, 373.
Goldschmidt, St. & Weber, R. (1957). *Hoppe-Seyler's Z. physiol. Chem.*, **308**, 9.
Gross, E. G. & Thompson, V. (1940). *J. Pharmac. exp. Therap.*, **68**, 413.
Gruber, C. M. & Keyser, G. F. (1946). *J. Pharmac. exp. Therap.*, **86**, 186.
Hayaishi, O. (1964). *Proc. Plenary Session, Sixth Int. Congr. of Biochem.*, New York, p. 31.
Kunz, W., Schaude, G., Schimassek, H., Schmid, W. & Siess, M. (1966). *Proc. Europ. Soc. Study Drug Toxicity*, VII.
Mason, H. S. (1957). *Adv. Enzymol.*, **19**, 79.
Orrenius, S., Ericsson, J. L. E. & Ernster, L., (1965). *J. Cell. Biol.*, **25**, 627.
Orrenius, S. & Ernster, L. (1967). *Life Sci.*, **6**, 1473.
Pringsheim, J. (1908). *Biochem. Z.*, **12**, 143.
Remmer, H. (1959). *Naturwissenschaften*, **46**, 580.
Remmer, H. (1962). *Enzymes and Drug Action*, Ciba Foundation Symposium. London: J. & A. Churchill, p. 276.
Remmer, H. (1963). *Arch. exp. Pathol. Pharmak.*, **244**, 311.
Remmer, H. (1964). *Proc. Europ. Soc. Study Drug Toxicity*, IV, 57.
Remmer, H. & Alsleben, B. (1958). *Klin. Woschr.*, **36**, 332.
Remmer, H., Estabrook, R. W., Schenkman, J. B. & Greim, H. (1968). *Arch. exp. Pathol. Pharmak.*, **259**, 98.
Remmer, H. & Merker, H. J. (1963*a*). *Science*, **142**, 1657.
Remmer, H. & Merker, H. J. (1963*b*). *Klin. Woschr.*, **41**, 276.

Remmer, H. & Siegert, M. (1964). *Arch. exp. Pathol. Pharmak.*, **247**, 522.
Remmer, H., Siegert, M. & Merker, H. J. (1964). *Arch. exp. Pathol. Pharmak.*, **249**, 71.
Schellhas, H., Hornef, W. & Remmer, H. (1965). *Arch. exp. Pathol. Pharmak.*, **251**, 2, 111.
Touster, O., Hollman, S., Pineda, O. & Shumaker, S. (1962). Metabolic factors controlling duration of drug action, *Proc. First Int. Pharmac. Meeting*, **6**, Ed. by Brodie, B. B. & Erdös, E. G. London: Pergamon Press.

DISTRIBUTION AND METABOLISM IN MAN OF SOME NARCOTIC ANALGESICS AND SOME 'AMPHETAMINES'

A. H. Beckett

Department of Pharmacy, Chelsea College of Science and Technology (University of London)

Many problems in the interpretation of drug metabolism and distribution studies are posed because of *apparent* large differences in results using various subjects. How are we to make progress in studies in man involving the passage of drugs across membranes (e.g. across the placenta); in the investigations of biochemical and metabolic changes if enzyme induction is involved; in the biochemical studies of any possible changes in drug metabolism when tolerance to drugs develops, and in the studies of the importance of stereochemistry in biological action in the *in vivo* system if we cannot control the large differences between individuals in normal conditions? The purpose of this paper is to outline steps to reduce differences in individuals in investigations in man so that some of these studies can be pursued in a logical manner. The presentation involves a consideration of narcotic analgesics and amphetamines, but, obviously, the approach can be used in many other fields.

Many basic drugs are concentrated extravascularly so that the concentration of these drugs in the blood is very low, in fact too low to allow quantitative assessments by most of our present methods of analysis. Consequently, urine is the most convenient biological fluid for the analysis of these drugs as a means of assessing absorption, distribution and metabolism (Beckett, 1966; Beckett &

Tucker, 1967 and see *Phychopharmac. Bull.*, 1966). In normal conditions, the rate of excretion of a base plotted against time after ingestion of the drug shows pronounced fluctuations which are a reflection of change in the pH of the urine; the more acidic the urine, the greater the rate of excretion (see Figure 1 for

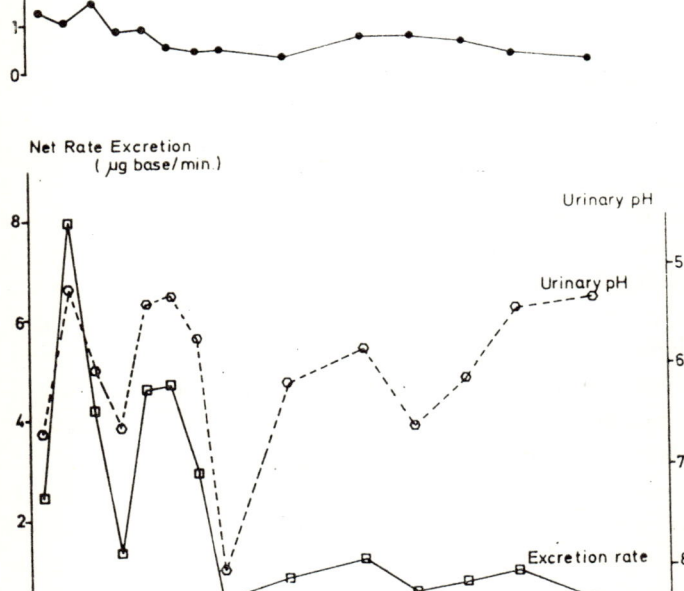

FIG. 1. The influence of urinary pH and urine output on the urinary excretion of amphetamine in man (Subject E.J.T.) after oral administration of 15 mg. of (+)-amphetamine sulphate. (Similar patterns were observed in other subjects.)

amphetamine). If the urine is kept acidic (below pH 5) by the prior administration of ammonium chloride, then these fluctuations are abolished and, after the peak level has been obtained, the plot of the log rate of excretion against time is linear (Figure 2). Much more unchanged drug is excreted in acidic conditions than in normal conditions of fluctuating pH (Figure 2). In acidic conditions, the normal large inter and intra-subject variations (5–60% recovery of unchanged drug in twenty-four hours) in the urinary excretion of amphetamine in normal conditions is considerably reduced (Table 1).

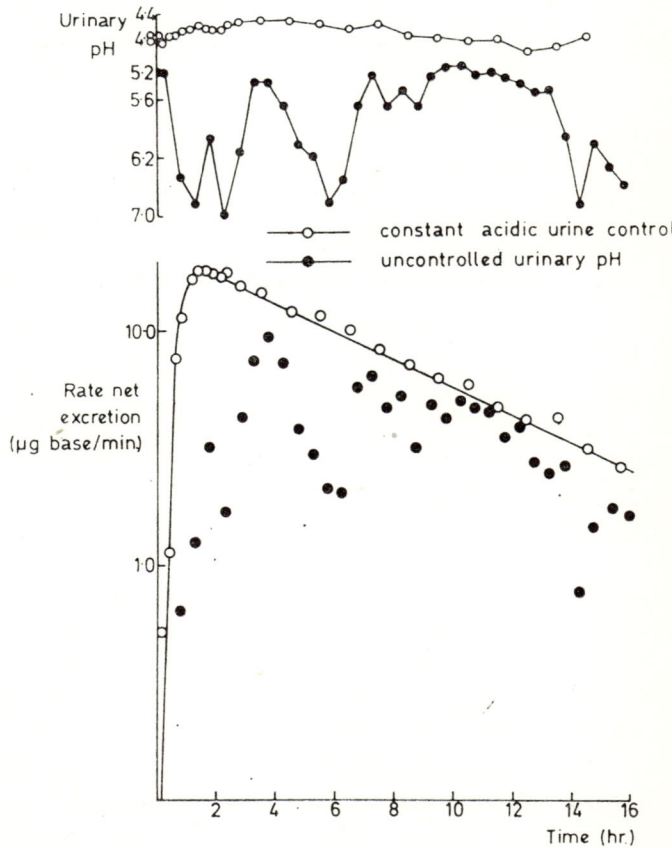

FIG. 2. Urinary excretion of amphetamine after oral administration of 15 mg solution doses of D-(+)-amphetamine sulphate. (Subject E.J.T.)

A similar situation occurs if methylamphetamine is administered (Beckett & Rowland, 1965) in normal conditions; the rate of excretion of drug plotted against time after administration

Table 1

Urinary excretion of amphetamine and elimination half-lives after oral administration of 15 mg D-(+)-amphetamine sulphate either as 'free' drug or in preparations representing essentially 'free' drug (acidic urine control)

Subject	Drug preparation	t/2 (hr)	Total % dose excreted
M.R.	Solution	5·02	63·6
N.B.	,,	4·75	61·5
E.J.T.	,,	4·93	83·5
C.M.L.	,,	4·32	63·6
A.C.M.	,,	4·60	71·1
,,	Free Pellets*	4·57	70·6
,,	,,	5·02	77·9
,,	Capsule containing free pellets**	4·70	72·8
G.T.T.	Free Pellets	5·06	78·5
,,	Capsule containing free pellets	5·31	81·9
J.F.T.	,,	6·04	79·9
,,	,,	6·50	76·0
T.M.J.	,,	4·18	74·7
	Mean	5·00	73·5

* Sugar pellets coated with drug
** Pellets as above contained in a hard gelatin capsule

is irregular, and the metabolite produced—amphetamine—also varies in its excretion pattern, as does the parent drug, the excretion of both being affected by the changes in urinary pH. Administering ammonium chloride to the subject to keep the urine acidic at below pH 5, abolishes the fluctuations and gives curves which can be used as a basis for kinetic considerations, e.g. Figure 3. Inter-subject variation in the amount of drug and metabolite excreted is also considerably reduced by this procedure. In conditions of different pH values of urine in the same individual, the accumulative excretion of methylamphetamine in man varies greatly (Figure 4), as does the duration of the biological response.

Although many basic drugs show pronounced pH dependence in their urinary excretions, not all drugs do so. For example, the excretion of methylephedrine (Beckett & Wilkinson, 1965) is greatly dependent on pH (Table 2); ephedrine excretion is not

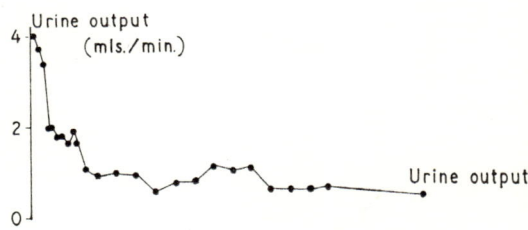

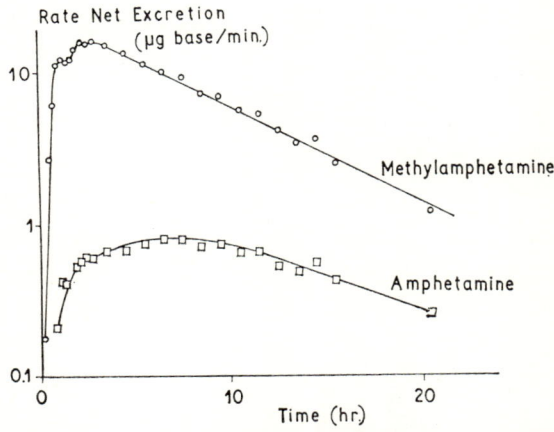

FIG. 3. Urinary excretion of methylamphetamine and amphetamine, urinary pH and urine output after oral administration of 11·0 mg of (+)-methylamphetamine and acidic urine control. (Subject E.J.T.)

Table 2

Urinary pH and excretion of ephedrine and derivatives in man

Subject	Compound administered (mg)		Route	Acidic urine (pH 4·5–5·0) % dose excreted in 24 hr as		Alkaline urine (pH 8·0 ± 0·5) % dose excreted in 24 hr as	
				Ephedrine	Norephedrine	Ephedrine	Norephedrine
N.B.	(−) Ephedrine	20·5	Oral	87·8	8·9	—	—
		25·0	Oral	85·8	10·4	21·8	24·4
		25·0	I.V.	86·7	7·2	—	—
G.R.W.		20·5	Oral	93·4	4·1	—	—
		25·0	Oral	92·0	3·7	24·3	10·9
		25·0	I.V.	99·0	3·0	—	—
R.W.D.		20·5	Oral	89·4	8·2	—	—
		25·0	Oral	73·9	8·1	34·7	19·4
N.B.	(−) Norephedrine	22·9	Oral	—	99·7	—	Approx. 98·0
G.R.W.				—	91·1	—	85·0
R.W.D.				—	94·2	—	90·0
N.B.	(−) Methylephedrine	27·1	Oral	63·7·*	1·7	1·8*	3·6
G.R.W.				75·3·*	N.D.	6·0*	1·4
R.W.D.				79·8·*	1·0	3·2*	1·7

Additional columns in Methylephedrine rows: 16·9, 10·0, 13·8 (Norephedrine acidic); 10·4, 5·9, 5·4 (Ephedrine alkaline).

* Methylephedrine

so pH dependent (Table 2), whereas acidic or alkaline urine makes very little difference to the excretion of norephedrine (Table 2). The pKa values of these three drugs are not very dissimilar;

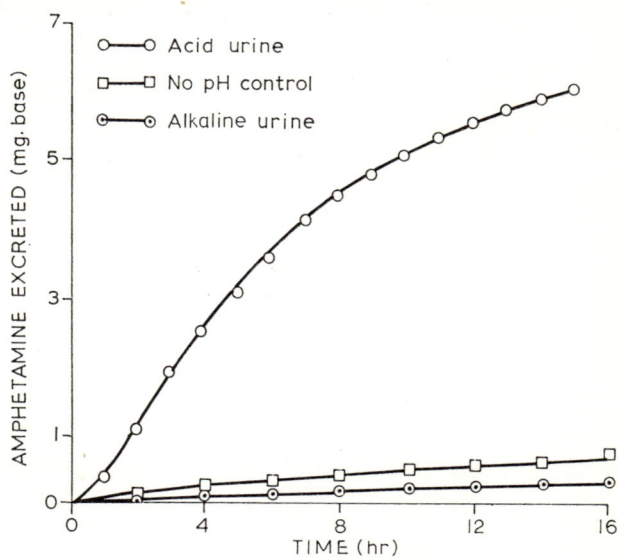

FIG. 4. Cumulative urinary excretion of amphetamine in man under varying conditions of urinary pH, after oral administration of 11·0 mg of (+)-amphetamine. (Subject M.R.)

the difference in pH sensitivity lies in the difference in the lipid solubility of the unionized form of the drug, i.e. unionized methylephedrine is very lipid soluble, ephedrine is less so, whereas unionized norephedrine is very soluble in water but is only slightly soluble in lipids. Similar results were obtained with the corresponding pseudo-ephedrines.

These results can be explained by assuming that the kidney tubules are selectively permeable to the *unionized* lipid soluble base rather than the ionized lipid insoluble cation of the base (Beckett, 1966; Beckett & Tucker, 1967). A diagrammatic presentation of renal tubular transport mechanism is shown in

Figure 5. The more lipid soluble the unionized base, the more rapid will be the partition between the aqueous solution and the kidney tubules and the lipid walls of the tubules, and both the pKa of the drug and the pH of the solution will influence the

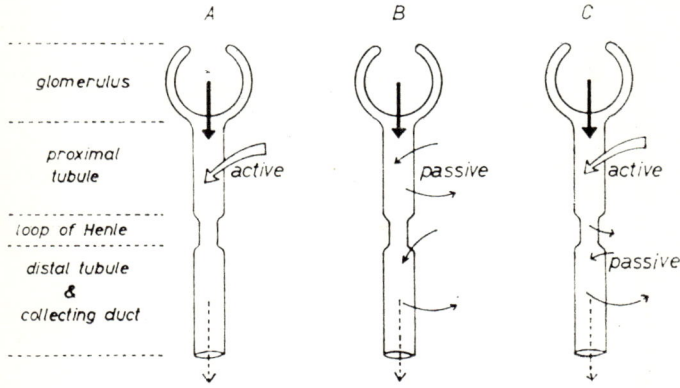

FIG. 5. Schematic presentation of renal tubular mechanisms of organic base transport.

concentration of ionized versus unionized forms. In certain circumstances, the rate of flow of the urine may influence the results, for it will have an effect on the concentration of the unionized base irrespective of the pH of the medium.

Narcotic Analgesics

Similar results have been obtained with the narcotic analgesics (e.g. Figure 6) in which the urine excretion of (+)-methadone in conditions of acidic urine and under uncontrolled urinary pH is presented (Beckett & Taylor, in the press). The recovery of unchanged drug (I) and its metabolite (II) resulting from mono-

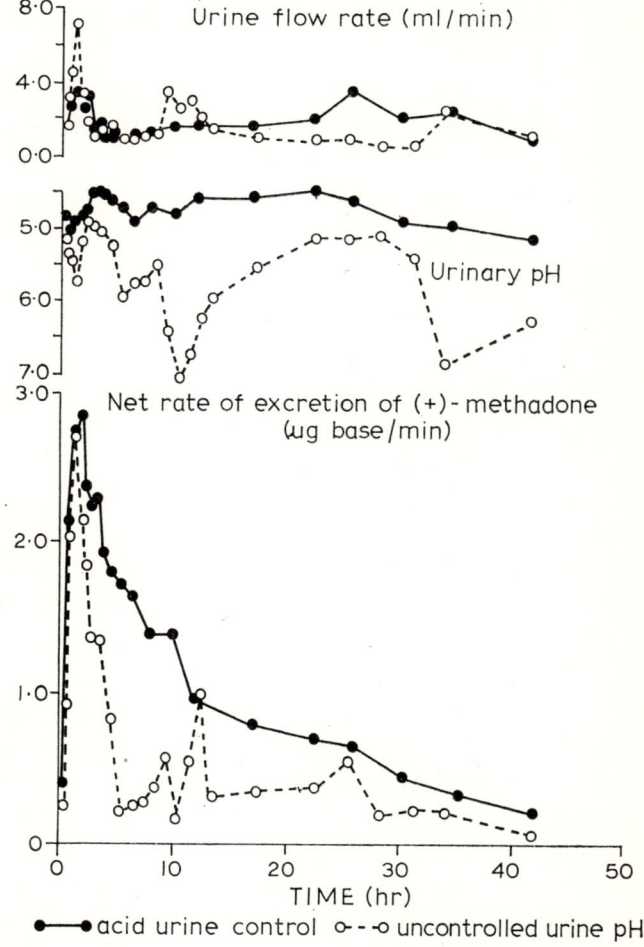

FIG. 6. Urinary excretion of (+)-methadone with corresponding urinary pH and urine flow rate after oral administration of 10 mg of (+)-methadone hydrochloride. (Subject J.F.T.)

N-demethylation of methadone followed by cyclization to give (I) is shown in Table 3. It should be noted that recovery of unchanged drug varies greatly with the pH of the urine, whereas the recovery of the metabolite does not. As will be seen later, the drug is substantially absorbed into a biological lipid at pH 7, whereas the metabolite is only slightly absorbed at this pH. Control of pH at an acid level for methadone does not give a straight line in the plot of log rate of excretion against time after intravenous injection in normal conditions (Figure 7). However, in conditions of enforced diuresis and acidic pH control, a straight

Table 3

Urinary recoveries of unchanged drug and metabolite produced by mono-N-demethylation after oral administration of (+)-methadone hydrochloride to man

Trial number	Subject	Control of urinary pH	% Recovery in 24 hr		
			Unchanged drug	metabolite	Total
A.1	J.F.T.	Acid (4·6–5·1)	22·2	21·3	43·5
U.1		None (4·9–7·1)	9·6	17·7	28·3
B.1		Alkaline (7·4–8·1)	0·5	18·0	18·5
A.6	E.J.T.	Acid (4·7–5·7)	18·5	13·0	31·5
B.2		Alkaline (7·5–8·1)	0·3	10·5	10·8

line is obtained for methadone excretion (Figure 8). The effect of the pH of the urine on the excretion of methadone and other narcotic drugs is also shown in Table 4.

If measurements of the urine excretion of unchanged drug and metabolite are used to attempt to elucidate the importance of differences in metabolism between individuals or between species, very misleading information can be obtained unless the pH of the urine is controlled. For example, the ratio of metabolite of methadone to unchanged methadone excreted in acidic conditions of urine is 1·0 whereas in alkaline conditions it is 40; the

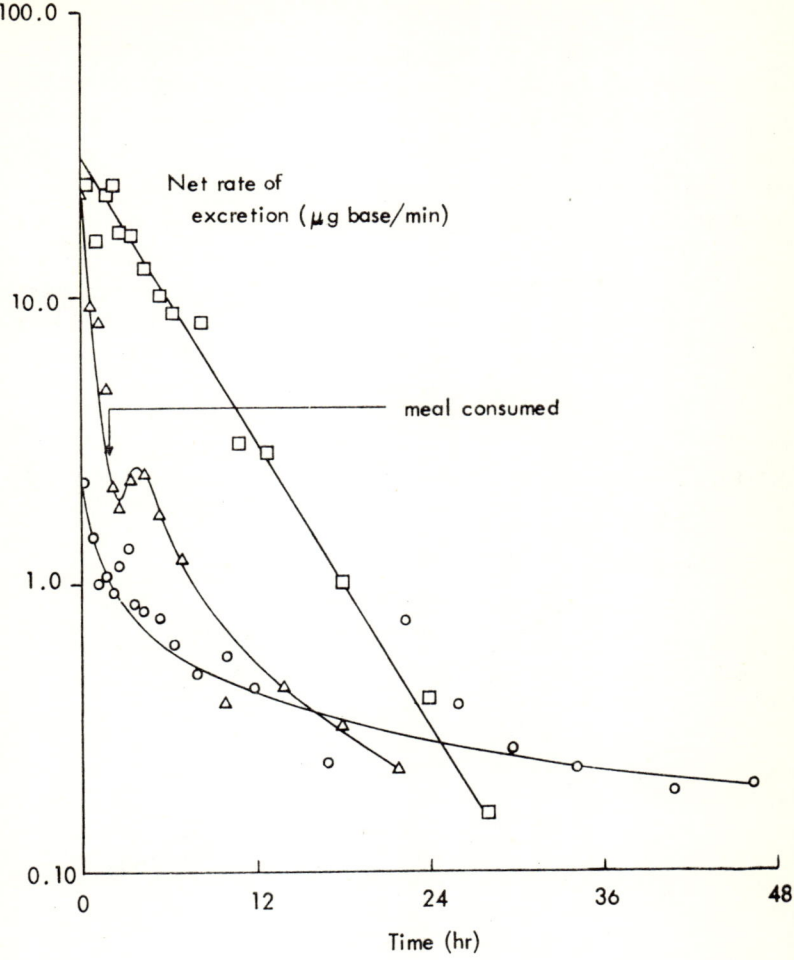

○ (+)-methadone HCl, 5mg, (subject EJT)
□ pethidine HCl, 50mg, (subject JFT)
△ pentazocine HCl, 20mg, (subject JFT)

Fig. 7. Urinary excretion of some analgesics after intravenous administration. Acid urine control.

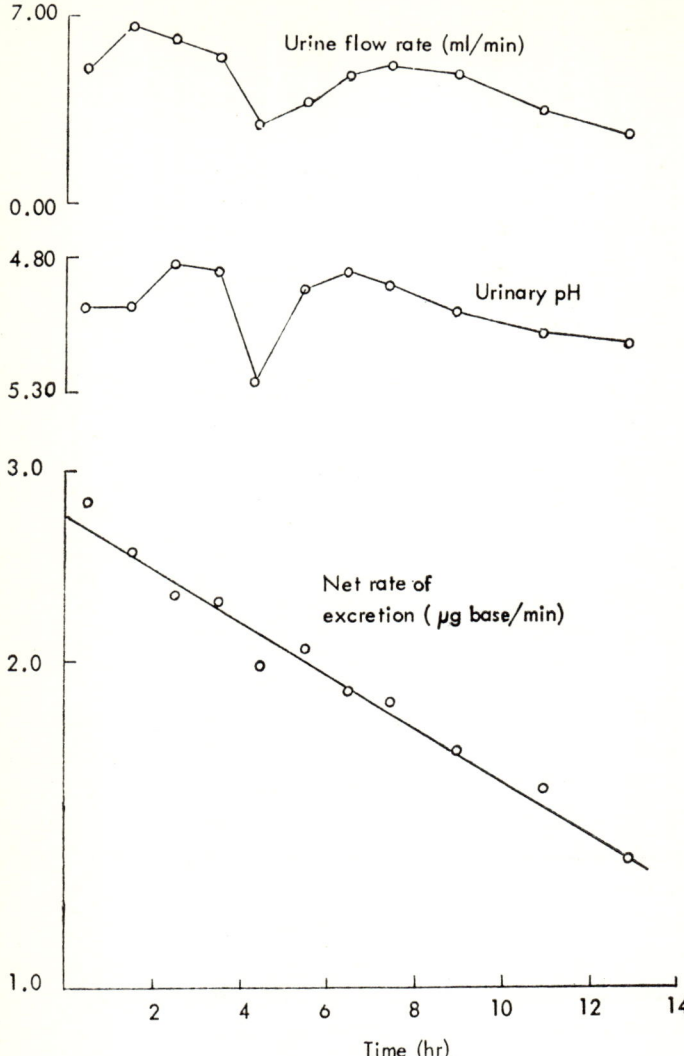

FIG. 8. Urinary excretion of methadone with corresponding urinary pH and urine flow rate after i.v. administration 10 mg of (+)-methadone HCl. Acid urine control and waterloading. (Subject J.E.T.)

ratio of the metabolite ephedrine to the unchanged drug methylephedrine is 0·25 in conditions of acidic urine and 5·0 in conditions of alkaline urine. It is thus obvious that any consideration of

Table 4

The effect of pH of urine on the excretion of some narcotic drugs

Percentage of drug excreted unchanged in the urine in 48 hr

Drug	Route	In normal conditions	In acidic conditions (approx. pH 5·0)	In alkaline conditions (approx. pH 8·0)
(+)-Methadone	Oral	About 10·0	25·0	0·5
	I.V.	N.D.	26·0	N.D.
(−)-Methadone	Oral	N.D.	35·0	N.D.
Pethidine	Oral	About 8·0	30·0	1·0
	I.V.	N.D.	31·0	N.D.
Pentazocine	Oral	N.D.	1·5	N.D.
	I.V.	N.D.	13·0	N.D.

species differences in metabolism, or of inter-subject variation in metabolism in the same species, in which the drug or metabolite is partially unionized at physiological pH is virtually worthless unless the pH conditions of the urine are controlled. For example, the average pH of rabbits' urine is about 8 whereas that of man on a reasonable protein diet is about 6·2; how can we consider, therefore, species differences in rates of metabolism in these conditions? Similarly, how can we talk about inter-subject variation in metabolism using urine data when humans on a very low protein diet have an average pH of urine of about 8 against the normal average of 6·2? Standardized conditions are essential if any comparative studies are to be made.

When the kinetics of metabolism in the whole body are established in acidic conditions, it is then possible to use analogue computer techniques (Beckett & Tucker, 1968; Beckett, Boyes & Tucker, 1968a and b) to predict excretion patterns in an individual in conditions of fluctuating pH, e.g. see Figure 9 for amphetamine. Because in controlled conditions reproducible results can now be obtained in an individual, it is possible to examine enzyme induction in man with precision, and to examine the relative

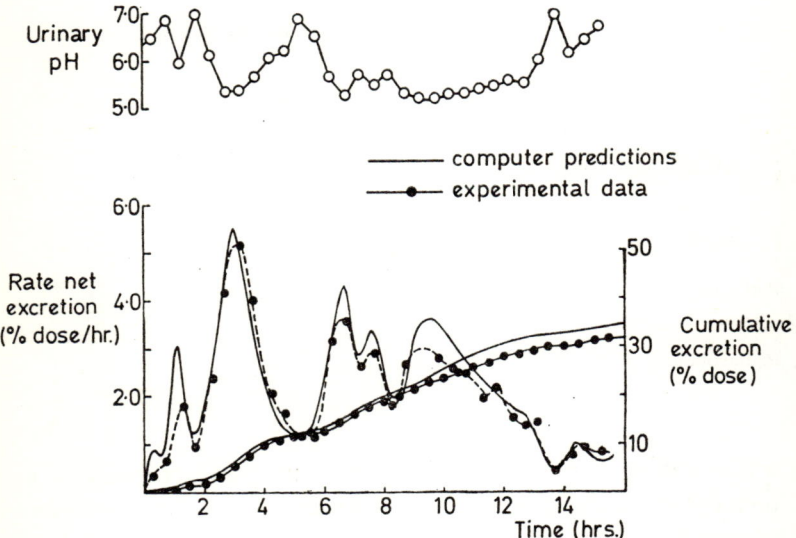

FIG. 9. A comparison of computer predicted and actual rates of excretion and cumulative excretion of amphetamine after oral administration of 15 mg of D(+)-amphetamine sulphate in solution. (Subject 1.)

importance of various metabolic routes in altering the structure and stereo-chemistry of the compound under examination.

Buccal tests of Drug Partitioning

It has been pointed out that, with some drugs, the plot of the log of the rate of excretion against time can be made to be linear by simply controlling the pH of the urine at an acidic level of 5·0, whereas other drugs, in addition to this pH control, require enforced diuresis to produce this straight line. The rate of partitioning of a drug into lipid is the controlling feature in the reabsorption in the kidney tubules of many drugs. Measurement

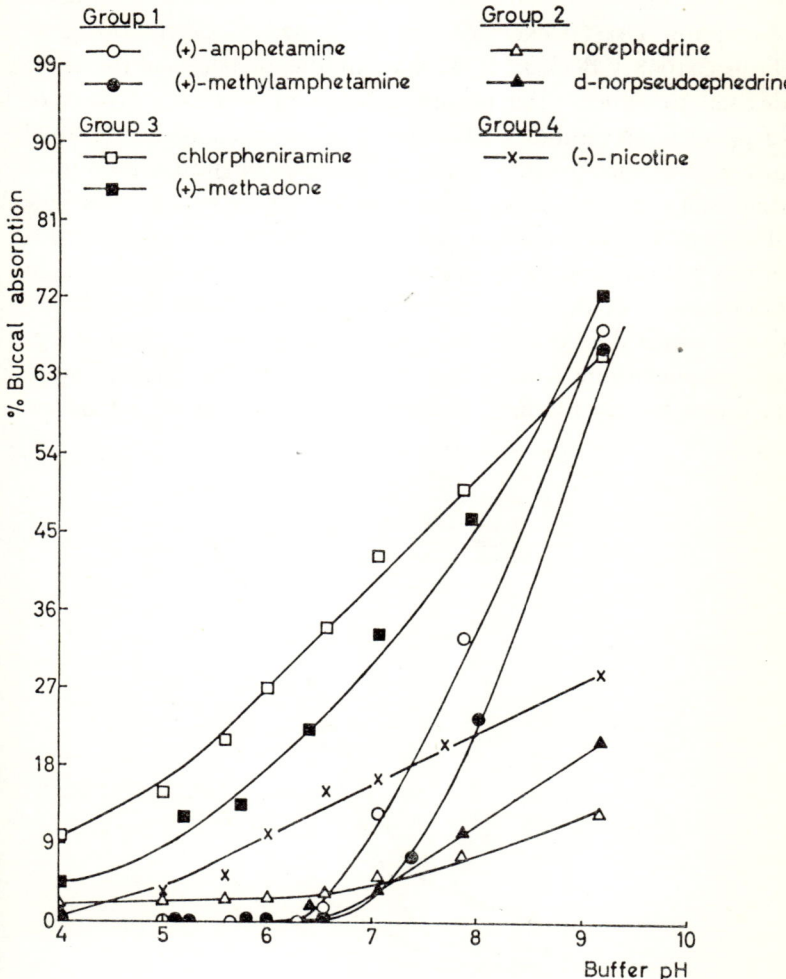

FIG. 10. Buccal absorption of some basic drugs representing different classes in the buccal absorption test.

of partition co-efficients of drugs between organic solvents and water or buffer solutions is not entirely satisfactory to classify drugs because the order of results in a series of drugs can vary with the organic solvent used. A simple test, namely, the buccal absorption test (Beckett & Triggs, 1967; Beckett, Boyes & Triggs, 1968; Beckett & Moffat, in the press), was therefore devised to indicate the possible re-absorption characteristics of drugs in kidney tubules. This test enables drugs to be classified in terms of their relative order of partitioning into a biological lipid; all subjects examined have placed a wide variety of drugs, always in the same relative order of partitioning. Typical results in this test, illustrating the various classes of drugs, are shown in Figure 10. The difference in the shape of the curve of norephedrine, which does not depend greatly on pH for its partitioning, and amphetamine which does, is to be noted. Similarly, Figure 11 shows the partitioning characteristics in this test of methadone

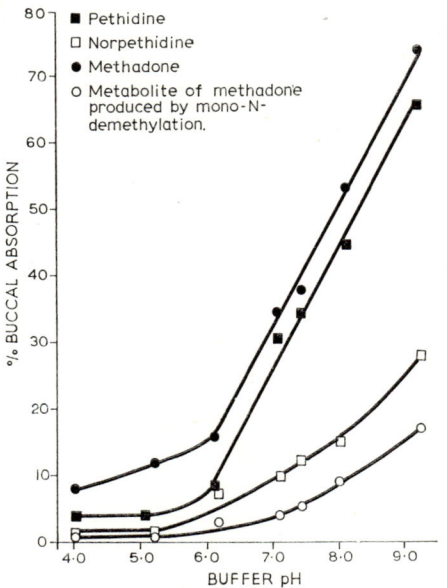

FIG. 11. Buccal absorption of some basic compounds.

Table 5

Maternal and cord blood levels after pethidine or pentazocine administration during labour

Drug	Patient	Dose (mg)	Route	Time interval before birth (hr-min)	μg analgesic base per/ml. blood		Ratio of cord level to maternal level	Average ratio	Ratio of the average ratio for pethidine to that for pentazocine
					Maternal	Cord			
Pentazocine	Mrs H.	48	I.M	1–50	0·25	0·11	0·44		
”	Mrs J. J.	48	”	1–05	0·25	0·15	0·60		
”	Mrs R.	{48 / 24	” / I.V	2–30 / 0–55}	0·31	0·23	0·74	0·59	
”	Mrs A. J.	48	I.M	6–15	0·12	0·07	0·58		1·67
Pethidine	Mrs E.	{120 / 120	” / ”	4–00 / 2–00}	0·77	0·58	0·75		
”	Mrs B.	120	”	1–50	0·56	0·37	0·66		
”	Mrs C.	120	”	3–15	0·27	0·27	1·00	0·98	
”	Mrs D.	120	”	1–50	0·27	0·32	1·19		
”	Mrs P.	{120 / 120	” / ”	5–25 / 3–00}	0·38	0·49	1·29		

Table 6

Maternal and cord blood levels after combined administration of pethidine and pentazocine during labour

Drug	Patient	Dose (mg)	Route	Time interval before birth (hr–min)	μg analgesic/ml. blood		Ratio of cord to maternal level	Ratio of cord/maternal ratio of pethidine to that of pentazocine
					Maternal	Cord		
Pentazocine & pethidine	Mrs H. S.	24 / 60	I.M	1–45	0·11 / 0·27	0·08 / 0·43	0·73 / 1·59	2·18
Pentazocine & pethidine	Mrs L. S.	24 / 60	,,	2–00	0·10 / 0·28	0·07 / 0·33	0·70 / 1·18	1·69
Pentazocine & pethidine	Mrs F. N.	24 / 60	,,	3–25	0·03 / 0·30	0·02 / 0·25	0·66 / 0·83	1·26
Pentazocine & pethidine	Mrs D. H.	24 / 60	,,	5–47 & 1–57	0·06 / 0·30	0·04 / 0·36	0·67 / 1·20	1·79
Pentazocine & pethidine	Mrs O. B.	24 / 60	,,	16–45 & 6–45	0·014 / 0·12	0·01 / 0·15	0·71 / 1·25	1·76
Pentazocine & pethidine	Mrs P. E.	24 / 60	,,	2–40	0·04 / 0·15	0·02 / 0·34	0·50 / 2·26	4·52

Average 2·2

and pethidine and their corresponding metabolites. This buccal absorption test indicates the sensitivity of partitioning of methadone to pH changes and the relative insensitivity of the partitioning of the metabolite to changes in the physiological pH range, results which are in accord with those reported above for the excretion of methadone and its metabolite. A similar but much smaller difference is to be noted for pethidine and its metabolite, norphethidine, again results which are in accord with the excretion data.

Detailed examinations of the relative partitioning of drugs can now be carried out with assurance with respect to the passage across the placenta in humans. It is known that the serum of the foetus is more acidic and in general there are wider pH variations than exist in the mother. Thus, the relative passage of drugs which are partially ionized at physiological pH could be influenced by pH differences between mother and foetus. Ideally, therefore, the two drugs should be given at the same time if true comparisons are to be made. Results (Beckett, Taylor & Kourounakis, unpublished), using the narcotics pentazocine and pethidine given separately and concurrently are shown in Tables 5 and 6 respectively. The results clearly indicate that pethidine crosses into the foetus more than does pentazocine relative to the concentration in the mother.

In conclusion, therefore, control of urinary pH is advocated. When this is done during pharmacological studies, conclusions about the induction of enzymes involved in drug metabolism become better established. Drug interactions, including those involved in drug-dependence, can be studied with greater certainty.

REFERENCES

Beckett, A. H. (1966). *Dansk Tidsskr. Farm.*, **40**, 197–223 and refs. cited therein.
Beckett, A. H., Boyes, R. N. & Triggs, E. J. (1968). *J. Pharm. Pharmac.*, **20**, 92–97.

Beckett, A. H., Boyes, R. N. & Tucker, G. T. (1968a). *J. Pharm. Pharmac.*, **20,** 269–276.
Beckett, A. H., Boyes, R. N. & Tucker, G. T. (1968b). *J. Pharm. Pharmac.*, **20,** 277–282.
Beckett, A. H. and Moffat, A. C. *J. Pharm. Pharmac.* In the press.
Beckett, A. H. & Rowland, M. (1965). *J. Pharm. Pharmac.*, **17,** 109S–114S.
Beckett, A. H. & Taylor, J. F. *J. Pharm. Pharmac.* In the press.
Beckett, A. H. & Triggs, E. J. (1967). *J. Pharm. Pharmac.*, **19,** 31S–41S.
Beckett, A. H. & Tucker, G. T. (1967). *J. Mond. Pharm.*, **3,** 181–202 and refs. cited therein.
Beckett, A. H. and Tucker, G. T. (1968). *J. Pharm. Pharmac.*, **20,** 174–193.
Beckett, A. H. & Wilkinson, G. R. (1965). *J. Pharm. Pharmac.*, **17,** 107S–108S.
See *Psychopharmac. Bull.* (1966). **3,** 21–62.

DEVELOPMENT OF NEW POTENT ANALGESICS

Paul A. J. Janssen

Janssen Pharmaceutica, Beerse, Belgium

The most potent analgesics known are pharmacologically and chemically related to morphine. The exact mechanism of action of these drugs is unknown. This is hardly surprising in view of the fact that the nature and range of the sensations covered by the word 'pain' elude precise definition (Sweet, 1959). Efforts to analyse the phenomenon of pain in neurophysiological or biochemical terms have yielded rather unsatisfactory results.

Basic pain mechanisms

Unequivocal proof of peripheral fibres that are specifically devoted to only one type of sensory modality—pain, touch, cold or warmth—has not been advanced so far. Correlation of cutaneous, somatic and visceral nerve endings or receptors with particular types of pain is at a similar elementary stage. Clinically important pain impulses seem to enter the spinal cord, exclusively by the posterior roots, and terminate around cells of the posterior horn. Pain impulse conduction within the cord seems to involve diffusely distributed unmyelinated as well as myelinated fibres, which ascend by multiple relays with crossing and recrossing. Most human pain fibres, however, seem to cross the spinal cord in the anterior commissure and ascend in the lateral spinothalamic tract, which projects not only to the ipsilateral and contralateral nucleus ventralis posterolateralis, but also to other thalamic nuclei, to the medullary, pontine and mesencephalic reticular formation, the corpora quadrigesima and the ipsilateral reticular nucleus. The invasion of these regions of the brain by impulses due to pain stimuli activates, in all probability, many ascending and descending functional systems (Martin, 1963).

Developing new analgesics

Classical approach. In view of the bewildering complexity of the problem, it is not surprising that a logical approach to the development of better potent analgesics is still inconceivable. The classical, empirical approach consists of synthesizing and screening new organic molecules that are chemically related to known analgesics (Janssen & Van der Eycken, 1968). This type of research is interesting in that it adds to the growing body of empirical data concerning the particular chemical features associated with a given pharmacological effect. It can also lead, if one is lucky, to a more useful analgesic. The crucial problem, therefore, is to find out how to predict relative clinical usefulness of an analgesic drug from animal data.

Type of analgesic needed. There are, of course, many clinical situations in which the relief or the prevention of pain is one of the problems. The prevention of all the undesirable consequences of the noxious and painful stimuli during major surgery calls for a potent analgesic, capable of producing complete surgical analgesia in all cases. The drug should have an immediate onset and a predictable, dose-related duration of action. Fentanyl is probably the most widely used drug for this purpose. A single intravenous injection of 0·5 mg of fentanyl will produce complete surgical analgesia in the adult within one minute. This state will last for about forty-five minutes and be followed by a gradual return to a state of normal susceptibility to painful stimuli over a period of several hours.

Fentanyl and morphine have many pharmacological properties in common: both drugs create a state of respiratory depression in which the respiratory centre is insensitive to carbon dioxide and the patient literally 'forgets' to breathe. Both drugs, by a spinal action, can create rigidity of the striated musculature, but this is easily overcome by curarizing agents. Both drugs are effectively antagonized by nalorphine-like agents. All these actions and properties are easily measurable in the experimental animal and are surprisingly predictable from animals to man. Fentanyl is much quicker and shorter acting than morphine, it does not release histamine and it is less emetic. With fentanyl it is much easier than with morphine and most other morphine-like drugs to eliminate completely all subjective, motor and autonomic effects of noxious and painful stimuli. Its analgesic peak effect is much more intense. Although the use of fentanyl presents no problems to the skilled anaesthetist, it is undoubtedly useful to try to improve upon it. One might, for instance, want to see a drug which is just as effective, but which has an even shorter-lived peak effect and with much less influence on respiration. Such a drug could conceivably be of even greater use than fentanyl in very short operations as well as in the treatment of various emergency situations associated with severe pain, such as myocardial infarction or renal colics. It should be pointed out, however, that the only drugs known to produce surgical analgesia in the conscious patient are all morphinomimetics and that efforts to separate morphine-like analgesic activity and respiratory depressant activity have not yet been successful.

In the treatment of severe post-operative pain it would be desirable to develop analgesics that are at least as effective as a parenteral dose of 10 mg of morphine or 100 mg of pethidine, but much safer in terms of side effect liability (nausea, vomiting, dizziness, respiratory depression, circulatory effects). The ideal drug should act quickly and have a predictable effect of at least six hours. In post-operative pain treatment, the abuse liability of the drugs used is known to be of secondary importance. Nalorphine, pentazocine and similar drugs cannot be considered superior to the morphine-like drugs in common use for the treatment of severe post-operative pain. Although they are perhaps equally active against moderate pain, they are unable to induce a state of surgical analgesia and are consequently less active against very severe pain. Furthermore, their liability to show side effects is at least as important. They are respiratory depressants and they produce dizziness, nausea, vomiting and even hallucinatory changes in a similar percentage of patients. The fact that they do not satisfy the peculiar needs of the morphine addict is rather irrelevant in this context.

What can be done, however, is to separate morphine-like analgesia from morphine-like emetic action. Piritramide, for example, is a typical morphine-like drug, chemically rather unrelated to the other narcotics in common use. A parenteral dose of 15 mg of piritramide produces almost exactly the same analgesic effect as 10 mg of morphine sulphate. Rather than inducing emesis and nausea through trigger zone stimulation, as morphine does, the standard dose of piritramide is antiemetically active in man. It blocks the chemoreceptor trigger zone.

Inadequacies of available analgesics. In the prolonged treatment of chronic patients with severe pain, there is a definite need for a much better strong analgesic. The available drugs suffer from a number of shortcomings. (*a*) Many, like morphine itself, are poorly active by the oral route. (*b*) Those that are regularly active against severe pain are all morphine-like drugs and produce respiratory depression, constipation, nausea and vomiting, dizziness, etc. They are poorly tolerated by ambulant patients, except in doses that are often analgesically inadequate. They induce tolerance up to the point at which tremendous doses are needed after a period of chronic administration to produce the same analgesic effect as the first dose. They induce a state of physical dependence and typical abstinence symptoms upon withdrawal after chronic administration of high doses. They tend to induce a state of psychological dependence and are likely to be abused by morphine addicts.

(*c*) Almost all potent analgesics known are, furthermore, too short acting, so that many patients with chronic severe pain are receiving parenteral doses at hourly intervals around the clock. Such patients, who do not sleep for more than a very short period at a time, rapidly deteriorate as a consequence. For such patients the administration in the evening of a single 5 mg tablet of bezitramide (R 4845) regularly produces a strong analgesic effect which lasts for about ten hours and enables these patients to

BEZITRAMIDE (R4845)

sleep well. This drug cannot be injected because of its very low solubility in aqueous media. It has a rather slow onset of action of about one hour and most patients can be kept free of severe pain on a b.i.d. schedule. Respiratory depression is not a major problem with R 4845. This is probably due to a sufficient degree of acute tolerance being built up during the onset phase, as seems to be the case with all slow acting morphinomimetic agents. The drug induces physical dependence of the morphine-type, but does not seem to be particularly attractive to morphine-addicts in that it fails to produce the quick and intense kick that the real addict expects to get out of his normal intravenous 'fix'. What we should be looking for, I feel, for the treatment of patients with chronic and severe pain, is an orally effective strong analgesic, as long acting as R 4845, but better tolerated, even when the patient is ambulant.

Summary

One could say that the most important shortcomings of the available strong analgesics have something to do with: inadequate onset and duration of action; insufficient intensity of the analgesic peak effect at well tolerated doses; incomplete oral activity; tendency to produce emesis, nausea, dizziness, constipation, respiratory depression, histamine release, circulatory effects, rigidity of the striated musculature, physical dependence, abstinence, physiological dependence and abuse liability.

The real medical problem, and therefore the most important challenge with which the medicinal chemist and the pharmacologist is confronted, is the adequate treatment of very severe pain or agony. We should not satisfy ourselves with a new analgesic which is only effective in slight or moderate pain, even when it is well tolerated. A number of such drugs already exist and more drugs of this type can only confuse the real issue.

REFERENCES

Janssen, P. A. J. & Van der Eycken, C. A. M. (1968). The chemical anatomy of potent morphine-like analgesics. *Drugs affecting the central nervous system*, **2**, Ch. 2, pp. 25–60. Ed. by Alfred Burger. New York: Marcel Dekker, Inc.

Martin, W. R. (1963). *Physiol. Pharmac.*, **I. A.**, 279.

Sweet, W. H. (1959). *Handbook of Physiology*, **I**, 1, 459.

SEARCH FOR ADDICTION IN A NEW ANALGESIC

J. MADINAVEITIA

Imperial Chemical Industries Limited, Pharmaceuticals Division, Macclesfield

MOST of the more powerful analgesics now available have the undesirable property of producing addiction. To find an analgesic free of this unwanted side action it is necessary to have methods to detect it in compounds found to be analgesic. The obvious type of addiction to look for is that of the opiate type, which is the type mainly dealt with in this paper. Potential analgesics may, like any other compound and especially those which act on the central nervous system, produce other types of addiction.

In experimental animals the methods to detect relief of pain have been studied more than the methods to detect addiction. The experimental methods to detect addiction of the morphine type have been surveyed by Halbach & Eddy (1963) who described in detail the qualitative and quantitative assessment of the determination of physical dependence. From the physical condition and the behaviour of an animal it is difficult, if not impossible, to know whether it is addicted to opiates when the drug is being given continuously. In some animal species it is possible, however, to detect addiction to opiates by the withdrawal symptoms which occur when the addicted animals are not given the drug for some time. Withdrawal symptoms are also produced by opiate antagonists such as nalorphine. These withdrawal symptoms can be relieved by giving the opiate which produced the addiction. The withdrawal symptoms are also relieved by giving opiates other than the one which produced the addiction.

In their review Halbach & Eddy (1963) mentioned that, at the Department of Pharmacology of the University of Michigan, a procedure has been developed to determine whether in monkeys addicted to morphine a compound behaves like the opiates in suppressing withdrawal symptoms. These workers gave the addicting morphine by injection. Monkeys can also be addicted to morphine by being given the drug in their drinking water. This procedure has been used in the present work. Animals which were given 500 mg of morphine sulphate daily behaved and gained weight normally. They were offered, and they drank, each morning and each afternoon about 500 ml of water in which 250 mg of morphine sulphate was dissolved. After about one month of this treatment the animals looked ill if they did not get their twice daily dose of morphine on three or four occasions. They lay on the bottom of the cage, sometimes in odd postures. When they sit they hold their abdomens as if they had cramp. They cried, yawned, lacrimated, had running noses and their faces were flushed. Their hair stood up and when challenged they were abnormally aggressive. The picture was similar, but clearer, when the animals had had morphine for several months.

Morphine and other opiates given orally or parenterally to monkeys in withdrawal have a dramatic effect. Within half an hour the animals look almost normal. After one hour they cannot be differentiated from normal animals. Nalorphine did produce withdrawal symptoms in our monkeys, but only in doses which had some slight effect on the behaviour of normal monkeys. In these animals parenteral nalorphine could be distinguished from saline.

It would be desirable to be able to test compounds for addiction in animals smaller and easier to handle than monkeys. Attempts have been made to determine whether in rats addicted to morphine a compound can replace the opiate in suppressing the withdrawal symptoms. It has been reported that withdrawal produces recognizable changes (review of Halbach & Eddy, 1963). This has not been confirmed with the animals and the conditions used in the work described here. In rats which for several weeks had morphine added to their food, no significant changes were seen on withdrawal. The most noticeable changes following an injection of nalorphine into these animals was a prompt increase in defecation. Defecation has been reported by many other workers as one

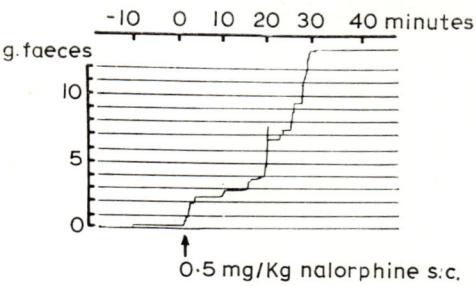

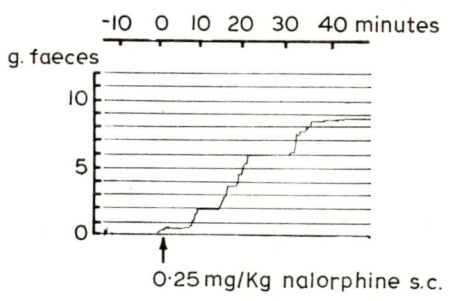

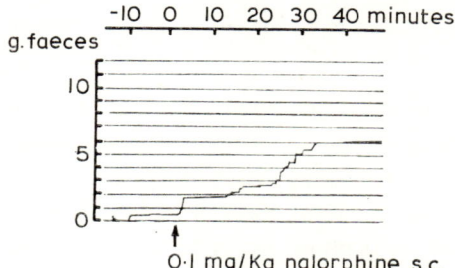

Fig. 1. Weight of faeces passed by groups of five rats addicted to morphine when injected subcutaneously with various amounts of nalorphine.

of the symptoms of withdrawal in addicted rats. The amount of faeces passed by the addicted rats in the first hour after injection of nalorphine depends on the dose (Figures 1 and 2). The obvious controls of giving saline to addicted animals and nalorphine to

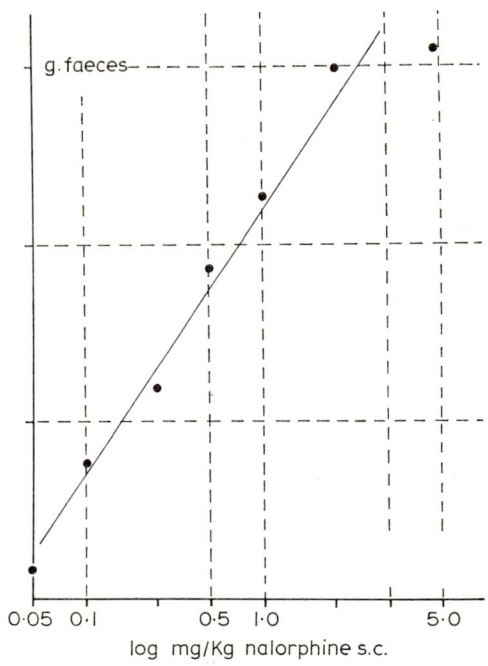

FIG. 2. Dose—response curve of the amount of faeces passed by groups of five rats addicted to morphine during the hour following subcutaneous injection of various amounts of nalorphine.

non-addicted ones were negative. Rats fed for some weeks on diets containing pethidine or codeine also respond to an injection of nalorphine by defecating. Levallorphan behaves like nalorphine in increasing the defecation of addicted rats.

The effect of nalorphine on defecation by addicted rats is sufficiently reproducible to obtain significant results with groups of five rats. Such groups pass between 5 and 10 g of faeces in the hour following an injection of 0·25 mg/kg of nalorphine. The faeces are reduced to less than 1 g if the animals are pretreated with 2·5 mg/kg of morphine. No pharmacological analysis has been made of this effect of nalorphine on addicted rats. The effect is not abolished by atropine. It has been reported (Kaymakçalan & Temelli, 1964) that morphine, but not nalorphine at comparable doses, produces a contracture of the colon of normal rats. In rats made tolerant to intraperitoneal morphine the position is reversed: their isolated colon contracts with nalorphine but not with morphine.

Monkeys and rats become addicted to morphine when they are forced to take the drug for a period of time. An attempt has been made to find out if rats choose to become addicted to morphine when the drug is available to them but they are not compelled to take it to survive. It is known that a proportion of monkeys choose to drink 0·1% morphine in preference to water and become addicted as measured by the symptoms following withdrawal of nalorphine (Claghorn, Nagy & Ordy, 1965; Deneau & Seevers, 1964).

In the conditions of our experiment the rats, to become addicted, had to overcome their distaste, if any, of a food which contained morphine. Rats, unlike monkeys, refuse to drink water that has only a trace of morphine. The rats will, however, eat a food which contains up to 0·1% morphine if there is no other food available. A group of fifty rats were given the choice to eat either untreated food or food to which 0·05% morphine had been added. Each animal was housed in a separate cage. For the first few days the animals ate mostly of the food without morphine, but all of them tasted the food with morphine (Figure 3).

Thereafter, with the exception of three animals they all ate almost exclusively of the food without morphine. The three animals which ate an appreciable amount of the food with morphine continued to do so for several weeks. At the end of three weeks these three animals responded to an injection of nalorphine with an increase in defecation. They were presumably addicted to morphine. The experiment was repeated with twenty-five rats, three of which became addicted as judged by the reaction to nalorphine. In both experiments all the rats had at

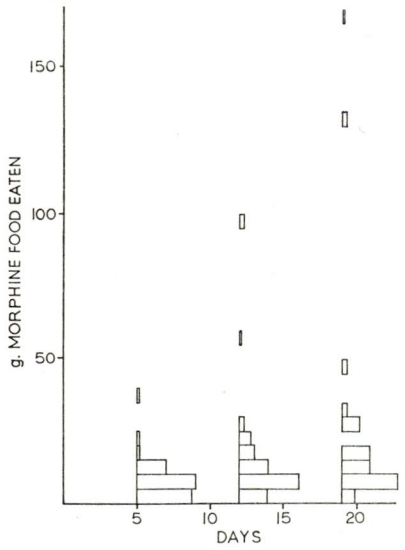

Fig. 3. Distribution at various times of the number of rats that choose to eat various amounts of a diet with 0·05% morphine when throughout the experiment they had access to this diet and the untreated diet. There were fifty animals in the experiment.

the beginning tasted the food with morphine. Because of some unknown predisposing factors about one in ten of them, actually six in seventy-five, did choose to become addicted by continuing to eat of the food with morphine.

It is known that treatment with morphine for a period of time increases the likelihood of human beings becoming addicts. The same appears to be the case in rats. Five of the animals which in the previous experiment had after three weeks not become addicted, were given morphine food only, without a choice, for one week. Then they were given the choice of foods with and without morphine. Three of these five animals chose to eat an appreciable amount of the food with morphine and become addicted, if increase in defecation by nalorphine is again taken as diagnostic for addiction (Figure 4).

The choice of food with and without morphine was given to twenty-five addicted rats which had had morphine in their food for six weeks. In the first few days they all ate a fair amount of the

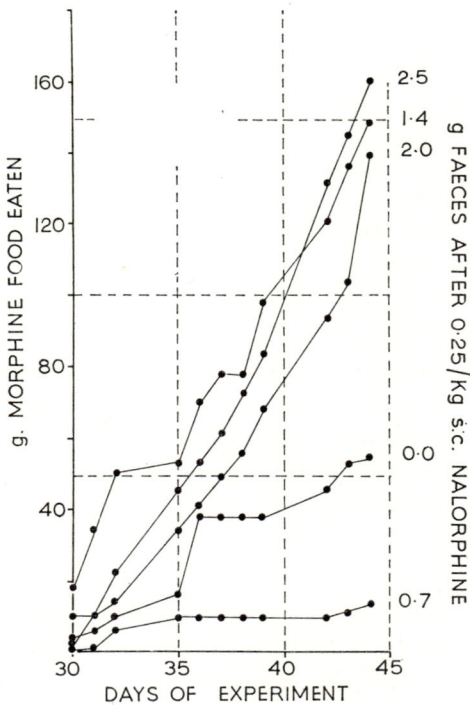

Fig. 4. Effect of feeding rats for one week on a diet containing 0·05% morphine. Weight of food containing 0·05% morphine that such rats choose to eat when both food with and without morphine was constantly available to them. Weight of faeces passed by each of these rats in the hour following a subcutaneous injection of 0·25% mg/kg of nalorphine after the animals had had the choice of food for two weeks.

food with morphine. Because of some unknown predisposing causes after three weeks eight of these twenty-five rats ceased to eat of the food with morphine. The rest continued to ingest morphine and remained addicted.

Work at the Pharmaceuticals Division of Imperial Chemical Inductries Ltd., has shown some tetrahydro-β-carbolines to be active in the animal tests that are usually used to detect analgesic action. Of a number of carbolines prepared in these laboratories

by Dr. R. Hull and Dr. J. D. Atkinson, (1965) isopropyl tetrahydro-β-carboline combines a relatively low toxicity with a moderate analgesic activity.

In the various animal tests for analgesia that we have used I.C.I. 49,455 was about as active as pethidine. In terms of dose this is not an outstanding discovery. There are many chemicals and drugs which are more active, but most compounds which are analgesic at doses lower than aspirin produce addiction of the opiate type. If the tetrahydro-carbolines of the I.C.I. 49,455 type could be shown in experimental animals to be unlikely to produce opiate-like addiction they would be of interest as potential analgesic drugs.

The tetrahydro-carbolines are chemically related to the alkaloids of the plant *Peganum harmala* which has had an important place in therapy with the Arabs. The properties of this plant have been reviewed recently (Hocking, 1966). The alkaloids of *P. harmala*, harman, harmaline, harmine and various others have been found to be inhibitors of the enzyme monoamino oxidase and this may account for some of the actions of the plant. These alkaloids are much less analgesic than the carboline I.C.I. 49,455, which is only a very weak inhibitor of monoamino oxidase. Although they have been known for a long time, the analgesic action of the tetrahydro-carbolines has not been reported. The lack of obvious chemical similarity between the carboline and the morphine ring systems does not mean that the tetrahydro-carbolines are certain to be free of opiate-like actions, including addiction liability. Compounds chemically so different as morphine, pethidine and methadone all produce the same type of

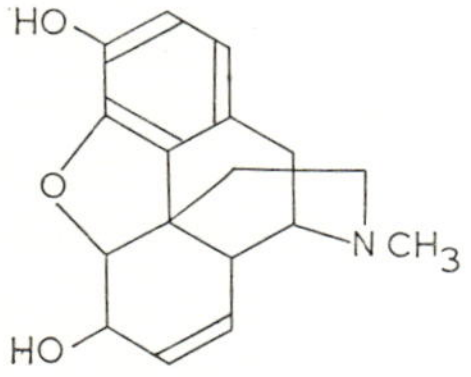

Morphine

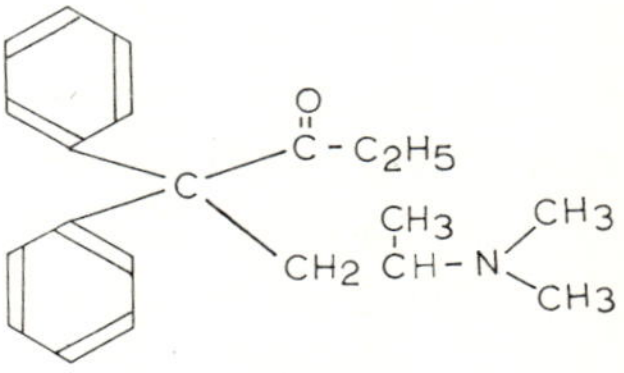

Methadone

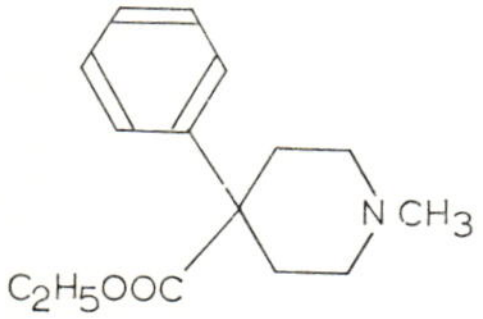

Pethidine

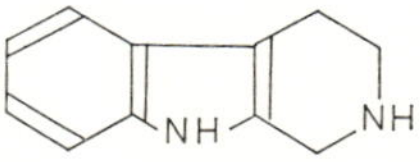

Tetrahydro-β-carboline

addiction. A compound so closely related to morphine as its non-allyl derivative does not produce addiction. Based on stereochemical considerations it has been claimed that the structures of morphine, pethidine and methadone have common features. The arguments used in these considerations (reviewed by Soine & Willette, 1966), which were made after the event, are not firm enough to enable one to predict with any degree of certainty whether the tetrahydro-carbolines are, or are not, likely to produce addiction of the opiate type. Furthermore these stereochemical arguments do not explain why morphine is addictive and nalorphine is not.

The animal experimental techniques discussed before indicate that I.C.I. 49,455 is unlikely to produce addiction of the opiate type. It does not produce tolerance, its analgesic action remaining unchanged even after thirty daily doses. The increase in reaction time that it produces in mice placed on a hot plate is not decreased by nalorphine. Since I.C.I. 49,455 does not depress respiration no antagonism of this effect by nalorphine could be observed. Unsuccessful attempts have been made to detect withdrawal symptoms in rats and in monkeys fed for a long time on a diet which contained I.C.I. 49,455. These animals did not respond to nalorphine. The tetrahydro-carboline did not stop rats addicted to morphine from defecating copiously after an injection of nalorphine. It had no effect on the withdrawal symptoms of monkeys addicted to morphine. These symptoms disappeared rapidly when morphine was given two hours after I.C.I. 49,455. All rats fed for many weeks on a diet containing I.C.I. 49,455 chose to eat of a drug free diet when a choice was offered to them.

All this may mean that isopropyl tetrahydro-carboline is a non-addictive analgesic more active than aspirin, perhaps as potent as pethidine. The real proof is yet to come if and when clinical trials show that I.C.I. 49,455 is in fact an analgesic and subsequent experimental and clinical work shows that it is not addictive in man.

REFERENCES

Claghorn, J. L., Nagy, A. & Ordy, J. M. (1965). Spontaneous opiate addiction in rhesus monkeys. *Science*, **149**, 440–441.
Deneau, J. A. & Seevers, M. H. (1964). Pharmacological aspects of drug dependence. *Advances in Pharmacology*, Ed. by Garattini, S. & Shore, P. A., **3**, 267–283.
Halbach, H. & Eddy, N. B. (1963). Tests for addiction (chronic intoxication) of morphine type. *Bull. Wld. Hlth. Org.*, **28**, 139–173.
Hocking, J. M. (1966). Harmala semen. *Q. J. crude Drug Res.*, **6**, 913.
Atkinson, J. D. & Hull, R. (1965) Brit. Pat. 105 5203.
Kaymakçalan, S. & Temelli, S. (1964). Response of the isolated intestine of normal and morphine-tolerant rats to morphine and nalorphine. *Arch. int. Pharmacodyn.*, **151**, 136–141.

Soine, T. O. & Willette, R. E. (1966). Analgesic agents. *Text Book of Organic Medicinal and Pharmaceutical Chemistry*. 5th ed. Ed. by Doerge, R. F., Gisvold O. & Wilson, C. O. pp. 640–668.

DISCUSSION

McLean: I feel that when I am invited to open the discussion I am a delegate for the audience. An audience can demand of a scientific communication that it should be either useful (that is, the audience can go away and use the data in laboratory or clinic), or else it should have an intellectual content that the audience appreciates; one might call this amusement value. Dr. Mulé has shown us a number of experiments that we need not do ourselves. Does he not think, seeing that brain morphine levels were steady for eight hours, long after the effect had worn off, that this approach was not fruitful?

Mulé: My reply to Dr. McLean's question is as follows.

The study was primarily conducted to ascertain:

(1) whether morphine was localized at a specific anatomical site in the CNS;

(2) the disposition and metabolism of the drug in the CNS with respect to time in the nontolerant dog;

(3) whether the development of tolerance, antagonism of the pharmacological action of morphine, or abstinence alters disposition or metabolism of the drug.

An interesting and fruitful observation was an apparent lack of correlation between levels of drug in the CNS and duration of analgesia. However, one questions whether this lack of correlation is due to sensitivity limitations in analgesimetry as compared to the detection of radio labelled morphine in brain or directly due to receptor fatigue.

McLean: It seems to me that Professor Remmer's studies on habituation to barbiturates at the liver level cannot account for barbiturate withdrawal fits. Also, are the doses used in man likely to cause stimulation of microsomal enzyme activity?

Remmer: (1) Withdrawal fits occur if the barbiturate level in the habituated individual decreases rapidly as is the case after the intake of shorter acting barbiturates such as cyclobarbitone and nembutal which are nearly completely oxidized by inducible enzymes in the liver. It is conceivable that their increased metabolism and the more rapid decrease of the level in the organism during tolerance support the appearance of withdrawal fits and intensify the convulsions. These are, however, an indication of a severe change in the reaction of the CNS due to an adaptation of the CNS to high levels of barbiturates in the brain.

(2) Induction of drug-metabolizing enzymes in man can only be produced by a high level of the barbiturates in the liver. This is achieved if an overdose of shorter acting compounds is used or if a therapeutic dose of a long acting barbiturate, such as phenobarbitone, accumulates during prolonged treatment. There is some evidence that the drug metabolizing enzymes in the liver can be more easily induced and the conversion of drugs significantly accelerated in patients whose barbiturate oxidation in the liver is normally slow.

McLean: Professor Beckett has emphasized urinary excretion, but often drugs do not have a urinary metabolite, and the metabolism of the drug will have to be followed in the plasma. Also, the metabolism of a drug may be predominantly hepatic and show great variability between individuals—phenylbutazone is one such drug—so that his computer cannot make any predictions with the data on urinary pH that he gives to it.

Beckett: It is true that the procedures I have described apply to those drugs which are excreted at least 40% unchanged in the urine.

Please note that I centred my talk and my methods on narcotic analgesics and amphetamines and these are basic drugs. Little inter- or intra-subject variation in the excretion of these drugs is seen, provided kidney tubular reabsorption is reduced as I described. We can therefore make use of computer studies for these basic drugs and predict what will happen in normal conditions from our studies carried out in controlled conditions.

I accept that there are great differences between individuals when differences in metabolism are genetically controlled, but we have not met such problems with the classes of compounds described in my paper.

Ginsburg: In some of Dr. Mulé's experiments he observed that the uptake of radioactivity in the brain, after injection of labelled morphine, was less in tolerant animals than in non-tolerant animals. To what extent can this observation be explained by the presence of unlabelled morphine in the brain in tolerant animals at the time of injection of the labelled drug, and the consequent dilution of radioactivity subsequently taken up in the brain?

Mulé: In the tolerant dogs which received a single labelled injection of morphine, one would expect some isotopic dilution with non-labelled morphine present in the CNS. This dilution effect would contribute to the lower values observed in the tolerant dogs, especially at the early time interval. However, labelled morphine was administered consecutively to non-tolerant and to tolerant dogs so that all the morphine in the CNS was radioactive. At eight hours after the drug, the concentrations in the CNS of the tolerant dogs were significantly lower than those observed for the non-tolerant dogs. Therefore, the egress of free morphine from the CNS of consecutively injected dogs was still similar to that observed for those that received a single dose, although the absolute levels of drug were different.

Collier: Dr. Remmer distinguished tolerance to barbiturates developing at a fairly specific receptor site in the CNS, from a non-specific tolerance arising from the activation of liver enzymes. Since ethanol and barbituates are cross-dependent, I should like to ask Dr. Remmer whether cross-tolerance towards ethanol develops at the receptor site in the CNS.

Remmer: Cross-tolerance between ethanol and barbiturates is due to a diminished sensitivity at the receptor site in the CNS. Since chronic treatment of rats with alcohol induces an increased oxidation of barbiturates, the tolerance of alcoholics towards barbiturates should be reinforced by an increased breakdown (see my Table 2). On the other hand, barbiturates do not enhance the oxidation of ethanol. Individuals who are dependent on barbiturates, therefore, should never metabolize alcohol faster. The cross-tolerance with alcohol is only due to a decreased response of similar receptor sites.

Collier: Does the β-carboline that Dr. Madinaveitia spoke of act centrally or peripherally? Does it suppress responses to mechanonociceptive stimuli, as morphine does, or does it depress chemonociceptive stimuli as aspirin often also does? Does it depress respiration?

Madinaveitia: It is not known how the isopropyl β-tetrahydro-carboline acts. It does not depress respiration in non-toxic doses.

Lister: (1) As Dr. Madinaveitia gave his drugs orally, is there any possibility that the defecation observed after nalorphine, and used as an index of dependence, is a measurement of a local effect on the gut and not of true CNS dependence?

(2) Did Dr. Madinaveitia observe the writhing syndrome in his rats following nalorphine as demonstrated in monkeys, and if so does he think that this reflects an effect on mechanisms similar to those which he studied?

Madinaveitia: (1) The defecation observed after parenteral nalorphine is likely to be a local effect on the gut (Kaymakçalan & Temelli, 1964). It was used as an index of addiction because it is an easy way of differentiating between untreated rats and animals which were fed for some time on a diet containing morphine, and which were therefore presumably addicted.

(2) With the higher doses of nalorphine, all sorts of movements originating in the abdominal region of the rats were observed. They are probably due to the animals completely emptying their colon in ten to twenty minutes after injection.

I suspect that the symptoms of abdominal discomfort seen in addicted monkeys after injection of nalorphine are due, like the defecation in rats, to nalorphine unmasking the effect that chronic administration of morphine has on the gut.

S. A. Lewis: While accepting that since the rats did not continue to take the tetrahydro-β-carboline it does not have addictive properties, why did none continue to eat the treated food? On a chance basis it would be expected that 50% would—the test of addictive properties being a significantly greater proportion than that continuing on the treated food.

Madinaveitia: Rats did not continue to take the food with tetrahydro-β-carboline because they disliked this food. The amount of tetrahydro-carboline in it was such that rats would eat the medicated food if they had no other food available. When the choice of medicated and plain food was given the animals chose to eat plain food only.

After rats had eaten a diet with morphine for some time (weeks) they chose to continue to eat the morphine-containing food when the choice of plain and medicated food was given to them. Naive rats ate the morphine food when they had no choice, and the vast majority of them ate the plain food when the choice was given.

The failure of rats which had eaten the carboline food for some time to continue to do so when choice of medicated and unmedicated food was given, is taken as an indication that the tetrahydro-β-carboline may not be addictive. The addictive morphine behaves differently.

Paton: Does tolerance develop to the analgesia produced by your compound?

Madinaveitia: No tolerance developed to the analgesia produced by tetrahydro-isopropyl carboline. In a parallel experiment tolerance to the analgesia produced by oral morphine was demonstrated.

Paton: Could you give more detail of the method used for assaying the analgesic effect?

Madinaveitia: I have used a number of well known methods such as the increase in the time of response of mice to heat stimuli applied to their tail or to their paws (hot plate method). I have also used the method based on the decrease of the number of responses that mice produce when injected intraperitoneally with diluted acetic acid. The improvement of the posture of the rats with a chronic inflammation of their hind legs was also used for assaying the analgesic effect.

Kumar: There is the possibility that on successive choice tests an increased consumption of the food containing morphine could be due, for example, to desensitisation of taste mechanisms, and that the rats ate more of it because they were less able to discriminate the bitter taste. This could be tested by giving injections of morphine immediately before the choice tests and seeing whether the proportion of 'drugged' food eaten was correspondingly reduced; or another way would be to run control experiments with food containing quinine. Has Dr. Madinaveitia done such tests?

Madinaveitia: The tests suggested by Dr. Kumar have not been carried out. There is no evidence that indicates that rats fail to distinguish between the bitter tastes of quinine and of morphine, nor that these two compounds substitute each other in desensitising taste mechanisms.

The rats had a choice of foods during the whole of their normal nightly feeding periods. It is difficult to interpret the effect of injections of morphine which are known to stop non-addicted animals from eating for some hours.

Richter: The concept of tolerance is an important one in considering the actions of drugs. Some speakers have discussed the time-course of tolerance as if tolerance were established uniformly in all parts of the brain at the same time. But I think there is evidence that some systems in the brain develop tolerance more readily than others. In clinical practice it is not uncommon to find a patient, often an old alcoholic, who reacts to barbiturates by showing manic excitement instead of sedation. In such cases it seems that the inhibitory mechanisms are affected more strongly than the excitatory mechanisms, suggesting that tolerance is not achieved in both systems at the same time. It might be helpful if, before this meeting is concluded, the concept of tolerance could be more clearly defined.

Neal: To reply to Dr. Richter's question, why barbiturates cause increased restlessness in patients in pain: I think he is quite correct when he suggests that barbiturates act first on inhibitory centres in the brain. Magni has shown that local perfusion of the caudal R.F. with thiopentone produces an arousal type of EEG response while perfusion of the more rostal R.F. produces only a low frequency high voltage ('sleeping') type of EEG. Brazier has shown the same sequence of EEG changes in man on giving a slow intravenous injection of dilute thiopentone solution, i.e. first an 'arousal' pattern followed by a 'sleeping' pattern.

The initial selective depressant action of barbiturates on the caudal inhibitory part of the R.F. seems to provide a neurophysiological explanation for the hyperalgesic action of barbiturates in animals and also their clinical effect in increasing restlessness in patients suffering pain. However, I do not think this phenomenon is really concerned with tolerance to barbiturates.

McIlwain: Can Dr. Janssen give further details of the biological assays used in guiding the synthesis of the new analgesics which he described?

Janssen: These details are described in the following publications.

REFERENCES

Janssen, P. & Jageneau, A. (1956). Mydriatic activity of analgesics in mice. *Experientia*, **12**, 293.

Janssen, P. A. J. (1960). *Synthetic Analgesics*. Part I: diphenylpropylamines. London: Pergamon Press.

Janssen, P. A. J. (1961). Pirinitramide (R 3365), a potent analgesic with unusual chemical structure. *J. Pharm. Pharmac.*, **13**, 513.

Janssen, P. A. J., Niemegeers, C. J. E. & Dony, J. G. H. (1963). The inhibitory effect of fentanyl and other morphine-like analgesics on the warm water induced tail withdrawal reflex in rats. *Arzneimittel-Forschung*, **13**, 502.

Janssen, P. A. J. & Van der Eycken, C. A. M. (1968). The chemical anatomy of potent morphine-like analgesics. In *Drugs Affecting the Central Nervous System*, Ed. by Burger, A., New York: Marcel Dekker, Inc. **2**, Ch. 2, pp. 25–60.

Session III

LABORATORY STUDIES OF ANIMAL AND HUMAN BEHAVIOUR

Chairman: HANNAH STEINBERG

CHAIRMAN'S INTRODUCTION

Laboratory experiments on behaviour can be regarded as a bridge between the pharmacological and biochemical approaches discussed in the two previous sessions and the clinical and social problems which are dealt with in the next session. It is not always easy to know how far such experiments provide useful models of real life situations, but at the very least information can be obtained in closely controlled conditions and factors which might affect dependence can be identified.

That animals can become 'drug addicts' at all is remarkable. But once this is accepted it is perhaps less surprising to find that animals become dependent on much the same drugs as man. They may become dependent as a result of having a drug repeatedly administered to them by the experimenter, or almost incidentally while satisfying a natural need such as hunger or thirst. They can learn to administer drugs to themselves if given the opportunity. Their behaviour is influenced by changes in their physical or social environment; for example, rats can be re-addicted to morphine more quickly in the laboratory where they originally became dependent than elsewhere. Among problems which might be further investigated are: why do some animals become dependent so much more readily than others, and in what conditions will dependent animals learn to accept non-drug substitutes?

Experiments on man have to be more limited in scope; one reason for this is that it is obviously not feasible deliberately to addict a person for experimental purposes, and so subjects must be used who are already taking drugs more or less regularly. Again, drugs can either be administered by the investigator or else by the subjects themselves, and as one might expect, alcohol, barbiturates and amphetamines are probably most readily studied. It is interesting that alcoholics can be shown to drink less alcohol the more work they are required to do to obtain it and that risk taking does not necessarily increase with increased consumption. Sleep, dreams and eye movements can all be changed by the repeated use of drugs and by their abrupt withdrawal. Investigations on man are also our principal source of information on subjective reactions to drugs and on how far it is possible to disentangle 'pharmacological' and 'placebo' effects.

DRUG SELF-ADMINISTRATION AND CONDITIONING

TRAVIS THOMPSON AND ROY PICKENS

Psychiatry Research, University of Minnesota, Minneapolis, Minnesota

DRUG dependence is a complex phenomenon involving several inter-related conditions. A drug dependent organism may be physically dependent, behaviourally dependent and/or it may self-administer the drug on which it is dependent. Physical dependence refers to a condition produced by chronic drug administration in which a characteristic syndrome of illness occurs when drug administration is discontinued; behavioural dependence refers to a comparable state characterized by behavioural disruption on discontinuing drug administration. Human drug addiction, which has been known for more than 3,000 years (Terry & Pellens, 1928) usually involves all three kinds of dependence, though many drugs that are self-administered produce neither physical nor behavioural dependence.

Despite man's substantial experience with drug dependence, it was only recently that the relation between drug taking and basic conditioning phenomena was recognized. In 1955 it was shown that morphine could serve as a reward or reinforcer for physically dependent rats (Headlee, Coppock & Nichols, 1955), much as food is a reward for a hungry animal. The fact that drugs can serve as reinforcing consequences for instrumental or operant responses has now been widely confirmed. Procedures which provide animals with the opportunity to inject themselves with (Davis, 1966) or to drink drug solutions (Wikler, Martin, Pescor & Eades, 1963; Masserman & Yum, 1964; Casey, 1960; Meisch & Pickens, in the press) have been exploited for this purpose and are called *self-administration* methods. Figure 1 shows an intravenous self-administration method for the rat, and Figure 2 shows a similar preparation for rhesus monkeys.

The largest body of evidence on drug self-administration which falls within the framework of operant conditioning is based on opiate self-administration by physically dependent rats (Weeks, 1962; Weeks & Collins, 1964) and monkeys (Thompson & Schuster, 1964; Deneau, personal communication; Schuster & Thompson, 1962). More recent studies have shown that other types of drugs will serve as reinforcers as well (Deneau, personal communication; Davis & Miller, 1963; Pickens, Meisch & McGuire, 1967; Pickens, 1968; Pickens & Thompson, 1968). Sufficient data are now available to justify a more systematic examination of factors governing the ability of drugs to serve as reinforcers. An understanding of the ways in which these factors function in controlling drug-reinforced behaviour is fundamental to understanding basic behavioural mechanisms underlying drug self-administration.

If the analysis of drug dependence outlined is correct, factors known to control acquisition, maintenance, and elimination of other operant responses should also control acquisition, maintenance, and elimination of drug-reinforced responses. Through an understanding of acquisition of behaviour reinforced by drug injection, we may come to understand the initial development of drug dependence. By investigating factors influencing maintenance of already learned operant drug-reinforced responses we may have a better understanding of the maintenance of previously established drug dependence; and by studying factors known to contribute to the elimination of operant behaviour we may come to understand basic mechanisms involved in the elimination of drug dependence. Finally, by studying the interaction of drug self-administration with other kinds of behaviour it may be possible to understand some of the factors which contribute and are related to the reinforcing effects of drugs. This paper systematically explores the possible role of the principal classes of factors known to influence other operant responses as they might relate to drug-reinforced behaviour.

Acquisition and maintenance of drug dependence

Antecedent variables

An array of procedures carried out before introducing organisms to an experimental situation can influence the acquisition and maintenance of operant responses. Among the most important factors are the organism's past history and the current motivational conditions. When dealing with drugs as reinforcers, an additional antecedent consideration is the pharmacological status of the organism, i.e. the degree of tolerance, the chronicity of drug treatment and the presence of other drugs.

Experience with the reinforcer and the particular mode of its presentation are important in initial acquisition. A common procedure used in the laboratory to establish new operant responses is called 'magazine training'. In this method, a hungry animal is given experience with the reinforcing food pellets by being repeatedly presented with food in a way which is not contingent on his behaviour. Training of this sort greatly facilitates later learning of a response which is to be reinforced by food pellets. By the same token, repeated infusion of a potentially reinforcing drug solution, non-contingent on the organism's behaviour, has the functional status of magazine training. It provides the organism with some experience of the reinforcing drug, and of its specific mode of presentation (route of administration). Presumably such magazine training with drugs can markedly influence the initial establishment of drug dependence. Hospitalized patients often receive drugs in this manner. This experience with potentially reinforcing drugs can provide the basis for subsequent drug dependence (Kolb, 1962).

Specific learning histories have been shown to facilitate the reacquisition of operant responses reinforced by food, water and shock avoidance (Keller & Schoenfeld, 1950). The same is true of reinforcing drugs. Rats which have a history of intravenous morphine reinforcement and are then withdrawn, reacquire the self-administration response far more quickly than matched subjects which receive the same amount of morphine, but which have not previously learned a response which produces drug infusion (Weeks, 1967).

Motivational conditions are also critical in the conditioning and maintenance of operant behaviour. Some minimal level of food deprivation is necessary for food to act as a reinforcer. Once the food-reinforced behaviour has been acquired, the level of performance varies directly as a function of food deprivation conditions (Lawson, 1960). The role of drug deprivation conditions has been explored in physically dependent rats and monkeys. Monkeys were deprived of morphine for 24 h, and this produced an approximately ten-fold increase in morphine-reinforced responding (Thompson & Schuster, 1964). Chemically-induced morphine deprivation was affected by administration of nalorphine, which antagonizes the effects of morphine, thereby effectively placing the physically dependent organism in a state of deprivation. Morphine-reinforced responding increased in proportion to the dose of nalorphine (Weeks, 1962; Weeks & Collins, 1964; Thompson & Schuster, 1964).

Another procedure for studying motivational or deprivation conditions consists of 'pre-feeding' an animal shortly before a work session in which food will be used as the reinforcer. Generally, diminution in food-reinforced responding co-varies with the amount of pre-feeding (Skinner, 1938). Similar experiments have been conducted in which morphine is administered to an animal shortly before the normal work period is due. An orderly diminution in morphine-reinforced responding was produced, comparable to the results obtained by pre-feeding in a food-reinforcement experiment (Thompson & Schuster,

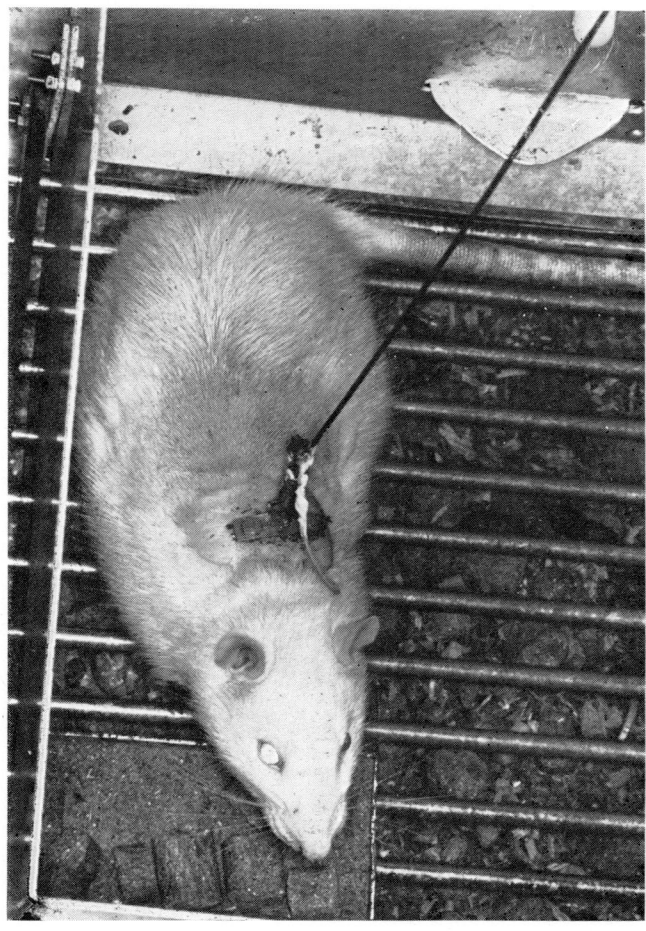

Fig. 1. A chronic preparation permitting intravenous self-administration of drugs by rats. A flexible stainless steel harness is attached to a piece of needle tubing connected to a remote infusion pump. The end of the needle tubing is cemented to silicone rubber tubing which runs subcutaneously and is inserted into the external jugular vein.

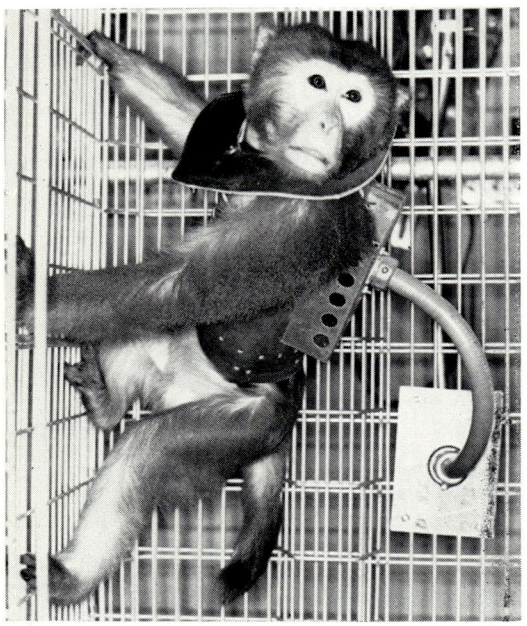

Fig. 2. A chronic preparation permitting intravenous self-administration of drugs in partially restrained rhesus monkeys. Silicone rubber catheter tubing runs inside a heavy flexible conduit through a hole in the custom fitted leather vest, and runs subcutaneously to the internal jugular vein. The vest and conduit have been described in detail by Pickens, Hauck and Bloom (1966).

1964). Substitution of a related drug (etonitazine) diminished morphine-reinforced responding, supporting the notion that the effective degree of drug deprivation can alter drug-reinforced responding (Weeks & Collins, 1964).

When non-opiates are used as the reinforcing drugs, the role of drug deprivation conditions is open to conjecture. Minimum deprivation intervals between successive drug administrations may be necessary for specific drugs to act as reinforcers. Presumably, the lengths of such deprivation periods will vary as a function of the dose per reinforcement.

Current circumstance

Not all people taking addicting drugs become drug addicts, and so drug dependence cannot be due to drug action alone. In all likelihood, drugs must act in combination with other factors to become reinforcers, just as food and water are not reinforcers in their own right but become so only when certain conditions prevail (Cofer & Appley, 1964). Little experimental attention, however, has been paid to the role of current circumstances in the development and maintenance of human drug dependence. Perhaps the most important of these factors are the social influences which comprise the organism's immediate stimulus environment. Just as the effects of antecedent conditions are not the same for all classes of self-administered drugs, neither are the environmental factors influencing drug dependence expected to be the same for all drugs. While one type of environment may increase the tendency to self-administer one drug, it may decrease the tendency to self-administer a second drug and have little or no effect on the self-administration of a third. Besides influencing the tendency for drug self-administration, a specific environment may be the necessary condition for the development of self-administration of certain drugs. For example, amylobarbitone and alcohol have been shown not to be self-administered in one environment, but are actively self-administered in other circumstances (Davis

& Miller, 1963; Masserman & Yum, 1946). Clearly, therefore, drug self-administration is dependent at least to some extent on the environment of the organism.

An aversive environment is reported to be a significant factor in the development of human drug addiction (Ausubel, 1963). It has been hypothesized that drugs serve as reinforcers in such environments by their ability to decrease the effects of aversive stimulation (Davis & Miller, 1963). The influence of sensory deprivation or isolation on behaviour also seems to be similar to that of aversive stimulation (Miller, 1948; Berlyne, 1955;

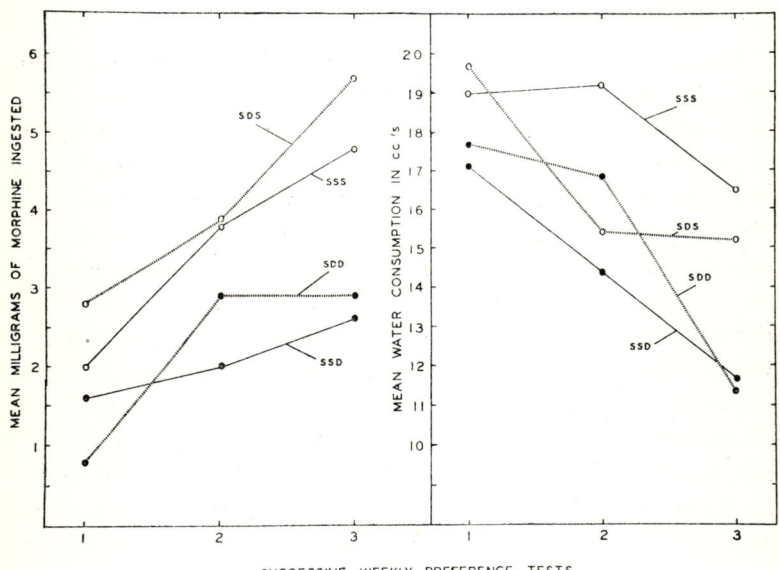

FIG. 3. Oral morphine self-administration by rats as a function of the environments in which they were withdrawn and readdicted, following prior establishment of physical dependence. Curves labelled SDS and SSS were addicted and readdicted in the same environment whereas those labelled SDD and SSD were readdicted in a different environment from that in which original addiction occurred. Note that animals readdicted in the same environment ingested more morphine than animals readdicted in a new environment. (Thompson & Ostlund, 1965.)

Welker, 1956). Consequently, drugs which change sensory input (e.g. analgesics, hypnotics, hallucinogens, etc.) may become reinforcing in these conditions.

Social factors in the organism's environment are also thought to play a significant role in the development of drug dependence. Indeed, it would seem fair to say that human drug addiction, at least initially, is outstandingly social in character. Social reinforcement contingent on drug taking, reinforcement of imitation (Miller & Dollard, 1941) and social enhancement of effectiveness of a drug (Lundin, 1961) might all contribute to the role of social interaction in drug dependence.

The importance of current circumstances in drug dependence is illustrated by a study (Thompson & Ostlund, 1965) in which rats were orally addicted, withdrawn, then half were readdicted in the same environment and half in a new environment. Changing the environment significantly diminished the rate of readdiction (Figure 3). Thus, a specific history of drug-reinforced behaviour in a given set of conditions profoundly altered subsequent reacquisition of the previously learned response.

Reinforcement variables

It is well known that certain substances are more effective as reinforcers than others (Cofer & Appley, 1964). Thus, while food, electrical stimulation of the brain, and a flash of light will all serve as reinforcers, they vary widely in their effectiveness to reinforce and maintain operant behaviour (Kish, 1955; Olds, 1958), and are influenced to different degrees by changes in experimental conditions such as satiation and extinction (Brady, Boren, Conrad & Sidman, 1957; Seward, Uyeda, & Olds, 1959; Crowder, Morris, Dyer & Robinson, 1961). There is evidence which suggests that some drugs are more reinforcing than others, as reflected in the clinical observations that heroin has a greater 'addiction liability' than morphine, morphine has a greater addiction liability than phenadoxone, etc. (Eddy, Halback &

Braenden, 1957). Addicts are also known to prefer certain drugs and combinations of drugs to others and will work more actively to obtain them (Ausubel, 1963).

Inexorably tied to the question of the kind of reinforcement

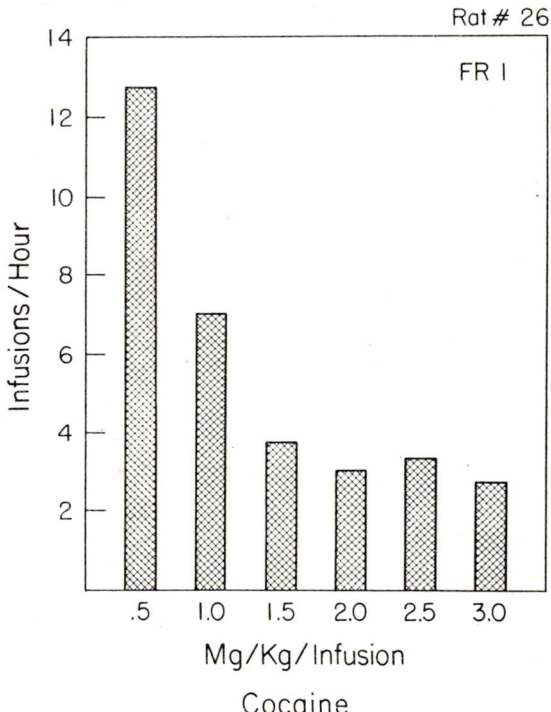

FIG. 4. The effects of magnitude of cocaine reinforcement (dosage per infusion) on the number of infusions taken per hour by a rat. The apparatus shown in Fig. 1 was used and each lever press produced an intravenous infusion. There is an inverse relation between magnitude of reinforcement and number of infusions per hour (Pickens & Thompson, 1968).

is that of the amount of reinforcement. A large amount of a normally less preferred substance may be a more effective reinforcer in maintaining an instrumental response than a small amount of a highly preferred substance (Crespi, 1942). In general, increases in the amounts of food and water reinforcement are known to result in increases in the level of performance (Kimble, 1961); however, with other reinforcers (e.g. heat, sucrose), curvilinear relationships have been found between the amount of reinforcement and performance (Guttman, 1953; Weiss & Laties, 1961). A curvilinear relationship has been observed between the dose of the drug (amount of reinforcement) and the frequency of self-administration of morphine by animals when the dose range is less than that necessary to produce observable physical dependence (Schuster, 1967). At higher doses and with physically dependent animals, the frequency of morphine self-administration is seemingly linearly related to the infusion dose (Weeks & Collins, 1964). With cocaine, a drug which does not produce physical dependence, only a limited range of infusion doses (0·5–3·0 mg/kg) will maintain drug self-administration (Figure 4), both higher and lower doses producing ragged performance or a complete cessation of drug self-administration (Pickens & Thompson, in the press). Comparable effects have not been reported with morphine or other drugs which produce physical dependence (Beach, 1957; Weeks, 1962; Deneau, personal communication). The number of reinforcements is also known to influence the strength of an instrumental response. During the initial acquisition, the more frequently a response is reinforced, the greater the tendency for the response to recur (Lawson, 1960). Thus, presumably, the more experience an organism has with a reinforcing drug, the greater will be its degree of 'dependence' upon it.

The time interval between the occurrence of a response and the appearance of the reinforcement is known to influence instrumental conditioning (Weeks, 1962; Weeks & Collins, 1964; Thompson & Schuster, 1964). Responses immediately followed by reinforcement are learned more quickly than those where reinforcement is delayed (Perin, 1943). The addiction liability of narcotic drugs is known to be related to the method of their administration and to their duration and peak of action. Oral administration with a rather long delay before the peak of action yields a low addiction liability, while parenteral administration with a relatively rapid peak produces a much higher addiction liability (Goodman & Gilman, 1963). Experimental evidence with barbiturate self-administration corroborates this clinical observation (Davis, Lulenski & Miller, 1968). While it would thus seem that the intravenous route would always be the favoured method of drug administration among addicts, such is not the case. In fact, of the most commonly self-administered drugs, morphine, heroin and cocaine are almost always injected intravenously, while pentobarbitone, amphetamine, alcohol and caffeine are taken orally and marijuana and nicotine are inhaled as smoke (Way, Wilner & Kassebaum, 1965). This apparent discrepancy between theory and fact has not yet been investigated, but it seems likely that at least part of the discrepancy may be related to the forms in which the drugs are readily available, and to the untoward effects involved in the administration of the various compounds (e.g. abscesses formed by pentobarbitone in the subcutaneous tissues).

Drugs are rarely freely available to human addicts. More usually, drugs are available at specified times, and after the completion of a specified amount of work (usually expressed in terms of an amount of money earned). Stated in terms of contingencies for reinforcement, one can say that the addict is reinforced on an interval* and/or ratio† schedule of reinforcement (Ferster & Skinner, 1957; Morse, 1966). It would be very surprising if the schedule of drug reinforcement were not equally important in the maintenance of drug self-administration behaviour. The evidence so far accumulated indicates that at least some of the schedules of reinforcement investigated using food

* A reinforcement schedule in which the first response after a fixed time interval following the last reinforced response will produce reinforcement.
† A reinforcement schedule in which the first response after a fixed number of responses following the last reinforced response will produce reinforcement.

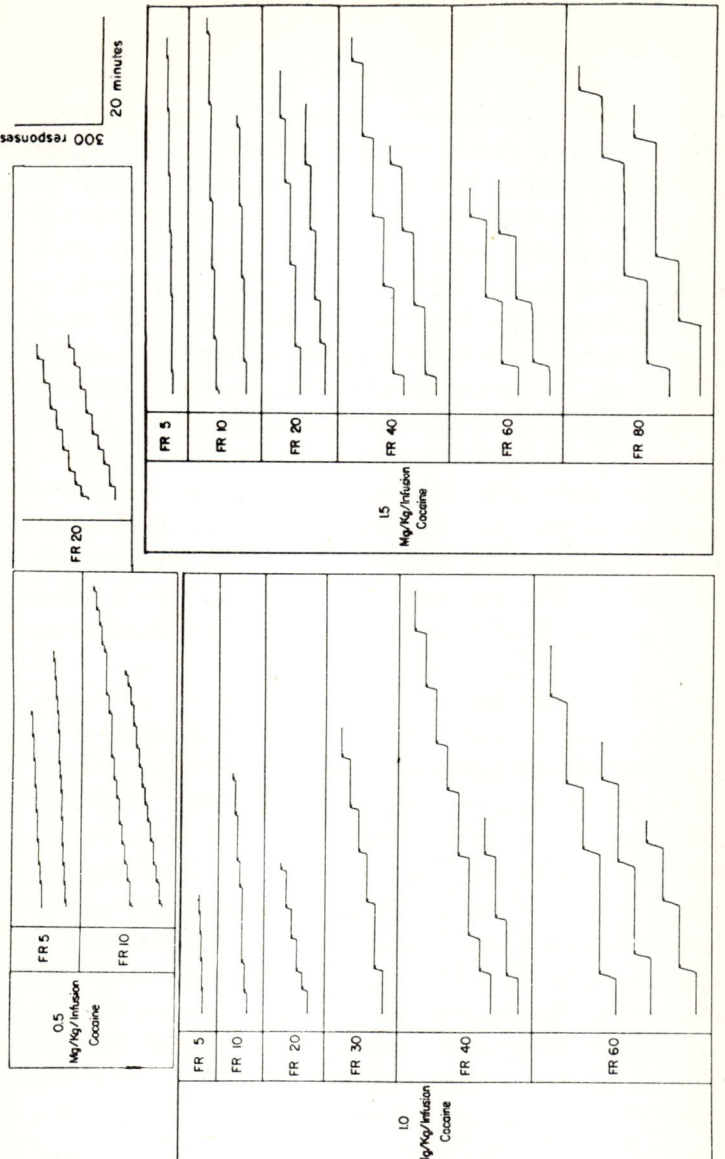

FIG. 5. Sample cumulative reponse records showing the effects of magnitude of cocaine reinforcement and value of a fixed ratio schedule of reinforcement on the pattern of intravenous cocaine-reinforced responding by a rat. The data shown are for all reinforcement magnitudes and ratio values which would maintain responding (Pickens & Thompson, 1968).

and water as reinforcers generate similar patterns of drug-reinforced responding. Generally, characteristic fixed-ratio performance using morphine as a reinforcer has been reported, although the temporal characteristics of performance were quite different (Weeks, 1962; Weeks & Collins, 1964). Variable-interval morphine reinforcement produces a characteristically low steady rate of responding, much as has been observed with other reinforcers (Woods, 1967). Across an array of fixed-ratio values, cocaine reinforcement produces characteristic fixed-ratio runs, alternating with regular pausing (Pickens & Thompson, in the press) (Figure 5). The pause duration is very reliable, but far longer than might be expected with other reinforcers. A chained schedule of morphine reinforcement (a reinforcement schedule in which satisfying the contingencies of a first component produces a stimulus, in the presence of which satisfying a second set of contingencies leads to reinforcement) produces characteristic schedule control. The contingencies in this case were a fixed interval two minute-fixed ratio 25 chain (Thompson & Schuster, 1964).

Stimuli paired with reinforcers gain reinforcing properties of their own. Such conditioned reinforcers are thought to be responsible for maintaining complex sequences of responses both inside and outside the laboratory (Kelleher, 1966). Repeated pairing of drug administration with other reinforcing stimuli (e.g. food, shock, social stimuli) may cause drugs to be reinforcing in their own right. For example, dogs were infused with acetylcholine, noradrenaline or adrenaline before they received a painful shock. Soon the infusion of the drug alone led to the performance of a response which would terminate infusion and so to the avoidance of the painful shock. Thus, not only did the drug infusion act as a warning stimulus, but its removal was reinforcing (Cook, Davidson, Davis & Kelleher, 1960). Similarly, cats were conditioned to avoid the arm in a T-maze that was associated with infusion of noradrenaline, when injection of that drug had been followed by painful shock (Sharpless, 1961). The circumstances under which many drugs (e.g. alcohol, marijuana) are taken by humans are social, and one might therefore expect that these drugs would gain their reinforcing properties, in part, because of being paired with social reinforcement.

Not only may drugs gain reinforcing properties when paired with other reinforcing stimuli, but other stimuli which were not initially reinforcing may come to be reinforcing because they are paired with drug infusion. A light paired with drug infusion has been shown to be capable of maintaining responding when morphine reinforcement was stopped (Schuster & Thompson, 1962; Schuster, 1967). Presumably a great many stimuli associated with drug reinforcement may come to be reinforcing and may be responsible for maintaining much 'drug seeking' behaviour, even in the non-physically dependent organism. The role of such conditioned reinforcers in maintaining drug-reinforced behaviour is essential to understanding, and to ultimately controlling drug dependence.

Interactions of drug self-administration with other behaviour

Clinical evidence suggests that drug dependence can have a pervasive influence on the organism's behaviour. The nature of this influence partly depends on the type of drug on which the organism is dependent. For example, opiate addiction decreases behaviour concerned with the attainment of food, sex and social stimulation, while barbiturate or alcohol dependence does not (Wikler, 1953). Experimental evidence also indicates an interaction between drug self-administration and other behaviour in animals. Morphine self-administration and abstinence have been found to interact with food-reinforced and shock-avoidance behaviour in monkeys (Thompson & Schuster, 1964). In conditions of morphine abstinence, food-reinforced and shock-avoidance behaviour were disrupted, but recovered again after the reinstatement of drug self-administration. Stimuli

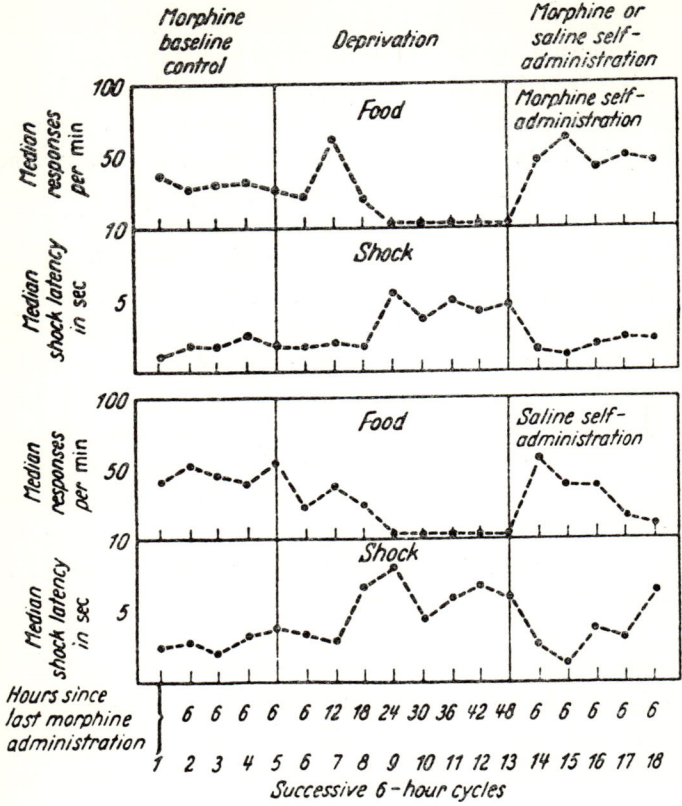

FIG. 6. The effect of morphine abstinence on food-reinforced and shock avoidance behaviour in a rhesus monkey which self-administered morphine intravenously. The upper two graphs show normal baseline performance for food (FR-35 schedule) and signalled shock avoidance based on four food and shock avoidance trials per six-hour period. At the first vertical line (cycle 6) the opportunity to self-administer morphine (1·0 mg/kg/6 hr) was discontinued. At the second vertical line (cycle 13) morphine self-administration was reinstituted. Notice the disruption of food and shock avoidance behaviours during abstinence. The lower two graphs show a replication of this experiment in which saline was substituted for morphine when self-administration was reinstituted, and a light which had been paired with morphine injections, was illuminated during each saline self-administration, there was a temporary placebo effect (Thompson & Schuster, 1964).

FIG. 7. A chronic preparation for intravenous drug self-administration via radio transceiver in unrestrained rhesus monkeys. The aluminum back pack contains a radio receiver, miniature infusion pump and a drug reservoir. The pump can be activated by a remote transmitter, permitting several animals to live in the same cage, each with receivers tuned to different frequencies.

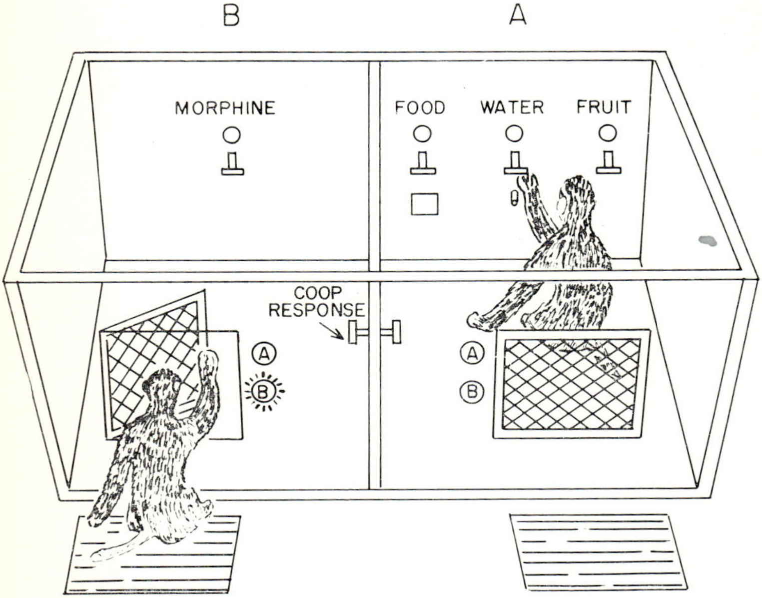

FIG. 8. Two adjacent cages connected to an outer large cage by two solenoid locked doors. One cage is used for obtaining morphine by radio-telemetry as shown in Fig. 7, and the adjacent cage to obtain food, water and fruit. Access to the cages is controlled by weight sensitive platform scales located in front of each door. The monkey in compartment A stood on the scale when the appropriate signal light was illuminated (A), entered and closed his door. This illuminated signal light B on compartment B, which unlocks door B when the correct monkey stands on the scale. Once both monkeys are in their respective compartments response keys on the wall separating the animals must be operated simultaneously to make their respective reinforcers available (see Fig. 9).

paired with morphine infusion were also capable of reinstating the disrupted behaviour, though only temporarily (Figure 6). No investigation of this sort has been conducted with drugs which are non-narcotic and/or do not produce physical dependence.

Detailed analysis of interactions between drug self-administration and other kinds of behaviour becomes extremely complex, particularly when social behaviour is involved. An experiment with freely moving monkeys in a multicompartment space illustrates such interactions. Three monkeys obtained all food, water and fruit, and in addition self-administered morphine intravenously through a radio-controlled infusion pump (Figure 7). Food, water and fruit could be obtained in one compartment and morphine in an adjacent compartment (Figure 8). In order for either monkey to obtain a reinforcer (e.g. morphine), another monkey must emit a co-operative switch-holding response, and vice versa (Figure 9). In this way a pattern of social dependencies was established for each monkey such that one monkey co-operated in earning food and another in obtaining morphine. To establish such a stable social system in which a drug is one of the major controlling reinforcers is technically difficult, but nevertheless, it is a powerful method for studying the role of drug dependence in controlling and interacting with other forces of behaviour.

Elimination of drug dependence

The common methods for eliminating operant responses are punishing the unwanted response, discontinuing reinforcement or satiation with the reinforcer. The traditional treatment for drug addiction, on the other hand, has mainly involved depriving the addict of the drug. This technique is based on the observation that abstinence leads to elimination of physical dependence, which in the case of the opiates and barbiturates is associated with diminished frequency of drug self-administration. Experimental investigation of the effectiveness of abstinence

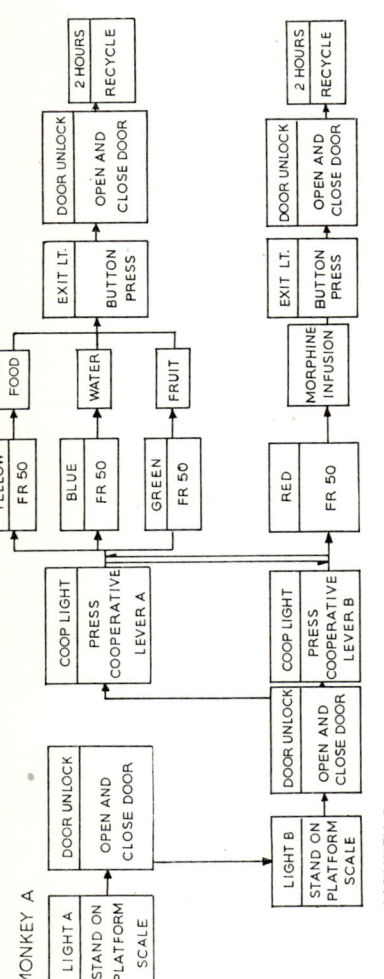

FIG. 9. Summary diagram of behavioural sequence involving social interdependencies between two monkeys in which one works to gain access to food, water and fruit (A) providing the paired animal with the opportunity to self-administer morphine. The sequence of events proceeds from left to right, with the conditions necessary for occurrence of each event (e.g. discriminative stimulus) indicated in the enclosed box at the top of each event. On completion of the above sequence a two-hour rest period is programmed followed by recurrence of the procedure in which monkey A works to obtain morphine, while a third animal (C) cooperates with A, providing C with access to food, water and fruit. Thus, for monkey A, one animal is uniquely paired with obtaining morphine (C) while another animal is uniquely associated with obtaining food, water and fruit (B). Subsequent portions of the study are concerned with discriminative stimulus and reinforcing properties of animals B and C (Thompson & Bigelow, unpublished).

in eliminating drug dependence has only recently been initiated. Animals withdrawn and repeatedly given the opportunity to self-administer morphine take the drug with reliability (Weeks, 1967). Such data suggest that abstinence alone is not a sufficient condition to eliminate drug reinforced responding.

Punishment is perhaps the most commonly used procedure for eliminating unwanted forms of behaviour (Azrin & Holz, 1966). The general procedure consists of presenting some consequence following a response, and so decreasing the frequency of the

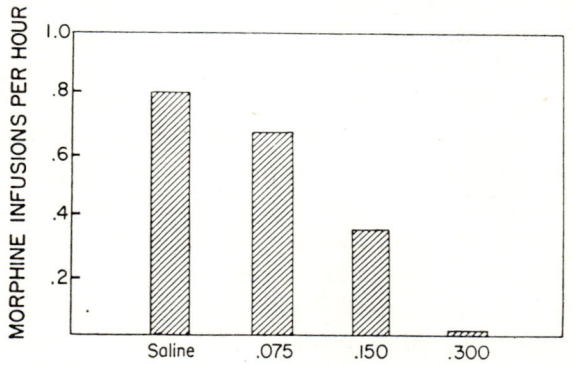

FIG. 10. The effects of hourly injections of methadone on intravenous self-administration of morphine by a physically dependent monkey. At 0·300 mg/kg/hr intramuscularly, morphine self-administration virtually ceased, but food intake and other gross behavioural indices appeared normal.

response that produced it. For example, if each food-reinforced response produces a brief shock, the food-reinforced response will tend to decrease in frequency. Such aversive stimulation is said to suppress the ongoing food-reinforced response.

Substituting methadone for morphine or heroin in the opiate-dependent addict has received increasing attention in the past few years (Dole & Nyswander, 1955). This procedure is essentially one of satiating the addict so that opiates will not function as reinforcers. Satiation has the effect of suppressing the instrumental response which has been maintained by that reinforcer. Methadone has been shown to reduce morphine self-administration in the monkey (Figure 10). This method for controlling drug self-administration is effective as long as the treatment is given, and may be useful for certain therapeutic purposes.

Behaviour is seldom entirely eliminated by punishment or by satiation. If one wants truly to eliminate an instrumental response, it is usually necessary to extinguish it—that is, to allow the response to occur but to go unreinforced. By using various extinction procedures it may be possible to effect long-term suppression of subsequent drug-reinforced responding. One approach is to allow the animal to continue responding for the drug but to decrease the dose obtained per reinforcement. Insufficient reinforcement with drugs such as cocaine, dexamphetamine and methamphetamine (Pickens & Thompson, in the press; Pickens, Meisch & McGuire, 1967; Pickens & Thompson, 1968) indicate that responding ceases rather abruptly, and ceases altogether if the amount of reinforcement is decreased to a minimum. Comparable manipulations with morphine produce prolonged responding, suggesting that the reduced dose retains potent reinforcing properties.

Finally, if one hopes to eliminate drug-reinforced behaviour, it will also be necessary to weaken the effectiveness of stimuli associated with drug administration. The importance of such stimuli in maintaining behaviour cannot be over-emphasized. For example, it was found that chimpanzees would emit as many as 120,000 responses per food reinforcement, when every 400th response produced a stimulus which had been paired with food. In the absence of these conditioned reinforcers, lever pressing ceased altogether (Findley & Brady, 1965). It seems evident that the extended behaviour sequences called 'drug seeking' are maintained by and large by stimuli paired with drug administration. To eliminate such behaviour it is necessary to stop presenting stimuli associated with drug administration, much as the elimination of lever pressing requires that the presentation of stimuli paired with food be stopped.

Summary

Knowledge of the variables controlling a particular operant behaviour is a prerequisite for an understanding of the behavioural mechanisms by which a drug influences that behaviour (Thompson & Schuster, 1968). In drug self-administration, the drug can be viewed as one variable in the network of interacting factors controlling the drug-maintained operant. Antecedent conditions, current stimulus circumstances, qualitative and quantitative properties of the reinforcing drug as well as stimuli associated with drug administration, all have the status of 'behavioural' variables affecting the drug-reinforced response. In this paper we have reviewed the roles of each of these classes of factors as they relate to the initial development of drug dependence (acquisition), to the maintenance and to the elimination of drug dependence. Finally, the interactions between drug-reinforced responding and behaviour controlled by other reinforcers and contingencies have been examined. The body of evidence indicates that drug self-administration and dependence can be profitably analyzed within this framework, suggesting basic mechanisms underlying drug dependence.

Acknowledgement: This research was supported in part by U.S. Public Health Service research grants to the University of Minnesota.

REFERENCES

Ausubel, D. P. (1963). *Drug addiction: Physiological, psychological and sociological aspects.* New York: Random House.

Azrin, N. H. & Holz, W. C. (1966). Punishment. In *Operant behavior: Areas of research and application,* Ed. by Honig, W. H. New York: Appleton-Century-Crofts.

Beach, H. D. (1957). Morphine addiction in rats. *Canad. J. Psychol.,* **11**, 104–112.

Berlyne, D. E. (1955). The arousal and satiation of perceptual curiosity in the rat. *J. comp. physiol. Psychol.,* **48**, 238–246.

Brady, J. V., Boren, J. J., Conrad, D. & Sidman, M. (1957). The effect of food and water deprivation upon intracranial self-stimulation. *J. comp. physiol. Psychol.*, **50**, 134–137.

Casey, A. (1960). The effects of stress on consumption of alcohol and reserpine. *Quart. J. Stud. Alchol.*, **21**, 208–216.

Cofer, C. N. & Appley, M. H. (1964). *Motivation: Theory and research.* New York: John Wiley & Sons.

Cook, L., Davidson, A., Davis, D. J. & Kelleher, R. T. (1960). Epinephrine, norepinephrine, and acetylcholine as conditioned stimuli for avoidance behavior. *Science*, **131**, 990–991.

Crespi, L. P. (1942). Quantitative variation of incentive and performance in the white rat. *Am. J. Psychol.*, **55**, 467–517.

Crowder, W. F., Morris, J. B., Dyer, W. R. & Robinson, J. V. (1961). Resistance to extinction and number of weak-light reinforcements. *J. Psychol.*, **51**, 361–364.

Davis, J. D. (1966). A method for chronic intravenous infusion in freely moving rats. *J. exp. Anal. Behav.*, **9**, 385–387.

Davis, J. D., Lulenski, G. C. & Miller, N. E. In the press. Comparative studies of barbiturate self-administration. *Int. J. of Addictions*.

Davis, J. D. & Miller, N. E. (1963). Fear and pain: their effect on self-injection of amobarbital sodium by rats. *Science*, **141**, 1286–1287.

Davis, W. M. & Nichols, J. R. (1963). A technique for self-injection of drugs in the study of reinforcement. *J. exp. Anal. Behav.*, **6**, 233–235.

Dole, V. P. & Nyswander, M. (1965). A medical treatment of diacetylmorphine (heroin) addiction. *J. Am. Med. Ass.*, **195**, 646–650.

Eddy, N. B., Halback, H. & Braenden, O. J. (1957). Synthetic substances with morphine-like effects. *Bull. Wld. Hlth. Org.*, **17**, 569–863.

Ferster, C. B. & Skinner, B. F. (1957). *Schedules of reinforcement.* New York: Appleton-Century-Crofts.

Findley, J. D. & Brady, J. V. (1965). Facilitation of large ratio performance by use of conditioned reinforcement. *J. exp. Anal. Behav.*, **8**, 125–129.

Goodman, L. S. & Gilman, A. (1963). *The pharmacological basis of therapeutics.* New York: Macmillan.

Guttman, N. (1953). Operant conditioning, extinction, and periodic reinforcement in relation to concentration of sucrose used as a reinforcing agent. *J. exp. Psychol.*, **46**, 213–224.

Headlee, C. P., Coppock, H. W. & Nichols, J. R. (1955). Apparatus and technique involved in a laboratory method of detecting the addictiveness of drugs. *J. Am. Pharm. Ass.* (Sci. ed.), **44**, 229–231.

Kelleher, R. T. (1966). Chaining and conditioned reinforcement. In *Operant behavior: Areas of research and application*, Ed. by Honig, W. H. New York: Appleton-Century-Crofts, 160–212.

Keller, F. S. & Schoenfeld, W. N. (1950). *Principles of psychology.* New York: Appleton-Century-Crofts.

Kimble, G. A. (1961). *Hilgard and Marquis' conditioning and learning*. New York: Appleton-Century-Crofts.

Kish, G. B. (1955). Learning when the onset of illumination is used as reinforcing stimulus. *J. comp. physiol. Psychol.*, **48**, 261–264.

Kolb, L. (1939). Drug addiction as a public health problem. *Sci. Monthly*, **48**, 391.

Kolb, L. (1962). *Drug addiction: A medical problem*. Springfield, Illinois: Thomas.

Lawson, R. (1960). *Learning and behavior*. New York: Macmillan.

Lundin, R. W. (1961). *Personality: An experimental approach*. New York: Macmillan.

Masserman, J. H. & Yum, K. S. (1946). An analysis of the influence of alcohol on experimental neurosis in cats. *Psychosom. Med.*, **8**, 36–52.

Meisch, R. A. & Pickens, R. (1967). A new technique for oral self-administration of drugs by animals. NAS-NRC Meeting of Committee on Problems of Drug Dependence.

Miller, N. W. (1948). Studies of fear as an acquirable drive. I. Fear as motivation and fear-reduction as reinforcement in the learning of new responses. *J. exp. Psychol.*, **38**, 89–101.

Miller, N. E. & Dollard, J. (1941). *Social learning and imitation*. New Haven: Yale University Press.

Morse, W. H. (1966). Intermittent reinforcement. In *Operant behavior: Areas of research and application*. Ed. by Honig, W. H. New York: Appleton-Century-Crofts, 52–108.

Olds, J. (1958). Satiation effects in self-stimulation of the brain. *J. comp. Physiol. Psychol.*, **51**, 675–678.

Perin, C. T. (1943). A quantitative investigation of the delay-of-reinforcement gradient. *J. exp. Psychol.*, **32**, 37–51.

Pickens, R. & Harris, W. C. In the press. Self-administration of d-amphetamine by rats. *Psychopharmacologia*.

Pickens, R., Meisch, R. & McGuire, L. E. (1967). Methamphetamine reinforcement in rats. *Psychon. Sci.*, **8**, 371–372.

Pickens, R. & Thompson, T. (1968). Cocaine-reinforced behavior in rats: Effects of reinforcement magnitude and fixed-ratio size. *J. Pharm. exp. Ther.*

Popovic, V. & Popovic, P. (1960). Permanent cannulation of aorta and vena cava in rats and ground squirrels. *J. appl. Physiol.*, **15**, 727.

Schuster, C. R. (1967). Classically conditioned morphine withdrawal and influence of morphine on effects of other reinforcers. Paper presented at Mid-western Psychol. Ass., Chicago.

Schuster, C. R. & Thompson, T. I. (1962). Self-administration of morphine in physically dependent rhesus monkeys. *Lab. Psychopharm., Univer. of Maryland*, Tech. Rpt. No. 62–29.

Seward, J. P., Uyeda, A. & Olds, J. (1959). Resistance to extinction following cranial self-stimulation. *J. comp. Physiol. Psychol.*, **52**, 294–299.

Sharpless, S. K. (1961). Effects of intravenous injection of epinephrine and norepinephrine in a choice situation. *J. comp. physiol. Psychol.*, **54,** 103–108.

Skinner, B. F. (1938). *The behavior of organisms.* New York: Appleton-Century-Crofts.

Slusher, M. A. & Browning, B. (1961). Morphine inhibition of plasma corticosteroid levels in chronic venous-catheterized rats. *Am. J. Physiol.*, **200,** 1032.

Spragg, S. D. S. (1940). Morphine addiction in chimpanzees. *Comp. Psychol. Monogr.*, **15,** No. 7.

Terry, C. E. & Pellens, M. (1928). *The opium problem.* New York: Bureau of Social Hygiene.

Thompson, T. & Ostlund, W. (1965). Susceptibility to readdiction as a function of the addiction and withdrawal environment. *J. comp. physiol. Psychol.*, **59,** 388–392.

Thompson, T. & Schuster, C. R. (1964). Morphine self-administration, food-reinforced and avoidance behaviors in rhesus monkeys. *Psychopharmacologia*, **5,** 87–94.

Thompson, T. & Schuster, C. R. (1968). *Behavioral pharmacology.* Englewood, N.J.: Prentice-Hall.

Waller, M. B. & Waller, P. F. (1962). Effects of chlorpromazine on appetitive and aversive components of a multiple schedule. *J. exp. Anal. Behav.*, **5,** 259–264.

Way, E. L. (1965). Control and treatment of drug addiction in Hong Kong. In *Narcotics*, Ed. by Wilner, D. M. & Kassebaum, G. G. New York: McGraw-Hill.

Weeks, J. R. (1962). Experimental morphine addiction: Method for automatic intravenous injection in unrestrained rats. *Science*, **138,** 143–144.

Weeks, J. (1967). Self-administration of opiates by rats. Paper presented at Mid-western Psychol. Ass., Chicago.

Weeks, J. R. & Collins, R. J. (1964). Factors affecting voluntary morphine intake in self-maintained addicted rats. *Psychopharmacologia*, **6,** 267–279.

Weiss, B. & Laties, V. G. (1961). Behavioral thermoregulation. *Science*, **133,** 1338–1344.

Welker, W. I. (1956). Variability of play and exploration in chimpanzees. *J. comp. physiol. Psychol.*, **49,** 181–185.

Wikler, A. (1953). *Opiate addiction. Psychological and neurophysiological aspects in relation to clinical problems.* Springfield, Illinois: Thomas.

Wikler, A., Martin, W. R., Pescor, F. T. & Eades, C. G. (1963). Factors regulating oral consumption of an opioid (etonitazene) by morphine-addicted rats. *Psychopharmacologia*, **5,** 55–78.

Woods, J. (1967). Parametric studies of morphine self-administration by monkeys. Paper presented at Midwestern Psychol. Ass., Chicago.

PSYCHOGENIC DEPENDENCE IN MONKEYS

Gerald A. Deneau

Southern Research Institute, Birmingham, Alabama

Drug abuse occurs when a subject self-administers a drug for non-therapeutic purposes to the extent that he becomes mentally or physically incapacitated by the effects of the drug. Being no longer productive, the subject is at least a burden, if not an outright menace, to society.

Certain aspects of drug abuse have been studied in experimental animals for many years. Thus, the phenomena of physiological dependence and tolerance, while not well understood, are at least well known. It is clear, however, that these are not essential aspects of drug abuse, since such widely abused drugs as cocaine, the amphetamines, marijuana, and LSD do not induce physiological dependence. The only aspect of abuse common to all drugs is what I shall call psychogenic dependence.

The only way in which psychogenic dependence can be demonstrated is to allow the experimental animal to demonstrate by its behaviour that it desires to receive the drug. Spragg (1940) made the first study of this sort. He made chimpanzees physiologically dependent on morphine and showed that at a time when abstinence signs began to appear, the chimpanzees would choose a box (white) containing a hypodermic syringe filled with a solution of morphine rather than a box (black) containing a banana or orange. Unfortunately, it was not clear from these studies whether the chimpanzees preferred to be under the influence of morphine or whether they had learned that this was a means of avoiding, or escaping from, the distressing abstinence syndrome. Later, Nichols, Headlee, & Coppock (1956); Beach (1957) and Wikler, Martin, Pescor & Eades (1963) conducted studies in rats which drank solutions of narcotic analgesics. Unfortunately, some drugs which are abused, such as the barbiturates, taste so bitter that they cannot be studied in this manner.

Weeks (1961) developed a method using rats which had chronic indwelling intravenous catheters. Such rats, having been made physiologically dependent on morphine by programmed injection, soon learned to maintain their dependence by pressing a lever to activate the injector after the automatic injections had been stopped. Yanagita, Deneau & Seevers (1965) developed a method which permits programmed or self-administration of drugs to rhesus monkeys with indwelling intravenous catheters. Thompson & Schuster (1964) also developed a similar technique with rhesus monkeys. With the intravenous techniques, the problems associated with bitter-tasting solutions are avoided. If naive monkeys voluntarily initiate and continue to self-administer a drug, it is believed that this demonstrates psychogenic dependence.

Methods

A single apparatus is utilized for the long-term intravenous administration of drugs to the monkey, either by a programmed schedule determined by the investigator or by a self-administration schedule determined by the experimental subject. The apparatus consists of a restraining arm and harness which serves to confine the monkey in an open-faced cage as well as to connect the animal with an injector. An electric switching unit allows the injector to be activated either by a timer or a switch which can be operated by the monkey.

Apparatus

The harness is made of stainless steel tubing the size of which can be adjusted to fit the particular monkey. A housing box on the back of the harness serves a three-fold purpose: as a junction point connecting the monkey to the restraining arm; as a junction point between the monkey's intravascular catheter and the tube which leads from the injector through the tubular restraining arm, and as a barrier which prevents the monkey from grasping the short length of the exposed catheter as it emerges from the subcutaneous tissue at a point on the monkey's back directly beneath the housing box.

The restraining arm is made of stainless steel tubing. It serves to keep the monkey within the confines of the open-faced cage as well as to provide a protective conduit for the silicone rubber tube which conveys the drug solution from the injector to the monkey. Swivel joints at both ends of the arm and in the middle allow the monkey to move freely within the cage except for rotation in a complete circle. Rotation is limited to 300 degrees to prevent fouling of the catheter.

The injector consists of a motor-driven syringe which is connected via a three-way solenoid valve to the tubing which leads to the monkey and to a reservoir of drug solution. The motor can be activated by a timer in the control unit for programmed drug administration or, in self-administration experiments, it can be activated by the monkey when it presses the lever switch which is located on the wall of the cage. The injector delivers a predetermined volume of solution at each activation. The volume is determined by setting a microswitch which reverses the motor when a given amount has been delivered. As the motor reverses, the solenoid valve disconnects the monkey from the syringe and connects the syringe to the reservoir. The syringe thus refills automatically.

A hot stylus event recorder records the time at which the monkey depresses the lever and at which injections are delivered.

General procedure

Monkeys are placed in the harness for several days during which they become accustomed to wearing the harness and to the limitation of incomplete rotation imposed by the restraining arm. This period also serves as a time of observation during which the harness can be adjusted if signs of irritation are observed at the monkey's shoulders.

When the monkey has become adapted to this new environment, it is anaesthetized with a short-acting barbiturate, removed from the cage and catheterized. A silicone rubber catheter is inserted into the superior vena cava via either jugular vein. When the catheter has been properly located, it is tied into the vein and then led subcutaneously to the dorsal thoracic region where it passes through a stab wound in the skin and is secured to a connector in the housing box of the harness. The monkey is then reattached to the restraining arm and the tube leading from the injector is connected with the intravascular catheter. Injections of saline are administered on a programmed schedule for several days during which it can be determined that the injector and catheter are functioning properly, and during which the monkey recovers from the surgical procedure. If the experiment is one which involves programmed administration of drugs, it can be started at this point. If the experiment is intended to involve self-administration of drugs by the monkey, further training procedures are carried out.

One blank panel of the cage wall is replaced by another panel on which are mounted a signal light and a lever switch. The light, when on, indicates to the monkey that he can activate the injector by pressing the lever switch. For the first few days a clear lens, indicating the availability of injections of physiological saline, is placed over the panel light. During this period the monkey, which is a naturally curious animal, will depress the lever either by accident or on purpose, and so control values for lever-pressing activity are obtained.

When the lever-pressing activity has stabilized, the saline solution is replaced by a drug solution and a coloured lens is placed over the panel light. The next depression of the lever by the monkey results in the injection of a test drug, and if the drug produces any subjective effects, the monkey quickly learns to associate lever-pressing with the drug effects. If the drug effects are positively rewarding, the monkey will press the lever repeatedly, and a pattern of self-administration of the drug is initiated. If the monkey maintains this pattern of self-administration at levels above those of the previous saline control period, psychogenic dependence is said to have been established.

If there is a danger that too frequent injections of the particular test drug may result in toxic or fatal effects, a deprivation period of any selected duration can be interposed after each injection. The duration of the deprivation period is set on an electric timer in the switching unit. The panel light is off during this period and the injector does not work. The monkey soon learns that the illumination of the panel light is associated with availability of the drug.

During the saline control period some monkeys may stop pressing the lever entirely and, not yet having learned the significance of the panel light, they may not press the lever for several days after the saline has been replaced with a test drug. When the lever-pressing behaviour has been extinguished in this manner, it is necessary to prompt the monkey into pressing the lever once more in order that he may experience the effects of the test drug. This is done by taping a raisin or a small piece of candy to the lever with transparent cellulose tape. In his efforts to obtain the raisin, the monkey will activate the injector. If the test drug is positively rewarding, two or three such trials serve to teach the monkey that lever pressing is associated with drug effects. If the drug is negatively rewarding, the monkey will not attempt to extricate raisins or candy from underneath the tape in subsequent trials, even though he will take raisins from the investigator's hand.

Monkeys demonstrate variability in the readiness with which they learn to associate the presence of an illuminated panel light with availability of a drug and also the colour of the panel light with a particular drug. Selected animals can be used to determine an approximate rank ordering of drug preference by using Skinnerian progressive ration techniques in which drug injections are effected after progressively increasing ratios of lever presses per activation of the injector. The persistence of lever-pressing activity can be correlated with the desirability of the subjective effects of various drugs in this manner.

When a monkey fails to initiate self-administration of a test drug, it is pertinent to ask whether psychogenic dependence might develop after further exposure to the drug's effects. To test this possibility, injections are programmed automatically at constant intervals while at the same time the injector can also be activated by the monkey. If the monkey's initial indifference to the drug effects changes to a positive preference, this change is indicated by monkey-activated injections during the intervals between the programmed injections. If self-administration does not begin within a month however, the monkey is assumed not to have developed psychogenic dependence to the particular drug.

There are situations in which self-administration behaviour can be induced, but in which it must be concluded that the monkey is exhibiting escape-avoidance behaviour rather than psychogenic dependence. An illustration of this would be with a monkey which failed to initiate self-administration during the course of a month of programmed injections of a drug which would be expected to produce physiological dependence. If the programmed injections are suddenly stopped and the monkey then begins self-administration as abstinence signs develop, it is more likely that the self-administration has begun in order to ameliorate the distress of abstinence rather than as a result of positively rewarding aspects of the drug effects.

Results

The techniques described were developed for the specific purpose of studying the phenomenon of psychogenic dependence. From studies so far, it may be stated that drugs which definitely produce psychogenic dependence in the rhesus monkey (*Macaca mulatta*) include: morphine, codeine, cocaine, dexamphetamine, pentobarbitone, ethanol and caffeine. Drugs to which psychogenic dependence does not develop include: nalorphine, mixtures of nalorphine and morphine, chlorpromazine, and also physiological saline.

The monkey shows a similar range of susceptibility to drug abuse as does man, in that some animals are highly susceptible, some are only moderately so, some are indifferent, and some are completely resistant.

Discussion

Programmed or self-administration of drugs is an easy way to establish physiological dependence on drugs which possess this capacity. Although this technique has not been employed for this specific purpose, it would be ideally suited for establishing the physiological dependence capacities of drugs which act for a very short time and thus require frequent administration. The method would likewise be suitable for drugs which produce severe local tissue irritation at intramuscular or subcutaneous sites of injection.

Additional applications of this technique include acute and chronic pharmacological and toxicological studies in the monkey. There is no need here to reiterate the advantages of a primate species for pharmacological experiments. It should be pointed out, however, that the monkey is a nervous animal and that the acts of catching and injecting it by conventional means may produce residual behavioural effects which partially mask or enhance the actions of the drug. This artifact can be avoided by injecting the drugs unbeknown into animals which have been previously prepared with intravascular catheters.

Since the catheters are stable for many months, these preparations offer an opportunity to study many drugs in conditions of chronic administration. By means of such studies, several potential problems could be properly predicted before expensive and disappointing clinical trials. Phenomena such as tolerance, intolerance or sensitivity, physiological dependence and interactions with adjuvant therapy, as well as somatic and behavioural toxicity, could all be established by such studies.

The technique which I have described provides many demonstrated and potential advantages for pharmacological evaluation of new drugs. There are, however, some limitations of applicability and inherent hazards which should not be overlooked. One serious limitation is that only those drugs which are readily soluble in water can be administered intravascularly for prolonged periods. Many drugs cannot be evaluated properly by this technique because of their low water solubility. A significant hazard inherent in the technique is that of infectious complications. The most common complication of these experiments is bacterial endocarditis with subsequent fatal pulmonary emboli. Since the cost of the experimental animals, physical facilities, and man hours involved in experiments of this nature is large, it is in the investigator's own interest to take every possible precaution to ensure asepsis from the initial surgical procedure and by using sterile equipment and drug solutions.

Summary

(1) The development of psychogenic dependence is felt to be the most important factor in the initiation of drug abuse. (2) The voluntary initiation and continuation of self-administration of drugs by monkeys is a laboratory model of psychogenic dependence. (3) With those drugs tested so far, monkeys develop psychogenic dependence on the same drugs that man abuses and do not develop dependence on drugs which man does not abuse. (4) Monkeys show individual variation in that some quickly develop psychogenic dependence on a particular drug, others develop dependence more slowly, and some never do.

REFERENCES

Beach, H. D. (1957). Morphine addiction in rats. *Canad. J. Psychol.*, **11**, 104–112.

Nichols, J. R., Headlee, C. P. & Coppock, H. W. (1956). Drug Addiction I. Addiction by escape training. *J. Am. Pharmaceut. Ass.*, **45**, 788–791.

Spragg, S. D. S. (1940). Morphine addiction in chimpanzees. *Comp. Psychol. Monogr.*, **15**, 1–132.

Thompson, T. & Schuster, C. R. (1964). Morphine self-administration, food reinforced and avoidance behaviors in rhesus monkeys. *Psychopharmacologia (Berl.)*, **5**, 87–94.

Weeks, J. R. (1961). Self-maintained morphine 'addiction'—a method for chronic programmed intravenous injections in unrestricted rats. *Fed. Proc.*, **20**, 397.

Wikler, A., Martin, W. R., Pescor, F. T. & Eades, C. G. (1963). Factors regulating oral consumption of an opioid (etonitazine) by morphine-addicted rats. *Psychopharmacologia, Berl.*, **5**, 55–76.

Yanagita, T., Deneau, G. A. & Seevers, M. H. (1965). Evaluation of pharmacologic agents in the monkey by long-term intravenous self- or programmed administration. *Excerpta Med. Int. Congr. Ser.*, No. **87**, 453–457.

HOW RATS CAN BECOME DEPENDENT ON MORPHINE IN THE COURSE OF RELIEVING ANOTHER NEED

R. KUMAR,[*] HANNAH STEINBERG AND I. P. STOLERMAN

Department of Pharmacology, University College, London

ABOUT two years ago we surveyed the literature dealing with experiments on drug dependence in animals (Steinberg, Kumar, Kemp & Bartley, 1968). We were surprised how little of it seemed to have been directly inspired by prevalent social and clinical problems, although since then, as might be expected, this state of affairs has changed somewhat.

Provided the validity of animal models of drug dependence can be established, experiments with animals have obvious implications for man. It becomes possible to investigate in controlled conditions problems which, for ethical and other reasons, cannot be experimentally examined using human subjects.

Methods of inducing dependence

Among the most convincing techniques are those in which animals are given opportunities for administering drugs to themselves, either by eating them mixed with their diet (Madinaveitia, this volume, p. 161), by drinking solutions (Nichols, Headlee & Coppock, 1956; Nichols & Davis, 1959), or by pressing levers which release intravenous injections through implanted catheters (Weeks, 1962; Deneau, this volume, p. 201).

This paper reports new findings made while we were developing a method for oral self-administration of morphine solutions

---

[*] Beit Memorial Research Fellow.

by rats. Our procedure was an amalgam of what we considered to be the most important characteristics of methods of oral self-administration described in the literature (Nichols, Headlee & Coppock, 1956; Wikler & Pescor, 1967): our aim was to induce a marked dependence quickly and reliably, and if possible in all the animals used.

Until recently, it was thought necessary to premedicate animals before they would learn to administer drugs to themselves. The experimenter usually gave daily injections of increasing doses of morphine for two to three weeks in order to make the animals 'passively' dependent on the drug; injections were then stopped and the animals developed withdrawal symptoms (Martin, Wikler, Eades & Pescor, 1963; Akera & Brody, 1968) which could be relieved by more morphine. In this state of deprivation the animals would learn to administer the drug to themselves. Monkeys will, however, learn to press levers for intravenous injections even without premedication, though such learning is much slower, and sometimes raisins have to be taped to the lever for the learning to occur at all (Deneau, this volume, p. 203). Some monkeys will also voluntarily drink morphine solutions, which are bitter, but others persistently reject them without premedication (Claghorn et al., 1965).

The experiments reported here show that in rats it is possible to dispense with premedication altogether and yet to convert an initial aversion for the bitter morphine into a clear preference, as measured by the proportion of morphine solution drunk when both morphine and water are available. By a clear preference is meant that more than 50% of the total liquid intake is voluntarily drunk in the form of morphine solution. In our experiments (Kumar, Steinberg & Stolerman, 1968) the preference seemed to be more consistent and greater than any previously reported, even with premedicated rats. The preference persisted for several weeks, again irrespective of whether it had initially developed following premedication or not.

Our method involved making the rats accustomed to satisfying their normal thirst during a limited time each day, and then substituting morphine solutions for the water normally given. The results have been substantially confirmed by later work.

A procedure for inducing dependence

Male hooded rats aged 60–90 days were housed singly at an ambient temperature of 70–74°F, with unlimited quantities of food pellets (diet GR/R/3) always available; but they only had access to water between 10 a.m. and 5 p.m. They quickly became accustomed to relieving their normal thirst during these seven hours, and after a slight initial drop in body weight, they continued to grow normally. The interval of seventeen hours between the daily drinking periods was chosen so as to be long enough (Martin, Wikler, Eades & Pescor, 1963) for the daily development of withdrawal symptoms at a later stage of the experiment, when morphine solution was to be substituted for the drinking water. On the sixth day of restricted drinking the rats were divided into three groups. Group 1 (six rats), the premedicated group, was given morphine injections twice daily (60 mg/kg at 10 a.m. and at 5 p.m.); group 2 (four rats) was given saline injections twice daily, and group 3 (seven rats) was not injected. From the sixteenth day onwards the dose of morphine given to group 1 was doubled in order to allow for tolerance. Although these doses of morphine may seem large in relation to the usually quoted ED_{50}'s for analgesia, they are typical of the doses used for premedication in dependence experiments.

After 20 days of the restricted drinking no more morning injections were given; instead the rats in groups 1 and 2 were either offered both morphine solution (0·5 mg/ml.) and water in separate bottles throughout their daily seven hour drinking period ('choice' trial), or morphine solution only ('forced' trial).

The first and every third day were 'choice' days, and the intervening two days were 'forced' days. Furthermore, in order to augment withdrawal symptoms on the following day in group 1, no evening injections were given before choice days; evening injections were retained before forced days in case the amount of morphine solution consumed by drinking alone, usually not less than 20 ml., was not enough to maintain a state of dependence. Group 3, which had not been injected, was given quinine solution (0·5 mg/ml.) instead of morphine solution in order to serve as a control for repeated access to a bitter solution of a drug not associated with dependence; the concentration was that used by Nichols (Nichols, Headlee & Coppock, 1956). The amounts of the various liquids consumed were determined by weighing the drinking bottles before and after each drinking period. The bottle containing the drug solution was allocated to either side of the cage on a random basis. The hydrochlorides of morphine and quinine were used throughout.

Results

On the first choice day, the rats drank very little of their fluid intake in the form of drug solution. This is consistent with previous findings (Nichols, Headlee & Coppock, 1956; Nichols & Davis, 1959). On each of the following two days (which were forced trials) the mean consumption of morphine solution was approximately 20 ml., which is a little below the consumption of water in comparable conditions. Figure 1 shows that on the succeeding choice trials—interspersed with two forced days as described—the premedicated group quickly increased its voluntary intake of morphine solution (for trials 1–10, $F = 6·17$, $P < 0·001$); this confirms earlier work (Nichols, Headlee & Coppock, 1956; Nichols & Davis, 1959). They rapidly developed a clear preference for morphine: they took much more than 50% of their liquid intake in the form of morphine solution, and maintained this preference even when no more injections were given (choice trials 11–18). From choice trial 19 onwards, forced trials were discontinued altogether, and the animals were given choice trials daily. Nevertheless, the preference persisted, even

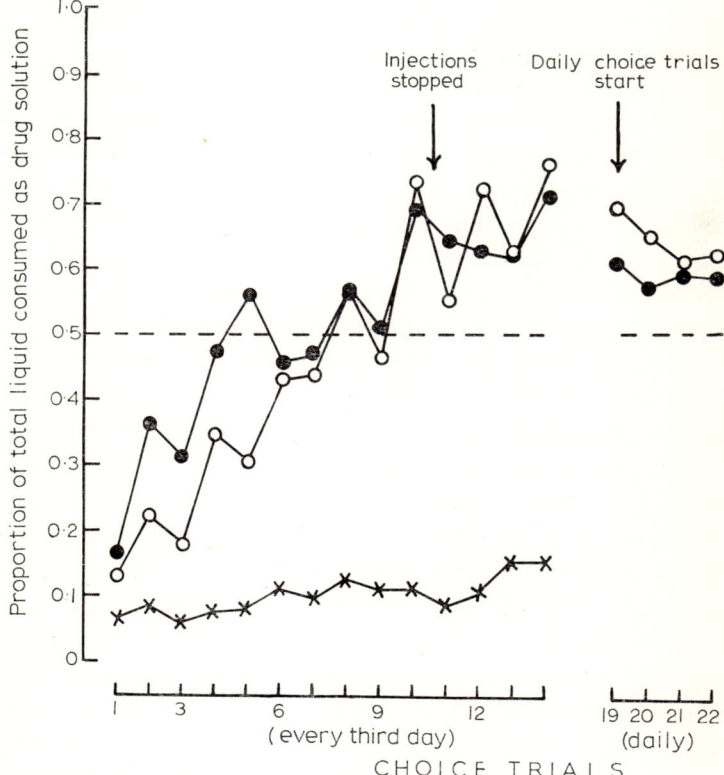

FIG. 1. Development of preference for morphine in rats given a choice between morphine solution and water every third day. On the intervening days morphine solution only was available. Premedicated rats (group 1: ●—●) had had morphine injections for 15 days before drinking trials began and up to the tenth choice trial. Unpremedicated rats (group 2: ○—○) received saline injections only. A clear preference for morphine developed in both groups and they continued to drink more morphine solution than water even when water was available as an alternative to morphine every day. No preference developed in a control group given quinine solution (group 3: ×—×).

though the rats could have reverted to their original rejection of morphine since water was simultaneously available every day.

Surprisingly, the rats injected with saline also increased their morphine intake ($F = 9.36$, $P < 0.001$), and developed a preference which was not significantly different from that of the premedicated group either overall ($F = 0.63$, $P > 0.2$) or at any stage (group × trial interaction $F = 0.94$, $P > 0.2$). Daily choice trials were continued for several weeks and both groups regularly drank significantly more than 50% of their liquid intake in the form of morphine solution (for example, for trials 19–28, $t = 3.77$, $P < 0.01$). The average dose of morphine drunk on choice days amounted to approximately 30 mg/kg. Such a marked and consistent preference does not previously seem to have been reported even in premedicated rats, possibly because most investigators (e.g. Nichols, Headlee & Coppock, 1956; Nichols & Davis, 1959; Thompson & Oslund, 1965) did not continue experiments beyond a few choice trials. Moreover, it has been usual to accept *any* substantial increase in the voluntary consumption of drug solution as evidence for the development of dependence, even though the volume actually drunk fell short of 50% of the total liquid intake. Increases to above 50% are, however, more satisfactory; only then can one speak of a genuine preference. They also exclude the possibility that the increases in morphine consumption are entirely caused by progressive desensitization of taste mechanisms; in our case the rats were obviously able to discriminate between the two liquids if they chose to drink more of the morphine solution than of the water.

Very little of the quinine solution offered to group 3 was drunk, although there was a slight increase with repeated trials ($F = 2.15$, $P < 0.05$). This increase may be attributed either to an effect on taste itself or, to a learnt association between a bitter taste and the relief of thirst; but the overall difference between the quinine group and the two morphine groups combined was large and statistically highly significant ($t = 8.68$, $P < 0.001$).

We had used a quinine solution which was of the same concentration as that used by Nichols *et al.* (1956) because they had attempted to match it for bitterness with a morphine solution which was similar to ours. However, in the conditions of our own experiments the concentration of quinine seemed to be too great because even during the first choice trial the rats drank less of it than of the morphine solution, and during forced trials they drank much less. We therefore repeated the experiments with a weaker quinine solution (0·25 mg/ml.—roughly five times the strength of tonic water). Again no preference developed. The failure of quinine at either concentration to induce a preference is consistent with the assumption that the preference for morphine was due to dependence.

Experiments with dependent rats

In order to obtain additional validation of the preference for morphine as an index of a dependent state which has some characteristics in common with dependence in man, other experiments were carried out.

Rats which had been made dependent by the method described were injected subcutaneously thirty minutes before their daily choice tests either with one of three doses of morphine or with saline. Each rat received each treatment once in a balanced order according to a Latin square design. The results in Fig. 2a show that the bigger the pre-injected dose, the lower the proportion of the total liquid intake which was subsequently drunk in the form of morphine solution. The downward trend was significant ($P < 0.01$). The total liquid intake, however, remained constant (Fig. 2b): the injections of morphine in this dose range do not seem simply to have depressed drinking.

Another experiment was concerned with withdrawal. Our dependent rats, when not in a state of withdrawal, continued to gain weight; in addition, we did not find any evidence of the self-mutilation which has sometimes been reported, or any other

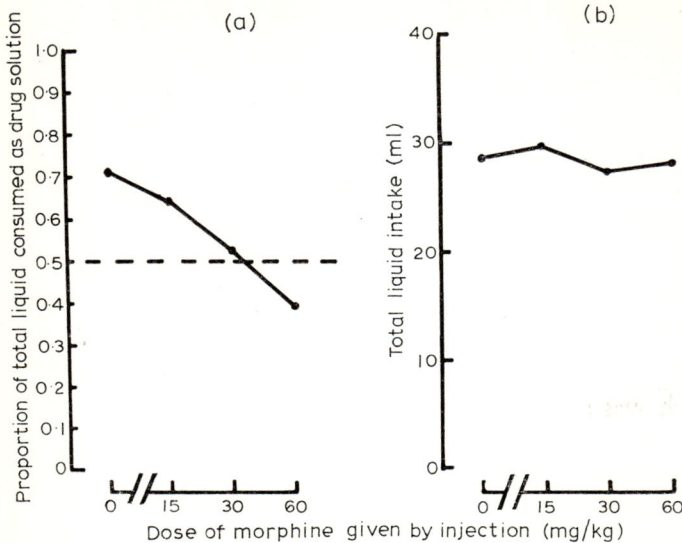

FIG. 2. Injections of morphine 30 min before choice trials selectively reduced the amount of morphine solution drunk by dependent rats (*a*), but the total fluid intake during the 7 hr was unaffected (*b*). Eight rats were injected subcutaneously with either saline or one of three doses of morphine (15, 30 or 60 mg/kg) and each rat received each treatment once according to a Latin square design.

obvious signs of ill-health. After the rats had been maintaining a stable preference on daily choice trials for some weeks, the morphine solution was abruptly withdrawn and only water was made available during the daily seven hour drinking period. As Fig. 3 shows, their body weights fell precipitously for forty-eight hours and then gradually recovered. The quinine group (cf. Fig. 1) was at the same time abruptly deprived of quinine solution and was given access to water only: they continued to gain weight normally.

Discussion

The development of dependence and its recent epidemic spread (Rathod *et al.*, this volume, p. 331) is extremely complicated, and only after prolonged and patient analysis can some predisposing factors be isolated (Willis, this volume, p. 301; Vaillant, this volume, p. 341). As has been discussed elsewhere in this symposium, there is still much speculation as to why certain individuals are led to take drugs; how far

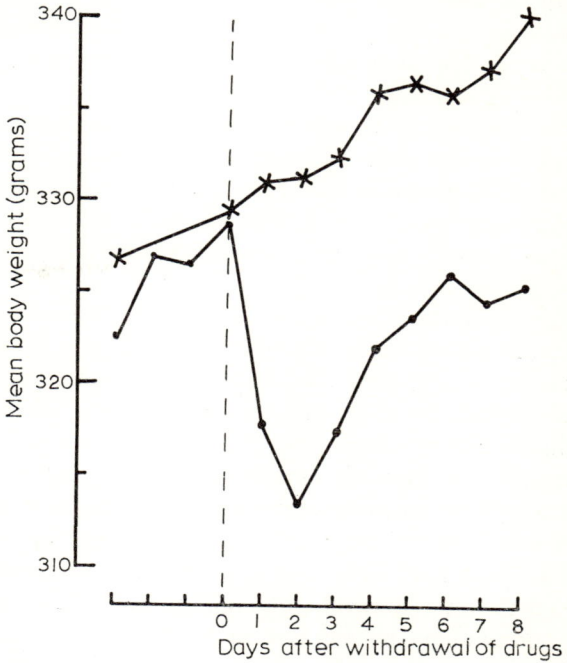

Fig. 3. Depriving morphine-dependent rats of the drug (•—•, seven rats) produces a marked loss of weight. After these rats had been drinking morphine solutions in preference to water daily for several weeks, the morphine solution was abruptly withdrawn and only water was made available. A control group 'withdrawn' from quinine solution in a similar manner continued to gain weight normally (×—×, seven rats).

is the responsibility theirs or society's? How far are they exploited by 'pushers' seeking expanding markets, or do addicts largely create their own demands? How important is 'escalation', and does it occur at all? Do drugs that are misused have some special pharmacological properties or psychological effects in common? What part is played by a search for novel stimulation? How can effective substitutes for drugs be found?

If it is reasonable to regard animal models of drug dependence as valid for human addiction, they should help to throw light on some problems of this kind.

Dr. Deneau has already reported that monkeys will self-administer only those drugs that are usually associated with human drug dependence (this volume, p. 206).

Our own experiments have shown that, as in man, premedication with morphine is not necessary for the development of dependence; if morphine self-administration is repeatedly made a condition for the satisfaction of a different need, in this case thirst, rats will overcome their aversion for bitter morphine solutions and eventually prefer them to water.

The results illustrated in Fig. 2 could be regarded as evidence that to some extent the rats were regulating their total daily dose of morphine; but the amount of morphine solution drunk did not decrease as might have been expected if the dose injected had precisely substituted for the morphine which would otherwise have been obtained by drinking. By drinking, the rats normally obtained about 30 mg/kg of morphine daily; but after, for example, pre-injection with 30 mg/kg of morphine they obtained a further 20 mg/kg by drinking. The greater total intake of morphine may have been due to a number of factors, such as differences in the time course of action of the drug, because of both the different routes and the different rates of its administration. Thompson has obtained essentially similar results with a different method for inducing dependence (this volume, p. 194); pre-injection with methadone reduced the amount of lever pressing for morphine rewards in monkeys.

In addition, when only water was available to our morphine-dependent rats they had withdrawal symptoms and abruptly lost weight, whereas the quinine controls continued to grow normally. Loss of body weight after withdrawal of the drug seems previously to have been reported only when morphine was withdrawn from rats which had first been made 'passively' dependent by repeated pre-medication with the drug (Martin *et al.*, 1963; Akera & Brody, 1968). We agree with Akera & Brody that weight loss is probably the most reliable sign of withdrawal in the rat, and it is also one of the most objective and easy to determine.

How did the action of morphine and the conditions of our experiment interact to induce dependence? Tolerance and withdrawal eventually occur after repeated forced drinking of morphine solution; thus the bitter morphine solution, in addition to reducing thirst, presumably takes on another powerful rewarding property, that of relieving withdrawal symptoms. Nichols had found that premedication followed by withdrawal was crucial for the subsequent development of morphine dependence. In our somewhat different conditions, premedication had little effect on the eventual outcome (choice trials 19–22, Fig. 1). Results reported by Deneau (this volume, p. 205) and by Thompson (this volume, p. 185) are consistent with an earlier suggestion by Beach (1957) that morphine might in addition produce in animals, as in man, 'pleasurable' effects. In our experiments any such effects could not have occurred on the first choice trial, since on that occasion the rats did not drink the bitter drug solution at all. But after the first few forced trials pleasurable effects could well have influenced the consumption of morphine.

The results which we have described suggest that our morphine-dependent rats were indeed governed by needs which are in some ways similar to those believed to operate in human addicts, and that our animal model of dependence has many features in common with the human syndrome.

Our current experiments are particularly concerned with a more detailed analysis of factors leading to morphine dependence. Thompson and Ostlund (1965) have already established that rats are readdicted more quickly in an environment in which addiction originally occurred. We are particularly interested in the possibility of studying 'escalation' in animals; could the continued use of one drug facilitate the development of dependence on a drug of a different kind? Finally, the influence of social and environmental factors on drug dependence in animals seems to us to deserve more attention than it has hitherto received.

We wish to thank Mr. Barry Hutchings, Mr. David Blundell and Miss Marion Dorr for help with carrying out the experiments described, Mr. John Hall for statistical advice, and Prof. H. O. Schild and Dr. M. Lader for discussion. The work was supported by grant MH-03313 from the U.S. Public Health Service, and by a grant from the Medical Research Council.

REFERENCES

Akera, T. & Brody, T. M. (1968). The addiction cycle to narcotics in the rat and its relation to catecholamines. *Biochem. Pharmac.*, **17,** 675–688.

Claghorn, J. L., Ordy, J. M. & Nagy, A. (1965). Spontaneous opiate addiction in rhesus monkeys. *Science, N.Y.*, **149,** 440–441.

Kumar, R., Steinberg, H. & Stolerman, I. P. (1968). Inducing a preference for morphine in rats without premedication. *Nature, Lond.*, **218,** 564–565.

Martin, W. R., Wikler, A., Eades, C. G. & Pescor, F. T. (1968). Tolerance to and physical dependence on morphine in rats. *Psychopharmocologia*, **4,** 247–260.

Nichols, J. R. & Davis, W. M. (1969). Drug addiction II. Variation of addiction. *J. Am. pharm. Ass. (Sci. Ed.)*, **48,** 259–262.

Nichols, J. R., Headlee, C. P., & Coppock, H. W. (1956). Drug addiction 1. Addiction by escape training. *J. Amer. Pharm. Ass.*, 788–791.

Steinberg, H., Kumar, R., Kemp, I. & Bartley, H. (1968). Animal behaviour studies and some possible implications for man. *Proc. symposium on the pharmacological and epidemological aspects of adolescent drug dependence*, pp. 29–40. Oxford: Pergamon Press.

Thompson, T. & Ostlund, W. (1965). Susceptibility to readdiction as a function of the addiction and withdrawal environment. *J. comp. physiol. Psychol.*, **59,** 388–392.

Weeks, J. R. (1962). Experimental morphine addiction; method for automatic intravenous injections in unrestrained rats. *Science, N.Y.*, **138,** 143–144.

Wikler, A. & Pescor, F. T. (1967). Classical conditioning of a morphine abstinence phenomenon, reinforcement of opioid-drinking behaviour and 'relapse' in morphine-addicted rats. *Psychopharmacologia, Berl.*, **10,** 255–284.

AN ANALYSIS OF THE MECHANISMS INVOLVED IN THE TASTE FOR DRINK

C. W. M. Wilson

Trinity College, University of Dublin

Any discussion of the incidence, severity or effects of alcoholism generally founders on the difficulty of defining an alcoholic. Classification of alcoholism as a disease process is based on the appearance of a typical sequence of symptoms (Jellinek, 1946; 1953). Although Jellinek discussed the clustering of these symptoms, it has now become common practice to describe alcoholism as a series of drinking and associated experiences arranged in a sequence culminating in loss of control of alcohol consumption and the appearance of frequent blackouts. However, Alexander (1963), in a discussion of alcoholism as a behavioural disorder, has pointed out that classifications based on the description of overt directly observable behaviour of large numbers of cases are of little value for meaningful definition or etiological understanding of the condition.

An alternative method of classifying the characteristics of the alcoholic depends on a description of the pharmacological effects of alcohol. Alcohol may pharmacologically influence the central nervous system, it may act as a source of energy and it may influence metabolism. Forsander, Kohonen & Suomalainen (1958) suggest that the desire for alcohol arises from one of these pharmacological actions of alcohol; a person may want to produce the intoxicating effect of alcohol, to use it as a nutrient or to satisfy the subconscious needs of his metabolism. It is stated that one of these effects cannot be produced without the other two also appearing. Forsander (1962) admitted that not much is known about the degree to which metabolism affects human drinking habits, but he concluded that it is reasonable to assume that metabolism is the basis on which drinking habits develop in man. When discussing the reasons for the desire for alcohol, Forsander *et al.* (1958) maintained that the only effect resulting from the pharmacological actions of alcohol which the senses can clearly identify is that on the central nervous system. Unfortunately they do not amplify this statement and do not make it clear whether they are referring to the senses of the animal which is taking alcohol or the senses of the individual, or individuals, who are observing his consumption of alcohol.

Another method of classifying individuals who consume alcohol is based on attempts to define the limits between the drinking which characterises the real alcoholic and that of other individuals who also consume alcoholic drinks (Marconi, 1959). Drinkers can be classified according to certain characteristics, the quantity and types of alcoholic drinks usually consumed, the time intervals between consumption of the drinks, the effects produced by ingestion of the drinks, and the etiological factors which induce the drinking. The last are difficult to define with any exactitude, and it is therefore hard to devise methods for measuring them. They include the physical and psychological characteristics of the drinking individuals, and social factors in their environment which influence their drinking habits. The social factors have been discussed by Leake and Silverman (1966) as an aspect of the pharmacology of alcohol in relation to the community. Wilson (1968) has defined social pharmacology as the factors which influence the use and abuse, effects and control of drugs by the medical profession and the public. Alcohol is a compound which is used and abused by the public and which has pharmacological properties which affect the health of the individual in society and the health of society as a whole. In consequence it must be included in this definition like other drugs of dependence, and it must be appreciated that there is a need to design animal models to illustrate the social pharmacology of alcohol consumption, as well as the need to study it in different human cultures.

Alexander (1963) claimed that the chaotic and uncritical correlation of highly differentiated and heterogeneous variables throws little light on the complex problem of alcoholism. Perhaps this conclusion rests to a large extent on the fact that it is difficult to relate measurements of the effects of alcohol on metabolism to the taste for it. Although it is possible to measure the quality and quantity, and the frequency, of consumption of alcoholic drinks by human beings, it is very difficult to measure the influence of social factors on alcohol consumption in man; and the absence of any animal model which can serve as a basis for estimating their importance in man makes it impossible to evaluate the relationship between central nervous activity and influence of stimuli originating in the individual or from the social environment.

Investigations of individuals who drink alcohol, and of alcoholics, have in general been based on the assumption that the desire to drink is wholly related to the effects produced by the compound on the individual after absorption of the alcohol into the blood stream. It is believed that the subjective, but undefinable appreciation of the pharmacological effect of alcohol on the central nervous system is the principal reason for the consumption of alcoholic beverages. The presence of other individuals may affect the consumption of alcohol through visual and other types of peripheral-sensory discrimination, but the importance of this factor in the pattern of alcohol consumption has hardly been considered scientifically as an etiological factor and few attempts have been made to measure it. The fact that individuals have preferences for particular drinks, or different concentrations of alcohol has been known for a long time and this personal drinking behaviour has been used to characterise them. However, their selection of particular qualities and quantities of alcohol on drinking occasions is probably mainly based on their taste appreciation, and this depends on peripheral sensory, and central nervous activity. Both visual appreciation of social factors and taste discrimination influence central nervous activity immediately before and at the instant of the consumption of alcohol. The factors which cause stimulation of these sensory organs can be measured and I describe here how these measurements can be performed, and the light which they throw on the reasons for the consumption of alcohol.

The social pharmacology of drinking

Wilson & Mapes (1965) have studied the effects of group size and composition on the actions of sedative and ulcerogenic drugs in rats. They found that alteration in both these group parameters had significant effects on the degree and quality of drug action. Rick & Wilson (1966) have shown that rats preferentially select alcohol at a concentration of 5·5% when they are housed in groups of six. In these conditions a significant increase in the daily consumption of alcohol occurred during the six months of the experiments. Dr. Rick and I have extended the observations on the relationship between alcohol consumption and social grouping among rats in order to investigate the possibility of providing an animal model to investigate the characteristics of social drinking among humans.

Alcohol consumption was studied in male rats grouped eight, four and two to a cage and in rats caged individually, in both forced and choice conditions. Food consumption was not limited in any way. Fluid consumption was recorded during a period of ninety-six days and all the groups were placed in one of three fluid conditions. These conditions consisted of water alone, 5·5% alcohol alone, or a choice between water and 5·5% alcohol. A total of twenty-four rats was examined in each of these conditions. Each cage was of standard dimensions and contained two graduated drinking bottles. For the groups in choice conditions the two bottles were interchanged randomly throughout the experimental period. The results were calculated in terms of fluid consumed per twenty-four hour period by eight rats in each of the fluid conditions, and the means and standard deviations of

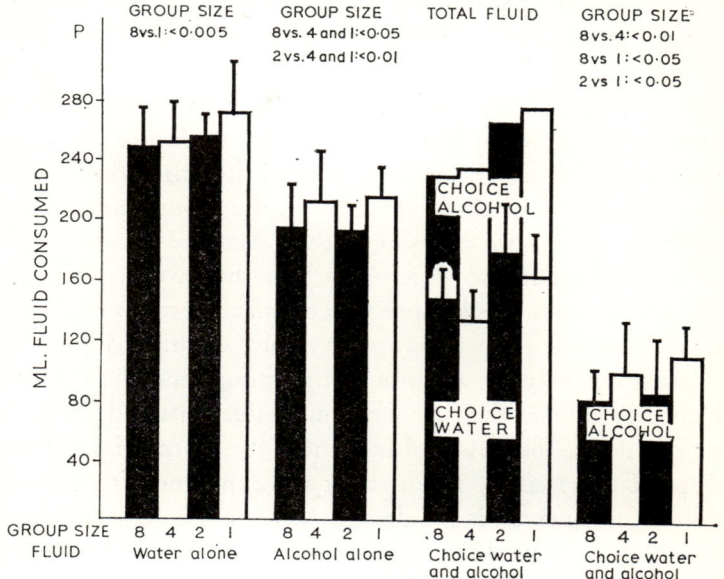

FIG. 1. The alcohol and fluid consumption of rat groups of various sizes. The means and standard deviations of the fluid consumed per twenty-four hour period by groups containing eight, four, two and one rats per group. The animals were provided with water alone, alcohol alone and a choice between alcohol and water. The total fluid consumption by the rats in the choice situation, divided into water and alcohol, is shown in the third block, and the proportion of the total fluid consumed as alcohol is shown in the fourth block. The significance of the comparisons between the fluid consumed by the different group sizes is shown in the top line.

alcohol consumed during the whole experimental period by the different groups are shown in Figure 1.

Among the rats which received water alone, fluid consumption was significantly greater in those housed individually. Rats kept in groups of four and one in a cage drank significantly more of the 5·5% alcohol solution than the rats housed eight and two to a cage. In conditions in which the rats had a choice of water and 5·5% alcohol in their cages, the pattern of consumption of alcohol by the groups resembled that when they were given alcohol alone; in these circumstances, however, the total volume of alcohol was less than half as much as in the non-choice condition. In choice conditions the total fluid consumed by the different groups resembled the consumption of water when there was no choice; single rats drank significantly more fluid than the other groups. The consumption of water alone by all the groups in the choice conditions was significantly less than that by groups which had no choice; it also differed in that the groups containing eight and two rats drank more water than the groups containing four rats and one rat per group. In choice conditions there was a relationship between the size of the groups and the extent to which they diluted their alcohol—individual rats and groups of four rats drank their alcohol in a more concentrated form than groups of other sizes. Throughout the experiment there was a chronological increase in the alcohol consumption of the individual rats, and those housed in groups of four and eight. This increase did not occur in those grouped two to a cage or in those drinking water alone.

The implications of group drinking

It is clear from these results that the social environment among rats affects the quantity and concentration of alcohol which they consume. Their alcohol consumption is a manifestation of group size. This is apparent from the fact that consumption of water alone, and total fluid consumption, are influenced by group characteristics in an entirely different way from alcohol consumption. Forsander (1966) considers that alcohol self-selection by animals can be most satisfactorily explained in terms of the different species' and individuals' metabolic alcohol tolerance, but he does not attempt to explain the mechanism by which the self-selection is determined by the metabolic requirements. In the experiments just described all the animals had the same caloric opportunities. In consequence the metabolic explanation alone does not seem adequate to account for the results. It must therefore be concluded that the visual and social stimuli engendered by the different group arrangements were transmitted to the brain and induced sufficient changes in the alcohol metabolism of the individuals in the groups to make them change their patterns of alcohol consumption with respect to the characteristics of their group formation. Forsander (1966) suggests that the appetite regulating centre is the central control mechanism which regulates the appetite for alcohol and its rate of metabolism. This indicates that the metabolic alterations in the animals result from a series of changes which originate through sensory perception of social environmental stimuli.

Lester (1966) has discussed the possibility of developing animal models for the human alcoholic. He wrote: "Although efforts have been directed towards producing in an animal species those features which distinguish the human alcoholic, such as loss of control and the intoxicated state, these attempts through self-selection experiments have not been successful. This is because the investigator appears to imply that he is in some way privy to the bases on which the animal makes its choice of one fluid or another." The present results and previous experiments (Rick & Wilson, 1966) have demonstrated that there is a relationship between the company in which alcohol is ingested, the concentration which is consumed, and the quantity which is drunk. It seems possible that the experimental method could be used and interpreted as an animal model resembling the human situation. However the perception and interpretation of social stimuli by animals, and by humans, have been little investigated and can only be measured crudely. The mechanisms by which they influence alcohol metabolism can only be surmised.

The pharmacology of the taste for alcohol

One of the principal factors which characterizes the consumption of alcohol among individuals and races is the taste for drink. This becomes obvious when the quantities and types of alcohol drunk by different cultures are compared (Lolli, Sevianni Golder & Luzzatto-Fegiz, 1958; Sadoun, Lolli & Silverman, 1965). In these surveys the quantities of different types of alcohol drunk have been related to the risk of alcoholism in the groups (Leake & Silverman, 1966). In none of these surveys, however, has the taste for alcohol been measured in practice even among samples of the population under investigation.

During the past three years the taste for alcohol has been measured among staff and students in the University of Dublin by asking individuals to taste different concentrations of alcohol in water ranging from 0·25% to 64% absolute ethyl alcohol (McAirt, O'Brien, Rolfe & Wilson, 1968). The method for measuring and confirming the taste threshold for alcohol was based on that developed by Harris & Kalmus (1949) for determining the taste threshold to phenylthiocarbamide (PTC).

Two different tastes for alcohol can be detected. At lower concentrations alcohol and water mixtures are differentiated from water by the development of a sweet taste in the mixture. This taste is sometimes described as being like an almond or as slightly bitter. Although it is difficult to define with accuracy, it can be differentiated from water quite definitely at a mean threshold of $2·4 \pm 0·7\%$ alcohol in the 167 observations made in the Irish sample under investigation. At higher concentrations of alcohol the sweet taste changes to a burning taste. The taste threshold for the burning taste is $13·6 \pm 1·1\%$ absolute alcohol in water (Figure 2). The sweet taste may however change to bitter-sweet as the alcohol concentration increases. The appearance of the burning taste is quite definite and the sweet taste is merged, or disappears, into the former when it is detected. The burning taste appears to be an all-or-none phenomenon. It can be compared with the all-or-none phenomenon of pain in the skin whereas the sweet taste can be compared with the qualitative sensation of touch in the skin. The burning taste is usually recognized in fortified drinks, although it is also a necessary ingredient

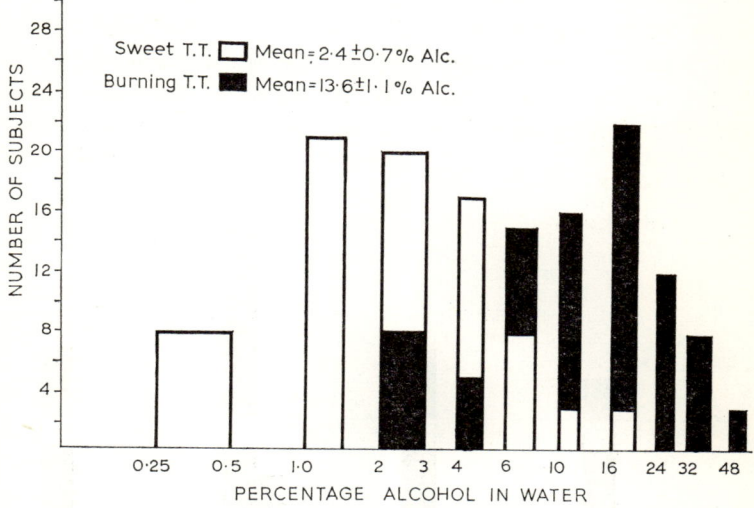

FIG. 2. The frequency distribution of the taste threshold for sweet and burning tastes of alcohol. Total number of subjects in sample for sweet threshold was fifty-eight. Total number of sample for burning threshold was eighty-nine.

for producing the 'kick' or palatable taste which characterises wines and sherries and which differentiates them from a mixture of essential oils and colouring matter in water.

The taste-threshold to PTC was also investigated in the subjects examined in Dublin. They had the characteristic bimodal frequency distribution for this compound which is found in sample populations described elsewhere (Harris & Kalmus, 1949). Metronidazole, like PTC has a lingering kind of bitter taste though its persistence is not so great as that of the other compound.

Unlike PTC metronidazole was found to have a unimodal frequency distribution curve. Neither of these compounds has the capacity of alcohol to produce a definite change in taste as the concentration is increased.

Although it is possible to assess the appreciation of taste for alcohol, this does not necessarily give an indication of its relevance to the desire of individuals to drink alcoholic beverages. It has been reported that metronidazole reduces the desire for alcoholic drinks among some invididuals (Bonfiglio & Donadio, 1967), although there is no evidence that it has any effect on alcohol

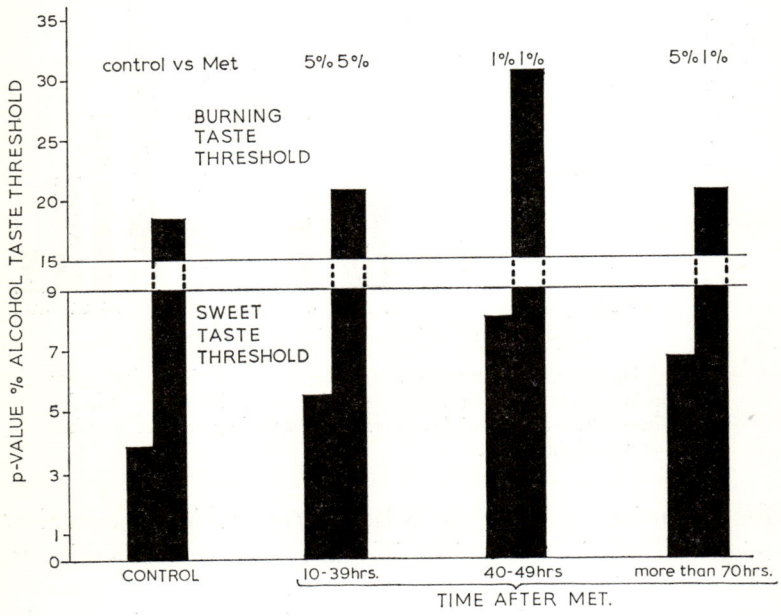

FIG. 3. The effect of metronidazole on the sweet and burning taste thresholds to alcohol. The mean sweet taste thresholds are indicated in the left hand columns; the mean burning taste thresholds are indicated in the right hand columns. The levels of significance of the control taste threshold values in comparison with the taste thresholds at various times after the last administration of metronidazole are shown in the top line. Metronidazole was administered orally in a dose of 200 mg four times during the twenty-four hour period following the control tests.

metabolising enzymes *in vivo* (Fried & Fried, 1966). Observation of patients has suggested that it may alter their appreciation of the alcoholic drinks which they consume.

During the past three years in Dublin the effect of metronidazole on the taste threshold to alcohol has been examined. The sweet and burning taste thresholds to alcohol were measured in forty subjects before the administration of 200 mg of metronidazole four times during a twenty-four hour period. The taste threshold was then measured again within four hours of the time of taking the last tablet and at intervals thereafter. The effects of metronidazole on the taste threshold to alcohol are shown in Figure 3.

This figure shows that metronidazole significantly increases both the sweet and burning taste threshold to alcohol. The effect reaches its maximum forty to sixty nine hours after administration of the drug. Although the taste threshold is beginning to diminish after seventy hours, more extended studies indicate that the taste threshold may still be high for five days or longer after the last administration of the drug. Further unpublished evidence indicates that at least part of the effect of metronidazole on the taste for alcohol is produced by a direct effect on the taste receptors in the mouth. This is understandable because it has been shown that metronidazole is excreted in the saliva.

Conclusions

It has been demonstrated that differences in the sizes of groups of rats have a significant effect on their consumption of alcohol. The experiments were designed in such a way that this social influence could not primarily be attributed to a metabolic effect as Forsander (1966) has defined the term. In his experiments, in which the effects of hormones on the metabolism of alcohol were investigated, the rats were caged individually or in groups of a standard size. In normal circumstances rats, like humans, are accustomed to the formation of social groups. It can therefore be concluded that social environmental stimuli are normally affecting behaviour, and the experimental results which have been described demonstrate that these are sufficiently powerful to influence alcohol consumption.

Although Richter (1956) has investigated and measured the concentrations of alcohol which rats are prepared to drink, and many other workers have elaborated on his original methods, the interpretation of the experimental findings has raised many difficulties, the chief of which has been that of relating the acceptance or refusal of alcohol in rats to a comparable physiological measurement in man. Lester (1966) admits that "both taste and smell influence the selection of alcohol, but rats and mice may be affected to differing degrees". The same comment could be applied to man. In spite of these observations, all the investigations in both human beings and animals up to the present have attempted to interpret refusal or consumption of alcohol in terms of metabolic, endocrine, or genetic factors. The difficulty in interpreting Richter's observations lies in the fact that the sense of taste in animals cannot be appreciated or measured by human experimenters.

The demonstration, in the experiments described here, that the sense of taste to alcohol can be measured in man and has characteristics which separate it from the taste of other compounds, suggests that Richter's hypothesis about the existence of a taste threshold to alcohol in animals is correct. Metronidazole alters the taste for alcohol significantly in human beings, and human beings under treatment with metronidazole state that their appreciation of alcoholic beverages is so altered that they prefer not to drink them. It is possible that the different effects produced on alcoholic consumption in mice by the administration of sugars having different sweetnesses may be explained by alterations in the ability of the animals to appreciate and select the alcohol which they were offered at the same time (Iida, 1960).

It is therefore clear that sensations which occur in the peripheral sense organs, of a visual, auditory and tactile nature in response to external stimuli, or which occur as a result of olfactory (Kahn & Stellar, 1960; Rodgers & McClearn, 1962) or of taste stimulation, are capable of producing significant effects on alcohol consumption in individuals in normal circumstances. Forsander (1966) has pointed out that the two principal factors which influence the consumption of alcohol are the environment and soma. The principal and primary problem in studying the etiology of alcohol consumption, and subsequently, the development of alcoholism, lies in understanding and assessing how the activity of the sense organs influences the intake of alcohol, in turn how this affects somatic function, and finally how intoxication ensues. Several interacting forces influence the consumption and effects of alcohol, but neither the interplay of these forces nor their form has ever tentatively been worked out (Lester, 1966). An attempt to analyse the forces which are in action and their mutual relationships is presented in Figure 4.

The factors which have been defined here and by other workers, and which influence the intake of alcohol, are shown on the left side of the figure as the environmental factors. These factors excite somatic activity in specific sensory organs. In appropriate circumstances environmental stimuli can excite an appetite for alcohol through the appetite regulatory centre. This causes alcohol to be consumed but the degree of stimulation and response of the taste organs will determine the quantity of alcohol actually drunk. The activity of these organs is directly or indirectly under the control of various specific control centres in the brain stem. Consumption of alcohol produces various psychological effects in the upper part of the brain, through indirect mechanisms. The principal physiological effect is the appetite for alcohol. This, in turn, stimulates endocrine and enzyme activity which enables the body to metabolise the alcohol which has been consumed. As the appetite for alcohol is increased,

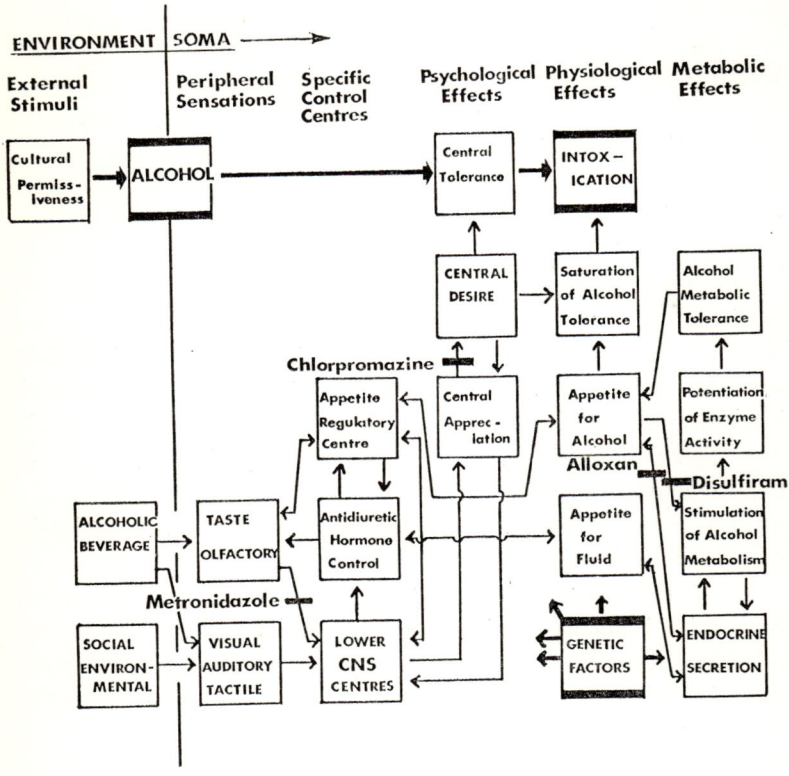

FIG. 4. The interacting forces which influence consumption and effects of alcohol. The external stimuli which excite specific sensory organs are indicated on the left side of the figure. The chain of events by which initial consumption of alcohol initiates the sensory stimuli which activate control centres in the brain stem are shown. Psychological effects arise in the higher brain centres in response to the central nervous stimulation. Physiological effects subsequently occur in the body tissues in response to the intake of alcohol; these can be interpreted in terms of the metabolic and endocrine changes shown on the right side of the diagram. The points where some of the drugs, which are used to control the consumption of alcohol, may act in interrupting the chain of interacting processes are shown. The forces generally considered to be of prime importance in the alcohol-taking culture are indicated by heavy blacks.

enzyme activity is potentiated and the alcohol metabolic tolerance is raised. If, however, the alcohol tolerance is saturated, intoxication ensues. Various drugs are known to influence the consumption of alcohol, including metronidazole, chlorpromazine, disulfiram and alloxan. The points at which they probably exert their effects are shown in Figure 4.

The responses of a cell to any external stimuli are genetically determined, and so these built-in factors which influence all physiological mechanisms are shown in the lower right corner. Leake & Silverman (1966) have pointed out that the intensity of action of alcohol at social levels, as at cellular or organ levels, depends on dose and on the mass of alcohol per mass of living material. When the environmental factors alone are analysed in relation to the quantity of alcohol consumed by individuals in the culture, the cultural incidence of alcoholism and intoxication are generally considered only in relation to genetic factors which are ill-defined with respect to alcohol consumption. These factors are indicated in heavy blocks in the figure. When the relationship of the external stimuli to the cultural characteristics is analysed with respect to the activity induced in individual sensory organs, and the subsequent physiological and metabolic chain reaction is traced, the interaction of the social pharmacological, and the individual pharamacological effects of alcohol will become clearer and the mechanisms by which the actions of drugs prevent the occurrence of alcoholism in the culture might be understood.

REFERENCES

Alexander, F. (1963). Alcohol and behavioural disorder—alcoholism. In *Alcohol and Civilisation*, pp. 130–141, Ed. by Lucia, S. P. London: McGraw-Hill.

Bonfiglio, G. & Donadio, G. (1967). Results of the clinical testing of a new drug 'Metronidazole' in the treatment of chronic alcoholism. *Brit. J. Addict.*, **62**, 349–255.

Forsander, O., Kohonen, J. & Suomalainen, H. (1958). Physiological alcohol consumption. *Quart. J. Stud. Alc.*, **19**, 379–387.

Forsander, O. (1962). Everybody does not like alcohol. *Alkohopolitik*, **25**, 186–188.

Forsander, O. A. (1966). Metabolism of rats as related to voluntary alcohol consumption. *Psychosomatic Medicine*, **28**, 521–528.

Forsander, O. A. (1966). The role of metabolism in alcohol consumption. In *Biochemical Factors in Alcoholism*. London: Pergamon Press.

Fried, R. & Fried, L. W. (1966). The effect of Flagyl on xanthine oxidase and alcohol dehydrogenase. *Biochem. Pharm.*, **15**, 1890–1894.

Harris, H. & Kalmus, H. (1949). The measurement of taste sensitivity to phenylthiourea (P.T.C.). *Ann. Eugen.*, **15**, 24–31.

Iida, S. (1960). Experimental Studies on the craving for alcohol III. The relationship between alcoholic craving and carbohydrate metabolism. *Jap. J. Pharmac.*, **10**, 15–20.

Jellinek, E. M. (1946). Phases in the drinking history of alcoholics. Analysis of a survey conducted by the official organ of Alcoholics Anonymous. *Quart. J. Stud. Alc.*, **7**, 1–88.

Jellinek, E. M. (1952). Phases of alcohol addiction. *Quart. J. Stud. Alc.*, **13**, 673–684.

Kahn, M. & Stellar, E. (1960). Alcohol preference in normal and anosmic rats. *J. Comp. Physiol. Psychol.*, **53**, 571–575.

Leake, C. D. & Silverman, M. (1966). *Alcoholic Beverages in Clinical Medicine*. Chicago: Year Book Medical Publishers Inc.

Lester, D. (1966). Self-selection of alcohol by animals, human variation, and the etiology of alcoholism. *Quart. J. Stud. Alc.*, **27**, 395–438.

Lolli, G., Sevianni, E., Golder, G. M. & Luzzatto-Fegiz, P. (1958). Alcohol in Italian Culture. Monograph 3. Connectient: Yale Center of Alcohol Studies, New Haven.

Marconi, J. I. (1959). The concept of alcoholism. *Quart. J. Stud. Alc.*, 216.

McAirt, J. P., O'Brien, C., Rolfe, D. A. H. & Wilson, C. W. M., in the press. A taste for drink and its control. *Irish J. Med. Sci.*

Richter, C. P. (1967). Production and control of alcoholic craving in rats. *Neuropharmacology;* Transactions of the First Conference, Ed. by Abramson, H. A., pp. 39–146. New York: Josiah Macey Jr. Foundation.

Rick, J. T. & Wilson, C. W. M. (1966). Alcohol preference in the rat: its relationship to total fluid consumption. *Quart. J. Stud. Alc.*, **37**, 337–458.

Rodgers, D. A. & McClearn, G. E. (1962). Alcohol preference of mice. In *Roots of Behaviour*. Ed. by Bliss, E. L., pp. 68–95. New York: Hoeber.

Sadoun, R., Lolli, G. & Silverman, M. (1965). Drinking in French Culture. *Monograph* 5. New Jersey: Rutgers Centre of Alcohol Studies.

Wilson, C. W. M. & Mapes, R. E. A. (1964). The effects of group composition on drug action. In *Animal Behaviour and Drug Action*. Ed. by Steinberg, H., de Reuck, A. V. S. & Knight, J. London: J. & A. Churchill.

Wilson, C. W. M. (1968). Drug dependence or drug abuse? In *Adolescent Drug Dependence*, pp. 139–158. Ed. by Wilson, C. W. M. London: Pergamon Press.

APPENDIX

CANNABIS AND ALCOHOL: IS THERE A SCIENTIFIC BASIS FOR COMPARISON?

An advertisement appeared in the London *Times* on July 24, 1967 advocating reform of the law controlling the smoking and possession of cannabis. This advertisement stated that cannabis is taken by normal persons for the purpose of enhancing sensory experience, and implies that they wish to use it wholly as a pleasure-giving drug. A section of society is therefore attempting to alter the law so that cannabis can be used as a means of enjoyment (Knaffl-Lenz, 1952) or in order that it can be used by individuals so as to induce a desirable state of supernormality (Wilson, 1965). To justify this type of use for pleasure, the advertisers state that the pharmacological properties of cannabis are sufficiently outstanding to warrant its therapeutic use in medical practice.

The proposed therapeutic uses of cannabis are as a sedative and anti-depressant in psychiatry and for treatment of the abstinence syndrome (Rolls and Stafford-Clark, 1954). Other proposals are as an anti-bacterial agent for local application as ear-drops, in the prevention of obstetric staphylococcal mastitis, and as a prophylactic ointment against infection in veterinary surgeries and mortuaries (Krejčí, 1965). It is claimed that scientific evidence substantiates the advertisers' statement. On the basis of their statement the advertisers make a plea that the law controlling the use of cannabis should be altered.

Stockings (1947) said that cannabis itself is satisfactory for the treatment of depressive states but is incapable of producing complete or lasting remission of symptoms. As several specific and effective drugs have recently been produced for the treatment of the abstinence syndrome (Fink *et al.*, 1968), it appears that the time for using cannabis by inhalation in the treatment of narcotic withdrawal has long been past. WHO has examined the possibility of using cannabis extract for its anti-bacterial properties, and does not consider that there is any justification for the medical use of such extracts (United Nations Secretariat, 1961). I, therefore, know of no scientific or clinical evidence which justifies the use of cannabis or its derivatives for therapy at present, and an extensive period of laboratory investigation will be necessary before their pharmacological actions are sufficiently defined to warrant their future use.

Following the *Times* advertisement it has become the fashion to try to justify the social use of cannabis by drawing comparisons between the actions and use of cannabis and alcohol. It is claimed that "Cannabis is less harmful than alcohol". Supporting evidence for this claim is not provided. Its analysis is difficult because the chemical constitution of the two compounds is totally different, relatively little is known about the chemical pharmacology of cannabis and there is no known method of comparing them in terms of their clinical pharmacology. Clinical, epidemiological, and social evidence must, therefore, be used to examine the validity of the assertion. Use of such evidence could be criticised because the data about cannabis must be drawn largely from population samples which differ ethnically or culturally from those in the western civilisation which drink alcohol. The justification of the validity of such comparisons lies in the fact that the cultures which are being compared have each been using their specific drug for a long period and so the drug effects in the different samples can be assessed and evaluated.

Damage to the Individual

In terms of damage to the individual caused by cannabis, the mean incidence of patients diagnosed as having schizophreniform psychoses or specific cannabis psychoses following cannabis self-administration was 22.5% among psychiatric hospital admissions in Brazil, India, Morocco and Nigeria in 1957 and 1964 (Wilson, 1968).

In terms of damage to the individual caused by alcohol, the

evidence about patients diagnosed as having alcoholic psychoses in relation to hospital admissions has been analysed by Walsh (1968) for England and Wales, Scotland and Ireland. He found that the crude rates for first admissions to psychiatric facilities in Dublin, Ireland, with a diagnosis of either alcoholic addiction or alcoholic psychosis were 40.2 for males and 7.8 for females per 100,000 population giving an overall rate of 34.4. This value was twice that for Scotland and five times that for England. The Irish figures corresponded to a first admission rate of 25% for males and 5% for females of all admissions to psychiatric facilities in Dublin, who had a diagnosis of alcoholism and alcoholic psychosis.

Damage to Society

Damage to society caused by cannabis and alcohol also can be analysed in relation to *the incidence of crime* committed while individuals are under the influence of these drugs. Lambo (1965) has shown that 53% of those who committed crime, in three West African countries, carried it out while under the influence of cannabis and that culpable driving and burglary were the most frequent offences. Of the male users of cannabis admitted to psychiatric hospitals in Nigeria, Lambo (1965) concluded that 30% had disorders of behaviour and character. In Brazil, Cordeiro de Farias (1955) came to the conclusion that a person with criminal propensities may translate his criminal thoughts into action under the influence of cannabis; Charen and Perelman (1946) quote examples of this in the USA, and Ames (1958) cites an example in South Africa. In an analysis of British ex-prisoners, Maule and Cooper (1966) have shown that 56% were heavy drinkers. Of these, 89% considered that alcohol played a part in causing them to commit their last crime, and 29% of them stated that theft, breaking and entering or fraud was the last offence. Gerchow (1964) has carried out a careful analysis of the relationship between the occurrence of crime and the consumption of alcohol and has found that 10-20% of crimes which are committed in Germany, Holland and Britain are associated with consumption of alcohol. He has also shown amongst Germans that about one third of the offences were associated with theft. Gerchow concludes from his analysis that criminal impulses are facilitated, caused and furthered by alcohol.

Disturbances in marital and family relationships may be caused by cannabis and alcohol, and in this way both drugs can cause damage to the social culture. In Morocco, Benabud (1957) has shown that 38.5% of 824 patients with a positive Wasserman test were cannabis users, 41% of his cases were unmarried and 19% were divorced. In the USA there was 100% sexual promiscuity among 19 cannabis users (Markovitz and Myers, 1964), and a recent survey in Britain (Linken, 1967) shows a prevalance rate of 18.2% drug use among a sample of adolescents attending a VD centre. Their drug of choice was hashish. Lambo (1965) has shown that 26% of the criminal offences in West African countries among cannabis users were of a sexual nature. Maule and Cooper (1966) found that 70% of their ex-prisoners who were heavy drinkers, and who had ever been married, had broken marriages. The relationship between alcohol and sexual offences particularly those in which children were involved has been examined by Gerchow (1964) who has shown that 11-25% of individuals carrying out the offences were under the influence of alcohol, and that about 50% of the offenders attributed their action to the influence of the alcohol.

Social Welfare and Work Capacity

Another way in which these drugs can produce effects detrimental to an individual's contribution to the social welfare is through their action on his work capacity. Markovitz and Myers (1944) and the Mayor's Committee on Marijuana (1944) found that marijuana users had extremely poor and irregular work records. Wilson and Linken (1968) have analysed the relationship between intellectual ability and psychiatric states in cannabis users and their evidence appears to show that the use of cannabis impairs intellectual and social performance particularly among students. Glatt and Hills (1965) have analysed the occupational behaviour patterns among English alcoholic employees. Their evidence shows that alcoholism caused loss of working time, and diminished efficiency and social performance.

In relation to society, therefore, cannabis, like alcohol, can produce anti-social behaviour among an unidentifiable proportion of the culture which uses it, and gives rise to impaired intellectual ability which lasts for a variable period among the majority of users.

No evidence can be adduced to justify alteration of the law controlling the use of cannabis on the grounds of its therapeutic usefulness. Comparison of the effects of alcohol and cannabis on the individual and society demonstrates that they are equally harmful. The fact that western society has learned the dangers and disadvantages of alcohol after long use does not justify removal of control from cannabis so that western culture can start to use it. This would merely allow the introduction of an equally dangerous, but hitherto unknown, second social drug into the western culture. Cannabis has a further serious disadvantage in comparison with alcohol; namely its consumption is associated with the use of other more damaging and dangerous drugs (Wilson and Linken, 1968; Wilson, 1968). I therefore, consider that there is no scientific or social justification at present to support the demand that the law controlling the use of cannabis should be modified in any way.

REFERENCES

Ames, F. (1958). *J. Ment. Sci.*, **104**, 972–999.
Benabud, A. (1957). *Bull. Narcotics*, **9**:4, 1–20.
Charen, S. and Perelman, L. (1946). *Am. J. Psychiat.*, **102**, 674–682.

Cordeiro de Farais, R. (1955). *Bull. Narcotics*, **7,** 5–19.
Fink, M., Zaks, A., Sharoff, R., Mora, A., Bruner, A., Levitt, S., & Freedman, A. (1968). Committee on Problems of Drug Dependence, thirtieth Meeting, 5306–5313, Washington: Nat. Acad. Sci.
Gerchow, J. (1964). Proc. 27th Int. Congr. on Alcohol and Alcoholism, **2,** 49–60.
Glatt, M. M. and Hills, D. R. (1965). *Brit. J. Addict.*, **61,** 71–78.
Knaffl-Lenz, E. (1952). *Bull. Narcotics*, **4,** 1–8.
Krejčí, Z. (1965), in Ciba Foundation Study Group, **21,** 49. London: Churchill.
Lambo, T. A. (1965). *Bull. Narcotics*, **17:1,** 3–13.
Linken, A. (1967). Young Minds at Risk. London: Nat. Assoc. for Mental Health.
Markovitz, E. and Myers, H. J. (1944). *War Medicine*, **6,** 382–391.
Maule, H. A. and Cooper, J. (1966). *Brit. J. Addict.*, **61,** 201–212.
Mayor's Committee on Marijuana (1944). Lancaster, U.S.A.: Jacques Cattrell Press.
Rolls, E. J. and Stafford-Clark, D. (1954). *Guy's Hosp. Rep.*, **103,** 330–336.
Stockings, S. T. (1947). *Brit. med. J.*, **1,** 918–922.
United Nations Secretariat (1961). *Document E/CN 7/409.*
Walsh, D. (1968). *J. Irish Med. Ass.*, **61,** 153–156.
Wilson, C. W. M. (1965). *Lancet*, **2,** 496–7
Wilson, C. W. M. (1968). in *Adolescent Drug Dependence*, 381–488, Ed. by Wilson, C. W. M. Oxford: Pergamon Press.
Wilson, C. W. M. and Linken, A. (1968), in *Adolescent Drug Dependence*, 93–138, Ed. by Wilson, C. W. M. Oxford: Pergamon Press.

ADDICTIVE DRUGS CAUSE SUPPRESSION OF PARADOXICAL SLEEP WITH WITHDRAWAL REBOUND

Ian Oswald, J. I. Evans and S. A. Lewis

Department of Psychiatry, University of Edinburgh

Drugs of addiction are taken because, initially at least, they make possible an escape from reality. Those most vulnerable are people whose personalities bring them conflicts and anxieties, but little solace, from contacts with the real world. Given access to the drugs, they are enabled to escape to a less harsh world, a world more removed from reality and nearer to dreams. Formerly we thought of two principal states of our lives, the waking state and the sleeping state. We must now accept that there are three basic life states—the waking state and two different sleep states (Oswald, 1962; Snyder, 1963; Hartmann, 1967). The last two states differ sharply not only in their physiological but in their psychological characteristics. The one is accompanied by a measure of mental life left over from the waking state and is reality-based. The other is accompanied by what Freud called primary process thinking—dreaming, and escape from reality.

Drugs and sleep

The wealth of recent research into the two kinds of sleep has led to an examination of the relation between drugs which produce escape from reality and the state of sleep accompanied by dreaming, which is most commonly termed paradoxical sleep or REM (rapid eye movement) sleep. The present evidence suggests that all the common *drugs of addiction at first suppress paradoxical sleep and that after their withdrawal a rebound excess occurs*, and that this second disturbance of brain physiology may take weeks to disappear. Whether we should regard the effect of such drugs on paradoxical (or dreaming) sleep as a basic correlate of their capacity to produce reality-escape and addiction, or whether we should regard it as a largely irrelevant phenomenon which has attracted interest merely because it is conveniently measurable, is unsettled. The evidence, however, steadily lends endorsement to the first conclusion.

It will be as well to mention why it has now had to be accepted that there are three basic organismic states. We will not dwell upon the differences between wakefulness and the sleep states but will outline differences between the two kinds of sleep. Let us first emphasize that one is not 'light' sleep and the other 'deep' sleep, for either adjective could be applied to each state, depending upon the variables chosen—the two adjectives are better avoided. The two forms of sleep, orthodox (slow wave or NREM sleep) and paradoxical (desynchronized or REM sleep) differ. In paradoxical sleep the EEG appearances are nearer to those of wakefulness, the eyeballs make recurrent rapid conjugate movements (Dement & Kleitman, 1957), the skeletal muscles are much more flaccid (Berger, 1961; Jacobson *et al.*, 1964), the anterior horn cells being subject to descending inhibitory impulses (Pompeiano, 1967) and the spinal monosynaptic reflexes almost abolished (Hodes & Dement, 1964). Yet there are more brief body movements (Oswald *et al.*, 1963), the blood flow to the brain is doubled to a higher flow than that of wakefulness (Reivich *et al.*, 1968), the respiration, blood pressure and heart rate become irregular (Snyder *et al.*, 1964), the penis becomes erect (Fisher *et al.*, 1965; Karacan *et al.*, 1966), urine output decreases (Mandell *et al.*, 1966), plasma free fatty acids rise (Gottschalk *et al.*, 1966) as does whole body oxygen consumption (Brebbia & Altshuler, 1965) and the accompanying mental life is readily discriminable from that reported after deliberate awakening from orthodox sleep (Monroe et al., 1965) and has the character of dreaming.

The two kinds of sleep alternate and in man there are about five periods of paradoxical sleep nightly, totalling about 23% of sleep. Orthodox sleep comes first and lasts about an hour. The transition to paradoxical sleep is generally abrupt, with the signs of loss of muscle tone, a low voltage EEG, often with saw-tooth frontal waves, and rapid eye movements. The reverse transition is usually marked by a body movement and a brief period of drowsiness (stage 1 sleep) before orthodox sleep (stage 2) with EEG spindles is resumed. The percentage of paradoxical sleep in the whole night, the delay to its first onset and its distribution through the night provide measurable indices of brain function. The effect of drugs can be studied as follows: a first laboratory night is undertaken but the results discarded because of a small 'first-night' effect (Agnew et al., 1966). A series of placebo nights then provide mean base-line values. The drug is next given and the altered pattern of sleep quantified. The drug may be continued for several nights or for weeks and the gradual disappearance of its first effect seen. Withdrawal of the drug, if followed by recordings of sleep for several nights or weeks, reveals deviations from the base-line means assessable by elementary statistical procedures, or, frequently, extreme deviations far outside the normal range.

The first application of this type of procedure to the study of addiction revealed that when patients addicted to dexamphetamine, dexamphetamine-barbiturate mixtures, or phenmetrazine, continued to take their accustomed drugs, the proportion of whole-night paradoxical sleep was normal. When the drug was withdrawn, abnormalities appeared. When the drug was restored, these abnormalities of brain function disappeared, and reappeared when the drug was withdrawn once again. The abnormalities included excess whole-night paradoxical sleep, with a particular excess in the early part of the night, and abnormally early onset of paradoxical sleep—the normal forty-five minute minimum delay between orthodox sleep onset and first rapid eye movements being reduced to as little as four minutes (Oswald & Thacore, 1963). Up to two months elapsed before these abnormalities resolved (Figure 1). The fact that amphetamine suppresses paradoxical sleep when first given, was demonstrated by Rechtschaffen and Maron (1964), so that, in the case

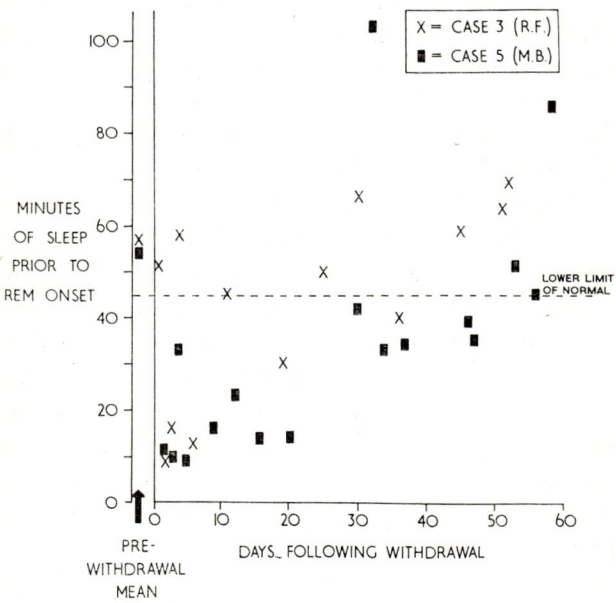

FIG. 1. After withdrawal of dexamphetamine (case 3) and Drinamyl (case 5) there are very short delays between first falling asleep and first rapid eye movements (REMS) of the first period of paradoxical sleep. Case 5 on the eighteenth and twentieth days still had values as short as 14 min. Slowly, abnormal values disappear and normal values of over 45 min appear established after 50 days (from Oswald and Thacore, 1963).

of the previously mentioned addicts, the normal amount of paradoxical sleep while taking the drug must be interpreted as a manifestation of tolerance.

The experiments illustrated the naivety of the then current distinction between drugs of addiction and drugs of habituation. Only the former were supposed to provoke 'physiological' abnormalities on drug withdrawal, so that the Interdepartmental Committee on Drug Addiction of the Ministry of Health (1961) had not accepted that amphetamine was an addictive substance. The distinction between 'physiological' and 'psychological' dependence was a relic of a past in which medical men regarded the body and soul as dichotomous, whereas today we believe that mental events are determined by brain (physiological) events. The most characteristic feature of any abstinence syndrome is the craving. As this was merely 'psychological' it was accorded little importance. It is, however, absurd not to recognize that it has a basis in brain function, as yet unascertainable, just as all drugs which are said to produce 'psychological dependence' do so because they affect brain physiology and change the person's feelings and thoughts. Given sophisticated techniques for measuring brain function, 'physiological' features of dependence and abstinence will inevitably become more and more frequently reported—the amphetamine and phenmetrazine evidence was but an early example.

Hypnotics

The barbiturates also suppress paradoxical sleep, not merely reducing its duration and delaying its onset but reducing also its intensity, as judged by a significant reduction in the profusion of accompanying rapid eye movements (Oswald *et al.*, 1963; Baekeland, 1967). The profusion of rapid eye movements is correlated with the degree of 'activity' of the accompanying dream (Dement & Wolpert, 1958; Berger & Oswald, 1962).

Withdrawal of amylobarbitone sodium following its regular administration for eighteen consecutive nights led to rebound abnormalities comparable to those after amphetamine withdrawal (Oswald & Priest, 1965). Despite the short period of

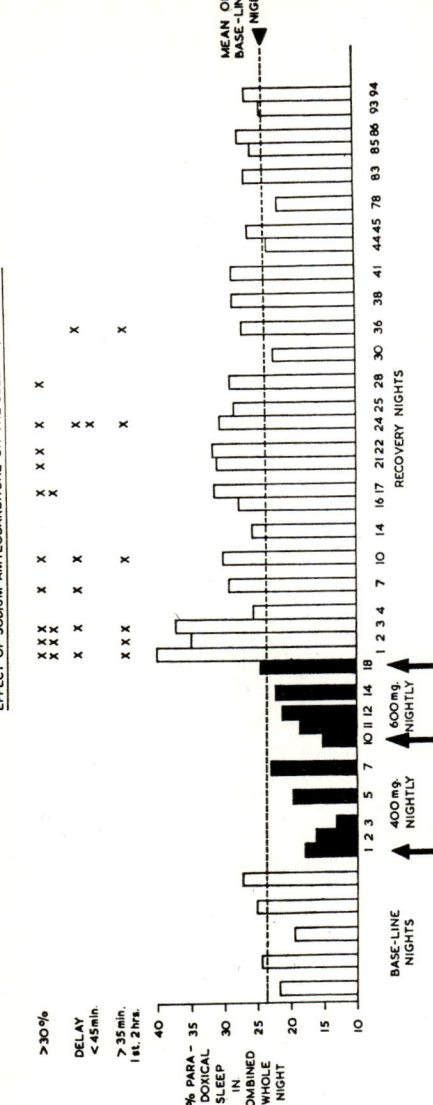

FIG. 2. Effect of sodium amylobarbitone on the sleep of two men who serve as their own controls. The hypnotic at first causes suppression of paradoxical sleep and withdrawal a rebound increase. The time scale is not linear. Where either or both volunteers spent over 30 per cent of the whole night in paradoxical sleep, had a delay of less than 45 min between first falling asleep and first rapid eye movements of paradoxical sleep, or spent more than 35 min of the first two hours of sleep in paradoxical sleep, a cross has been placed over the night concerned. The crosses, which indicate extreme or frankly abnormal values, are seen only after drug withdrawal and peter out in the sixth recovery week (from Oswald & Priest, 1965).

exposure to the drug, abnormalities did not completely subside till the sixth week after withdrawal (Figure 2). Similar findings were made in a parallel study of the non-barbiturate hypnotic, nitrazepam. In each case withdrawal of the drug was accompanied, among other unpleasant subjective effects, by nightmares. We had earlier seen vivid nightmares provoked by withdrawal of tranylcypromine from an addict (Le Gassicke et al., 1965).

Withdrawal of all three drugs had caused a very early onset, and an early-night excess of paradoxical sleep. Taken in conjunction with other observations, in which tryptophan had been found to cause both nightmares and increased paradoxical sleep in narcoleptics, we were led to postulate that increase of 'pressure' towards paradoxical sleep could increase the intensity of the accompanying dream experience (Evans & Oswald, 1966). Corroborative evidence was obtained by Lewis (1968) who re-scrutinized the records of the nitrazepam experiment and found that the profuseness of rapid eye movements had been increased above baseline levels by drug withdrawal, consistent with more 'active' dreams. Kales & Jacobson (1967) have observed similar nightmare induction by withdrawal of pentobarbitone and also withdrawal of methyprylon (Noludar). At Edinburgh also we have observed nightmares in all-night studies of withdrawal of drugs from patients addicted to barbiturates (Evans & Lewis, unpublished observations). Pivik & Foulkes (1966) also found that increased 'pressure' towards paradoxical sleep, induced by behavioural techniques, was associated both with increased profusion of rapid eye movements and increased vividness and bizarreness of dreams. The commonly encountered patient who has been taking barbiturates for years, when studied in the laboratory, and when his drugs are withdrawn, reveals a big rebound into high levels of paradoxical sleep, with nightmares. Restoration of the drug within a few nights restores sleep to normal while re-withdrawal of the drug causes a return to the abstinence abnormalities (Figure 3).

We wish to draw special attention to the raised anxiety level of patients whose hypnotics have just been withdrawn. The anxiety is manifest by day, as well as in their nightmares. It is anxiety literally caused by the medication they had been given for possibly only brief periods, but it must be seen as a potent factor

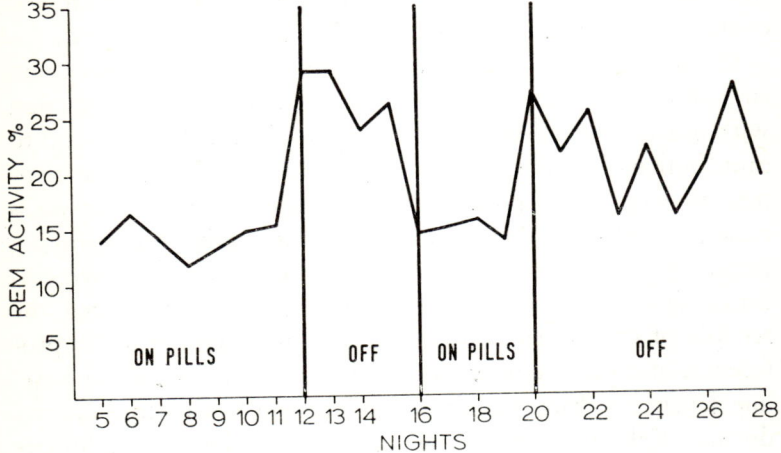

Fig. 3. Subject habituated to 600 mg of Tuinal nocte (quinalbarbitone 300 mg and amylobarbitone 300 mg). Nights on drugs contain low normal quantities of rapid eye movement (REM or paradoxical) sleep. On withdrawal of the drug, there is a marked increase in REM sleep which returns to previous values when the drug is restored. Similarly REM sleep increases when the drugs are finally withdrawn on night 20. (Reproduced from Evans et al., 1968.)

making for prolonged dependence upon hypnotic drugs. To suppose that hypnotics have effects limited to a few hours, or to, at the most, the 48 hours of detectable blood levels is a common error. Rebound sequelae may last for many weeks.

One must further conclude that the vast and increasing consumption of hypnotics is iatrogenic. Consumption of barbiturates doubled in Britain between 1954 and 1959, it doubled in Czechoslovakia between 1958 and 1965 (Vondracek et al., 1968), the absolute expenditure on hypnotics in Australia doubled between

1961 and 1965 (Commonwealth Director General of Health, 1962, 1966), while in the U.S.A. "from 1952 to 1963, the retail sales of sedatives and tranquillisers increased 535 percent" (Department of Health, Education and Welfare, 1967). A major corollary of all this, and one which throws an increasing burden on medical services, is the rise in the use of such drugs for deliberate self-poisoning, admissions for which have increased about tenfold in 10 years in both Edinburgh (Matthew, 1966) and Western Australia (Oswald, 1966) even though successful suicide rates have varied little.

Other drugs

Freeman *et al.*, (1965) reported that meprobamate in clinical doses suppresses paradoxical sleep. Its withdrawal provokes a rebound as illustrated in a study in our laboratory (Figure 4).

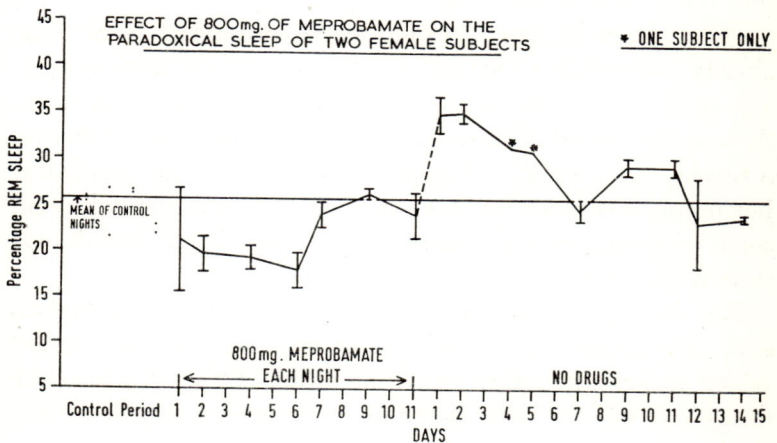

FIG. 4. Effect of meprobamate on paradoxical sleep. After four control nights, the two tablets of drug (800 mg) were given regularly for eleven nights. Initially it suppressed rapid eye movement (REM) sleep but this returned to baseline values by night 7. Withdrawal of the drug was accompanied by a 'rebound' effect, and REM sleep was increased; subsiding to baseline level in a fluctuant way by night 14. (Evans & Lewis, 1968.)

Gresham *et al.*, (1963) reported that alcohol suppressed paradoxical sleep. Despite the great practical difficulties in making prolonged studies of patients entering *delirium tremens*, the work of Gross *et al.*, (1966) and Greenberg & Pearlman (1967) makes it clear that in these circumstances, as with tranylcypromine withdrawal (Le Gassicke *et al.*, 1965; Cramer & Ohlmeier, 1967) the 'pressure' towards paradoxical sleep is dramatic and extreme and that wakefulness may be succeeded directly by paradoxical sleep and nightmares, paradoxical sleep accounting for even 100% of all sleep. Confirmatory observations have been made in our laboratory. It is possible to speculate that the disoriented and terrified state of *delirium tremens* itself may represent a 'breaking through' into the waking state of the mechanisms responsible for paradoxical sleep, and it appears that drugs effective in the treatment of the delirium are drugs which reduce paradoxical sleep (Evans & Lewis, in the press).

Other drugs known to cause dependence, apart from those already mentioned, which cause suppression of paradoxical sleep, are methylphenidate (Baekeland, 1966) and diethylpropion. At least the second of these two provokes a withdrawal rebound (Oswald *et al.*, 1968). Morphine has recently been studied at Lexington, Kentucky by D. C. Kay and his colleagues who find again suppression with subsequent rebound on withdrawal (Kay *et al.*, 1968).

We have emphasized the *rebound increase* of paradoxical sleep as a nocturnal correlate of that unpleasant daytime mood which makes the patient crave his drug. Other psychoactive drugs have different actions and one, reserpine, is notable for the unpleasant mood it induces at a time when its administration (and not withdrawal) is provoking increased paradoxical sleep at night (Hartmann, 1966). It would be wrong to assume that increased paradoxical sleep is always associated with intensification of mood in the direction of unpleasure. There could be circumstances where it was associated with intensification of other emotions such as sexual emotion (Oswald *et al.*, 1966). We should note that there are potent psychoactive drugs which do not induce dependence. Even though these may cause an initial suppression of paradoxical sleep, they have been said not to provoke a rebound on withdrawal, e.g. amitriptyline (Hartmann, 1968), and nialamide (Jouvet, 1967). Interestingly ECT, also used to treat depression, suppresses paradoxical sleep but causes neither rebound (Zarcone *et al.*, 1967) nor addiction. Phenothiazines again are different, small doses of chlorpromazine enhancing, and larger doses decreasing, paradoxical sleep, without obvious rebound (Evans & Lewis, unpublished observations). Although drugs like amitriptyline and chlorpromazine are potent and valuable drugs we may note that they do not give the patient an immediate escape from reality and do not invite abuse.

At present we are able to say that the study of sleep, and especially the phase associated with divorce from reality, has provided a tool for the study of addictive drugs and has made it possible to demonstrate neurophysiological consequences of their administration which extend far into the postwithdrawal period. The drug LSD, while liable to abuse, is generally not regarded as addictive in a manner comparable with amphetamine, but as belonging, perhaps like cannabis, to a different category of mind influencing drugs. Muzio *et al.*, (1965) showed that LSD is unusual in that it enhances paradoxical sleep. Following the initial effect there was again a rebound (in this case a rebound decrease of paradoxical sleep). There is no evidence available for cannabis.

Among the slimming drugs known to cause dependence, amphetamine, phenmetrazine and diethylpropion share the usual effects on paradoxical sleep. In contrast, the new slimming drug fenfluramine, though chemically related, has no effect on paradoxical sleep (Oswald *et al.*, 1968). It will be a matter of interest to see whether or not time will prove fenfluramine to cause dependence, for this would provide one test of the proposition that drugs capable of causing dependence are drugs which both suppress paradoxical sleep and provoke a rebound enhancement of paradoxical sleep when withdrawn.

Finally we should point out that the man who, in puzzling fashion, switches from morphine one day to amphetamine the next and alcohol on the third day is actually maintaining a constant effect on his sleep functions.

Time alone can clarify the link between addictive properties and effects on paradoxical sleep. The link may be direct, it may be chance, or it might be connected with the phenomenon of the rebound and the rapidity of onset of the rebound. An abrupt rebound, manifest in paradoxical sleep, could simply reflect the abrupt rebound distortion of numerous other (less easily measurable) features of central nervous activity.

REFERENCES

Agnew, H. W., Webb.W. B. & Williams, R. L. (1966). The first night effect: an EEG study of sleep. *Psychophysiology*, 2, 263–266.

Baekeland, F. (1966). The effect of methylphenidate on the sleep cycle in man. *Psychopharmacologia (Berl.)*, 10, 179–183.

Baekeland, F. (1967). Pentobarbital and dextroamphetamine sulfate: effects on the sleep cycle in man. *Psychopharmacologia, Berl.*, 11, 388–396.

Berger, R. J. (1961). Tonus of extrinsic laryngeal muscles during sleep and dreaming. *Science*, 134, 840.

Berger, R. J. & Oswald, I. (1962). Eye movements during active and passive dreams. *Science*, 137, 601.

Brebbia, D. R. & Altshuler, K. Z. (1965). Oxygen consumption rate and electroencephalographic stage of sleep. *Science*, 150, 1621–1623.

Commonwealth Director General of Health (1962). *Annual Report 1961–62*. Canberra.

Commonwealth Director General of Health (1966). *Annual Report 1965–66*. Canberra.

Cramer, H. & Ohlmeier, D. (1967). Ein Fall von Tranylcypromin-und-Trifluoperazine-(Jatrosom)-Sucht: Psychopathologische, schlafphysiologische und biochemische Untersuchungen. *Arch. Psychiat. NervKrankh.*, 210, 182–197.

Dement, W. C. & Kleitman, N. (1957). Cyclic variations in EEG during sleep and their relation to eye movements, body motility and dreaming. *Electroenceph. clin. Neurophysiol.*, 9, 673–690.

Dement, W. C. & Wolpert, E. A. (1958). The relation of eye movements, body motility and external stimuli to dream content. *J. exp. Psychol.*, **55**, 543–553.

Department of Health, Education and Welfare (1967). *A report to the President on medical care prices.* Washington, D.C.: U.S. Government Printing Office.

Evans, J. I., Gibb, I., Me, H., Cheetham, M. & Lewis, S. A. Sleep and barbiturates, *Brit. med. J.* in the press.

Evans, J. I. & Lewis, S. A. Treatment of a drug withdrawal state: an EEG sleep study. *Archt. gen. Psychiat* (in press).

Evans, J. I. & Oswald, I. (1966). Some experiments in the chemistry of narcoleptic sleep. *Brit. J. Psychiat.*, **112**, 401–404.

Fisher, C., Gross, J. & Zuch, J. (1965). Cycle of penile erection synchronous with dreaming (REM) sleep. *Arch. gen. Psychiat.*, **12**, 29–44.

Freeman, F. R., Agnew, H. W. & Williams, R. L. (1965). An electroencephalographic study of the effects of meprobamate on human sleep. *Clin. Pharmac. Ther.*, **6**, 172–176.

Gottschalk, L. A., Stone, W. N., Gleser, G. C. & Iacono, J. M. (1966). Anxiety levels in dreams: relation to changes in plasma free fatty acids. *Science*, **153**, 654–657.

Greenberg, R. & Pearlman, C. (1967). Delirium tremens and dreaming. *Am. J. Psychiat.*, **124**, 133–142.

Gresham, S. C., Webb, W. B. & Williams, R. K. (1963). Alcohol and caffeine: effect on inferred visual dreaming. *Science*, **140**, 1226–1227.

Gross, M. M., Goodenough, D., Tobin, M., Halpert, E., Lepore, D., Perlstein, A., Sirota, M., Dibianco, J., Fuller, R. & Kishner, I. (1966). Sleep disturbances and hallucinations in the acute alcoholic psychoses. *J. nerv. ment. Dis.*, **142**, 493–514.

Hartmann, E. (1966). Reserpine: its effect on the sleep-dream cycle in man. *Psychopharmacologia, Berl.*, **8**, 242–247.

Hartmann, E. (1967). *The Biology of Dreaming.* Springfield, Illinois: Charles C. Thomas.

Hartmann, E. (1968). The effect of four drugs on sleep patterns in man. *Psychopharmacologia, Berl.*, **12**, 346–353.

Hodes, R. & Dement, W. C. (1964). Depression of electrically induced reflexes (H-reflexes) in man during low voltage EEG 'sleep'. *Electroenceph. clin. Neurophysiol.*, **17**, 617–629.

Jacobson, A., Kales, A., Lehmann, D. & Hoedemaker, F. S. (1964). Muscle tonus in human subjects during sleep and dreaming. *Exp. Neurol.*, **10**, 418–424.

Jouvet, M. (1967). Mechanisms of the states of sleep: a neuropharmacological approach. *Res. Publ. Ass. nerv. ment. Dis.*, **45**, 86–126.

Kales, A. & Jacobson, A. (1967). Mental activity during sleep: recall studies, somnambulism, and effects of rapid eye movement deprivation and drugs. *Exp. Neurol.* Suppl. 4, 81–91.

Karacan, E., Goodenough, D. R., Shapiro, A. & Starker, S. (1966). Erection cycle during sleep in relation to dream anxiety. *Arch. gen. Psychiat.*, **15**, 183–189.

Kay, D. C., Eisentein, R. B. & Jasinski, D. R., in the press. Morphine effects on human REM state, waking state and NREM sleep. *Psychophysiology*, 5.

Le Gassicke, J., Ashcroft, G. W., Eccleston, D., Evans, J. I., Oswald, I. & Ritson, E. B. (1965). The clinical state, sleep and amine metabolism of a tranylcypromine ('Parnate') addict. *Brit. J. Psychiat.*, **111**, 357–364.

Lewis, S. A. (1968). The quantification of rapid eye movement sleep. In *Drugs and Sensory Functions*, a Biological Council Symposium, Ed. Herxheimer, A., pp. 287–298. London: Churchill.

Mandell, A. J., Chaffey, B., Brill, P., Mandell, M. P., Rodnick, J., Rubin, R. T. & Sheff, R. (1966). Dreaming sleep in man: changes in urine volume and osmolality. *Science*, **151**, 1558–1560.

Matthew, J. (1966). Poisoning by medicaments. *Brit. med. J.*, **2**, 788–790.

Ministry of Health and Department of Health for Scotland (1961). *Drug Addiction. Report of the Interdepartmental Committee.* London: H.M.S.O.

Monroe, L. J., Rechtschaffen, A., Foulkes, D. & Jensen, J. (1965). Discriminability of REM and NREM reports. *J. Pers. soc. Psychol.*, **2**, 456–460.

Muzio, J. N., Roffwarg, H. P. & Kaufman, E. (1966). Alterations in the nocturnal sleep cycle resulting from LSD. *Electroenceph. clin. Neurophysiol.*, **21**, 313–324.

Oswald, I. (1962). Sleep mechanisms: recent advances. *Proc. roy. Soc. Med.*, **55**, 910–912.

Oswald, I. (1966). Preventing self-poisoning. *Brit. med. J.*, **2**, 301. (One page report.)

Oswald, I., Ashcroft, G. W., Berger, R. J., Eccleston, D., Evans, J. I. & Thacore, V. R. (1966). Some experiments in the chemistry of normal sleep. *Brit. J. Psychiat.*, **112**, 391–399.

Oswald, I., Berger, R. J., Jaramillo, R. A., Keddie, K. M. G., Olley, P. C. & Plunkett, G. B. (1963). Melancholia and barbiturates: a controlled EEG body and eye movement study of sleep. *Brit. J. Psychiat.*, **109**, 66–78.

Oswald, I., Jones, H. S. & Mannerheim, J. E. (1968). Effects of two slimming drugs on sleep. *Brit. med. J.*, **1**, 796–799.

Oswald, I. & Priest, R. G. (1965). Five weeks to escape the sleeping pill habit. *Brit. med. J.*, **2**, 1093–1095.

Oswald, I. & Thacore, V. R. (1963). Amphetamine and phenmetrazine addiction: physiological abnormalities in the abstinence syndrome. *Brit. med. J.*, **2**, 427–431.

Pivik, R. & Foulkes, D. (1966). 'Dream deprivation': effects on dream content. *Science*, **153**, 1282–1284.

Pompeiano, O. (1967). The neurophysiological mechanisms of the postural and motor events during desynchronised sleep. *Res. Publ. Ass. nerv. ment. Dis.*, **45**, 351–423.

Rechtschaffen, A. & Maron, L. (1964). Effect of amphetamine on the sleep cycle. *Electroenceph. clin. Neurophysiol.*, **16**, 438–444.

Reivich, M., Isaacs, G., Evarts, E. & Kety, S. (1968). The effect of slow wave sleep and REM sleep on regional cerebral blood flow in cats. *J. Neurochem.*, **15**, 301–306.

Snyder, F. (1963). The new biology of dreaming. *Arch. gen. Psychiat.*, **8**, 381–391.

Snyder, F., Hobson, J. A., Morrison, D. F. & Goldfrank, F. (1964). Changes in respiration, heart rate, and systolic blood pressure in human sleep. *J. appl. Physiol.*, **19**, 417–422.

Vondráček, V., Prokupek, J., Fischer, R. & Ahrenbergova, M. (1968). Recent patterns of addiction in Czechoslovakia. *Brit. J. Psychiat.*, **114**, 285–292.

Zarcone, V., Gulevich, G. & Dement, W. (1967). Sleep and electroconvulsive therapy. *Arch. gen. Psychiat.*, **16**, 567–573.

AN EXPERIMENTAL APPROACH TO THE EXAMINATION OF DRINKING PATTERNS OF ALCOHOLICS

Nancy K. Mello,* Jack H. Mendelson* and
H. Brian McNamee†

*The Stanley Cobb Laboratories for Psychiatric Research
Department of Psychiatry, Massachusetts General Hospital
and Harvard Medical School, Boston, Massachusetts and
The National Center for Prevention and Control of Alcoholism
National Institute of Mental Health, Chevy Chase, Maryland*

Introduction

The aim of this investigation was to study the drinking patterns of chronic alcoholics with particular reference to gambling and motivation for alcohol.

The chief reasons for studying the drinking patterns and behaviour of chronic alcoholics in an experimental situation are as follows.

(1) The periodicity of drinking can be measured directly and, on the basis of these data, inferences can be made about some broader questions concerning alcoholism. At the phenomenological level, it would be of interest to determine whether there are consistencies in drinking patterns within the behaviour of a single individual, or between individuals with comparable histories of alcoholism.

(2) At a more theoretical level, experimental examination of drinking patterns is necessary if the factors which maintain

* Present address: National Center for Prevention and Control of Alcoholism, National Institute of Mental Health, Chevy Chase, Maryland.
† Present address: Department of Psychiatry, The University, Dundee, Scotland.

and perpetuate drinking in an alcoholic person are to be analyzed. The lack of data on the motivational factors which maintain alcoholism has led to the use of concepts like 'need' and 'craving', which are defined by the behaviour that they are used to explain. Motivational factors can be examined by giving subjects a choice between alcohol and money for performance of an operant task. A second approach to establishing an index of motivation for alcohol is to manipulate the requirements of the operant task so as to increase the amount of work or the frustrations encountered in the performance of the task. Operant procedures also permit the comparison of the rate at which alcohol is earned with the rate at which it is consumed—a 'craving' hypothesis would predict consumption of the alcohol as soon as it becomes available. The extent to which changes in these behavioural indices of motivation for alcohol parallel fluctuations in blood alcohol levels, might clarify the biological aspects of motivation. A previous study (Mendelson & Mello, 1966) has suggested that once alcoholics have achieved their relatively high concentration of alcohol in their blood, they are able to titrate the alcohol intake in such a way as to maintain a constant blood alcohol level. This notion is in direct opposition to the prevailing concept of acute loss of control and that an alcoholic rapidly attempts to achieve a state of oblivion by drinking.

(3) Perhaps the most important reason for studying drinking patterns and behaviour of chronic alcoholics in an experimental situation is to allow a systematic examination of the many untested assumptions about how and why an alcoholic drinks. Little attention has been paid to the fact that these assumptions have been derived primarily from retrospective accounts during intervals of sobriety. Apart from the fact that alcoholics are not noted for their truthfulness, it is unlikely that recollection of events during a drinking phase could be accurate.

Observation of the effects of sustained alcohol consumption in man has only been attempted by two groups of investigators.

Doctor & Bernal (1964) conducted a physiological study of two male alcoholics and observed changes in social behaviour during a drinking period of fourteen days. They found that both subjects were silent and uncommunicative when sober, while after drinking they became much more talkative and also demanding and assertive in their general behaviour. Mendelson and his co-workers, in the past seven years, have been concerned with direct observation of the effects of prolonged free alcohol ingestion by alcoholic subjects, in experimental conditions (Mendelson, 1964). Some of their major findings are as follows.

(a) Alcohol withdrawal symptoms occurred as a result of ceasing to drink and not as a consequence of nutritional deficiency, confirming the findings of Isbell *et al.* (1955).

(b) The psychomotor disturbances often designated as physiological criteria for alcohol withdrawal (i.e. tremor, nystagmus and alteration of deep tendon reflexes), may be present also during periods of active alcohol consumption. Their data indicated that the significance of these criteria as specific manifestations of alcohol withdrawal needs to be re-evaluated.

(c) Altered liver and kidney function (other than diuresis) were associated with alcohol consumption, the postulate being that alcohol, in large amounts and without concomitant nutritional deficit, has a direct hepatic and renal toxicity. However, the toxic derangement is reversible.

(d) The observed relationship between alcohol consumption and withdrawal and the onset of alcohol gastritis suggested some new hypothesis concerning the association of alcoholism with gastric disease. Specifically gastro-intestinal tolerance may be an extremely important determinant of the amount and periodicity of ethanol ingestion by the alcoholic individual.

(e) Derangement of memory function during heavy alcohol ingestion and subsequent withdrawal was frequently limited to a selective lacunar amnesia for recent events with relatively little impairment of remote memory processes.

(f) Anxiety and depression increased rather than decreased as subjects consumed alcohol over a long period of time. This finding is in direct opposition to the prevailing notions about the effect of alcohol on the alcoholic.

Drinking patterns in chronic alcoholics have now been examined by giving subjects an opportunity to obtain unlimited alcohol for the performance of a simple operant task. Motivation for alcohol was examined both by direct observation of the rate of drinking and by manipulating the requirements of an operant task so as to increase the amount of work or frustration involved in performance in order to obtain alcohol. The experiment was concerned with the following specific questions.

(1) What is the pattern of alcohol consumption, during a seven day period, of alcoholics given an opportunity to earn as much alcohol as they wished at any time? (2) Given an opportunity to work either for alcohol or for money, will the alcoholic show a consistent preference for one or the other? (3) Does risk-taking behaviour (gambling) vary as a function of blood alcohol level?

Methods and material

Subjects

Fourteen male volunteers between the ages of thirty and forty-five were selected from among a group of inmates at a correctional institution. All the subjects were selected according to the following criteria. (1) A history of chronic alcoholism characterized by spree drinking for a period of at least five years. (2) A past history of alcohol withdrawal symptoms. All had at least experienced tremulousness, nausea and vomiting, following cessation of drinking. Eleven of the subjects had delirium tremens in the past. (3) No evidence of any current major physical illness. (4) No evidence of psychosis or subnormal intelligence. (5) No history of drug addiction or of any current use of medication. (6) No previous convictions for assaultive or aggressive behaviour. (7) The subjects were matched as closely as possible with regard to recent social and economic histories. All were either unmarried or estranged from their spouses and had been sporadically employed in a variety of semi-skilled or non-skilled jobs, with the exception of one subject. All had repeated voluntary admissions or court commitments to the correctional institution for drunkenness. (8) No subject had taken alcohol for at least two weeks before the beginning of the study.

A detailed description of the screening assessment has been given by Mendelson (1964). The alcoholic subjects studied in this experiment are most appropriately classified as 'gamma' alcoholics, according to Jellinek's criteria (1960).

Procedure

Subjects were brought to the psychiatric ward of the Massachusetts General Hospital immediately after completing a court sentence for public drunkenness, or at the end of a period of voluntary commitment. A full explanation was given of the exact nature and length of the experiment and subjects were assured that they could leave at any stage of the project. The subjects were not under any degree of legal confinement or restraint, nor was there any pending litigation at the time of the study.

There was an average of twenty patients, mostly female, in the psychiatric ward. The alcoholic subjects were not segregated from the other patients and shared a wide variety of recreational facilities in the ward. Each patient had a single bedroom which was adjacent to the experimental room.

Subjects were required to eat a well balanced diet, averaging 2,000 calories a day with daily multiple vitamin supplements. Their caloric intake was charted daily in addition to their weight and vital signs. One packet of cigarettes was provided daily for each subject. Detailed psychiatric interviews were carried out each day.

The experimental booths for the operant studies were in a separate room adjacent to the subject's bedroom. Each subject had his own key to the room so that he could work at the operant booths whenever he wished. No one else was allowed in the experimental room. The experimental programme was divided into three consecutive phases: pre-drinking, drinking and post-drinking.

In the pre-drinking phase a thorough assessment of psychiatric history and mental state was carried out. In addition, a physical examination and a variety of investigations were performed including routine blood and urine analyses, a rapid Hinton test, and a chest x-ray and a B.S.P. (bromsulphalein) test.

The drinking phase was a seven day period of drinking during which the subjects had free access to the operant instruments. During this phase, blood alcohol levels were determined twice daily (8 a.m. and 5 p.m.) with a breathalyzer. The accuracy of breath alcohol values obtained with this instrument has been validated by comparison with serum alcohol levels determined by the enzymatic method of Bucher and Redetski (1951).

During the post-drinking phase the subjects remained in hospital until there was a complete remission of withdrawal symptoms. This recovery period usually lasted five days. During this time adequate medication, namely paraldehyde and chlordiazepoxide (Librium) was given to help control withdrawal symptoms. B.S.P. tests were repeated and the subjects were discharged from the hospital only if there was no evidence of any liver dysfunction. The subjects were encouraged to seek further help through the alcohol clinic and the social service department of the Massachusetts General Hospital and appropriate arrangements were made if they so desired. Admission to a half-way house at Boston City Hospital for one to two months was also offered.

Operant procedures

During the drinking phase, operant conditioning procedures were used to study drinking patterns. This technique was similar to a real life situation in that the subject could control both the amount and rate of his alcohol intake. It assured that drinking behaviour would not be affected by interactions with a staff attendant assigned to administer alcohol. Also, because alcohol is not usually available to most alcoholics without some expenditure of effort or money, it seemed realistic to require the subject to perform a simple operant task in order to obtain his alcohol.

A schematic diagram of the apparatus used in this experiment is presented in Figure 1. The experimental programme was con-

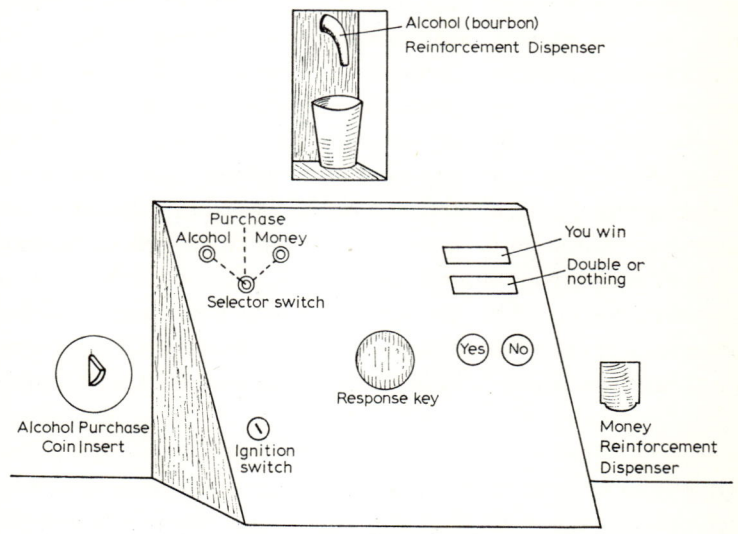

FIG. 1. Schematic diagram of the gambling apparatus.

trolled by transistorized circuitry located in an adjoining cubicle. Transistorized circuitry was used because it was electrically and mechanically silent and had the advantage of rapid (about 8 msec) operating time.

Each man was given access to an instrument from which he could obtain either alcohol or money directly. The subjects were told that the apparatus was a 'gambling machine' and that they should try to learn how to 'beat' the machine. The task was to press a response key within 0.5 sec of the appearance of a stimulus light. The instrument was programmed so that the subject could not predict exactly when the light would appear. Failure to respond, or responding when there was no light, resulted in a loss of the accumulated points. If the subject responded correctly following a predetermined number of consecutive light appearances, he received either 10 c.c. of 86 proof whisky (bourbon) or 15 cents. The subject could choose to work for alcohol or money. The money earned could be used to purchase alcohol which was automatically dispensed from the instrument. A total of 15 cents could buy 10 c.c. of alcohol. This was based on the current retail value of whisky in the local taverns usually frequented by the subjects. Following each series of successfully completed responses, the subject was allowed to choose whether he wished to receive his award or if he wished to gamble on a double or nothing basis. If he elected to gamble, the instrument was programmed so that he could win on an unpredictable fifty-fifty chance basis. The men were told that they could operate the machines at any hour of the day or night, and drink as much or as little alcohol as they wished at any time.

Results and discussion

It was found that the average blood alcohol level achieved by each subject was related to the amount of work required for alcohol reward (reinforcement). Subjects who were required to make sixteen consecutive correct responses in order to obtain one alcohol reinforcement (10 c.c. of 86 proof bourbon) had approximately twice the blood alcohol levels of those subjects who were required to make thirty-two correct responses. These data indicated that subjects who had to work twice as hard for their alcohol drank half as much as comparable subjects in an identical situation. These limitations on consumption reflect a form of control over drinking behaviour. The implication of these findings are that, given access to alcohol, alcoholics do not drink the maximum amount of alcohol available and in the conditions of this expriement did not drink to achieve a state of oblivion. These findings may lend support to the work of Davies and others concerning the ability of some alcoholics to resume social drinking (Davies, 1962; Kendall, 1965).

Most subjects did not work for money reinforcement, even though this would have permitted a sustained period of drinking dissociated from working, since money earned could be used to buy alcohol. However, the men studied in this experiment had histories of little or no gainful employment. Therefore, their pattern of obtaining alcohol was consistent with their pattern of drinking outside hospital.

Risk-taking behaviour (gambling) was not correlated with blood alcohol levels. It is often assumed that various kinds of socially deviant behaviour are associated with states of drunkenness which impair judgment about the nature and severity of risks involved.

In a previous study it was found that alcoholic subjects could titrate their alcohol intake to produce stable values for long periods of time. This was not confirmed in this study, but other findings were consistent with data obtained in previous investigations of experimentally induced intoxication in alcoholics (McNamee et al., 1968; Mello & Mendelson, 1965; Mendelson, 1964; Mendelson & Mello, 1966). The subjects' expectancies expressed about their drinking behaviour and about the effects of alcohol on themselves did not predict the actual behaviour observed during a drinking period, e.g. subjective levels of anxiety and depression appeared to increase rather than decrease as the men continued to consume alcohol. The usual signs of intoxication occurred only rarely, and there was very little disruptive behaviour. Marked impairment of motor function was not observed and response efficiency at the operant instrument tended to increase rather than decrease as the experiment progressed.

Summary

The drinking patterns of fourteen male alcoholic subjects were studied in an experimental drinking situation for a period of seven days. The men could obtain whisky or money rewards (reinforcements) by performing a simple operant task. Also, the subjects could choose to gamble for a double reward which was programmed on a fifty-fifty chance basis.

Contrary to expectation it was found that the amount of work required to obtain alcohol could exert some control over the amount and rate of drinking. The tendency to take risks (gambling) was not associated with blood levels of alcohol. Most of the subjects did not choose to work for money rewards.

The findings of this investigation cast doubt on some of the previously untested assumptions about the phenomenon of alcoholism. These data highlight the need for further work on experimentally induced chronic intoxication and withdrawal in alcoholics, and perhaps also in drug dependence in general.

Acknowledgements: This research was supported in part by Research Grant MH-10247 from the National Institute of Mental Health and the Hall Mercer Hospital Fund. H. Brian McNamee was in receipt of a Wellcome Trust Travel Grant.

The investigators are grateful for co-operation and assistance to the resident and nursing staff of the department of psychiatry at the Massachusetts General Hospital; to Mr. John Metevier of the social service division of the Massachusetts Correctional Institution at Bridgewater; and to Miss Clare Corbett, Mr. R. R. Ballard and Mr. David Latham, research assistants. We thank the staff of the Alcohol Research Unit of the Boston City Hospital for providing a half-way house facility for the subjects of this experiment.

The full report of these results appears in *Clinical Research in Alcoholism* (J. O. Cole, ed.), Psychiatric Research Report No. 24, American Psychiatric Association, Washington, D.C. (1968).

REFERENCES

Bucher, T. & Redetski, H. (1951). Eine spezifische photometrische bestimmung von athylakol auf fermentativem. *Wege. Klin. Wschr.*, **29**, 615–616.
Davies, D. L. (1962). Normal drinking in recovered alcohol addicts. *Quart. J. Stud. Alc.*, **23**, 94–104.
Doctor, R. R. & Bernal, M. E. (1964). Immediate and prolonged psychophysiological effects of sustained alcohol intake in alcoholics. *Quart. J. Stud. Alc.*, **25**, 433–450.
Isbell, H., Fraser, H. F., Wikler, A., Belleville, R. E. & Eisenman, A. J. (1955). An experimental study of the aetiology of 'rum fits' and delirium tremens. *Quart. J. Stud. Alc.*, **16**, 1–33.
Jellinek, E. M. (1960). *Disease Concept of Alcoholism.* New Haven: Hillhouse Press.
Kendall, R. E. (1965). Normal drinking by former alcohol adicts. *Quart. J. Stud. Alc.*, **26**, 247–257.
McNamee, H. B., Mello, N. K. & Mendelson, J. H. (1968). Experimental analysis of drinking patterns: concurrent psychiatric observations. *Am. J. Psychiat.*, **124**, 1063–1069.
Mello, N. K. & Mendelson, J. H. (1965). Operant analysis of drinking patterns of chronic alcoholics. *Nature*, **206**, 43–36.
Mendelson, J. H. (Ed.) (1964). Experimentally induced chronic intoxication and withdrawal in alcoholics. *Quart. J. Stud. Alc.*, Suppl. 2.
Mendelson, J. H. & Mello, N. K. (1966). Experimental analysis of drinking behaviour of chronic alcoholics. *Ann. N.Y. Acad. Sci.*, **133**, 828–845.

QUANTITATIVE ESTIMATES OF DEPENDENCE ON THE SYMBOLIC FUNCTION OF DRUGS

C. R. B. JOYCE

Department of Pharmacology and Therapeutics, London Hospital Medical College

WE are seeing an outstanding and widespread symbolic dependence upon a drug that is of value in closely defined circumstances, such as rheumatoid arthritis, at the present time. The phenomenon is not merely British but international: the phenomenon of dependence on gold. Analogy must not be pressed too far, but it is of interest that for gold, as for heroin or amphetamine, there are two markets—the therapeutic and the illicit. One major difference between the two 'illicit' markets, both created from intense pressure by the consumer, is that that for gold has been recognized officially and so made licit. It is unlikely that we shall see anything of the kind for other drugs—at least as far as heroin is concerned. But our concern here is with dependence upon chalk and sugar and salt, rather than upon the gold into which the alchemist sought to transmute them.

What I have to say in this paper is intended to be consistent with the definition of dependence given earlier by Paton (this volume, pp. 31 to 47).

Placebo reactivity

Earlier controversy about the consistency of the placebo-reactor or non-reactor (Wolf, 1959; Joyce, 1959), though still not resolved, has diminished. This may be because of indirect clinical evidence that an individual's experiences with drugs have cumulative effects, so that people who have had one favourable outcome from drug treatment will more probably experience such an outcome on subsequent occasions as well; and those whose experience has been disappointing will perhaps have become conditioned to give negative reactions in the future (Joyce, 1968). To confirm this hypothesis directly, a longitudinal study of individual experiences with drugs is needed. At least half of this is obviously difficult to acquire, because doctors tend, understandably, not to change a treatment that is proving useful. The alternative is to prospect in the same individual for further episodes of other illnesses requiring treatments of different nature. This has not so far been done. There are however, many observations, made in the course of clinical trials, that even drugs known to be active work better if given before a placebo. The relevance of laboratory to clinic is suggested by the repeated observation (Beecher, 1959; Joyce, 1962) that the proportion of patients who prefer placebo approximates to the number of experimental subjects reporting that the dummy they had received was an active drug, namely about one in three. Moreover, one in six patients with rheumatoid arthritis each treated for successive one month periods with placebo, phenylbutazone and a new compound, preferred the treatment they had been receiving before the trial began at all to any of these (Joyce, 1962). Two generalizations can be safely based upon such studies. First, many patients are satisfactorily treated with placebo; second, many patients are attached to the medication they are receiving. When the generalizations are combined, the question is: what proportion of patients is attached to placebo? Or, put rather more generally, what proportion is dependent upon the symbolic functions of a drug? Estimates of this proportion based on information from various sources now follow.

Estimates of placebos prescribed

First, Evang (1960) has shown that the half turnover time of drugs in the Scandinavian Pharmacopoeia is about five years.

But we do not know what proportion is dropped because it is toxic and what because it is inactive. It would be only a wild guess that the proportions may be fifty-fifty, and the number of

Table 1

Estimates of Placebos Prescribed—I

Class	No. of prescriptions (millions)			Cost (£ millions)		
	1964	1965	1966	1964	1965	1966
Total (all prescriptions)	209·4	244·3	262·0	72·0	86·4	95·8
Antacids	6·9	8·1	8·6	1·2	1·5	1·6
Gastro-intestinal sedatives	2·5	2·7	2·9	0·3	0·4	0·4
Tonics	2·4	2·5	2·4	0·3	0·3	0·3
Laxatives	3·6	4·2	4·4	0·5	0·6	0·7
Antipyretic analgesics	14·9	18·7	20·4	2·6	4·0	5·3
Local anaesthetics, counter-irritants	3·6	4·7	4·6	0·6	0·7	0·7
Local action on u.r.t.	5·7	6·8	7·0	0·6	0·7	0·7
Expectorants, cough suppressants	16·2	19·5	22·0	2·0	2·5	2·9
Other preparations	6·2	7·5	8·1	2·5	3·1	3·5
Preparations for allergic conditions	5·6	6·3	6·9	1·3	1·4	1·6
Antipruritics, etc.	5·6	6·9	7·3	1·0	1·3	1·6
Miscellaneous, including individual formulations	4·8	4·7	4·7	0·5	0·5	0·5
Total	78·0	92·6	99·3	13·4	17·0	19·8
Percentage of grand total	36·1	37·9	37·9	18·6	19·7	20·6

From Ministry of Health Pamphlet: *Cost of Prescribing: Notes for Lecturers* (undated).

prescribable placebos at any time is not validly estimated in this way. However, a second estimate (Table 1) is based on Ministry of Health Statistics. If it is assumed that only half the prescriptions listed (for tonics, laxatives, and individual formulation, etc.) are in fact functioning as placebos—no doubt an over-estimate for some categories and an under-estimate for others—nearly one in five of *all* prescriptions may be written by general practitioners in the Health Service for their symbolic functions. With the possible exception of antipyretic analgesics, no drugs active on the central nervous system have been included in the list, half of the cost of which, incidentally, is about twelve million pounds per annum, or 10% of the total drug cost.

A third line of evidence comes from a study of the prescribing and attitudes of more than 300 general practitioners in three large industrial towns in the north of England (Joyce, Last & Weatherall, 1968). A random one-in-three sample were asked what proportion of their prescriptions they thought were for placebos (Table 2). The median estimate in the three towns was

Table 2

Estimates of Placebos Prescribed—II
Study of doctors in three towns (Joyce, Last & Weatherall, 1968)

Town	n	(1) Median percentage of prescriptions for placebos %	(2) Median percentage expecting medicine %	Product (1 × 2) Median %	Range %
A	24	15	80	16	1–40
B	25	10	70	8	1–32
C	44	15	80	11	0–68

15%, 10% and 15%—a not very dissimilar figure from that just quoted, and also perhaps an under-estimate. In the same study, another question asked was: "What proportion of your patients expect to be given some kind of medicine as a token?" or, more crudely, "What proportion are 'bottle or pill conscious'?". In reply to this question, the median estimates were 80%, 70%

and 80%. These are, of course, the doctors' own subjective estimates: but they were made after serious reflection. Now, if the estimates by each doctor are multiplied together, the median product, or percentage of 'symbol-dependent' patients to whom these doctors consider they are prescribing placebos, is 16%, 8% and 11%. (It is interesting that the study to which these findings were incidental showed that the doctors of town B appeared significantly more aware of the social and psychological needs of their patients than did those of the other two towns, and were more inclined to take a 'whole-person' view of the medical problems presented to them.) Of the doctors sampled in the three towns 4% estimated that they were prescribing placebos to the dependent on more than half the occasions when they prescribed at all, and 50% were so prescribing on more than 10% of all occasions. If these figures can be generalized, and assuming that each general practitioner in Britain sees an average of forty patients a day, at least 50,000 medicine-expecting patients a day are being prescribed for in this way. If each makes contact with his general practitioner on average twice a month, there is a minimum of half a million such people in the country. These figures, though speculative, involve assumptions that are all extremely conservative: as, for example, that the two attitudinal estimates provided by the doctor are independent of each other. (The correlation between them is in fact extremely low.)

Repeat prescribing

It may be argued that most of these self-conscious prescriptions for placebo, even if real, are each for a single course of the drug and so do not represent evidence of psychological dependence. A counter-argument is provided by a smaller, but more intensive study of prescribing in progress at the present time (Balint & Joyce, 1968). This strongly suggests that a very large proportion of prescriptions is in fact written repeatedly for the same patients. Approximately one hundred successive medical contacts of each of ten general practitioners were studied (Table 3). The doctors were taking part in a postgraduate training seminar in the application of psychotherapeutic methods to general practice (Balint, 1957). These doctors form a highly selected group, though possibly not one strongly biased towards the routine use of drugs (Table 3). Rather more than one in four of all their contacts

Table 3

Duration of Main Prescriptions for 998 Patients (Balint and Joyce, 1968)

	No. contacts	Percentage of all contacts
No prescription:	75	7·5
Single prescription:	665	66·5
'Repeat' prescription:		
< 1 month	47	
< 2–12 months	51	14·0
1–2 years	41	
> 2 years	119	12·0
Total	998	100·0

received a prescription identified by the doctor as being intended as a 'repeat' prescription (the alternatives from which this description could be chosen were: 'new, change, repeat or no prescription'). Fewer than one in ten patients received no prescription at all and two in three had a 'new' prescription. Some at least of these will have represented the initiation of a repeat prescription.*

Strikingly, more than one in ten received a repeat prescription that had been running for more than two years, and prescriptions that had been running for more than eight years were not uncommon. However, we may regard any drug given for more

* If, as one would suppose, the proportion is a quarter—and the follow-up study in progress will reveal if this assumption is correct—the total on repeat medication at any time is actually $(\frac{1}{4} + \frac{1}{4} \times \frac{2}{3})$ or 42%.

that two years as containing a large symbolic component. Just under 45% of these (Table 4) were for drugs acting upon the

Table 4

Character of 'Two Year Plus' Prescriptions (Balint & Joyce, 1968)

C.N.S.*	52
Cardiovascular and Respiratory	24
Genitourinary and Infections	15
Metabolic	10
Others	18
Total	119

*Barbiturates	27
Tranquillizers	7
Analgesics	7
Antidepressives	7
Others	4

central nervous system, of which about a half were for barbiturates. Four were for morphine and four for an amphetamine. Twenty per cent of patients receiving repeat prescriptions for other than centrally-active drugs had a primarily psychiatric diagnosis. A rather larger proportion (27%) of those given centrally-active drugs had a mainly organic diagnosis. Both observations confirm the likelihood that symbolic medication is widely used. If these general practitioners are representative the assumptions made previously lead to an estimate that between one and one and a half million patients are being treated in this way in the country as a whole.

We are trying to tease out some of the factors that are associated with the patient treated by a repeat prescription rather than by a more comprehensive attempt to formulate and deal with his problem. Of course, a repeat prescription for maintenance with insulin or a cardiac glycoside, or for a prophylactic antibiotic, may be an adequate treatment. Hence we are examining (Table 5) the characteristics of patients receiving central and other repeat prescriptions separately. They have been compared with those of all patients consulting, for whatever reason and however treated. Though there are only trivial differences between the

Table 5

Some Characteristics of Patients on 'Two Year Plus' Repeats in 998 Patient Study

	Repeats for Drugs Acting on		All patients consulting
	C.N.S.	All other systems	
n	(52)	(67)	(998)
	%	%	%
Women	63	57	62
Men	37	43	38
Single	10	23	35
Married	50	52	51
Widowed	30	21	10
Divorced, etc.	10	4	4
Age < 20 years	0	14	27
21–40 years	15	9	30
41–60 years	37	29	20
> 60 years	48	46	21
Initiation by a G.P.	90	75	—
Initiation by consultant	6	25	—
< 5 contacts/year	27	24	63
6–25 contacts/year	63	73	34
> 25 contacts/year	10	2	2

sexes, and in the proportion of those married, the number of repeats is significantly greater for all drugs, but especially central, for those widowed. This may be in part due to the afflictions of age, but the significantly more frequent treatment of those divorced or separated with centrally active drugs is independent of age. However, the repeated use of centrally active drugs begins earlier, and continues to increase more rapidly. Prescriptions for only 6% of such drugs are initiated by a consultant, against 25% for all others. But, though the patient's own general practitioner has initiated half the prescriptions for a sedative, a tranquillizer or an anti-depressant and for almost as many of the other drugs, this form of defence may not be very effective. Patients with repeat prescriptions consult four or five times as frequently as the general rate for all patients, those with prescriptions for centrally active drugs most frequently of all. The consultation may be briefer, it may even be by telephone or by proxy: but in sum, it may take a great deal of the doctor's yearly time. Nevertheless, the doctor tends to regard the doctor-patient relationship as having improved significantly since the point at which the repeat prescription was initiated. Whether the patient agrees, we do not yet know: but it is possible that in many cases he may.

That we live in a drug-using and drug-dependent society is well known; that we live in a symbol-dependent society is becoming better known. That we live in a society in no small measure dependent upon drugs as symbols appears a factor worth recognizing, so that it may be taken into account when we evaluate the uses, both positive and negative, that society makes of its drugs.

Summary

Estimates of the extent to which general practitioners prescribe placebos and other drugs suggest that there is a large number of patients dependent upon the symbolic functions of medication. One survey of the attitudes of nearly one hundred general practitioners leads to a minimal estimate, for the entire country, of five hundred thousand such patients. An intensive study of the prescribing habits of ten other general practitioners gives an even larger estimate.

Acknowledgements: I am grateful to several colleagues for permission to quote from observations made in collaborative work, especially to Dr. J. M. Last, of the Department of Social Medicine, University of Edinburgh, Dr. Michael Balint and the group of ten general practitioners.

REFERENCES

Balint, M. (1957). *The Doctor, His Patient and the Illness*. London: Pitman.
Balint, M. & Joyce, C. R. B. (1968). Unpublished.
Beecher, H. K. (1959). *J. Am. med. Ass.*, **159**, 1602.
Evang, K. (1960). *Health Service, Society and Medicine*, London: O.U.P.
Joyce, C. R. B. (1959). *Brit. J. Pharmac.*, **14**, 512.
Joyce, C. R. B. (1962). *J. chron. Dis.*, **15**, 1025.
Joyce, C. R. B. (Ed.) (1968). *Psychopharmacology: Dimensions and Perspectives*, Chapter 7. London: Tavistock.
Joyce, C. R. B., Last, J. M. & Weatherall, M. (1968). *Brit. J. prev. soc. Med.*, **22**, 170.
Wolf, S. (1959). *Pharmac. Rev.*, **11**, 689.

DISCUSSION

Hinde: I should like to ask several questions. First, to Dr. Thompson. In the experiment showing that animals tested in the same environment as that in which they learnt to take the drug became re-addicted more rapidly than animals tested in a strange environment: was their proportional intake of the drug solution also greater than that of the latter group? Presumably the difference is not merely one of lowered total intake in a strange environment? This seems to be crucial if relevance of these results to human subjects is to be considered.

Thompson: Drug intake was expressed both in terms of absolute amounts of morphine consumed and as a ratio of morphine volume to the total fluid intake. Using both measures, animals consumed greater amounts of morphine when left in their original familiar environments than if transferred to a new environment during the re-addiction period.

Hinde: Dr. Thompson's data seem to indicate that stimuli associated with drug self-administration become secondary reinforcers. This would be important in understanding drug taking behaviour both in animals and perhaps in human addicts as well.

Thompson: The importance of stimuli associated with drug self-administration cannot be over-emphasized. Monkeys will continue to respond to a light previously paired with morphine self-administration for as long as sixty days after the drug infusion has been stopped. In recent experiments, social stimuli (e.g. the presence of another animal) have been paired with self-administration, and we have data which indicate that such social stimuli become important, both in setting the scene for drug-administration and for subsequent maintenance of 'drug seeking' behaviour. Certainly, if one hopes to eliminate the elaborate sequences of behaviour which culminate in drug injection, it will be necessary to weaken the effectiveness of these conditioned reinforcers as well.

Hinde: Dr. Deneau, I am worried about the dangers of the term 'psychogenic dependence'. It is being used as a blanket term, to cover diverse drugs in diverse organisms, and may obscure, or distract attention from, differences in mode of action.

Deneau: I have no special brief for the term 'psychogenic dependence' and should be glad to accept another term if you can suggest one. We do need some general term, however, to indicate that a person or an animal has demonstrated that he prefers to be under the influence of a drug. This is the first and essential step in the development of all forms of drug abuse. You are quite right that, with different drugs, we should be aware of differences in mode of action.

Hinde: I should like to ask what is known about the time delay between the intake of the drug by mouth and its reaching the site of action and producing its effects there. In the very remarkable and interesting results obtained by Dr. Steinberg and her colleagues, the unpremedicated group, as well as the premedicated group, steadily increased their morphine intake in spite of its distastefulness and in spite of the fact that they were not pre-addicted. And yet presumably the difference between the reward values of drinking the drug solution and those of drinking water or quinine solution cannot operate for a long time after intake. The mode of action of such a long delayed reinforcement is of interest to students of learning as well as students of addiction.

Kumar: The delay between the response of drinking the bitter drug solution and obtaining some relief of withdrawal is of the order of three minutes. This has been reported by Wikler for etonitazine solutions of comparable potency. As you suggest, this creates difficulties for interpretations in traditional learning theory terms. The most likely explanation is that since the rats are thirsty they continue to drink for a fairly long time. During the course of this drinking to relieve thirst, they experience the effects of the drug which was drunk a few minutes earlier and so the response of drinking the drug solution becomes rewarding not only because of relief of thirst but also because withdrawal symptons are relieved.

Malleson: It is a clinical observation that medical practitioners who are self-addicted to narcotics, deteriorate much less than the typical junkie in his different social environment. Dr. Deneau's monkeys, in their comfortable cages, would seem to be more like the addicted M.D.s. Do they deteriorate in learning tasks generally, and in their social relations, dominance ratings and the like?

Deneau: Monkeys which are well fed and are supplied with adequate amounts of sterile morphine solutions show no obvious signs of physical or behavioural deterioration.

S. A. Lewis: Several speakers have commented that some animals will not become addicted of their own volition. This must be of importance for studying differences between addicts and non-addicts who have had equal opportunity. Has Dr. Deneau any comment to make about these non-addicting animals?

Deneau: Yes, we are very interested in finding out why some animals will and other animals will not abuse drugs. We make many behavioural studies of all monkeys before they have an opportunity to take drugs, in the hope of correlating personality with their subsequent tendency to abuse drugs. To date, we have found no definite personality traits which mark a monkey as a potential user or non-user.

Pickersgill: Dr. McNamee found that alcoholics who had to make thirty-two consecutive correct responses by pressing a key within 0·5 sec of the occurrence of a light in order to obtain alcohol maintained a blood alcohol level which was approximately half that found in subjects who had to make only sixteen such responses. He suggested that this result implied that the former group of subjects were not willing to work harder to gain the same amount of alcohol, but an alternative possibility might be that the task chosen was beyond their capacity. I should like to ask whether there are control data for the performance of alcoholic subjects concerning the ability to make sixteen and thirty-two consecutive correct responses when there is no alcohol reward?

McNamee: In this experiment there was no clear correlation between blood alcohol level and response efficiency for any of the fourteen subjects. Five of the subjects performed at a consistent level of response efficiency throughout the seven day period, irrespective of their blood alcohol levels. The other nine subjects improved their response efficiency during the course of the experiment. The operant task appeared to meet the necessary requirement of simplicity in so far as the subjects were able to continue to work and to earn alcohol irrespective of the blood alcohol levels reached. The relative contribution of the ease of task and practice effects cannot be clearly distinguished in the present experiment.

Rosenthal: Concerning Dr. McNamee's paper, the problem of 'artifact' is significant. Putting a 'machine' on a psychiatric ward, where new social pressures are created, may in part account for the new drinking trends that occurred.

McNamee: The data obtained in this experiment certainly must be interpreted in the light of a number of limitations imposed on the research design by the experimental method. The experimental technique used made it impossible to replicate closely the milieu conditions in a non-experimental situation. However, if even the volume or periodicity of drinking can be consistently manipulated by systematic variations of some aspects of the operant task, such data have greater potential utility for analysis of 'motivational factors' than would experimental parallels to real life drinking patterns.

I believe Dr. Solomon of Boston City Hospital is at the moment studying alcoholics in an experimental drinking situation where the role of the social set-up is one of the main factors of interest.

Collier: In one of Dr. Joyce's lists of drugs, the only category acting centrally was that of antipyretic analgesics. I wonder if this exception could be removed, for Lim has made a good case that drugs of this type act peripherally as analgesics, and recent evidence suggests that aspirin acts as an antipyretic by preventing endogenous pyrogen entering the brain. Although aspirin may have central effects in large doses, I wonder if the doses are large enough for this to apply in the case Dr. Joyce quotes.

Joyce: I suggested that antipyretic analgesics might act centrally in order to keep my estimate of symbolic prescribing as free as possible from contamination by drugs with obvious, direct actions on the central nervous system. Despite the evidence to which Dr. Collier refers, the possibility remains that aspirin at least has such an action. I was thinking of the demonstration, by Pfeiffer and his colleagues, that aspirin has effects upon the human EEG that resemble those of 'anti-anxiety' drugs.

Paton: I remember being told by a medical man who had been a prisoner-of-war, that in the prison camps, different nationalities 'specialized' in different diseases: the pattern was (if I remember correctly); the French, afflictions of 'la poitrine'; Germans, of the heart; Russians, of the back; and the English, indigestion. It makes me wonder whether it is not so much the drugs that patients take that function as symbols, but the diseases for which they may be given. There would be slightly different connotations if it is not the pill or tablet itself which is the object of a patient's symbolic interest, but the recognition by society (through the doctor) that he labours under a handicap (some disease) for which treatment is needed and therefore allowances should be made.

REFERENCES

Goldstein, L. & Hopkins, M. (1966). *Fed. Proc.*, **25,** 503.
Pfeiffer, C. C. (1965). *J. new Drugs*, **5,** 260.

Session IV
SOCIAL AND CLINICAL FACTORS
Chairman: SIR DENIS HILL

CHAIRMAN'S INTRODUCTION

In this session we turn our attention from the biological to the social and clinical aspects of drug dependence. In Britain the problem is a comparatively recent one and few can claim extensive experience of it. We do not understand the circumstances which have given rise to the increasing spread of heroin abuse which now threatens to assume epidemic proportions. The facts as they became known to the Interdepartment Committee in 1965 and the actions proposed to meet this threat are outlined by Dr. P. H. Connell. It had been shown that a very small number of overprescribing doctors could encourage an epidemic of drug taking where a socio-cultural demand expresses itself. It is the nature of this socio-cultural demand of which we are ignorant. The papers in this session are by experts who have had first hand experience of the problem, both in communities in which it had not occurred before, and as a therapeutic problem, in populations where drug dependence is well established.

The natural history of opiate addiction is unknown, indeed it may not exist, for it varies with the socio-cultural milieu in which it develops, and the way society responds to it. Thus there is little evidence that addiction is a disease in the biological sense, although it is clear that once physical dependence, craving and 'total personal involvement', to use Chein's phrase, has developed, the addict continues if the supplies of drug are available to him. At this stage whatever social and psychological factors may have determined the onset of drug use, the whole life pattern of the addict is directed to obtaining supplies; he identifies himself with others in a similar plight and becomes a member of an addict subculture. Dr. J. H. Willis who reports a study of comparing hospitalized heroin addicts in New York and in London shows that if patients are categorized in terms of their personal involvement, craving and physical dependence, there are definite differences between the groups studied in the two countries. But, as he points out, the differences in the socio-cultural factors in the two countries are immense. The American addict tends to be a socially and economically deprived individual, one of a minority group, a first generation native born urban dweller of immigrant parentage. The majority are coloured. It is suggested that the parent-child cultural disparity is a significant factor. While the first experiments with drug taking occur among teenagers, in the majority in both societies it is clear from the preliminary studies reported in this session by Mr. Zacune and by Dr. de Alarcon and their colleagues that the British heroin user has different origins and a different background from his American counterpart. He is again quite different from the British heroin addict of even five years ago. At that time most patients were in middle age and addiction was consequent upon therapeutic use of the drug; now the majority are adolescent and have acquired their first contacts with heroin from sources other than therapeutic ones. In the two provincial towns described in this session where heroin use had rapidly spread, the subjects differed between the two towns as to social class origin, and probably also as to intelligence. Many, despite above average intelligence, had been failures at school. As in the studies from the United States many had a previous record of minor delinquencies and school truancy. The relationship between drug abuse and delinquency is complex and still obscure. It may not be the same in different cultural settings.

The decision in Britain not to follow practice in the United States and to avoid all measures of compulsory detention and treatment of heroin addicts has been taken after careful deliberations for reasons outlined by Dr. Connell. As a result many people believe that with the arrangements for voluntary treatment in a regulated psychiatric setting, overprescribing and the dangers of a criminal black market will be avoided. Equally important, as a consequence of these liberal and permissive measures, an opportunity will be provided, which is denied most investigators in the United States, of making enquiries in depth into the aetiology and pathogenesis of addiction and the individual and social factors which operate in its spread. Dr. George Vaillant who describes a fifteen year follow up study of patients released from Lexington, however, makes a case for compulsory hospitalization and detention for a prolonged period and emphasizes the value of a constructive parole period. Although nearly all patients treated in this way relapse on discharge almost immediately, there is in time a tendency for a proportion to become and to remain abstinent. The characteristics of those who do so are beginning to emerge, and in Dr. Vaillant's series these include experience of substantial periods of compulsory detention and subsequent parole. Nevertheless, there are individual psychological factors also operating and it is difficult to determine which is the most important—the psychological structure and the potentialities of the patient or what is done to him. It is reassuring to know, however, that heroin addicts can become abstinent and remain so. Dr. D. L. Davies reports that alcoholic addicts can resume normal drinking and that addiction to this drug can become controlled, i.e. that the dose is not progressively increased. There is of course a basic sociological difference between alcohol and heroin usage, for in western societies alcohol usage is socially acceptable and widespread while heroin usage is not.

It is a common idea that once started there is an inevitable escalation in drug use, despite the considerable evidence that there are many who have not become drug dependent even when observed for a considerable time. There have been few attempts to differentiate the characteristics of those who are dependent from those who are not, but take drugs casually and intermittently. Dr. Beryl Geber reports her attempt to examine this issue and the difficulties of sampling, particularly of the non-dependent subjects who are rarely known to social agencies. As in most studies the subjects were found to be taking many different drugs, both hard and soft, and reliable data about which drugs and dosages were difficult to obtain, particularly when the method of enquiry was the questionnaire, even though lightly structured and allowing the subject considerable latitude to express himself. It is evident that both field studies and individual enquiries in the form of 'depth interviews' in the patient's own habitat are required if this and other related problems are to be tackled.

A challenge to the current American concept that hospitalization, compulsory detention and parole are the most effective therapeutic methods, is provided by the development of special therapeutic communities, such as Synanon in California, Phoenix House and Daytop Village in New York. The administration, organization and structure, the functions and the purposes of Phoenix House are described by Dr. Mitchell Rosenthal. It is clear that only some addicts can be treated in such communities; they have to be adequately motivated to take part or they cannot enter. Only preliminary results are available, but it is clear that therapeutic efficacy can only be assessed by the most careful and detailed follow up studies, not only of those who are accepted for this treatment but also of those who are rejected, and not only of those who stay the course but also of those who fall out.

It seems likely, as several of the speakers in this symposium indicate, that the contemporary methods of clinical, psychological and social enquiry, administered within the artificial framework of the clinic or hospital setting, are inadequate to throw light on the spread of drug addiction, or on the social and cultural milieu in which drug abuse starts and flourishes. There is no dearth of hypothesis and theory to account for it but there are very few hard facts. The report of Mr. Zacune and his colleagues on their attempt to assess the heroin usage in a provincial town provided a much larger number of drug users than was suspected. The methods used were almost certainly responsible for this result.

It suggests that the investigator while taking his skills with him must be prepared to leave his clinic and his laboratory and examine the drug user within the social environment in which he uses it. He must adopt the research practices of the social anthropologist rather than those of the clinician. Only in this way, by examining the phenomenon of drug use within the context of social networks, of friendships and personal relationships does it seem likely that the interwoven factors of personal vulnerability and cultural determination will be specified and understood.

DRUG DEPENDENCE IN GREAT BRITAIN: A CHALLENGE TO THE PRACTICE OF MEDICINE

P. H. Connell

*Drug Dependence Clinical Research and Treatment Unit,
The Bethlem Royal and the Maudsley Hospital*

In this the last session of a symposium during which we have heard a number of stimulating, provocative and academic papers I present this paper with considerable humility, for I have no research data or original clinical material to present.

It seemed to me that at this crucial time, when new methods of dealing with the problem of drug dependence in this country are about to be instigated, it might be profitable to attempt to examine the thinking behind them and take a look at the problems which beset the physician who is to deal with drug dependent patients. This attempt might be of some value as a short historical statement.

Development of the problem

The numbers of non-therapeutic narcotic addicts known to the Home Office began to rise slowly in 1958 and by 1963 it was realized that if trends continued a major epidemic was likely. The Second Report of the Interdepartmental Committee on Drug Addiction was published late in 1965 following deliberations which had begun when the Committee was re-convened in July, 1964. Evidence presented to the Committee made it clear that the heroin being used by addicts was available because of gross overprescribing by a small number of general practitioners. Efforts on an informal basis to stop such overprescribing were fruitless, and so action had to be taken. This led to the Dangerous Drugs Act, 1967, which requires any doctor who comes into a professional relationship with a person addicted to certain drugs must notify certain basic particulars to the Chief Medical Officer at the Home Office (regulation brought in on February 22, 1968). The Act also denies the right of doctors to prescribe heroin or cocaine to addicts unless they hold a special licence to do so (regulation operative from April 16, 1968). The latter requirement has been delayed until a time when new treatment centres will be operating which, it has been calculated, should be able to deal with the number of addicts seeking help.

Rationale of the new approach

The rationale of the new approach, which includes the concept of prescribing heroin to addicts who do not wish to be withdrawn from the drug, can be summarized as follows.

(1) The prescribing of heroin to addicts must be under some tighter control than before.

(2) There is no evidence of a criminally organized heroin supply in the country and this must be avoided at all costs.

(3) If supplies of heroin to addicts are stopped abruptly there is a strong chance that a criminally organized black market will spring up, for the numbers of heroin addicts are approaching the level at which it would be financially worthwhile for criminal organizations to move in.

(4) When heroin is solely available in a criminal black market it has to be purchased, and the need to obtain money to purchase it drives the addict into criminal activities in order to obtain the money to maintain his dependence and to avoid withdrawal symptoms.

(5) Heroin provided free at special treatment centres will obviate the need for the addict to commit crimes to obtain money for the drug.

(6) Hospital clinics staffed by 'experts' are much less likely to overprescribe and licensing regulations will allow for a doctor's licence to be withdrawn where necessary, for the licences are to be renewable yearly.

(7) The treatment centres will be oriented towards eventual withdrawal of the patient from the drug and will be backed by special in-patient units. Regular contact between the addict and the doctor of the centre gives the opportunity for a relationship to be built up which may eventually lead to the addict requesting to be taken off the drug.

(8) The pure, British made heroin which the addict will receive is less likely to cause complications and death than the impure material which circulates in a criminally organized supply system. This hypothesis may well be untenable in the light of recent findings (Bewley *et al.*, 1968).

(9) If the hospital clinics do prescribe more closely to the actual dose taken by the addict there will be much less 'spare' heroin circulating to involve more uncommitted individuals.

(10) The addict is a sick person and properly comes within the ambit of medical practice. His dependence on the drug and his craving is so strong that he is unable to behave rationally.

(11) Punitive detention of the addict under a penal system has not been shown to be successful in curing addiction in other countries and should not be adopted hastily.

(12) Although it may well be that a population of addicts exists who can only be helped by compulsory detention in hospital (under, let us say, a new provision of the Mental Health Act) it is wiser to delay asking for such powers until the size of the population requiring such an approach and the features which distinguish this population from other addicts can be delimited. Too hasty provision of such compulsory powers might well lead to their widespread use where not necessary and such widespread use has not been found effective in other countries—notably the U.S.A.

The diagnostic problem

Since the treatment of heroin dependence is now to be passed over to special centres it may be as well to look at the diagnostic problem confronting the physicians working in the centres.

The physician wishes to establish a number of facts, including (a) is the patient taking heroin at all; (b) if he is taking it what is the dose; (c) is he taking other drugs; (d) is he taking it continuously or sporadically?

Here the physician turns to his colleagues concerned with chemical pathology, biochemistry and pharmacology and finds, to his dismay, that quantitative assessments are not possible in an out-patient setting (and the addict usually does not want to be admitted for observation) and that qualitative methods such as the use of thin-layer chromatography cannot be done quickly. A result in twenty-four hours is the most he can hope for when the chemical pathology services have been developed. There is the nalorphine test to demonstrate morphine and heroin use (Way et al., 1963; Way et al., 1966) which is used extensively in California, but this has its limitations and snags. The physician, therefore, who is supposed to be an expert, has no immediate expertise to help him. He must, therefore, try to play a waiting game in which he attempts to gain the co-operation of his probably hostile and suspicious patient, in an attempt to bring him back when urine test results are available (many of the patients are unable to pass urine in sufficient quantity). In the meantime he must try and keep the patient going by giving a drug such as methadone to prevent possible withdrawal symptoms, should the patient actually be taking heroin! This is an unenviable state of affairs. Test doses of heroin or barbiturates could be given to demonstrate the presence or absence of tolerance but this method is time consuming and requires standardization. Individual differences are likely to be wide.

The physician is therefore facing a patient who may be an

addict. The addict nearly always asks for more than he needs, partly because of his fear of being without any drug, and partly because he may wish to have extra to give to friends or sell for money. He is a skilled manipulator who plays on the kindness and weakness of doctors. During a month's visit to the U.S.A. in November, 1967, I asked several groups of addicts what a British doctor should do in this situation to prevent overprescribing, and I was told to divide the dose demanded by two or by three. Should this be taken as a guide in dealing with the British addict?

The physician, in the special centre, has to face the fact that if he puts too many requirements on the addict such as daily attendance, spending an hour each time he attends and so on, the addict may become fed up and seek a black market even though the drug may be costly. Should enough addicts feel thus, a black market would be worth while for the criminal organizations.

Thus physicians, chiefly for medico-social reasons, have agreed to take part in a treatment setting which includes maintaining a heroin addict on heroin, which is a very bad drug for maintenance purposes because of its short lived action. If taken intravenously it can lead to a number of serious medical complications (Louria, 1967; Bewley & Ben-Arie, 1968) and to a high mortality rate (Bewley et al., 1968). The diagnostic armamentarium available to the physician is minimal

The interim period

The past few months, during which clinics have been opening and taking over patients from general practitioners who have been prescribing for addicts, have been difficult, since only from April 16, 1968, will these clinics be the only places at which addicts can receive their heroin or cocaine. In the interim it is likely that there has been a good deal of overprescribing. This might be due to case load pressures; to the physician obtaining experience in handling the addict and because of the need to be thought of highly enough by the addict to encourage continued attendance when alternative sources of supply are still available.

The numbers of addicts who will come forward on or after April 16, 1968 cannot be assessed, though what evidence there is would suggest that the numbers are unlikely to be as large as has been predicted in some quarters.

The situation will require much careful evaluation during the four months from April, 1968, and geographical redistribution of addicts to more conveniently situated centres may eventually be necessary if contact between the centre and rehabilitation and social services is to be established.

The dangers inherent in the new approach

There are many dangers in the new approach which have to be faced and are better stated in order to avoid a drift into disaster and a breakdown of the new approach. I will draw attention to these by stating certain propositions.

(1) It has already been shown that a very small number of overprescribing doctors can encourage an epidemic of drug-taking where a socio-cultural demand expresses itself.

(2) The experts in the special centres are not infallible and have no accurate tools to assess dosage of the drug.

(3) All professional classes contain weaker brethren.

(4) The number of doctors in London who are actually going to prescribe heroin to addicts is several times more than the number of general practitioners who undertook this task.

If these propositions are accepted then it must be acknowledged that without careful evaluation and careful practice it would be possible for the situation to become much worse than when general practitioners were free to prescribe these drugs to addicts.

Safeguards to prevent untoward developments

There are two main requirements for cutting down the pool of 'free floating' or excess heroin which has been used to involve the as yet uncommitted.

First, it is necessary to recognize that there is a need to cut down the dose of drugs already being prescribed to addicts. This could best be effected by agreement by those working in the treatment centres that when they are working smoothly and preferably on an appointed day *all clinics* will reduce the amount of heroin prescribed over a period of, say, a month to about a half.

Second, it must be agreed that no heroin addict will ever receive a dose higher than that considered to be necessary during the first few attendances at the clinic. This measure, in particular, would provide protection to those who with the best of motives might be led to increase the dose by pressure from the addict. This agreement would recognize the fact that addicts have two needs; the physiological need to prevent withdrawal symptoms and the psychological need to increase the dose to obtain pleasant effects. This latter need is the need that gets doctors into dose escalation difficulties and requires combatting.

Other measures which will be essential in order to keep a close watch on developments will include the careful keeping of records of the quantities of drugs prescribed in each centre; the prevention of transfer of a patient from one centre to another without full details of doses taken; agreement that no addict will ever be prescribed heroin as an emergency; that only methadone is given to prevent emergency withdrawal symptoms; and agreement that after April 16, 1968 no addict will be prescribed heroin until it has been established that he is in fact taking heroin, and until attempts have been made to evaluate the smallest dose which will prevent withdrawal symptoms. This is particularly relevant to the situation of post-addicts who claim that they have been re-addicted and are only too easily prescribed the same high dose that they used to get before they were taken off the drug.

The future

If all goes well and the heroin problem is contained and then diminished in size, it has to be recognized that there is still a socio-cultural pressure to take drugs. These pressures are worldwide and not just specific to Great Britain.

It is likely, therefore, that this demand will lead to an increase in the taking of other drugs, notably the psychedelics. But the amphetamines which have been widely abused in Japan and more recently in Sweden will need to be watched, as will the barbiturates. In this context it is only realistic to point out that amphetamines are very widely prescribed by medical practitioners in large amounts, often where the real indications for their use are lacking (Connell, 1968) and that Schedule IV of the poisons rules does not provide adequate supervision or recording of prescriptions. Furthermore, the regulations relating to manufacture and distribution are such that it is very difficult to keep track of the drugs and relatively easy for the drugs to be stolen. Much tighter regulations with regard to manufacture, distribution and the recording of prescriptions might well be imperative if escalating misuse of these drugs is to be prevented.

The challenge to British medicine

What are the challenges? Some of these can be enumerated as follows.

(1) The challenge to physicians in the treatment centres to work together and adopt a reasonably uniform approach. This might mean agreement to give up the complete right to do exactly what the physician wishes in some circumstances.

(2) The challenge to the biochemist, pharmacologist and chemical pathologist to produce as quickly as possible some method of assessment of drug dosage on a quantitative basis and to develop some test for clinical usage, and also to explore urgently the possibility of a quick qualitative test so that the clinician can be in a position to know the drugs taken during the consultation.

(3) The challenge to physicians to produce hard data relating to treatment programmes in order that most effective methods can

be delimited. This research should not be left to just one or two special research units, but should ideally be by joint participation of all the centres. Follow up studies are important here.

(4) The challenge to the epidemiologists and sociologists to produce by careful research, data relating to the causes of drug taking, methods of spread and suggestions relating to prevention.

This country is in a unique and exciting position in relation to drug dependence. An epidemic has developed but the numbers of narcotic users are still small. It would be a tragedy if the opportunities given to us were lost because of lack of interest, lack of co-ordination, lack of support or rivalries and jealousies. We in this country need answers to many questions relating to drug dependence if we are to be in a position to deal wisely with the problem and if we are to advise the legislators. The U.S.A. and other countries are looking with interest at our new methods—though with some scepticism concerning prescribing heroin. Let us hope that we are all equal to our task.

REFERENCES

Bewley, T. H., Ben-Arie, O. & James, I. P. (1968). *Brit. Med. J.*, **i,** 725–726.
Bewley, T. H. & Ben-Arie, O. (1968). *Brit. Med. J.*, **i,** 727–730.
Connell, P. H. (1968). *The Practitioner*, **200,** 234–243.
Dangerous Drugs Act (1927). London: H.M.S.O.
Louria, D. B., Hensle, T. & Rose, J. (1967). *Ann. Int. Med.*, **67,** 1–22.
Ministry of Health & Scottish Home and Health Department (1965). *Drug Addiction*. The Second Report of the Interdepartmental Committee. London: H.M.S.O.
Way, E. L., Elliott, H. W. & Nomof, N. (1963). *Bull. Narcotics*, **15,** 29–33.
Way, E. L., Benjamin, P. N. M. O. & Quock, C. P. (1966). *Clin. Pharmac. & Therap.*, **7,** 300–311.

THE NATURAL HISTORY OF DRUG DEPENDENCE: SOME COMPARATIVE OBSERVATIONS ON UNITED KINGDOM AND UNITED STATES SUBJECTS

J. H. WILLIS

York Clinic, Guy's Hospital, London, S.E.1

Introduction

THE problem of narcotic dependence, particularly on heroin, is comparatively recent in this country. Formerly a medical curiosity confined to middle aged 'therapeutic' patients dependent on morphine, the condition has in the last ten years emerged as one in which the population involved is predominantly youthful, 'non-therapeutic' in origin and dependent on heroin (Bewley, 1965, 1966). For these reasons the literature relating to the demography and natural history of addiction in this country has been sparse.

Schur (1962) reviewed the British addiction problem and compared British policy towards addicts with that prevalent in America. He also examined some of the characteristics of British addicts. In the twenty-one addicts studied he found confirmation of the then official view of the problem, noting a heavy representation of the medical and allied professions, the age distribution (mainly older than thirty) and in general the relative insignificance of the problem. He contrasted it with the situation in America where addiction is predominantly a condition associated with minority groups living in conditions of considerable material deprivation. He also commented on its links with a delinquent drug-using subculture.

Schur's findings have been reviewed and criticized by Gillespie et al. (1967) who drew attention to a change in age distribution, a wider social class distribution and a different sex distribution. They also found no preponderance of medical and allied personnel. Hewetson & Ollendorf (1966) had found a similar social class and sex distribution.

This report forms part of a study of British and American addicts in which certain demographic and psychiatric aspects of heroin addicts are compared with hospitalized non-addict controls and non-hospitalized, non-addict controls.

A major part of the enquiry was concerned with the natural history of drug use, for it was predicted that such information, though difficult to collect, may be crucial because our knowledge of the patterns of drug dependence can be based on assertion rather than observation.

Method of the enquiry

The subjects studied in the United Kingdom were all hospitalized inpatients who had been admitted to psychiatric hospitals for the treatment of heroin addiction. They were all under twenty-five, of both sexes, forty-two male, sixteen female; mean ages 20·3, 19·0.

The subjects studied in the United States were all hospitalized in-patients in the Morris J. Bernstein Institute of the Beth Israel Center in New York. This is one of the principal detoxification centres in New York City and has an annual admission of 8,000 heroin addicts. The fifty patients included in the study, thirty-five male and fifteen female, were all in the same age range; mean ages 22·6, 21·7.

Addiction

Subjects were identified as heroin addicts if they had a history of daily self injection with heroin for a minimum period of six months. In addition, addiction was regarded as being manifest by the presence of unequivocal evidence of physical and psychological dependence.

Natural history of drug dependence

Careful enquiry was made into the subjects' history of drug use. Although this was based on self report and is therefore subject to the criticisms inherent in such a method, it has to be recognized that it is difficult to devise any other method because objective verification is usually lacking. With this in mind the nearest possible check was made by the use of a structured interview which could be repeated.

The areas covered and reported in this part of the study include: modes of introduction to drug use; stated reasons for drug use; subjective evaluation of first heroin experience; mode of administration; duration of use; age at first exposure to heroin; age at first dose of heroin; duration of heroin use before daily use started; self imposed abstention from drug use; other drugs used; typology of addiction.

Natural history of drug use

Introduction to the use of heroin

In every case the subject was asked who introduced him or her to the use of heroin. Though the common response was 'a friend,' when this was investigated it was found that the term covered fellow addicts, more often than not casual acquaintances rather than close friends. This finding has some relevance when consideration is given to the possibility of the existence of a drug-using subculture. The term subculture may loosely be applied to people possessing a common behavioural characteristic, but it is probably an over simplified use of the term. To be identifiable a subculture must have accepted modes of behaviour, customs and value systems. The existence of a drug-using subculture in the United Kingdom is tentatively supported by the evidence of

Gillespie *et al.* (1967), but the strands and elements of such a sub-culture have yet to be identified. It is premature to identify a sub-culture purely on the basis of the existence of a characteristic such as drug dependence since it is easy to assign to people characteristics which they may not possess and then oblige them to identify themselves as such by behaving in a way which confirms society's expectations of them. In this way a 'sub-culture' may be seen to be an artefact. Table 1 shows the modes of intro-

Table 1

Introduction to heroin

Introduced by:	U.K. Male	U.S. Male	U.K. Female	U.S. Female
Friend	41	28	16	11
Spouse or cohabitee	1	0	0	0
Pusher	0	7	0	4
	n = 42	n = 35	n = 16	n = 15

duction to heroin. As might be expected the only incidence of introduction to drugs by a 'pusher' or professional peddler of drugs was found in U.S. subjects. This reflects the absence of professional peddling in the U.K. It should however, be emphasized that in many instances introduction by a 'friend' in the U.K. involves buying surplus heroin tablets from the individual concerned. The financial profit involved is for the individual and is not part of an organized traffic in drugs. This confirms similar findings by Gillespie *et al.* (1967).

Reasons for experimenting with heroin

All subjects were asked about their own evaluation of reasons for heroin use. This gave a wide range of replies involving more than the answering of an unsubtle question such as 'why do you take heroin?' However, it was possible to categorize the stated reasons under five general headings (Table 2).

Table 2
Stated reasons for taking heroin

	U.K. Male	U.S. Male	U.K. Female	U.S. Female
Curiosity about effect	19	23	7	9
Effect on depressed mood	18	3	9	5
Analgesic	0	0	0	0
Wish for elevation of mood above normal	9	6	4	1
Persuaded by others	0	4	1	1
	n = 42	n = 35	n = 16	n = 15

Curiosity about effects

Throughout the subjects, this was one of the most commonly made responses—it is almost the standard reply at first, but closer questioning usually reveals whether or not it is a prominent motive.

There seems to be little doubt that all drugs (like alcohol) have a reputation for producing a desired or unknown effect, and the wish to experience this can operate forcefully. There is curiosity about the effects of smoking for example. But in the case of opiates, curiosity has to operate against a long tradition of unfavourable attitudes towards the use of opiates in our culture. With hindsight many addicts speak regretfully of their curiosity but it is hard to evaluate the intensity of these feelings because such a statement is likely to encounter medical approval.

At the same time interviews with subjects not taking heroin but taking other drugs (e.g. amphetamines), do reveal apparent caution about the use of opiates among drug users. Thus a considerable amount of myth and collective belief surrounds drugs and their effects. The wish for a new experience too is not confined to drug users.

Effect on depressed mood

This aspect of drug use may not have received sufficient attention. Poorly sustained mood disturbance is common in the established addict and as often as not is linked with withdrawal distress. However, mood disturbance as a precursor of drug taking is difficult to be precise about because the subject will be reporting on an event in the distant past. Eighteen of the U.K. series of subjects reported mood disturbance as the chief reason for taking heroin. However, in only three of these patients was there any substantial evidence of manifest mood disturbance of any severity. Three of the U.S. subjects gave it as their chief reason. This represents a significant difference between the two groups of subjects. However, it is a difference that perhaps should not be regarded too seriously because of the difficulties inherent in its assessment.

Analgesia

This was reported by none of the subjects and reflects the absence of 'therapeutic' addicts. There was one male English patient who regularly took extra doses of heroin to relieve severe migrainous headaches, but this was not his main stated reason for first taking heroin.

Wish for elevation of mood above normal

Contrary to expectation this—the quest for true euphoria—did not emerge as the chief reason for drug use. Many subjects confirmed that the desired effect of heroin was not the traditionally described euphoria of medical and pharmacological texts, but conceded that a euphoric experience was something they valued but would achieve by the use of amphetamines or cannabis.

On the other hand all subjects admitted that the wish for euphoria had been or was still a central element in their personal lives regardless of whether heroin was involved. In fact the euphoric experience is very much a part of the addict life style. With this in mind it is surprising that euphoria did not emerge as a potent reason for first trying the drug. It might be supposed that the term 'curiosity' would overlap with 'euphoria' but as far as could be established this was not so.

Persuaded by others

Without exception all the subjects who gave this as their reason for first drug use were very ineffectual individuals of low intelligence who had moved into drug use as a way of achieving acceptance in peer groups.

Comment

Those who gave 'curiosity' as a reason were quite definitely describing a state in which they had very ill formulated expectations about drug effects—or so it appears.

Subject's evaluation of first heroin experience

Every subject was asked to evaluate his or her first injection of heroin in terms of its 'pleasantness' or 'unpleasantness', or to comment whether the first experience had been neutral.

The first injection is something that is rarely forgotten although six U.K. male subjects were unable to recall whether or not it was pleasant or not. The remaining subjects were quite definite and clear in their recollections and descriptions. Though in the case of the U.K. males, U.S. males and U.K. females the predominant description was of a significantly pleasant experience, this was not true of the U.S. female subjects (Table 3), whereas

Table 3

Nature of first heroin experience

	U.K. Male	U.S. Male	U.K. Female	U.S. Female
Pleasant	25	20	15	6
Unpleasant	11	15	1	9
Unable to remember	6	0	0	0
	n = 42	n = 35	n = 16	n = 15

fifteen of the sixteen U.K. females found the first injection a significantly pleasant experience. This striking difference is not easily explained. In the first instance the U.K. girls were as a group very disturbed personalities from families with considerable social and personal pathology, so that they well fulfilled the expectation of personal and social deviance as factors predisposing to drug use. It should be noted too that the U.K. subject's first experience of heroin is likely to be with pure heroin—not heavily adulterated as in the U.S., so that a more potent effect is likely.

Heroin: mode of administration

All subjects were (or had been) taking heroin intravenously at the time of study. Enquiry was made as to other modes of administration that had been employed before on a regular basis. Clear differences emerged (Table 4).

The first finding was that only four of the U.K. male subjects had taken it any other way but intravenously. This was in sharp contrast to the U.S. male subjects of whom twenty-five had used alternative modes as indicated in Table 4. There were no differences between the modes used by female patients.

Table 4
Modes of administration

	U.K. Male	U.S. Male	U.K. Female	U.S. Female
Intravenous (currently)	42	35	16	15
Intramuscular★	0	1	2	0
Nasal★	3	11	2	3
Skin★	1	16	2	5

★ = previously.

A common description by U.S. subjects was that they started by inhaling powdered heroin—then progressed via subcutaneous injection to the intravenous route. Because heroin is not available in powdered form in this country it is not surprising that inhalation is an unusual route. Among the American subjects there was almost general agreement that sniffing heroin was a safe way of starting.

Duration of heroin usage

As can be seen from Tables 5a and 5b, the striking finding here is the preponderance of U.S. male subjects who had been taking heroin for five years or more. This is a function of two factors; first, a discernible tendency for U.S. male subjects to start using heroin at an earlier age, and second, it is related to the fact that there was a bias towards the upper end of the under twenty-five age group in the U.S. males studied. A similar though less pronounced difference was seen between U.K. and U.S. female subjects.

Table 5
Duration of heroin use

	(a) Male			(b) Female	
	U.K.	U.S.		U.K.	U.S.
6/12+	4	0	6/12+	4	2
9/12	7	1	9/12	0	1
1 year	13	1	1 year	5	2
18/12	3	3	18/12	0	1
2 years	5	4	2 years	3	2
3 years	5	2	3 years	1	0
4 years	1	4	4 years	2	3
5+ years	2	20	5+ years	0	3
	n = 42	n = 35		n = 16	n = 15

Age at first exposure to heroin

It seemed to be important to try to estimate the age at which subjects had first been exposed to heroin. By exposure to heroin is meant the consistent presence in the subject's immediate environment of individuals regularly using heroin. Exposure is thus not merely brief acquaintance with someone who may or may not be taking the drug, but being regularly in the company of and associating—on a day to day basis—with drug users. Such exposure implies the acquisition of myths and information about drug use, drug effects and the ways in which drug users behave. Thus exposure implies familiarity with the mores and life styles of drug users. While it may be problematic to estimate the influence of such exposure it should be possible to estimate the age incidence of the exposures. Table 6a gives the

Table 6

Age at first exposure to heroin

Age at first exposure to heroin	(a) Male		(b) Female	
	U.K.	U.S.	U.K.	U.S.
12	0	1	0	3
13	0	3	0	0
14	0	8	3	3
15	3	15	3	5
16	19	7	5	2
17	13	1	1	2
18	3	0	0	0
19	1	0	2	0
20	7	0	2	0
	n = 42	n = 35	n = 16	n = 15

findings for male subjects. Of interest here are the consistently earlier ages at which such exposure appeared to have occurred in U.S. subjects, more than 50% of whom had been exposed to heroin by the age of sixteen. It should be noted, however, that heroin has been available for a shorter time in the U.K. The later exposure in U.K. subjects may therefore be a misleading figure.

In the case of the female subjects, (Table 6b) this tendency prevails, with a higher proportion exposed as early as age twelve. When the U.K. females are compared with the U.K. males it is found that the females show an earlier age of exposure. Indeed despite their differences there are more similarities between U.K. and U.S. females than between U.K. females and U.K. males in this respect.

Age at first dose of heroin

First dose in this context means first non-therapeutic dose—by any route (Table 7). The age distribution for age at first dose of heroin shows a wider scatter in the U.S. sample, whereas in the U.K. subjects 50% were in the seventeen–eighteen age group. No U.K. subject was encountered whose first dose was taken

Table 7
Age at first dose of heroin

Age at first dose of heroin	(a) Male		(b) Female	
	U.K.	U.S.	U.K.	U.S.
12	0	1	0	1
13	0	2	0	0
14	0	1	1	1
15	2	3	3	0
16	3	4	2	2
17	12	9	4	2
18	9	4	2	2
19	7	4	0	4
20	3	5	1	1
21	2	0	2	2
22	2	2	1	0
23	1	0		
	n = 42	n = 35	n = 16	n = 15

before the age of fifteen. It should be remembered that it was only as recently as 1960 that the first heroin addict under age twenty became known to the Home Office.

Here the interesting finding was the larger number in the older age range in the U.S. subjects. Because of the small size of the series this finding must be viewed with some caution.

Duration of heroin use before daily use started

This was thought to be crucial to the study of the natural history of drug use, since it has frequently been stated that heroin is a drug to which individuals rapidly become physically addicted.

All subjects were closely questioned about the period that elapsed after the first dose of heroin before they began to inject themselves daily. Obviously recollection about this may be faulty or influenced by the need to understate the severity of a drug habit—for a variety of reasons. Table 8 suggests the following:

Table 8

Duration of heroin use before daily self injection started

	U.K. Male	U.S. Male	U.K. Female	U.S. Female
Immediate	4	5	7	1
Up to 1/12	12	4	2	2
1/12 to 6/12	17	12	3	9
6/12 to 12/12	4	8	1	1
12/12 to 2 years	2	5	2	1
	n = 42	n = 35	n = 16	n = 15

U.K. subjects

(1) Of the fifty-eight U.K. subjects, eleven reported having begun daily injections immediately after the first injection. It is not without significance that seven of these were girls—who as a group showed a consistently higher level of personal and familial pathology. (2) Of the U.K. male subjects thirty-three (78%) had become daily users in less than six months. However, of this number seventeen had varied between one and six months before starting daily usage. (3) Two had injected themselves irregularly for up to two years.

U.S. subjects

The scatter was similar in U.S. male and female subjects, i.e. similar to U.K. males in over-all distribution.

Comment

The modal period of irregular drug use before daily self injection seems to be wide, ranging from one to six months. However, the extremes are worth comment. Immediate daily use may reflect severe personal pathology, easy availability of the drug and also the purity and strength of the drug. The pure English heroin as opposed to its heavily adulterated U.S. equivalent has often been incriminated as a more potent addictive substance, but these figures do not appear to support such a contention. The preponderance of U.K. females as immediate daily users is thought to be an index of their severe levels of psychiatric pathology.

Self imposed abstention from drug use

Questions about this must inevitably yield suspect results (Table 9) because subjects are likely to exaggerate the extent of their own efforts to abstain from taking heroin.

Table 9
Periods of self imposed abstention

	U.K. Male	U.S. Male	U.K. Female	U.S. Female
Under 1/52	30	34	14	12
1/52–3/52	10	6	3	3
1/12–6/52	2	3	1	1
2/12–3/12	4	3	3	4
4/12–6/12	1	4	1	1
7/12–12/12	2	4	0	0
Over 1 year	0	3	0	2

It is interesting that five U.S. subjects reported self imposed periods of abstention lasting more than one year. This may reflect the age difference bias in the U.S. series.

Other drugs used regularly

All subjects were questioned about the regular use of other drugs, either before or accompanying heroin use. 'Regularly' in this context means daily over periods of weeks or months with the exception of LSD. Similar enquiry was made about the use of alcohol (Table 10).

Amphetamines

Amphetamines refers to oral amphetamine and/or amphetamine/barbiturate mixture tablets. Intramuscular or intravenous methylamphetamine injections are not included. Amphetamine taking could be seen to be an almost universal practice in U.K. subjects (94%) as opposed to the U.S. subjects studied (28%).

Table 10
Other drugs used regularly

	U.K. Male	U.S. Male	U.K. Female	U.S. Female
Amphetamines	40	10	14	4
Marijuana	42	24	15	11
Other opiates	12	1	4	0
Pethidine	6	0	2	1
LSD	16	3	6	1
Cocaine	33	1	14	1
Alcohol taken excessively for weeks or months	17	6	6	8
	n = 42	n = 35	n = 16	n = 15

Marijuana

Though marijuana use was widespread in U.S. subjects, regular marijuana use was only admitted to by thirty-five (66%) as opposed to all but one of the U.K. subjects. This difference is difficult to account for. It is possible that subjects gave false answers. However, the proportion of regular users is the same in the U.S. male subjects as in the U.S. female subjects, which suggests that the responses can be regarded as correct.

At the impressionistic level it can be pointed out that attitudes towards marijuana may be different between the U.S. and U.K. subjects studied. In England at the time of the study marijuana still had the mystique of a cult surrounding it and the subjects were strongly motivated towards its use, whereas U.S. subjects appeared more matter of fact towards it. They could take it or leave it or so it appeared.

Other opiates

Here enquiry was made about morphine by injection and about preparations such as paregoric by injection; paregoric is used by U.S. addicts and is available as the camphorated opium tincture and injected after boiling. Other opiates also included substances such as codein by injection. With the U.K. subjects morphine was the only other opiate encountered. In all cases subjects resorted to other opiates when they were unable to obtain heroin. One U.K. subject claimed to have smoked opium (in France) but this was not substantiated.

Pethidine

Pethidine had been taken regularly by eight of the U.K. subjects and one of the U.S. subjects. None of the subjects were medical or paramedical workers so that the usual English finding of pethidine use among medical personnel was not reflected. As with 'other opiates', pethidine had been taken originally at a time when the subject had been unable to obtain heroin and then continued its use for a period of weeks—ultimately returning to heroin.

LSD

Twenty-two of the U.K. subjects had taken LSD as opposed to four U.S. subjects. All the U.S. subjects expressed misgivings about the use of LSD whereas among U.K. subjects it was spoken of with interest and enthusiasm. Again, as in the case of marijuana, it was thought to be something of a cult drug.

Cocaine

Forty-seven of the U.K. subjects had used it as opposed to only two of the U.S. Surveys of American experience such as that of Meyer (1952) and Ellinwood *et al.* (1966), suggest that cocaine is a less popular drug in the U.S. and this would appear to support this finding.

Alcohol

Alcohol abuse as a precursor of opiate use is well documented (Pescor, 1943). In the present series excessive drinking, i.e. uncontrolled drinking, was reported by twenty-two U.K. subjects and fourteen U.S. subjects. In the U.S. subjects—particularly among Puerto Ricans—the reported pattern was one of bouts of wine drinking at an early age, in some cases at the age of twelve or thirteen. In all cases (U.S. and U.K.) the subjects had become abstinent from alcohol since taking heroin regularly.

A typology of addiction

Study of even a small sample of patients defined as 'addicts' readily shows that the addicted person is more difficult to identify than appears at first sight. At the simplest level there are individuals whose level of physiological dependence is stronger than others and this may not be clearly related to dose levels. On the other hand, there are recognizable individuals whose way of life changes during drug use more profoundly than that of others. Finally, it is often recognized that there are other individuals whose intensity of desire or craving for the drug is more pronounced. These aspects of the meaning of the term 'addiction' have been reviewed by Chein (1964) who has proposed a typology of addiction. Relevant to this is Lindesmith's (1947) discussion of the definition of formal addiction. Lindesmith's criteria include the recognition of dependence by the individual himself, with a change in his own self percept. This is ultimately associated with a state in which the individual becomes considerably preoccupied with drug-seeking activity, and ultimately his entry into an addict sub-culture in which he develops a mode of behaviour, language, etc., which is centrally related to drug taking.

This alteration in the way of life has been called by Chein 'total personal involvement' with drugs. This is an important observation which may provide a link between drug use and personality structure. In fact Chein postulates a theory of human behaviour in which an individual develops interests and concerns which are related to the assurance of the conditions of satisfying recurring needs. As he puts it: "These enduring concerns come to play a larger role in the life of the individual than the needs that originally gave rise to them, and indeed they acquire independence of the needs. As concerns with the conditions of satisfying motives, they incorporate the individual's conception of the self and of the relevant physical and social environment, and they require the development of relevant knowledge, skills, statuses and personal relationships. They acquire manifold interdependences which serve to really bind them."

Three dimensions of the addictive process are recognized and enumerated as follows. (1) The presence or absence of detectable degrees of physical dependence. (2) The presence or absence of detectable degrees of total personal involvement. (3) The presence or absence of detectable degrees of craving.

If these three dimensions are compounded, Chein postulates, it is possible to conceive of eight types of individuals, seven of whom could be regarded as being 'addictive'. He further suggests that the first dichotomy could be reduced to lesser status because of its 'shorter range' thus leaving four types of addicts which can be enumerated as follows. (1) Those who are totally involved but have no craving. (2) Those who have craving but no total involvement. (3) Those who have both craving and total involvement. (4) Individuals whose drug habit is characterized by repeated phases of physical dependence.

It is a fact that this typology of addiction has not been used hitherto, nor indeed was it used in Chein's studies. It was considered worthwhile to utilize it in the present study for a variety of reasons. The first of these was that it might conceivably be a way of drawing comparisons between U.K. and U.S. subjects. Chein has suggested that there may be some differences in this respect between the two populations; for example, he suggests that a substantial proportion of British addicts who continue on maintenance doses of opiates may well be individuals who could be regarded as type (1) cases, that is to say people who are totally involved with drug use but show little craving. He further suggests that there is reason to believe that there is a large proportion of American addicts who are either type (1) or type (4) cases.

An attempt was made to identify the addicts in this study utilizing this framework.

Applying the typology

The three identification points of the typology, namely (1) physical dependence, (2) total personal involvement, and (3) craving, were defined as follows.

(1) *Physical dependence*

Physical dependence was recognized as being present if the patient had an unequivocal history of characteristic abstinence symptoms related to opiate withdrawal.

(2) *Total personal involvement*

This was recognized as being present if the patient showed a clear history of, first of all, alterations in his way of life which led him into what can now be regarded as an addict way of life. The question was asked of the patient, 'Did he regard himself as being an addict?', and further, how he recognized this. If the patient was able to demonstrate a significant degree of association with other addicts, the adoption of an addict way of life and a degree of self recognition as an addict, then he was said to show involvement.

In practice this proved comparatively easy to evaluate; individuals who did not show this degree of total personal involvement were easily recognizable, since they were usually anxious to identify themselves with individuals who had managed to keep their drug habit away from their normal existence, and were not identifying themselves with an addict sub-culture.

(3) *Craving*

Craving was identified using the definition proposed by Chein. He suggests that there are three aspects of craving as applied to the addict which distinguish it from normal likes and desires. The three distinguishing features are as follows. First, craving is held to imply an abnormal intensity of desire. Second, craving is held to imply an abnormal intensification of the reaction to the failure to fulfil the desire. In other words, failure to satisfy the craving is followed by intense opposite reactions. Third, craving is said to imply an abnormal limit on the ability to modify the desire, even though the results of experiencing it tend negatively to reinforce the consequences of the satisfaction sought.

This a relatively tight definition of craving which proved not easy to apply and certainly bears little relation to the simple question put to an addict, e.g. 'Do you crave drugs?'

Categorization of the subjects

Using the typology described the subjects were classified as in Table 11.

Table 11

Typology of addiction (after Chein et al.)

Category	U.K. Male	U.S. Male	U.K. Female	U.S. Female
1	6	10	2	3
2	1	10	2	3
3	31	12	8	5
4	4	3	4	4
	n = 42	n = 35	n = 16	n = 15

Category 1: Marked total personal involvement and no craving.
Category 2: Strong craving—little personal involvement.
Category 3: Strong craving and personal involvement.
Category 4: Neither craving nor personal involvement but repeated phases of physical dependence.

It will be seen that the majority (73%) of U.K. male subjects fell into category 3, that is addicts with both marked craving and total personal involvement, while U.S. male subjects showed a more even scatter through categories 1–3.

The finding of thirty-one U.K. male addicts in category 3 is interesting in view of comments by Chein *et al.* that the patients most likely to be successful in 'maintenance' methods of treatment would be type 1 addicts, i.e. patients with personal involvement but no craving. All the British subjects had been involved in a 'maintenance' treatment situation at one stage or another, and no doubt their presence in hospital could be regarded as an index of the lack of success of the method. Further studies (using this typology) on out patients never admitted to hospital should yield useful information. Chein *et al.* comment that "it seems to be important to select type 1 cases if the experiment (maintenance medication) is to be successful".

It has to be conceded that applying the typology is not easy, but it does seem necessary to have some method of identifying patterns of addiction if their natural history is to be studied and treatment methods evaluated.

General Conclusions

A comparison of the drug using habits of similarly aged groups of London and New York addicts showed an earlier onset of heroin use in the U.S. subjects, with earlier exposure to drug use. There were differences in initial modes of administration. Also, there was a tendency for daily use to develop earlier in U.K. subjects, and the U.K. subjects showed a greater tendency to use oral amphetamine preparations before starting to use heroin. Periods of self imposed abstention were generally similar in both groups. Application of a typology of addiction showed clear differences between U.K. and U.S. male subjects studied.

It is difficult to know how much can be learnt from these findings from a cross-cultural point of view because of the enormous socio-cultural differences, but the study does, it is thought, emphasize again the need for constant recognition that addiction is a state with a natural history which does not follow a predictable course.

Tentatively it is suggested that the earlier development of daily self injection in U.K. subjects is a direct pharmacological effect related to the pure heroin available to U.K. addicts as opposed to the adulterated preparations available in the U.S.

Acknowledgements: I should like to thank the following colleagues who were most helpful in case finding: Dr. T. H. Bewley, Dr. P. A. L. Chapple, Dr. Dale Beckett, Dr. J. Merry, Dr. G. F. Vaughan. Also particular thanks to Dr. Harold Trigg and numerous colleagues at the Morris J. Bernstein Institute, New York. Professor Michael Shepherd gave much encouragement and advice. Financial aid was generously provided by the South East and South West Metropolitan Regional Hospital Boards and the Board of Governors of Guy's and King's College Hospitals.

I should also like to express my thanks to the Nestlé Corporation for generously providing data processing facilities.

REFERENCES

Bewley, T. H. (1965). Heroin and Cocaine Addiction. *Lancet*, **i**, 808–810.
Bewley, T. H. (1966). Recent changes in patterns of drug addiction in the United Kingdom. *Bull. Narcotics*, **18**, 4, 1–13.
Chein, I., Gerard, D. L., Lee, R. S. & Rosenfeld, E. (1964). *Narcotics, Delinquency and Social Policy—The Road to H.* New York: Basic Books.
Ellinwood, E. H., Smith, W. G. & Vaillant, G. E. (1966). *Int. J. Addict.*, **1**, 2, 32–45.
Gillespie, D., Glatt, M. M., Hills, D. R. & Pittman, D. J. (1967). Drug dependence and abuse in England. *Brit. J. Addict.*, **62**, 155–170.
Hewetson, J. & Ollendorf, R. (1966). Preliminary survey of 100 London heroin and cocaine addicts. *Brit. J. Addict.*, **60**, 110.
Lindesmith, A. R. (1947). *Opiate Addiction.* San Antonio, Texas: Principia Press of Trinity University.
Meyer, A. S. (1952). *Social and Psychological Factors in Opiate Addiction.* Bureau of Applied Social Research, Columbia University, New York, N.Y.
Pescor, M. J. (1943). *A Statistical Analysis of the Clinical Records of Hospitalised Drug Addicts.* Pub. Health Report U.S. Suppl. 143.
Schur, E. M. (1962). *Narcotic Addiction in Britain and America.* London: Tavistock.

THE ASSESSMENT OF HEROIN USAGE IN A PROVINCIAL COMMUNITY

J. Zacune, G. Stimson, A. Ogborne, M. Mitcheson
and A. Kosviner

Institute of Psychiatry, Addiction Research Unit,
101 Denmark Hill, London, S.E.5

Drug addiction in the United Kingdom is now at a dangerous level and its rising incidence raises urgent problems for treatment and research (Bewley, 1965; The Second Report of the Interdepartmental Committee, 1965; Office of Health Economics, 1967). The Home Office records indicate that the number of therapeutically addicted opiate users has stayed quite constant from 1960 to 1966—an average of 332 persons. In the same time, the number of non-therapeutic addicts (persons whose addiction did not originate in medical treatment) increased from 128 to 998. While the first opiate addict under the age of twenty was reported in 1960, 329 addicts under twenty years of age were listed in 1966. Furthermore, most of the new users were addicted to heroin rather than morphine. These figures may be an underestimate of the extent of opiate abuse but they accurately document the trends in the United Kingdom since 1960. Therefore it is imperative that this symposium explore the question that Professor Paton posed in opening this conference: can we find the biochemical, psychological and social forces that predispose people to try, and continue to use, opiate drugs? To approach parts of this question, the Addiction Research Unit at the Institute of Psychiatry decided to launch an intensive investigation in a provincial university town. With the help of a local and already involved psychiatrist, the unit wanted to ascertain the extent and nature of heroin use in that community.

Investigations into the psychological and sociological aspects of drug abuse have principally made use of interview material gained in a formalized (often medical) setting, assessment of statistical records, or studies of institutionalized subjects. Although these methods have provided invaluable insights, they cannot fully assess the process of heroin addiction.

In a formalized setting the experimenter and the subject (or doctor and patient) have basic social roles to perform. These role performances restrict their interaction and limit the information that can be gained (Goffman, 1961). Expectations will influence what behaviour is reported by the subject and how this report is interpreted by the experimenter (Sarbin, Taft & Bailey, 1960; Rosenthal, 1964). Moreover, it is difficult to assess the relevance of studies in a formal setting to the processes at work in the street (Sherif & Sherif, 1964). The heroin user is seen apart from his social environment and his social interaction, both of which are acknowledged to play a vital role in the process of heroin addiction. With this vital interaction omitted, only fragments of the involvement with heroin can be reconstructed.

The exclusive use of existing records for study is fraught with difficulty. The Home Office has the most extensive files available on opiate use in the United Kingdom, but until February 22, 1968 these files were constructed only on a voluntary basis. Most of the heroin users reported were either receiving a prescription for heroin or had come to the notice of an official agency. The notification system was not standardized. The criterion for inclusion was not absolutely clear. With any existing statistics there are the problems of false names, sporadic reporting and confirming the current status of those on the list. Heroin users that are not known to official sources are missed out. Schur (1962) reports that few users immediately go onto a prescription and getting a prescription is seen by users as a major step.

Problems of using existing statistical records are discussed fully by Chein *et al.* (Chein, Gerard, Lee & Rosenfeld, 1964).

Studies of institutionalized patients, i.e. those in hospitals, prisons, Borstals, etc., give a ready, but unfortunately biased sample. Such a study will assess only those who have ended up in trouble or receiving treatment. This may be only one end of a large spectrum of heroin users. In any case it represents only a percentage of the current heroin users and may miss out the most important groups. It does not encompass those who are just beginning but have not yet encountered serious difficulty. Of course these studies have limitations imposed by formalized settings.

The combination of methods described in Dr. Rathod's paper (this volume, pp. 331 to 339) are obviously more promising. He was able to uncover and interview a greater addict population than was suspected by any single agency which he had consulted. Yet we must now look for a method that will follow the vital 'Counting' stage with data on the details of the living patterns and interactions of heroin users. If possible we want to study processes and gain prospective, rather than retrospective, data.

This review of previous methodology is far from complete and the introductory discussion should not be construed to imply that these various studies are of little value. Rather, we are trying to feel our way to an approach that will allow us to expand and amplify the findings of previous research. These previous findings are obviously invaluable, but it is time to ascertain whether they are relevant and true of the street. Our guideline is still essentially the construction of reliable and valid research.

In our study of a provincial town, we opted for a research strategy which would eliminate some of the biases mentioned earlier, and which would capture a picture of heroin users in their own social environment. It was decided to seek all current, and recent users of heroin who were permanent residents in the town, who were either regular or irregular users, and regardless of whether or not they were known to official sources. It was hoped this would cover a wide population of people in different stages of heroin use. Thus, this study includes users who were recently institutionalized but excludes people attending the local university, unless they resided in the town before admission to the university.

For the major part of our study, we lived in a set of rooms near the centre of the town. The rooms served the double purpose of providing a base for our research, and a place that could be visited at any time of the day or night by heroin users who wished to chat, read, have a cup of coffee, or just warm up. The rooms constantly functioned on both levels. After we became acquainted with four heroin users, we were introduced to a large number of their friends. We spent a great deal of time chatting in pubs, flats, and in our rooms. The purpose of our research was explained in a straightforward way and no financial inducements were used. As we gained the confidence of more people we administered a long structured interview to each person. The interview covered social and family background, past and present social functioning, drug use, medical and psychiatric history. Sections of the interview also covered the user's attitude to society, his family and to other drug users, his attitude to treatment and to himself. In addition, two self-completion personality inventories were used. These interviews lasted on average two and a quarter hours.

At the same time, we checked all available sources for possible heroin users. We were able to secure the co-operation of the medical and psychiatric hospitals, local general practitioners, medical officers of health, the police, and probation service as well as the co-operation of the heroin users themselves. From these various sources, lists were compiled and ultimately cases were confirmed or rejected after obtaining as many completed interviews as possible. Thus we found thirty-seven people who were currently or very recently using heroin. We were able to have complete interviews with thirty-one users and obtain basic information about the remaining six. Heroin use was confirmed by observing twenty-two users self-inject heroin. The other fifteen were confirmed by medical sources and heroin-using friends. In addition to the completed interview schedules, we collected a great deal of anecdotal information because the rooms were almost in constant use as a social gathering place by a substantial number of heroin users in the town.

We do not propose to present and discuss the data in great detail because they have been published elsewhere (Kosviner, Mitcheson, Myers, Ogborne, Stimson, Zacune & Edwards, 1968). However, we will present a brief synopsis of the results and argue a few of their important implications.

Our sample had thirty-one males and six females, 84% of whom were aged twenty-one or less, and only two were over twenty-five. The average age for females was eighteen, for the males 21·1 years.

Using a social class rating of parent's occupation, we found the sample skewed to the higher social classes. Using the Registrar General's classification with the highest social class being I and the lowest social class V, all of our sample, except for four subjects whose social class was unknown, were in the higher social classes I, II and III. Using a newer Registrar General's classification, and assuming that the four unknowns were in the lower social classes, the distribution of social class in our sample is significantly different from the distribution of social class in the town itself (General Register Office, 1966).

Most of our subjects had good educational opportunity. 57% attended grammar, direct grant, or independent schools, 30% went to secondary modern or comprehensives, for 13% school type was unknown. In our sample 51% went on to some form of higher education in university, technical college, or art school, but 68% of these subjects failed to complete the course they began.

Fourteen heroin users in the sample were in full-time employment, seven were full-time students, nine were unemployed and seven currently institutionalized. On the whole, the jobs of subjects in full-time employment tended to be a lower level than would be expected with their educational background.

Drug use varied widely. We did not employ a criterion of addiction because, first, there is no general agreement on a satisfactory definition, and second, it is very difficult to assess the degree of dependence outside a medical setting. In our sample, twenty subjects were using heroin daily, sixteen were using heroin irregularly (less than daily), and one subject's frequency of use was not certain. When the study began only five subjects were receiving prescriptions, while the rest were supported by an illicit market. There were enough supplies coming from London to sustain this substantial group which contained a high percentage of daily users. Yet drugs were not 'pushed' in the American sense of the word, but rather, the users took it in turn to supply each other as a friendly rotating duty. A change in local policy had allowed seventeen of the sample to be on prescriptions by the end of the study.

The natural history of drug involvement showed no consistent patterns. All the users had tried both cannabis and amphetamine before heroin, but the length of time and degree of involvement with these drugs varied considerably. The confused issue of drug escalation can only be resolved with a prospective study. The spread of heroin use seemed to be through several existing friendship groups. It appears that the various groups then became more integrated with each other because of the necessity to organize supplies. We believe that friendship patterns are crucial to an understanding of how heroin spreads through a community, and these patterns must be thoroughly investigated in future studies.

The relationship of heroin use to delinquency is complex and intriguing. In our study, unlike most American investigations, deliquency decreased, rather than increased, after heroin use. Ten subjects had convictions for petty non-drug crime but there was only one such conviction following heroin usage, and that person had been convicted on a similar charge before.

It is hoped that this presentation of results has shown the variety of findings within the sample and that this has helped to differentiate it from other samples which have been reported. Although it has not been possible to do justice to the data collected, the following points present a few of the study's implications.

This investigation demonstrates the practicality of studying the heroin user in his own social environment, and points the way to studying the processes of heroin addiction. New approaches to study in the field are possible and should be exploited quickly.

It is vital to understand that there is no such thing as a typical 'junkie' in England. The diversity within our sample and its differentiation from other samples, forces us to look for a typology of heroin users rather than to try to find a single cause on a biological, social, or psychological level.

The uncovering of substantial hidden groups makes us think that the problem is more widespread than hitherto expected. Our study indicates that a variety of people may be at risk and we know little about the composition of the vulnerable population. A further investigation of friendship patterns is vital. The social network plays a major role in starting and continuing heroin use. Similarly, the values and aspirations of such groups must be taken into account to understand the meaning of the drug for individuals within the group.

Heroin use is a complex all-involving activity and it will challenge our imaginations to devise viable alternatives to drug involvement. These alternatives will have to be offered in a context that interprets treatment as a much wider and longer process than simply withdrawing the drug. It will have to replace a whole physical, psychological and social complex of activities.

In summary, it is hoped that this research has opened up new possibilities of looking at the heroin user in his social environment and points the way to uncovering some of the processes involved in drug use.

REFERENCES

Bewley, T. (1965). Heroin addiction in the United Kingdom (1955–1964). *Brit. Med. J.*, **2**, 1284.
Chein, I., Gerard, D., Lee, R. & Rosenfeld, E. (1964). *Narcotics, Deliquency, and Social Policy*. London: Tavistock.
General Register Office (1966). *Classification of Occupations*. London: H.M.S.O.
Goffman, E. (1961). *Asylums*. Garden City, N.Y.: Doubleday Anchor Books.
Kosviner, A., Mitcheson, M., Myers, K., Ogborne, A., Stimson, G., Zacune, J. & Edwards, G. (1968). Heroin use in a provincial town. *Lancet*, i, 1189–1192.
Office of Health Economics (1967). *Drug Addiction*. London: Office of Health Economics.
Rosenthal, R. (1964). Experimenter outcome-orientation and the results of the psychological experiment. *Psychol. Bull.*, **61**, 405–412.
Sarbin, T., Taft, R. & Bailey, D. (1960). *Clinical Inference and Cognitive Theory*. New York: Holt, Rinehart & Winston.
Schur, E. (1962). *Narcotic Addiction in Britain and America*. London: Tavistock.
Sherif, M. & Sherif, C. (1964). *Reference Groups*. New York: Harper & Row.
The Second Report of the Interdepartmental Committee (1965). *Drug Addiction*. London: H.M.S.O.

OBSERVATIONS ON HEROIN ABUSE BY YOUNG PEOPLE IN CRAWLEY NEW TOWN

R. DE ALARCON, N. H. RATHOD AND I. G. THOMSON

Graylingwell Hospital, Chichester

THIS report outlines some of the work done by clinical psychiatrists, working in a community psychiatric service, when they were confronted with an acute problem of abuse of heroin amongst the young people in the new town of Crawley.

This is a town situated half-way between London and Brighton. During the past seventeen years the population has increased six-fold and in 1966 it stood at 62,130 with 45% younger than twenty-five. The increase was chiefly caused by young families moving in to find work in the expanding industries—Crawley has 120 factories—and accommodation in the new housing estates. (More than two-thirds of its 17,000 houses are Council owned.)

Two consultants on the staff of Graylingwell Hospital have been responsible for running the general psychiatric services in the area. This covers the new town of Crawley, the nearby town of Horsham and the surrounding rural districts, and the total population served is approximately 130,000. The service is predominantly community-based with a day hospital at Horsham as its headquarters.

Until March 1967, no heroin users were known to the service. We treated three patients for dependence on amphetamines in 1966 and only discovered later that they were using heroin at the time.

In March and April 1967, we were taken by surprise when four patients, all under twenty and from Crawley, were referred by their family doctors for the treatment of abuse of heroin. These four patients told us that there were many more like them in Crawley and also that these patients had shared experiences, such as being searched for the possession of heroin or suffering jaundice long before the abuse of heroin was revealed to the G.P.s. These, and such other clues, obtained during our day to day practice as clinical psychiatrists, presented us with a unique opportunity for clinical research in the problem of abuse of drugs. At the same time the local community was demanding urgent treatment facilities.

Research carried out in 1967

Signs and symptoms of use of heroin

In view of the disappointing results of treating chronic addiction, we felt early detection to be necessary. To achieve this we and others (G.P.s, parents, teachers and so on) in the community needed to know how to recognize this abuse. Medical literature, which abounds in accounts of withdrawal syndrome and the changes in the 'way of life' of an addict, did not prove very helpful.

Through the help of our experts (the patients and their parents) we were able to assemble consistent data which we found useful in answering whether or not a person was on heroin. The results have been published elsewhere (Rathod, de Alarcon & Thomson, 1967).

Prevalence study

Our second difficulty was to assess the size of the problem. From the remarks of our patients it appeared that the G.P.s, our normal channel of referral, did not come across the cases as early as other agencies did, and that there was an undetected pool of heroin users in the community.

To assess the size of the problem we carried out a prevalence survey using the following five screening methods. (1) Information from local probation officers on drug users. (2) Information from local police regarding searches and convictions for abuse of drugs. (3) Information from patients under treatment about other new users known to them. (The incentive of providing prescriptions of heroin was not used.) (4) A survey of all cases of jaundice between January 1966 and December 1967 in the age group fifteen to twenty-five. (5) A similar survey of admissions to the casualty department for overdose of amphetamines and/or barbiturates.

Names revealed by each screening method and those who were referred by the G.P.s were entered on a cumulative register, each entry being cross-checked against information revealed by other screening methods. Names thus collected were classified into four types of users.

(1) *Confirmed users*

Either (a) were examined and diagnosed by a doctor, or (b) admitted use of heroin to G.P., probation officer or police, or (c) were those whose names were revealed by at least three different screening methods.

(2) *Probable users*

Excluding (1), and those whose names were revealed by two independent screening methods.

(3) *Suspects*

Those who were named by one screening method only.

(4) *Non-users*

Suspects seen by us but found not to be using heroin.

Ninety-eight names were collected and of those fifty were confirmed users; five were probable users; thirty-seven were suspected users and six were classified as non-users (Table 1).

Prevalence rates were calculated for the year 1967 (January to December) for the age group fifteen to twenty; no cases were revealed in people older than twenty. The total population in this age group was 5,880, and of these 3,050 were males. Taking the confirmed users alone, the prevalence rate works out at 8·5 per 1,000 of the total population; a rate which is at least six times higher than that based on Home Office figures. If only males are considered, the rate works out at 14·75 per thousand.

Table 1

Observed prevalence of heroin use in people aged 15–20 in Crawley New Town in 1967 (population 5,880)

Category of use	No.	Rate per 1,000 population	
		For each category	Cumulative
Confirmed users	50	8·50	—
Probable users	5	0·85	9·35
Suspected users	37	6·29	15·64
Totals	92	15·64	15·64

The screening methods revealed cases which would have been missed had we relied on our normal channels of referral (Table 2). They also disclosed cases earlier than would otherwise have been possible. In addition each method provided confirmatory evidence for information by the other screening methods (Table 3).

The details of this part of the work are being presented elsewhere (de Alarcon & Rathod, 1968).

Research in progress

What follows is abstracted from studies in progress and the findings are therefore of a preliminary nature. Further research and use of controls, where necessary, will be needed before any conclusions can be attempted.

Table 2
The value of each screening method

First source of information about heroin use	No. of names detected	Category of use			
		Confirmed	Probable	Suspected	Non-user
Direct G.P. referral	8	8	—	—	—
Jaundice survey	20	9	4	7	—
Casualty survey:					
Amphetamines	7	6	—	1	—
Barbiturates	8	2	—	—	6
Heroin users in treatment	46	17	1	28	—
Police:					
Convictions	4	4	—	—	—
Other evidence	3	2	—	1	—
Probation officers	2	2	—	—	—
Totals	98	50	5	37	6

Table 3
Subsequent confirmation of earliest indicator of heroin use in fifty confirmed cases

First indicator of heroin use	No. of cases	Subsequent source of confirmation				
		G.P.	Jaundice	Casualty	Police or probation	Users in treatment
General practitioner	8	—	2	1	5	5
Jaundice	9	8	—	1	4	5
Casualty	8	4	3	—	2	4
Police or probation	8	2	1	—	—	4
Users in treatment	17	9	7	—	7	—
Totals	50	23	13	2	18	18

Characteristics of patients

Age. Of the thirty-nine patients seen so far, two are twenty-one, two are fifteen and the rest are between sixteen and twenty. It seems that abuse of heroin in Crawley is chiefly a teenage problem.

Sex. Boys appear to use heroin more often than girls. Of the thirty-nine seen, only six were girls; the male-female ratio being 5·5 to 1.

Intelligence. Assessment was based on school reports and the Mill Hill vocabulary and Progressive Matrices. Of the twenty patients investigated so far only one had an I.Q. of less than 100. Six had an I.Q. between 120 and 130, but none of these boys fulfilled their academic expectations at school.

Deviant behaviour (*before use of drugs*). The data is based on information from the patients and their parents, schools, police and probation officers. Twenty-four patients have been investigated so far.

Fifteen (60%) truanted regularly in the last one to two years at school. Twelve (50%) left school at the earliest opportunity, i.e. at fifteen, and eight were asked to leave school, mostly for misbehaviour. Nineteen had appeared before the courts; eight of them more than once, and the commonest crime was of an acquisitive nature. Whether the abuse of drugs is causally related to anti-social behaviour or is only an extension of anti-social tendencies may, possibly, be revealed by further research.

Development of drug habit. Drug habits of thirty-two patients (twenty-seven boys and five girls) have been investigated. Information obtained from the user in question is cross-checked with that supplied by other sources, e.g. other users, police and probation officers.

Pattern of initiation and spread. Initiation and supplying is done on a mutual aid basis with little room for commercial profiting. Users take it in turns to do shopping for each other. The shopping centre is nearly always said to be London.

In 1964 and 1965, three boys had their first experience of heroin and were initiated separately by people outside Crawley. They continued to live in Crawley but had little contact with each other. Twelve months or more elapsed after their first injection before they started to use the drug regularly.

Then came a marked change. One member of the group initiated three other friends in Crawley in 1966, and from then on a massive proliferation took place. Teenagers who knew each other through schools, neighbourhood, youth clubs, etc., began to initiate ('infect') each other. All the rest of the group was initiated in Crawley by a 'friend' in Crawley; and five boys between them shared the credit of initiating twenty others. Moreover, all these boys started using heroin regularly within three months of their first injection.

Drugs used

Use of multiple drugs at the same time has been reported by the patients—both by intravenous and oral routes. Besides heroin, cocaine was used intravenously by 41% (thirteen boys and no girls), and methedrine by 31% (nine boys and one girl). As far as oral use was concerned, besides cannabis and alcohol, amphetamines were used by 28% (seven boys and two girls); LSD by 21% (seven boys and no girls), and barbiturates by 18% (four boys and two girls). This suggests existence of a poly-drug problem.

Frequency of use

For most patients financial resources and the availability of the drug seemed to play an important part in determining both the frequency and the types of the drugs used. Many patients were users on three to four days a week, mostly at weekends. Some used more often and some less often. These observations apply to all drugs and especially to heroin. We hope to investigate the factors which differentiate the different groups of these users.

Dependence

It is difficult to decide on the degree of dependency in the patients studied, but almost all patients claimed to have suffered from withdrawal symptoms and have craved for heroin. Certainly in sixteen patients so far treated as in-patients, these phenomena have been validated by us.

Treatment programme

We hope to describe our programme in detail in the near future. Briefly, the treatment is directed at the following. (a) Understanding the individual patient's psycho-social difficulties which make him vulnerable to drugs, and to help reorientate him in his attitudes both to himself and to others around him. Individual and group psychotherapy are used. (b) Deconditioning the patient against the self-injection of drugs. To achieve this we are experimenting with succinyl-scoline-induced apnoea as an instrument of deconditioning (Thomson & Rathod, 1968). (c) Understanding the home environment and its effects on the members, and helping the parents with support and education, encouraging them to examine their relationships between themselves and the patient. Individual counselling both at home and at clinics. Individual and group psychotherapy are used towards this purpose. Ten mothers and ten fathers are taking part in group therapy. (d) Provision of continuous and regular follow-ups for discharged patients. If the patient fails to attend, a member of the staff will usually visit the patient at his home or at work. In this connection close liaison with the police, probation service and the mental welfare officers is proving very useful. We also ensure that the patient can contact a member of the staff at any time of need. (e) Establishing close contact with the future employers or teachers to encourage personal responsibility for the patient while working or attending school. (f) Discouraging patients from the use of any drugs which can produce dependence. No heroin is ever prescribed for out-patients; oral physeptone is prescribed in reducing dosage as out-patients but it is not dispensed to the patient. Parents of the patient have to come and collect the drug and they have to supervise its admission to the patient. Frequent spot checks on urine are made, both for out-patients and in-patients.

The treatment is carried out in three settings; out-patient; day hospital and in-patient at Graylingwell Hospital. Of the forty patients seen, thirty-two had accepted treatment and of these sixteen had to be admitted to Graylingwell Hospital.

Research into social factors. Miss Carter, our P.S.W. with the help of Miss B. Nelson and Dr. J. Grad from the M.R.C. Clinical Psychiatry Research Unit at Chichester, is in the process of completing a pilot enquiry into the family structure of the drug users under treatment. Factors like social class, personal background of parents, living conditions, both prior to and after moving into Crawley, mental illness in the families, anti-social tendencies in other members of the family, etc., are being looked into.

REFERENCES

Rathod, N. H., de Alarcon, R. & Thomson, I. G. (1967). *Lancet*, **ii,** 1411–1414.
de Alarcon, R. & Rathod, N. H. (1968). *Brit. Med. J.*, **ii,** 549–553.
Thomson, I. G. & Rathod, N. H. (1968). *Lancet*, **ii,** 382–384.

THE NATURAL HISTORY OF URBAN NARCOTIC DRUG ADDICTION—SOME DETERMINANTS

George E. Vaillant

Department of Psychiatry, Tufts University School of Medicine, Boston, Massachusetts

In recent years narcotic drug addiction has posed modern society a vexing challenge. Addiction has received the serious attention of law enforcement agents, psychiatrists, sociologists and public servants; yet in spite of this attention the etiology and cure of narcotic addiction has remained obscured behind a scrim of too much opinion and too little data. Students of human behaviour have understood for some time that cherished human goals or objects derive their value from a complex dynamic matrix. Too often the study of such goals (be they success, affection or drugs) has been confined to one situation at one point in time. That this approach is misleading is illustrated by the fact that cigarettes in post-war Berlin exerted a very different sort of control over human behaviour from that which they do at present in the Surgeon General's office in Washington, D.C. The control that a cherished object exerts over an individual's behaviour certainly depends upon its intrinsic value, its symbolic significance, the individual's conscious and unconscious needs and on the external environment. However, the control that the cherished object exerts over behaviour also depends on the regular sequence of events or contingencies under which that object is sought. In the literature on operant conditioning such a regular sequence of events or *temporal environment* is called a 'schedule'. There is no more graphic illustration of the interaction between cherished goals, behaviour, and temporal contingencies than that provided by the life history of the addict.

One of the difficulties, of course, in understanding people is that they differ from moment to moment; like symphonies, they are hard to conceive of in their entirety. If over long periods, however, aspects of lifetimes can be presented graphically, it is possible to see dynamic interrelations between behaviour and temporal variables. A redwood trunk in cross-section allows us to *see* a millennium of forest history in an instant: yet we must *listen* to a sixty-minute tape of an interview for several hours if we wish to conceptualize its chronology. The crystallization of time represented by the redwood trunk resembles both the *cumulative records* devised by B. F. Skinner (1953) and his students to graph the behaviour of animals over time and the *life chart* that Adolph Meyer (1919) used to help him visualize the lives of psychiatric patients. In the past decade, behavioural pharmacologists, especially Peter Dews and his co-workers at Harvard Medical School, have used Skinner's cumulative records to investigate the effect of drugs on behaviour over time. Their work demonstrated that the schedules of reinforcement maintaining the behaviour under study are just as critical in determining drug effects on behaviour as are the nature of the reinforcement or the drug itself. Their laboratory observations seem relevant to the real life narcotic addict.

This paper is concerned with the lifetimes of a hundred narcotic addicts. Twelve years after they left the United States Public Health Service Hospital for narcotic addiction at Lexington, Kentucky, a hundred urban addicts were followed-up (Vaillant, 1966a). This sample of addicts was biased in that it contained only male first admissions who were from New York City and less than fifty years old. Otherwise selection was by chance. On the average, such addicts were twenty-five on admission and had been addicted to heroin for two years. Seventy-five per cent had sought hospital admission voluntarily.

Life histories of addicts

The life of each addict was represented graphically and the variables of addiction, employment and imprisonment were charted as illustrated in Figure 1, which represents a schematic drawing of fifteen years of an idealized addict's life. As can be seen, simple relapse or non-relapse to drugs is no longer the chief question. The course of an individual's narcotic addiction usually involves multiple relapses and often spans a decade or more. Thus, the problem under study becomes: if most urban addicts relapse after treatment, which they do, how often, in what conditions and for how long are they abstinent? In this figure the three kinds of behaviour—*abstinence, addiction* and *work*—are the dependent variables. Data collection was made as objective as possible. Anamnestic data for work history and imprisonment were substantiated by obtaining records of social security payments and police department fingerprint records. Both these last sources provided prospectively gathered data that were not affected by geographic mobility, the use of aliases and, most important, by the distortions of individual memory. The use of such routinely gathered institutional records provides information relatively uncontaminated by either the investigator's bias or by the experience of 'being studied'. At a single point in time such data seem crude, but when plotted over time, the data summarized in Figure 1 provide patterns that become extremely meaningful.

Clearly, the history of abstinence and of drug use is more difficult to measure objectively than that of crime or employment. Information about addiction during the period 1952–1964 was obtained from multiple sources. First, most of the men were prospectively followed-up for the first three to six years after they left Lexington. Second, if the discharged addicts were readmitted to institutions—prisons or hospitals—the arrest records and the records of these institutionalizations provided information contemporary for that period in the addict's life. Twelve years after discharge, I tried to interview the relatives of all patients and to interview personally all addicts that appeared to be abstinent. In these ways information about abstinence or addiction was gathered at *five* or more different points in time for all but one of the men in the study still alive in 1955. Both with

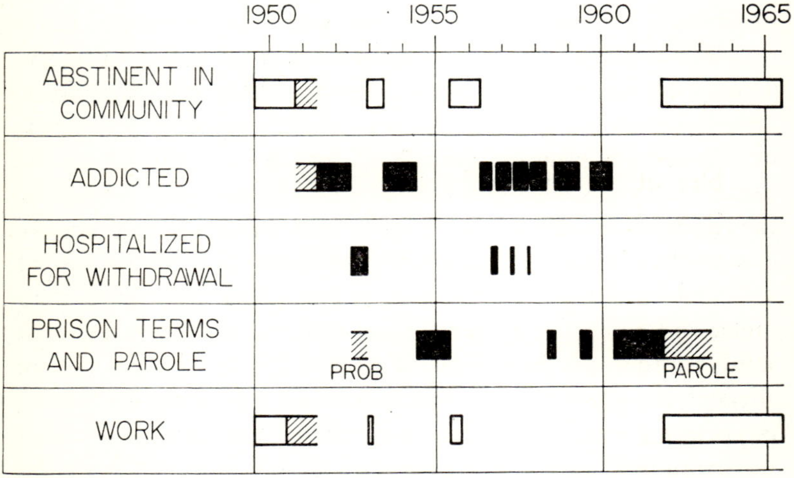

FIG. 1. An idealized case history to illustrate both the methods of data organization and the points that may be derived statistically from the life course of the hundred addicts in the study. By charting life events in this way, correlation between variables becomes apparent. The addict's work history deteriorated as he started to use drugs; and, then, when he was addicted, it ceased altogether. A long hospitalization produced a short community abstinence, but the reason why the addict remained 'voluntarily' hospitalized for so long was that he was under probation (Prob.). He relapsed and received a long prison term without parole. Again, he became abstinent, but prior punishment did not deter him long. Then, several short psychiatric hospitalizations followed; these diminished the likelihood of arrest but not of addiction. Subsequently, several short prison terms for possession again failed to alter his pattern of drug seeking. Neither medicine nor law alone could cure. In 1960, he was arrested for selling narcotics. He received an eighteen-month prison term and eighteen months more on parole, during which time, and, more important, afterwards, he was abstinent and gainfully employed.

the passage of time and with the chronicity of addiction, relatives and patients became more honest historians with regard to re-addiction.

Addiction patterns

Figure 2 represents an overall view of the general findings of the study. It represents the superimposed addiction patterns of one hundred addicts. In 1952, all hundred patients in the study had been using drugs daily, and 95% had been physiologically *addicted* as shown by the fact that they received narcotics during their withdrawal period at Lexington. Virtually all relapsed after leaving Lexington. As time passed, the number of actively *addicted* individuals decreased. So did those *institutionalized* (imprisoned or hospitalized for eleven months or more out of the calendar year). The number of addicts with a *marginal* adjustment remained more or less constant; such individuals were not addicted but either continued using drugs intermittently or engaged in illegal activities. The number of *abstinent* addicts steadily increased, but abstinence did not begin at any given age. There did not seem to be a special point in life when addicts spontaneously recovered. Addiction status in the group marked '*lost*' was not known with certainty. Most of these individuals however, were known to be working and had been abstinent when last heard from. Of the whole sample 47% were known to have been abstinent in 1964 or at the last contact. Thirty currently abstinent addicts had been abstinent for at least three years; the average of such abstinence was 7·7 years.

Why and how addiction develops

Figure 2 suggests the bold findings of the study, but does not tell us *why*. Addiction is a phenomenon that must be looked at in three parts: How does it begin? How is it maintained? How does it stop? Only when these answers are known, can we then *understand*, *predict* and *alter* the addict's fate.

Why *does* it begin? Addicts, indeed delinquents in general, have past histories of very unpatterned social behaviour. Several studies have shown that the young urban addict cannot be easily distinguished from the young urban delinquent. In the terminology of operant conditioning, both have had little experience

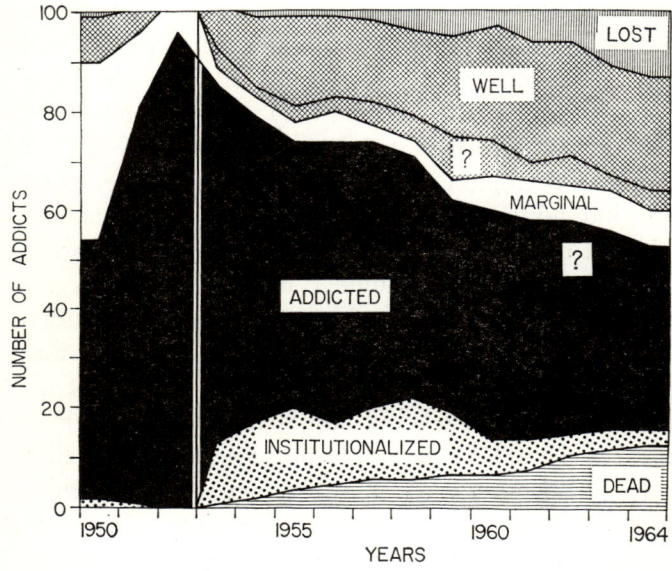

FIG. 2. Composite graph showing the proportion of addicts that fitted each clinical category each year after hospital discharge (indicated by the vertical line at the start of 1953). (Vaillant, 1966a.)

with stable schedules of reinforcement; they have been badly shaped and have been often exposed to conflicting stimulus control. In the vernacular of dynamic psychiatry they were orally deprived, exposed to double-blind communication and have inadequate parental introjects. In the language of everyday they have come from broken homes, where maternal supervision and affection in the pre-school years was inadequate, where the father was absent, where there was little family cohesion, where they were exposed to a 'do as I say, not as I do' morality, and where their efforts for independence were met with maternal ambivalence. These rather sweeping generalizations have been documented by comparing delinquents and addicts with non-delinquent, non-addict controls matched for variables like social class, place of residence, intelligence and ethnic background (Glueck & Glueck, 1950; Chein, Gerard, Lee & Rosenfeld, 1964).

The present investigation supported these observations (Vaillant, 1966a and c). Fifty per cent of the addicts in the study had lost their fathers before the age of sixteen and 20% had lost their mothers by the same age. Such figures are three times the national average. Like the Gluecks' delinquents, 64% of the addicts were first generation urban Americans. By this is meant that most of these addicts were born in New York City, although their parents were born abroad if they were white, or in the South if they were Negro (Vaillant, 1966e). By comparing data for these addicts with the census data for New York City males of similar age, it can be demonstrated that the likelihood of addiction among males born in New York of immigrant parents is three times that of addiction among immigrants (Figure 3). This relation holds good for different ethnic groups. Nevertheless, the immigrant who came to New York as a child encountered the same slums, the same prejudices, and the same drug using associates as a first generation New Yorker. In short, addiction occurred most often in families that were tangibly unstable either by parental separation or by parent-child cultural disparity.

More than half of the addicts in the study were known to have been delinquent *before* drug use. The majority of subjects had not qualified for the draft, or had been discharged as unfit. This was in spite of their own good general health and intelligence and the fact that the United States was engaged in the Korean war.

Although the average age on admission to Lexington was twenty-five, a third of the addicts had never worked for as long as a year; few had regular work histories before addiction. Despite intelligence superior to that found in other individuals from

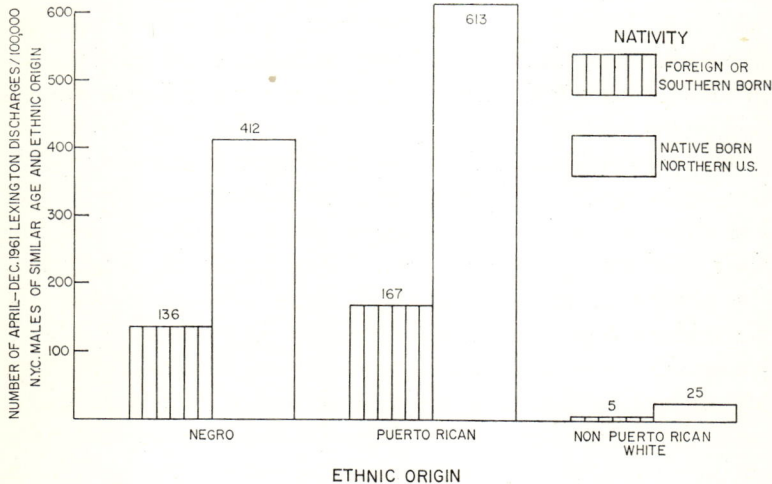

Fig. 3. Graph showing that the likelihood of addiction was greater for young New Yorkers born in the northern United States regardless of ethnic origin. The majority of these men had foreign or southern born parents (Vaillant, 1966e).

their socio-economic background, their length of schooling was inferior. Thus, the addict's inability to work or to conform to 'rules' preceded his addiction.

The background of the addicts supported the widely held clinical impression that addicts are unusually dependent and that this dependence stems from the quality of their relationship with their mother or mother surrogate. Of the hundred addicts in the study, twice as many as could be expected by chance were youngest children. Half of all the addicts continued to live with female blood relatives after age thirty.

In short, addicts become addicts not only through physiological dependence on opiates, by contagion from drug using or 'bad' associates, or from their wish to anaesthetize individual psychological problems; they also become addicts because of a life-long inability to maintain independent gratifying activities. The addict *begins* drug seeking behaviour more because he has very little tendency to engage in other competing forms of activity than because morphine or heroin *per se* is a powerful reinforcer or temptation.

After leaving Lexington in 1952, ninety of the hundred addicts,

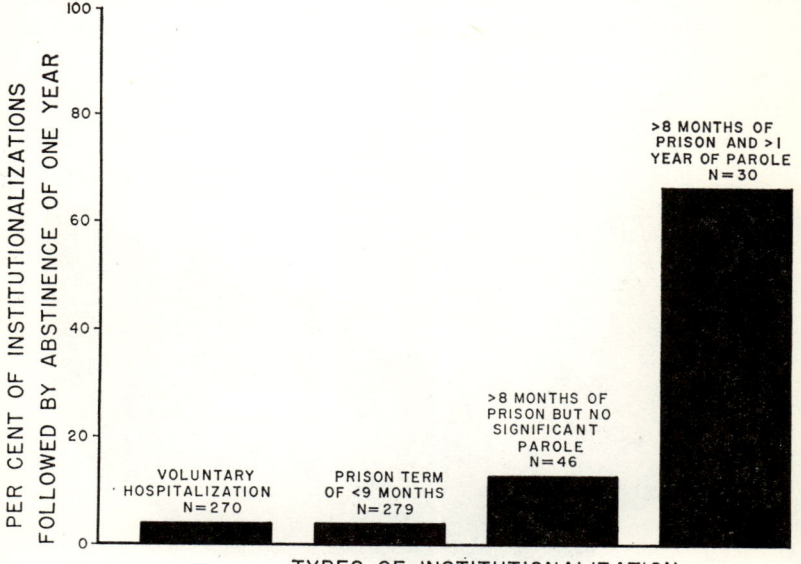

FIG. 4. Graph showing the relative frequency of abstinence following different types of institutional treatment (Vaillant, 1966a).

most of whom had voluntarily freed themselves from physiological dependence, quickly relapsed to the regular use of drugs. As can be seen in Figure 4, over the years almost 550 voluntary hospitalizations and short term imprisonments were ineffective in altering the drug seeking behaviour of these men. Thus, neither self-motivated withdrawal from physical dependence on narcotics nor being punished for using them produced abstinence. Conversely, since these men *were* repeatedly withdrawn from narcotics, physical dependence *per se* cannot be blamed for chronicity of addiction. Why, then, is addiction *maintained*?

Maintenance of addiction

First, addicts have trouble working. Existing evidence suggests that by the age of forty the average New York addict had spent only 20% of his adult life actively addicted, but he had spent 80% of this period unemployed (Figure 5) (Vaillant, 1966b). In

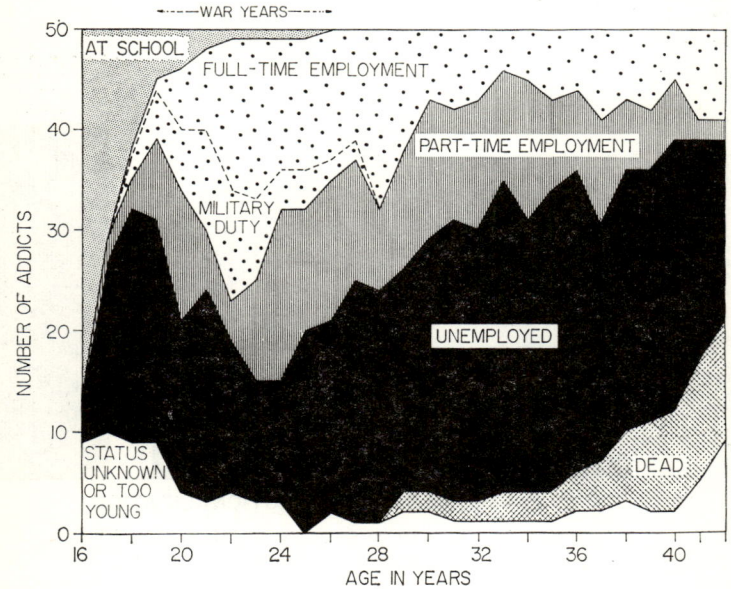

FIG. 5. Composite graph showing the proportion of New York heroin addicts that are employed at any given age. The graph is largely derived from their social security records; military duty was ascertained from other sources. The graph describes the employment careers of fifty consecutive admissions from New York to the Lexington Hospital in 1952 who would be at least forty in 1964. The average age of first addiction was twenty-five (Vaillant, 1966b).

someone whose daily life is unpatterned by a job, addiction imposes a very definite and gratifying, if rather stereotyped, pattern of behaviour. Addicts, many of whom have been misfits—both in school and in street gangs—do finally achieve a means of social reinforcement. Under present laws and conditions, if a man is addicted, he must work from morning to night to maintain the addiction. The ability to make a 'score' (successful theft) or 'cop a good bag' (obtain a *glassine* envelope of relatively concentrated heroin) is met with considerable peer group approval and personal satisfaction. Thus, drug addiction provides an Ersatz occupation—but a very absorbing one.

In the laboratory it has become increasingly apparent that 'schedules' are extremely important in determining the effects that different reinforcers *and* different drugs exert upon behaviour. In the case of clinical narcotic addiction these laboratory findings are borne out. The regular and predictable variables that affect the environment of the addict over time, i.e. 'schedules', exerted important effects upon drug seeking behaviour. For example, there is evidence that drug seeking behaviour with its associated indolence and petty crime takes precedence over competing schedules of behaviour (e.g. employment), but that this precedence cannot be explained by the sedative, euphoric or debilitating effects of narcotics alone. In highly structured and long maintained occupations like that of a physician or in an experimental but highly structured setting like the wards of the Addiction Research Center at Lexington, it is possible for an individual to be severely addicted with only minor impairment of his occupational efficiency. Thus, relatively high tissue concentrations of opiates *per se* do not preclude effective occupational functioning. Nor, despite claims in the popular press, can suppression of employment by addiction be solely attributed to drug cost; some addicts make roughly as much money when working as when engaged in crime. Rather, when addicted, the addict is on a schedule that demands immediate expenditure of as much money as is available. In this sense addiction is analogous to compulsive drinking. All the addict's financial resources are rapidly expended on drugs without effort to spread this expenditure out over time. When money is gone, it becomes necessary to obtain more within twelve hours or else suffer withdrawal symptoms. Characterized by immediate, if limited, financial payoff, petty crime is more suited to such a 'schedule' than a pay-check that comes only once a week.

But such a schedule is not always maintained by purely pharmacological determinants. In part, the addict's need for drugs is conditioned. First, it is not uncommon for an addict, who has sincerely told the admitting physician that he has a large habit, to discover that his withdrawal symptoms are much less severe than he expected. His worst suspicions are realized; for months his peddler had been selling him heroin that is virtually 100% milk sugar. Thus, a previous history of active addiction has conditioned the addict to respond to repeated injections of a placebo as if he were addicted.

Secondly, addiction is maintained by many 'conditioned reinforcers'. Friends, syringes, rituals of injection, and locations associated with addiction acquire reinforcing properties. Third, with chronic use, narcotics provide little or no conscious gratification; thus, once relapse has occurred, addiction is maintained in large part in order to avoid the discomfort of real or imagined withdrawal.

Yet there is evidence that withdrawal symptoms themselves are not simple physiological responses to the withdrawal of biologically active substance, but that they, too, are under considerable control of *schedules* and past *experience*. Let me first cite anecdotal illustrations. When nutmeg, a non-narcotic stimulant, is smuggled into the Lexington Hospital, the patients go through certain rituals, associated in time past with heroin disbribution, while dividing it among themselves. At such times, in anticipation of the nutmeg they may experience lacrimation, runny nose, yawning, goose flesh and muscular aches—in short, signs and symptoms characteristic of withdrawal. On finally having to leave the hospital, immature, dependent patients sometimes experience similar symptoms while going out of the hospital gate. On the research ward men who have been abstinent for months can experience acute craving and withdrawal symptoms while watching another addict receive an injection of narcotics. Finally, withdrawal symptoms at Lexington are often most severe among addicts who have a previous history of withdrawal in private hospital settings where a stormy withdrawal is often rewarded by excessive administration of substitute narcotics.

Experimental evidence supports these clinical impressions. For a short time the withdrawal symptoms of monkeys can be effectively relieved by injections of saline if the saline is administered in settings where morphine was given in the past (Spragg, 1940; Thompson and Schuster, 1964). The converse is also true. If morphine-addicted monkeys are given nalorphine, a morphine antagonist, withdrawal symptoms are abruptly precipitated. When morphine-satiated monkeys were given saline instead of nalorphine, withdrawal symptoms still occurred (Goldberg & Shuster, 1966). After several weeks without drugs rats will show signs of withdrawal in a setting where in the past they have often experienced withdrawal, yet in their home cages they will not show these signs (Wikler, 1965).

Studies in man suggest that the memory of abstinence and of the mental discomfort that in the past was relieved by opiates can evoke withdrawal signs. At Lexington *signs* as well as symptoms of withdrawal were produced in ex-addicts by hypnotic suggestion (Ludwig & Lyle, 1965). At the Rockefeller Institute, Dole & Nyswander (1965) reported that when some addicts were maintained on high doses of methadone, a synthetic opiate, they got no effect from heroin; but in the presence of psychological stress they still reported symptoms of withdrawal (yawning, sweating, malaise and nausea).

Having examined how the effects of narcotics and their absence can be conditioned in a Pavlovian fashion, it is useful to consider drug seeking as also conditioned in an operant fashion; by this is meant that behaviour can be maintained by its *consequences* as well as by its *antecedents*. The mere sight of a French restaurant may make a lover of continental cuisine salivate (Pavlovian conditioning), but in a strange city the same gourmet may repeatedly wander down side streets because in the past such behaviour had been associated with the discovery of French restaurants (operant conditioning). Neither behaviour need be conscious.

Abraham Wikler (1965) has suggested that drug seeking itself may be a gratifying life pattern that he calls 'hustling behaviour'. He suggests that 'hustling' *per se* is maintained because in time past it has had rewarding consequences—the relief of abstinence. For example, to ward off withdrawal the addict intravenously self-administers his total supply of narcotics. After the gratifying lassitude following such an intravenous injection has worn off, the penniless, drugless addict anticipating withdrawal will engage in his 'hustle', usually a stereotyped form of illegal activity, to get money for the next injection. This goal achieved, he will hurry off to locate a peddler; and then, rewarded by a second successful search, he will return to a favourite site for drug administration. After some social boasting to his peers of his success in getting a 'good bag', the addict engages in an enjoyable ritual of dissolving the heroin in a bent spoon or bottle cap of water, and of wrapping a belt around his bicepts to engorge the veins in his arm. Then, holding the belt taut with his teeth, he injects the drug via a cherished medicine dropper. Thus, each step in the cycle is causally related to the relief that follows.

I am not suggesting that opiates are not often obtained and administered in other ways; but in a given individual the temporal pattern or 'schedule' may be remarkably constant and maintained by tangible rewards all along the way. Most of these rewards have no direct pharmacological basis. Thus, it is not surprising that addicts, upon release from Lexington, despite firm conscious resolutions to the contrary, can relapse into the cycle of hustling almost as soon as they get off the train in New York. They will ascribe the relapse to an entirely unconscious process, to just accidently 'drifting' or to "It just happened before I thought what I was doing". Not only does a history of poorly patterned social behaviour, then, contribute to the initiation of addiction; but the substitute behavioural patterns that the addict evolves become strongly associated with its persistence.

Ways and means of abstinence

How does an addict *stop*? Figure 4 suggests that neither kindness nor punishment helps. But, several factors do appear to mitigate the addict's fate whether or not external intervention occurs. Figure 6 compares thirty addicts who during the twelve years after being at Lexington remained chronically addicted with thirty addicts who achieved a stable abstinence of three years or more. Statistically, addicts who had previously stable work patterns and addicts whose early family matrices were stable, were the ones who eventually became abstinent. The more 'scheduled' his early life had been, the more likely was he to recover from addiction. Ethnic background, delinquency, mental illness and family pathology had no bearing on prognosis. The variables in Figure 6 were all recorded in 1952 and provide a possible means of *predicting* long term outcome (Vaillant, 1966d).

The length of addiction before admission to Lexington correlated only weakly with prognosis. The amount of drug used (measured by the amount of narcotic required during withdrawal) was not at all correlated with outcome. Thus, once again, persistent drug seeking behaviour cannot be attributed solely to the result of the pharmacological effects of narcotics.

Effective treatment appeared to depend on the compulsory

alteration of the addict's behaviour for substantial periods of time. Figure 4 shows that long imprisonment was correlated with abstinence more often than short imprisonment or voluntary hospitalization. Long hospitalization was more effective

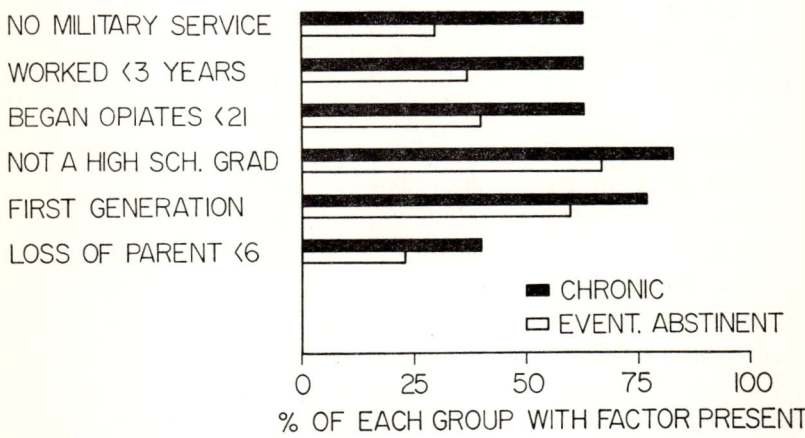

FIG. 6. Graph showing the significant differences at first admission in 1952 between thirty addicts who eventually became abstinent and thirty addicts who remained chronically addicted for the next ten years (Vaillant, 1966d).

than short hospitalization (Vaillant, 1966a). However, it is clear from the figure that a long prison term *coupled with a year of parole* was vastly more effective than any of the other three methods or treatment shown. This was in spite of the fact that (a) only the more severe offenders ever received sentences that included at least a year of parole; (b) virtually all such parole successes had previously relapsed after other forms of treatment; (c) the past histories of paroled individuals contained no more favourable prognostic factors than the histories of other prisoners, and (*d*) age was not a relevant variable (Vaillant, 1966*d*). Put another way, fifteen of the thirty best outcomes received a year of compulsory supervision but only three of the thirty worst outcomes ever received such treatment.

Significantly, eight other year-long abstinences also occurred during periods of prolonged probation or during a year or more of compulsory supervision following *short* imprisonments or hospitalization. None of the parole failures ever became abstinent after *any* form of treatment. Although after the addicts left Lexington in 1952, a social agency had attempted to follow them up regularly on a non-compulsory basis, in these circumstances virtually all had relapsed. Abstinent addicts, nevertheless, denied that parole was a factor in their recovery; and such a causal relationship would not be readily apparent by looking at addicts in one point in time.

The fact that abstinence was so enhanced by compulsory supervision is at variance with our intuitively derived knowledge of emotional difficulty in adults. Meaningful maturational change is difficult to impose on someone from without. Most people agree that motivation is important in determining response to psychiatric treatment. It is never enough to tell someone not to bite his nails or to stop being shy. Finally, addicts make it clear that they resent authoritarian approaches. If, however, we cease to conceptualize drug addiction as a more or less conscious use of a drug to provide either emotional solace or exquisite self indulgence, if instead we conceive of drug addiction as a whole constellation of conditioned, unconscious behaviours, then the relative success of parole over conventional psychiatric intervention begins to make sense. Drug seeking behaviour can persist both on the basis of conditioned withdrawal symptoms and on the basis of conditioned reinforcers like the ritual of 'belting up', the friendship of drug using associates, and the experience of purposeful behaviour that precedes each shot. Therefore, one reason why abstinence under parole is more enduring than abstinence achieved during voluntary hospitalization is that abstinence achieved in the community occurs in the presence of many conditioned reinforcers (other addicts, peddlers, community stresses, etc.). Such events lose their effectiveness in controlling the addict's behaviour most rapidly when they continue to occur but in the absence of any reinforcement. Thus, it may be most therapeutic for addicts to be required to give up drugs in a situation closely resembling the one where they took them in the past. This hypothesis is supported by the fact that less than a third of long abstinences were associated with the addict moving out of areas of high endemic drug use.

Substitutes for drugs

If we persist in trying to gaze at clinical phenomena through the useful, albeit limited, blinders of behavioural pharmacology, another virtue of parole appears—it provides a substitute for drugs. In no case did an adult become abstinent simply because he was unable to get drugs. Competent parole, however, does not demand that the addict abandon one habit without providing him with an alternative. Parole provides a fairly rigidly defined schedule of competing behaviour to the one the addict formerly pursued. In order to get parole the addict must earn it. To keep his parole the addict must not only avoid certain of his associates, but must maintain both stable employment and contact with a helpful, powerful authority figure. These are precisely the tasks that addicts have never performed in the past. Even in addicts with poor previous work histories, the correlation between parole and employment was dramatic. It was probably no accident that several addicts with no other history of regular employment successfully completed tours of duty in the supervised setting of the armed forces. After the 'crutch' of parole was removed, the rate of relapse was no greater than among addicts who had maintained an abstinence of a year or more without compulsory supervision. Thus, parole serves to alter the addict's pattern of behaviour in a lasting way.

There were, however, two other factors that were correlated with initiation of abstinence (Vaillant, 1966d). First, several addicts substituted alcohol for addiction. Many of these did this only in transition and at the time of last follow-up, 75% of the thirty best outcomes—no narcotic use for three years—were not misusing alcohol. Second, the formation of a stable relationship with a non-blood relative was often associated with abstinence. It appears that mothers of addicts gain gratification by the prolonged dependence of their children. Like the marital partners of alcoholics, mothers often tacitly participated in their child's addiction. In contrast, the human relationships associated with abstinence were often ones where another person was openly dependent on the addict or conversely trusted him to be independent. The importance of new relationships in facilitating abstinence can only support the psychoanalytical impression that in individuals with deprived childhoods, drug seeking becomes a substitute for more common avenues of satisfaction.

Conclusion

I wish to emphasize that addiction is a complex subject. First, the importance of psychodynamic factors and unconscious motivation in addiction cannot be denied. In this paper they have been shrouded in the terms of behavioural psychology but translation into more conventional psychiatric terminology is not difficult. Second, complex social and cultural variables are also important; for example, addiction is common in the slums of two north-eastern port cities, New York and Washington, but relatively rare in two others, Boston and Philadelphia. After obtaining heroin legally in England, one addict became permanently abstinent; for him rebellion against authority had been an important 'motivating' factor. Third, narcotics do work as effective tranquillizers; they often neutralize aggressive and sexual strivings. For many they also can serve as a means of frank self-destruction. Lastly, it must be kept in mind that the present findings refer only to New York addicts who came to Lexington in 1952. There are many other types of people who misuse narcotics.

Yet if behavioural psychology is too narrow to encompass all these complexities, it has demonstrated its heuristic worth. Addicts have often been called insane, incurable or both. But by visualizing their lifetimes as a whole they appear to be neither. Although mental aberrations do not always manifest themselves with such unmistakable landmarks, the present techniques can be applied elsewhere in psychiatry. I suspect that many aspects of character disorder, of perversions and maladaptive life patterns in general can be fruitfully studied in terms of the interaction between 'schedules' and behaviour. To do this, however, involves both reducing human behaviour to extremely simple components and, figuratively speaking, examining men's lives through the wrong end of the telescope. Nevertheless, if man is to learn to understand, to predict and meaningfully to alter his fate, the Meyerian macroscope offers as much promise as the Freudian microscope.

Acknowledgement: The preparation of this manuscript was supported by Grants MH-07084-06 and MH-02094 from the National Institute of Mental Health, U.S. Public Health Service.

REFERENCES

Chein, I., Gerard, D. L., Lee, R. S. & Rosenfeld, E. (1964). *The Road to H.* New York: Basic Books.

Dole, V. P. & Nyswander, M. (1965). A Medical Treatment for Diacetylmorphine (Heroin) Addiction. *J. Amer. Med. Assoc.*, **193**, 646–650.

Glueck, S. & Glueck, E. (1950). *Unraveling Juvenile Delinquency*. New York: Commonwealth Fund.

Goldberg, S. & Schuster, C. R. (1966). Classic Conditioning of the Morphine Withdrawal Syndrome. *Fed. Proc.*, **25**, 261.

Ludwig, A. M. & Lyle, W. H. (1964). The Experimental Production of Narcotic Drug Effects and Withdrawal Symptoms Through Hypnosis. *Int. J. Clin. exp. Hypnosis*, **11**, 1–17.

Meyer, A. (1919). The Life Chart. *The Commonsense Psychiatry of Dr. Adolf Meyer*, Ed. by Lief, A., pp. 418–422. New York: McGraw-Hill, 1948.

Skinner, B. F. (1953). *Science and Human Behavior*. New York: Macmillan.

Spragg, S. D. S. (1940). Morphine Addiction in Chimpanzees. *Comp. Psychol. Monogr.*, **15**, 1–132.

Thompson, T. & Schuster, C. R. (1964). Morphine Self-Administration, Food reinforced, and Avoidance Behaviors in Rhesus Monkeys. *Psychopharmacologia*, **5**, 87–94.

Vaillant, G. E. (1966a). A 12 Year Follow-up of New York Narcotic Addicts: I. The Relation of Treatment to Outcome. *Amer. J. Psychiat.*, **122**, 727–737.

Vaillant, G. E. (1966b). A 12 Year Follow-up of New York Narcotic Addicts: II. The Natural History of a Chronic Disease. *New Engl. Med. J.*, **275**, 1282–1288.

Vaillant, G. E. (1966c). A 12 Year Follow-up of New Narcotic Addicts: III. Some Social and Psychiatric Characteristics. *Arch. Gen. Psychiat.*, **15**, 599–609.

Vaillant, G. E. (1966d). A 12 Year Follow-up of New York Narcotic Addicts: IV. Some Characteristics and Determinants of Abstinence. *Amer. J. Psychiat.*, **123**, 573–584.

Vaillant, G. E. (1966e). Parent-Child Cultural Disparity and Drug Addiction. *J. Nerv. Ment. Dis.*, **142**, 534–539.

Wikler, A. (1965). Conditioning Factors in Opiate Addiction and Relapse. *Narcotics*, Ed. by Wilner, D. M. & Kassebaum, G. G. New York: McGraw-Hill.

STABILIZED ADDICTION AND NORMAL DRINKING IN RECOVERED ALCOHOL ADDICTS

D. L. DAVIES

The Maudsley Hospital, London

RESUMPTION of moderate drinking unaccompanied by harmful effects for the individual was reported (Davies, 1962) as one outcome of the treatment of alcohol addicts. It aroused considerable controversy at the time, and stimulated further interest in this kind of behaviour, which has been reported on more recently by Gerard *et al.* (1962), Kendell (1965), Gerard & Saenger (1966) and Bailey & Stewart (1967). It may be relevant to quote what Gerard & Saenger (1966) have to say about what has been variously called 'normal' or 'controlled' drinking:

"It might be proper logically and clinically to question or challenge the permanence or stability of this behaviour, but to deny its existence for a stated period of time is merely prejudice, not science."

The patient's own belief about the nature of alcohol addiction may play an important part in achieving, or preventing, normal drinking. It is interesting therefore to record the histories of four alcohol addicts who have deliberately aimed at normal drinking, on the basis of a philosophy which differs from that of Alcoholics Anonymous in that normal drinking is envisaged as within the grasp of alcoholics. The four men belong to a group of recovering Finnish alcoholics, centred on Vaasa, who call themselves the Polar Bears, and of whose beliefs on the subject of alcoholism more will be said later.

Case histories

Case 1. This fifty-four year old man (born in 1913) had a mother who was prone to much invalidism and a father who drank heavily. His two older sisters are well and there is nothing special of note in the family history.

Though his birth was difficult, he was a healthy child, brought up in a remote country area with no companions. He saw little of his father until the age of five because of the war, and developed into a shy child. He was an average scholar, studied in England and in Helsinki, and spent some time in the family business until the war, and his marriage in 1939. On leaving military service in 1944, he resumed business but was in constant difficulty because of his drinking and, since 1951, he has used his private means to further the interests of alcoholics. His four children are well.

His previous personality was marked by shyness. He always felt lonely, different from others, and with feelings of inferiority.

He began to drink at the age of seventeen, heavily from the onset. He would be drunk for three or four days at a time, with short intervals of sobriety in between. From the age of twenty-two (in 1935) this was causing difficulty with the family firm, and more troubles ensued on this account during his military service. At the age of thirty-seven (1950) he resolved to become abstinent, but resumed drinking three months later. Following the successful removal of a pituitary adenoma for acromegaly in the following year he underwent 'an emotional experience' through the personal influence of a person he met, at about the time when he became finally detached from the family business. He remained abstinent until June 1965, when he deliberately resumed drinking in the belief that he could drink normally. He now has up to four bottles of cider and perhaps a glass of sherry or liqueur three or four times weekly or even daily. In the family circle and on more formal social occasions he is well controlled in his drinking. With two or three men companions out together he has become more or less drunk, on about six occasions in the last year, but no prolongation into his former bouts has occurred.

Comment. This man's drinking began early, was excessive from the start, and arose in the setting of social isolation and adverse personality factors. After fourteen years of abstinence he has succeeded in achieving normal drinking in the family circle, but one cannot be sure after two years that his overall control extends fully to all drinking situations.

Case 2. This fifty-two year old man (born in 1914) is the second youngest of a poor family of nine children; there is no relevant history of mental or nervous disorder in the family. His birth and early development were normal, and after leaving school at the age of fourteen he became a labourer. At the age of twenty (1934) he did his military service, but after a further four years as a labourer he went into insurance work. Shortly afterwards he joined the Army (1939) and served until 1945, seeing a great deal of active fighting and rising to become a company sergeant-major. On demobilization he resumed his insurance work, which involved meeting many people socially, travelling away from home for many days at a time and living in commercial hotels. He was away from home some fifty days in every sixty. His marriage at the age of twenty-three (1935) to a woman six years older than he ended in divorce (because of his drinking) in 1956. He was married for a second time in 1957 to a woman four years younger than himself, and this has turned out well.

His previous personality was that of a very thorough, conscientious man. He had traits of tidiness and orderliness, but not to the point that they interfered with his efficiency. He resented injustice, prided himself on being fair and rarely losing his temper. He never had religious leanings. He was not regarded as being particularly different from others. His health was always good.

His drinking began at the age of sixteen to seventeen, taking the form of getting mildly drunk at parties, perhaps two or three times a month. It increased steadily when his work took him away from home for long periods as an insurance representative. By the age of forty (1954) he was drinking continuously and heavily. He needed to drink before rising, suffered 'blackouts', lost his wife and his job. He became a down and out. Though he frequently resolved to abstain he found himself unable to do so. In this state, at the age of forty-four (1958) he came under the influence of case 1, joined the Polar Bears, and became abstinent. He eventually rehabilitated himself professionally, and holds a senior post of responsibility equal to or greater than what he held before his downfall. He no longer needs to be away from home in the course of his work.

In March 1965 he resumed drinking, deliberately, in the belief that he could drink normally. He has had only occasional drinks since then, and has no urge to become drunk. In January 1966 he deliberately set out to get drunk, to test his reactions. He drank half a litre of rum, and achieved his aim. He did not go on to a bout. His reaction was one of disgust with the drunken state; it gave him no enjoyment. He believes that he has complete control of his drinking, which now amounts to a very occasional drink in a normal situation. His wife confirms this.

Comment. A man of good intelligence and previous personality, whose excessive drinking related chiefly to his occupational and social circumstances. After nearly seven years of abstinence he has successfully resumed normal drinking during the last two years in a changed occupational setting and with a new wife.

Case 3. A forty-two year old man (born 1925), the younger of two sons. His mother was a heavy drinker and two maternal uncles died in mental hospitals to which they had been admitted early in life with religious preoccupations. His maternal grandfather was an alcoholic.

This man's birth and early development were normal. On leaving school at the age of eighteen (1943) he joined the army, saw active fighting, and was demobilized in the rank of corporal. He married when twenty-three (1948) against the wishes of his family, and only drink has raised problems with his wife. His father made him give up the study of chemistry to join the family business, which proved irksome, and eventually this man prepared himself by part-time study for the teaching profession. At present part-time, he hopes soon to be a full-time teacher, and is studying for a higher degree.

His previous personality was that of an open, gay, sociable person, fond of sport, and not regarded as odd or queer in any way.

He first drank at the age of thirteen to fourteen (1938–1939). He was a normal social drinker until the age of 23 (1948), the time of his marriage, when he began to drink to excess. He became a bout drinker, these bouts lasting up to seven days. He frequently promised his wife to abstain, but was unable to keep his promise, even when this failure caused her the most serious mental anguish. He eventually developed a marked tremor, and had at least one spell in which he had visual and auditory hallucinations. After ten years of living in this way he joined the Polar Bears (1958) and became completely abstinent.

He resumed drinking after nearly seven years of abstinence (July 1965) because of his belief that he could now drink normally. He has occasional glasses of wine. With men friends he has been drunk on about five occasions in the last year. He found that he could not stop at the phase of mild elation, and had to go on to getting drunk, though he did not like it. In the family situation and normal social occasions he restricts himself to about half a bottle of wine, on which he does not get drunk, and which he regards as his limit. His wife confirms this account.

Comment. Though there is a bad family history, this man seems to have been of good previous personality, and to have become an excessive drinker at a time when he was in conflict with his family over marriage and work. These differences are now largely in the past, and after seven years of total abstinence he has resumed drinking for about two years. On ordinary occasions he has achieved success so far, but has been less successful with cronies, in a way which suggests that he is still vulnerable.

Case 4. A forty-three year old man (born 1924), an only child, in whose family, as far as is known, there was no nervous or mental disorder. At the age of two he lost his father, and at eleven his stepfather. The home atmosphere was good, and his birth and early development were normal.

After leaving school at the age of thirteen (1937) he became an errand boy, and then had a series of unskilled jobs until he joined the army at the age of eighteen (1942). He saw no action and was demobilized in the rank of a private in 1946. He became a truck driver, but managed to obtain some further technical training and became a map maker, which is his present trade.

His previous personality was that of a calm, relaxed person with few active interests. He got on well with people of both sexes, but always spent his spare time in convivial drinking.

When he was fourteen (1938), in company with high-spirited boys with whom he associated, he experimented with drink, and was drinking more than they at the age of sixteen (1940). From 1942 to 1946 he had little access to drink in the army, but after demobilization he began to drink more heavily. At twenty-six he married a woman twelve years older than he. She was an alcoholic, and they would get drunk together. It was when they were both down and out, sleeping on bare boards, that he had a change of heart, joined the Polar Bears, and became abstinent, in 1961. (His wife died in 1964.)

He resumed drinking in December 1965, because he believed that the initial weakness leading to his drinking had been obviated by his affiliation with the Polar Bears, and that he 'was no longer irresponsible'. He may go a month without a drink, or have three or four bottles of beer a night, for as many as three consecutive nights, without getting drunk. He has twice deliberately set out to get drunk experimentally, and has found that he could do so without going into a bout of drinking. He is satisfied on this score now, and believes he has his drinking completely under control.

Comment. This man's drinking reached excessive proportions after an early start before, and more so after, his marriage to an alcoholic. He achieved five and a half years of sobriety, followed by resumed drinking for the past eighteen months. So far he may be regarded as having achieved the controlled drinking he aimed at.

Discussion

The Polar Bears have some superficial resemblance to Alcoholics Anonymous, as a loosely associated group of recovering alcoholics who put emphasis on self-help. Their meetings are less structured than those of A.A., in that members do not recount their drinking histories. They often sit around a table, with no formal chairman, for general discussion in which the topic of drink is regarded as having no priority. Indeed, they regard the large emphasis which A.A. place on talking

STABILIZED ADDICTION AND NORMAL DRINKING

about drink as indicative of the fact that A.A. members have failed to achieve a balanced attitude on that matter.

In so far as the Polar Bears have formulated their views on the etiology of alcohol addiction, it would seem that they indict 'milieu damage' in childhood, resulting in maladjustment in adult life. They contrast this view with the irreparable state which addiction presents to A.A. To the Polar Bears, this maladjustment can be rectified by achieving insight through associating together, so that normal drinking becomes an attainable goal implying real independence of alcohol, as against 'the artificial sobriety' of A.A.

The quality of personal relationships in the Polar Bears would seem to transcend the sponsorship of A.A.

It must be emphasized that though the Polar Bears welcomed my account (1962) of resumed normal drinking, they had formulated their views on this matter earlier, and some of them were resolved to put themselves to the test in any event. Nor could they be dissuaded from so doing by the author when they approached him with their intentions.

In the event, the four men reported have all achieved success in varying degrees. There can be no doubt that all four were excessive drinkers, who suffered considerably in consequence, nor can it be doubted that all were addicted in that they had been unable to give up drinking and so mitigate the damage.

At the present time two of them (cases 2 and 4) have achieved complete success over periods of two years and one and a half years respectively. Both drink only occasionally, in a manner which can in no way be regarded as abnormal, and in any social situation. Both have deliberately tried the effect of getting drunk, and found that it did not precipitate them into a bout or make them feel that drunkenness is other than an unrewarding and unwished-for experience.

The other two men (cases 1 and 3) are somewhat different. The consumption of alcohol in the first of these is more regular than that of any of the others, being a daily intake of moderate amount. Both are free of difficulties of any kind as a result of their drinking; their drinking is unobjectionable on social occasions, such as in the family circle, where some external restraint may be thought to be operating. With cronies, however, there have been several occasions during two years in both cases, when inebriety has resulted, in a way which suggests loss of control, though these occasions have never been continued into bouts of drinking.

The different patterns of resumed drinking illustrated here raise the question of terminology. It may well be significant that Gerard & Saenger (1966) have eschewed the term 'normal drinking' for the phenomenon they have described, and instead have used the term 'controlled drinking'.

'Normal drinking' suggests drinking in accordance with the usage of the majority of people who take alcohol without ill-effect in a socially acceptable way, both as to amount and occasion, in contrast with the abuse of alcohol by a minority. It precludes overt addiction.

'Controlled drinking' suggests the phenomenon of 'stabilized addiction' which is well known to occur with narcotics, such as opium, as well as with other drugs. The individual leads a useful and fairly normal life while taking a regular (usually daily) amount of the drug, in small doses, which does not need to be increased. He is nevertheless dependent in that the dose cannot be reduced, or the drug withdrawn, without difficulties arising, usually withdrawal symptoms or craving or both. Excellent examples of this were given by the Brain Committee (1958) in referring to this topic.

It is almost certain that 'controlled drinking' in the sense of stabilized addiction to alcohol occurs in many alcohol addicts, some of whom may never be put to the test of withdrawal and so may never know of their 'true' state. Something of the sort occurs in the culture of wine-drinking countries such as France, and may well account in part for the unrecognized alcoholism of the kind to which Nolan (1965) has drawn attention.

It is proper therefore to try to distinguish the patterns of resumed drinking (in alcoholics) which do not make for difficulties for the individual, and to try to categorize these.

One can accept unreservedly the normal drinking pattern as described here, and illustrated in cases 2 and 4. Case 3 might be regarded as a variant of this, in that the individual appears to be vulnerable in a certain situation (drinking with cronies) although otherwise normal. Case 1 could be either a normal or a controlled drinker, who also is vulnerable in the same circumstances as case 3.

No doubt there are other patterns which might be revealed by clinical observation. Accepting continuous and bout drinking as the two principal types seen in alcoholics, regular controlled drinking might be viewed as an intermediate stage down from the former to normal drinking. A corresponding stage, of controlled bout drinking, might be imagined between the latter and normal drinking.

One may suspect the former intermediate stage when the normal drinking is regular and especially daily in frequency. However, to prove its occurrence one would need to show that interruption of this pattern by periods of abstinence is beyond the capacity of the individual and that the attempt is accompanied by psychological or physiological concomitants of an unpleasant kind.

Using these tests none of the four is a proved controlled drinker, and the possibility only arises in case 1.

Some idea of the relative frequency of these two possible outcomes may be arrived at by examining a larger series of resumed drinkers who are free from difficulties. The material is drawn from the publications from the Maudsley Hospital already mentioned, as well as from those by Davies, Shepherd & Myers (1956) and Scott (1967). These amount to fifteen cases. There are also the histories of the four Finns reported here, as well as three other Finns (not Polar Bears) whom I examined in Helsinki, at the same time as the others. This makes a total of twenty-two cases. Assessment of these in accordance with the criteria outlined would place fifteen in the category of normal drinkers. Of the remaining seven, four are daily drinkers of beer, who consume from one to two glasses up to (in one case) two to three pints in that period. These are very difficult to classify as possible controlled drinkers. One of the remaining three, a Finn aged fifty-one, formerly a continuous drinker, later became abstinent in A.A. However, for two years now he has resumed drinking which takes the form of having up to half a bottle of gin or vodka in a day, producing mild exhilaration. Apart from five to six days of this sort in a two year period, he has been totally abstinent. This pattern suggests the second of the two intermediate types of drinking envisaged above, i.e. controlled bout drinking.

In addition two out of the twenty-two showed limited vulnerability (to drunkenness but not to a bout) in certain social situations, but evidence on this point was not available in all the protocols.

It must be concluded that the use of the term 'normal drinking' is justified completely in fifteen out of the twenty-two cases (68%), and almost certainly in nineteen out of the twenty-two cases (86%). Appreciable doubt arises on this score in only three out of the twenty-two cases (14%) who might be suspected of controlled drinking (stabilized addiction), but in whom proof of this condition is not forthcoming.

If the Polar Bears were at an ideological advantage in their unique group experiment, A.A. members are at a corresponding disadvantage. While the A.A. doctrine of indefinite abstinence is clearly the most prudent, does acceptance of its premises put the therapist at a disadvantage when facing the alcoholic who feels unable to aim at that, but is prepared to co-operate in the achievement of normal drinking? Have some patients been unnecessarily deterred from achieving this by these views?

Moreover, the implications for the spouses of alcoholics must be considered. In the case of most of the seven Finns examined, all of whom were free from difficulties in their resumed drinking, wives continued to feel anxious about their husbands, not on the basis of experience but because of the A.A. view which they had accepted as universally true. How far has this anxiety been needlessly engendered?

Finally, what about the A.A. man who has one drink (or two)? Is a lapse from abstinence synonymous with a lapse from sobriety? Might he not as well be 'in for a penny, in for a pound'? Especially bearing in mind the investigations of Merry (1966) on the failure of alcoholics to respond as expected to small doses of alcohol in disguise, one wonders whether some A.A. members might have been saved from relapse if they had held less extreme views about the nature of their disability.

The excellent work of A.A. and the undeniable value of this movement is in no way decried. There is room, however, for other groups, similar in aims and structure, using different approaches, so that the alcoholic seeking help may receive this in the setting which best suits his individual needs.

Summary

Case histories of four alcoholics belonging to a group calling themselves the Polar Bears are given, which show that these men have had considerable success in resuming normal drinking deliberately with this aim, on the basis of their beliefs. A consideration of resumed drinking in twenty-two recovered alcohol addicts shows that normal drinking has been achieved in fifteen (68%) with certainty and nineteen (86%) if one includes cases where one cannot be completely sure. Only three cases (14%) might be suspected of being controlled drinkers (stabilized addicts), but proof that they are so is lacking.

REFERENCES

Bailey, M. B. & Stewart, J. (1967). Normal drinking by persons reporting previous problem drinking. *Quart. J. Stud. Alc.*, **28,** 305–315.

Davies, D. L. (1962). Normal drinking in recovered alcohol addicts. *Quart. J. Stud. Alc.*, **23,** 94–104.

Davies, D. L., Shepherd, M. & Myers, E. (1956). The two-year prognosis of 50 alcohol addicts after treatment in hospital. *Quart. J. Stud. Alc.*, **17,** 485–502.

Gerard, D. L., Saenger, G. & Wile, R. (1962). The abstinent alcoholic. *Arch. gen. Psychiat.*, **6,** 83–95.

Gerard, D. L. & Saenger, G. (1966). The out-patient treatment of alcoholism. pp. 110 and p. 172. Toronto: University of Toronto Press.

Kendell, R. E. (1965). Normal drinking by former alcohol addicts. *Quart. J. Stud. Alc.*, **26,** 247–257.

Merry, J. (1966). The "loss of control" myth. *Lancet*, **ii,** 167.

Ministry of Health and Dept. of Health for Scotland. Inter-departmental committee on drug addiction. First Report 1958. (Chairman: Sir Russell Brain). London: H.M.S.O.

Nolan, J. P. (1965). Alcohol as a factor in illness of university source patients. *Amer. J. med. Sci.*, **249,** 135–142.

Scott, D. F. (1967). Alcoholic hallucinosis—an aetiological study. *Brit. J. Addict.*, **62,** 113–125.

NON-DEPENDENT DRUG USE: SOME PSYCHOLOGICAL ASPECTS

Beryl A. Geber

*Department of Psychology,
London School of Economics and Political Science*

SOCIO-PSYCHOLOGICAL studies of drug use have usually concentrated on the dependent drug user (Chein, Gerard, Lee & Rosenfeld, 1964; Zinberg, 1967) examined at a time when dependence is already established. The process of becoming dependent is inferred retrospectively, and the people, who have tried drugs but have not become dependent users are not included in the studies. Thus the issue of selectivity in addiction—why some users become dependent and others are able to continue drug use in a casual and uncommitted manner—is not accounted for.

Theories formulated to explain addiction in psychological terms cannot easily account for those who do not become dependent on drugs despite frequent use. Explanations of dependent behaviour in terms of learning theory postulate that the use of drugs becomes associated with consequent satisfactions which reinforce drug taking. This leads to more frequent use. But this approach cannot differentiate the casual from the committed user (Ausubel, 1963). Attempts to explain dependence in cognitive terms are no more satisfactory. Lindesmith (1947) has suggested that a conscious realization of dependence is followed by changes in the concept of self and then by a constant preoccupation with the object of addiction. This stress on the 'conscious realization of dependence' as the pivotal point in differentiating the dependent from the non-dependent user of drugs still leaves unanswered the question of selectivity: why do some reach this realization and others not? Using the idea of individual differences, of differences in personality structure, as the chief variable explaining differences in dependence has not been satisfactory. Addicts show a wide range of personality types (Zinberg, 1967), and where variability has been estimated personality factors have accounted for a small percentage thereof. Chein *et al.* (1964) explained a large percentage of the variance in heroin use in New York youths by demographic and social variables. An adequate explanation of drug dependence will probably have to account for the interaction between social and personal variables, and it will also have to differentiate the dependent from the non-dependent user of drugs.

Studies of non-dependent drug users are rare. An attempt was made in 1967 as the result of dissatisfaction with the assumptions underlying popular views of the inevitability of escalation in drug use and the lack of information about informal social processes and interaction in drug taking. Conceived as a general exploration of the subject and a pilot study of some few specific dimensions, the study probed certain areas of concern without the precision—and often attendant limitation of range—of well formulated hypotheses. The results suggest some interesting relations which may be worth further exploration.

Method

A series of informal non-directed interviews was conducted by graduate psychology students with non-dependent, and dependent drug users and with people who had given up drugs. These users were extremely helpful and willing to talk about their drug experiences and habits. From these interviews grew a conviction that much of the information drug users could provide would be lost if the study was to impose a set frame of reference on the respondents, that incorrect use of prevailing drug jargon would alienate the drug users, and that sophisticated technical terminology would impose too formal a structure on the investigation. One of the first priorities therefore was to produce a questionnaire in parts flexible enough to allow the respondents to set their own individual framework about drug use and yet specific enough to gain information on specific 'areas of concern'.

The questionnaire was designed to cover, with varying degrees of thoroughness, the following: (a) demographic data and family ties; (b) natural history of drug use, (for example, see Appendix 1, p. 388); (c) details of present drug habits; (d) social network, and (e) attitudes towards drug use, anxieties about drugs, wider interests and personal future orientation. The questionnaire made use of 'closed' and 'open-ended' questions, a sentence-completion section, and an adjective checklist for self-description.

The questionnaire was self-administered and completed only by drug users. No attempt was made to find an equivalent non-drug taking control group, nor to use a dependent sample for comparison. This makes it impossible to draw specific conclusions about distinguishing characteristics of the non-dependent drug population. Since, however, the chief purpose of the study was exploratory and its area of interest deliberately that of non-dependent drug use, it was felt that within-sample comparisons would be most meaningful in this context.

The sample consisted of forty-three users who completed and returned the questionnaire. The respondents were generally found through a tenuous social network which produced a noticeable bias in the sample. This bias is consistent with the fact that the investigators were young students, and their social contacts were in part determined by this.

The age of the sample was eighteen to twenty-eight years (70% twenty-three years and younger) and 72% were males. Only 30% had parents rated as lower middle class (white collar workers) or working class, and the subjects' own occupations show the sample to be skewed towards high status occupations (33%

students, 19% artistic, 16% professional, 9% unemployed, 14% manual and clerical). Of the forty-three users 86% were single.

Results

Data were coded, and computed on a TAB XI programme, and the major variables were run against all the relevant items in the questionnaire. The sample was classified by three criteria: (i) frequency of drug use; (ii) type of drugs used, and (iii) numbers of drugs tried.

(i) Frequency of use was determined in two ways, one a subjective assessment rated on a four point scale ranging from 'very frequent' to 'rarely', the other a check on a list of actual use—once a day, once a week, once a month, etc. The objective and subjective assessment correlated highly, and the sample was therefore classified on the objective criteria. Three groups were defined: very frequent twenty-one, moderately frequent thirteen, occasional nine.

(ii) More difficult than rating frequency was the problem of differentiating within the sample in terms of the kinds of drug used. A wide variety of drugs was used and many individuals had used or were using a number of different drugs. Finally a rather uneasy classification was devised: (1) 'soft'—marijuana, amphetamines and barbiturates only; (2) 'soft + psychedelic'—as (1) but also mescaline and LSD; (3) 'multi'—as (1) and (2) but including opium and related drugs, such as heroin and cocaine.

This classification, however, did not really result in three discrete groups. The results indicate that the 'soft' group may well be independent, but that the other two groups are not clearly differentiated. This is because the 'multi' group contains a number of people who use 'psychedelic' drugs and therefore overlaps the 'soft + psychedelic' group and the inclusion of those with experience of the so-called 'hard' drugs does not distinguish a one-time-only experimenter from a more regular user. This multi-category therefore tends to be something like a blanket category. Thirty per cent of the subjects fell in each of the 'soft' and 'soft + psychedelic' categories, 40% in the 'multi' group.

(iii) Not only did the results indicate the use of many different drugs, but there was evidence of individual differences in the number of drugs tried.

There is quite a strong correlation ($r = 0.6$) between drug category and the number of drugs tried, but there is still variation within each category (Table 1).

Table 1

Category of drugs used by number of drugs tried

Category	1 or 2	3 or 4	5 or more	Total
'Soft'	9	3	1	13
'Soft + psychedelic'	1	5	7	13
'Multi'	0	5	12	17
Total	10	13	20	43

Using these three categories, comparisons were made between the category subgroups on dimensions relating to various areas of concern.

(a) Social factors

The questionnaire attempted to establish whether the users perceived themselves as part of a discernible 'drug group', whether friendships were established in close relation to drug taking and whether drug use disrupted friendships with non-users (Table 2).

A significant relation was found between category of drug used and the user's perception of himself as belonging to a consistent drug group. Those in the 'soft + psychedelic' group see themselves as part of a larger drug group, while the other groups do not admit to group membership of this sort.

When category of drugs was tested against friendship dimensions, significant relationships were again established, particularly when the users of 'soft' drugs alone were compared with a combined group of 'soft + psychedelic' and 'multi' users. The combined category claims to have made significantly more

Table 2
Group belongingness by category of drugs

Category	Group belongingness		
	Yes	No	Total
'Soft'	1	11	12
'Soft + psychedelic'	9	3	12
Total	10	14	24

$P < 0.05$, Fisher Yates test

Category	Group belongingness		
	Yes	No	Total
'Soft + psychedelic'	9	3	12
'Multi'	4	10	14
Total	13	13	26

$P < 0.025$, Fisher Yates test

friends through the drug experience than the users of 'soft' drugs alone, as well as feeling more cut off from non-users ($P < 0.001$) and believing more strongly that their friendships were deepened by drug use ($P < 0.05$) than the subjects in the 'soft' category. Comparing friendship categories and group membership with frequency of drug use did not, however, yield significant results.

(b) 'Escalation'

A number of questions were included in the questionnaire to establish a link between the number of years drugs had been used and an increase in use either in terms of frequency or in terms of moving to more dangerous drugs in a regular progression. There was no evidence to support the view that drug taking over time leads to increasing frequency of use, nor that the number of drugs tried relates to the number of years of use. The only marginally significant relationship elicited was between the number of years of use and the category of use ($P < 0.1$): that is, the longer drugs have been used, the more likely is it that drugs in wider categories have been tried. This really appears to indicate that many of those who had tried the more dangerous drugs had stopped using them, so that exploration of the drug field and continued use of drugs are not necessarily related.

In the responses to questions about the subjects' willingness to try any new drugs or to try 'hard' drugs there were no significant differences within the sample using each of the systems of categorization. Even those who had tried 'hard' drugs (i.e. the 'multi' category) were no more willing to use them again than others who had not yet tried them. Responses to questions about drugs used but given up gave no indication of a tendency to give up 'soft' drugs once more potent drugs had been used—often where people had used both 'hard' and 'soft' drugs it was the 'hard' drugs which were given up. There were also no significant differences across the sample with regard to anticipating a future without drugs.

It was expected that, where a drug had a diminishing effect on the user, he would take more of the same drug in order to get the original effect. This expectation was not supported. Indeed, an interesting tendency was noted: more frequent users of drugs and those in the 'multi' category appeared to take less of any particular drug when its effects lessen, rather than to increase the dose. Nor does the evidence suggest that they then move to a drug in a more potent category: the movement may be within the category rather than step-like (escalation) to a more dangerous drug.

(c) First Experience

It was anticipated (Becker, 1953) that the first experience of drugs would play a significant role in determining patterns of drug use. However, within this drug user sample there was no significant relation between people's enjoyment or dislike of their first drug experience and later use.

(d) Family

Seventy-four per cent of the parents of the sample lived together, and there was no significant relationship between the structure of the family and drug use or the frequency of use. In terms of relationships within the family, there was no significance in the reported closeness of attachment to father and mother and the use of drugs. Taking the sample as a whole, 54% felt close to the father and 56% to the mother. This does not appear to support any hypotheses about 'alienation' from the family as a correlate of drug use.

The subjects were asked about family reactions to their drug taking. Of those whose families were aware of their activity (twenty-seven of the forty-three subjects) nothing significant emerged in analyses of parental approval or disapproval in relation to the number of drugs tried or the frequency of use. However, a barely significant relation between family reaction and category of drug used did emerge ($P < 0.1$), suggesting that people in the 'soft' category had disapproving parents, while those in the 'multi' category had more approving or accepting parents.

(e) Attitudes

An attempt was made to relate attitudes to drug taking to a more general approach to living. The questions on moral and political values produced interesting responses but were not sufficiently probing or wide ranging to gather reliable results. Many in the sample professed to hold strongly to personal moral or belief systems, and political views tended to inactivity with ill-defined affiliations toward the left of the political spectrum.

It was hoped to assess the centrality of the drug activities to the subjects' way of life by getting some indication of the range and importance of other activities in which the subjects participated. The responses to the questions were generally inadequate and no results can be reported.

One problem which was thought to be of importance was the drug users' perception of risk. This risk could lie in the effects of the drug itself, or in the legal risks involved in illicit drug use or in the risk of family tensions arising out of anatagonism to drugs. Unfortunately the responses to questions were not very informative, and apart from a general reluctance to try certain drugs, presumably because of the risk to the user, no trends were discernible. There was, however, across the whole sample, no acceptance of the view that most drug users risk moving from less dangerous to more dangerous drugs: the percentage of the drug using population at risk was estimated at less than 9%, with no significant differences in estimates between the categories of the sample.

Attitudes to the use of alcohol and tobacco were tested to see whether use of other drugs made these drugs less attractive. There was no indication of a strongly negative attitude to either alcohol or tobacco, but comparison of the 'multi' group with a combined 'soft' + 'soft + psychedelic' group yielded a significant difference indicating that the 'multi' users were more negative to alcohol. Neither frequency nor variety of drug use was related to changes in smoking habits, and although there was some evidence to suggest that those who had tried a large number of drugs (five or more) decreased their cigarette smoking more frequently than those who tried fewer drugs, more than half of the people in that category had increased their use of tobacco.

One quite interesting line of investigation was into attitudes towards 'losing control'. Occasional users had significantly more negative responses ($P < 0.05$) to losing control over themselves than the moderate or very frequent users. The distribution within and between categories is shown in Table 3.

Included in the questionnaire was an adjective checklist: a series of adjectives described personal characteristics, and the respondents had to check how well each word listed described them on a four point scale ranging from 'very well' to 'not at all'.

Table 3

Losing control by frequency of use

Frequency	Attitudes towards losing control		Total
	positive and neutral	negative	
VF	9	3	12
MF	6	5	11
OCC	0	8	8
Total	15	16	31

$X^2 = 6\cdot3$; $P < 0\cdot05$

Table 4

a

Category	Ambitious describes me ...		Total
	very/fairly well	not at all	
'Soft'	5	8	13
'Soft + psychedelic'	10	2	12
Total	15	10	25

Significant at the 0·05 level on
Fisher-Yates exact probability test

b

'Soft'	5	8	13
'Multi'	11	5	16
Total	16	13	29

Significant at the 0·1 level on
Fisher-Yates exact probability test

c

'Soft'	5	8	13
'Soft + psychedelic + multi'	21	7	28
Total	26	15	41

$X^2 = 4\cdot9$, significant at the 0·05 level

'Ambitious' by category of **drug used**

The only word which showed any significant relation to differences in drug use was 'ambitious'. The 'soft + psychedelic' group marked themselves significantly higher on this dimension than the 'soft' group, and the differences between the 'multi' (which includes uses of psychedelic drugs), and 'soft' categories, though less significant, were in the same direction (Table 4*a*, *b* and *c*).

Discussion

This exploratory study of non-dependent drug use points to the need for a specification of the categories of drug users. Those who use drugs but are not dependent on them do not form a uniform group. One of the most difficult problems is classification. This study divided its small sample on the basis of three variables: frequency of use, number and type of drugs. Each of these variables discriminated among the sample on some dimensions, on others they were inadequate. It is not clear whether the categories formed are in fact discrete, and at some points there is overlap in the category subdivisions.

The most suggestive indication of distinction within the sample is in the results on group factors. The evidence shows that those who use only 'soft' drugs—chiefly marijuana, amphetamines and barbiturates, or combinations of these—do not perceive themselves as part of a drug-taking group. Those who use the so-called mind-expanding drugs do see themselves as belonging to a drug taking group, and regard drugs as an important part of the relationships formed within this group. This sense of belonging is possibly fostered by the growth of a distinguishable sub-culture, with its own press, art forms and clubs, and with drug use recognized as a central part of its activities. What is interesting is the feeling that friendships are enhanced and deepened by using drugs. Those who do not use drugs popularly regarded as psychedelic are frequently at pains to emphasize their non-belonging and the fact that drug use does not change people, or produce differences in attitudes. For a close examination of non-dependent drug use, a much more refined method of investigation is needed. Field studies, if they could be carried out, and depth interviews probing social networks could throw a great deal of light on this topic.

The process of 'escalation' also needs more detailed study. Some of those in the 'multi' group of drug-takers had tried opiates and heroin but had not continued to use these. Many of those in the other two groups had used drugs for a number of years and had not necessarily increased the frequency of their use, nor tried the more dangerous drugs. Length of time of exposure—both to drugs and to other drug takers—is therefore not a sufficient explanatory variable in studying dependence, nor is the idea of the centrality of the drug taking activity as the main criterion of dependence easy to estimate. Although the study did not really examine other interests and activities in detail or depth, many of those who used drugs frequently did in fact lead active lives and hold steady and dependable positions.

One investigation which could prehaps throw some light on the escalation process concerns the limits which drug users place on their drug taking. The subjects of this particular study seemed to be aware of the risks of using certain drugs and were determined not to try these. This may mean that they are unaware of the risks involved in the drugs they did use, but they appeared quite deliberately to set themselves limits. Although the evidence did not indicate that drug taking was seen as an age-related activity, at least a few respondents indicated that they found drug use ending as they grew older. The whole problem of giving up drugs is one which really deserves exploration; if drugs are used because of the satisfactions they provide, then presumably their use is discontinued because the reinforcements or rewards no longer follow, or because the rewards provided are gained in other ways or are no longer sought. But we are ignorant of the antecedents of this changed reinforcement value, and this study has achieved no more than simply to raise this problem. It also raises the problem of relating the end of the individual's drug use to the reactions of other members of his social network. It may be that once drugs are abandoned the social network of an individual changes, or it may be that drugs are only one aspect of the activities of an established social group and that the group does not change its composition when drugs are dropped.

As regards family ties, attitudes and personality description, a study which simply describes the responses of one particular sample is not sufficient. The results of this study of non-dependent drug use in these respects are difficult to interpret. It is not possible to differentiate the non-dependent from the dependent user or from the non-user on any of the dimensions examined. All that this study can indicate is that the particular sample studied does not show alienation from the family or an absence of some form of personal ambition in its members; at most this throws doubt on some commonly held assumptions about drug users.

The problems of sampling in studying non-dependent drug use are innumerable. The dependent users in contact with doctor, hospital or police are more accessible to the researcher than the non-dependent user. Non-dependent users are on no list, and there are no convenient ways of gathering subjects. The population from which any particular sample is drawn is unknown and there appears to be no easy way of specifying it. Attempts to find suitable subjects by random testing of populations thought to be at risk, such as school leavers in deprived areas, or students at various higher education institutions have yielded numbers too small for meaningful results. However, information about non-dependent drug users is highly important in socio-psychological research into drug dependence and in establishing a satisfactory psychological theory of dependence.

Acknowledgements: I wish to express my thanks to Denise Benusiglio, Adele Kosviner, Stephanie Pixner, Gerald Stimson and Jim Zacune with whom this project was carried out.

REFERENCES

Ausubel, D. (1963). *Drug Addiction: Physiological, Psychological and Sociological Aspects*. New York: Random House.

Becker, H. (1953). Becoming a marijuana user. *Amer. J. of Soc.*, **59,** 235–242.

Chein, I., Garard, D., Lee, R. & Rosenfeld, E. (1964). *Narcotics, Delinquency and Social Policy*. London: Tavistock.

Lindesmith, A. (1947). *Opiate Addiction*. Bloomington, Indiana: Principia Press.

Zinberg, N. (1967). Facts and fancies about drug addiction. *The Public Interest*, **6.**

APPENDIX 1

Drug use grid, as completed by a respondent

We would like to know the drugs you have used and some conditions under which you use them. (By drugs we do not mean those you have used for medical purposes.) We would like an *exhaustive list of all* the drugs and combinations of drugs you have taken *in the order in which you first tried them*. Put the drug you first tried under column '1', the next under column '2', etc.

Order in which drugs were tried:	1	2	3	4	5	6
Name of drug or combination of drugs	marijuana/hashish	amphetamine inc. methedrine	opium	LSD	cocaine/heroin inhaled	amyl-nitrite
Mark the drug you use most frequently F	F					
Mark the drug you most prefer P	P					P
Mark the drug you most easily obtained E	E					E
Mark the drug you take with alcohol A	A	A	A	A	A	A
Note for each how old you were when you first tried it	17	17	18	20	20	20
On the average how often do you take each *now* (e.g. once a day, month, week, etc.)	3 × week	1 × month	—	1 × 2 month	—	1 × month
Note for each how long you have been taking them with this frequency	5 years	2 years	2 years	2 years	—	2 years
With approximately how many	4?	Parties	—	3	—	?

Question						
they are mainly (a) close friends (b) acquaintances (c) newly met	a, b & c	a, b & c	a, b & c			a, b & c
Indicate for each drug if you *usually* take it with (a) the same people (b) different people	a	?			a	a
If with different people for what reason	—	No necessity to differentiate			—	—
Indicate for each drug whether they are in any way harmful. Please describe in what way they can do harm	No	Yes—addictive in certain circumstances	Yes—addictive in certain circumstances	Yes—can lead to acute paranoia	Yes—could lead to fixing it	Stimulating heart to excess if taken in excess
Indicate for each, if offered would you accept (a) always (b) usually (c) sometimes (d) rarely	Usually/ always	Sometimes	Rarely	Depends who offered it	No	Always
Please describe for each drug in which ways, if any, it is beneficial	Relaxing de-restricting, facilitates greater appreciation	Increases perception, physical boost	Relaxing	Liberating etc.	—	Kick

APPENDIX 2

Analysis of the use of amphetamines in the non-dependent drug users (a subsample)

Of the forty-three non-dependent drug users twenty-seven (63%) used some form of amphetamine. Of these twenty had used only one form, or had simply mentioned the generic name, six had used or mentioned two forms, and one had used four varieties.

The specific labels given were: amphetamine (thirteen users); methedrine (six users); dexamphetamine (six users); drinamyl (purple hearts) (five users); ephedrine (two users); 'blues' (two users); benzedrine (two users).

Few subjects mentioned the route of administration, but one specified the oral use of 'liquid' amphetamine and one mentioned the use of 'liquid' methedrine without indicating whether it was taken orally or by injection.

This subsample of amphetamine users was categorized by three criteria: frequency of use, the number of drugs tried, and the type of drug. Only five subjects limited themselves to amphetamines and marijuana, eight had used these and LSD or other 'mind-expanding' drugs, and the remaining fourteen had all tried a great variety of drugs, including heroin, morphine, cocaine or opium. This means that the subsample of amphetamine users accounts for 84% of drug users in the multiple use category, but for only 38% of those using 'soft' drugs alone. In terms of the number of drugs used, two used two, nine used three or four, and the other sixteen used five or more. The figures for the total sample are: one to two drugs, ten subjects; three to four drugs, thirteen subjects; five or more drugs, twenty subjects, so that amphetamine users account for 80% of the subjects in the group using most drugs, but for only 20% in the group using few. The same bias occurs with the frequency of use. Thus those who use, or have used, amphetamines tend to be among the most active of the drug users in this non-dependent sample. However, when the figures for actual amphetamine use are examined, it seems that continuous use of amphetamines accounts for only a small part of drug activities. Using the frequency of all drugs used the subsample is distributed as follows: six occasional users; eleven frequent users; and ten very frequent users. When, however, the sample is distributed in terms of frequency of amphetamine the picture is different: seventeen occasional users; three frequent users and no very frequent users. The remaining seven subjects had given up using amphetamines. This group will be discussed in greater detail later.

The surprising prevalence of the occasional use only of amphetamines suggested that these may be the first drugs tried and therefore dropped in favour of other drugs tried later in the subjects' drug career. In only eight cases, however, amphetamines were the first drugs tried. One subject had tried these drugs as late as fifth, and of other users three groups of six had tried amphetamines second, third and fourth. Thus there was no consistent pattern in the order of use of amphetamines, and the reasons for the minimal use of these drugs must lie elsewhere. The answer may be in the bias of the sample; most subjects appeared to prefer marijuana in some form to the other drugs. Further research may support the suggestion that 'pill users' and 'pot users' are discrete groups, and thus indicate that these particular non-dependent users are drawn from the population of marijuana users.

Three further aspects were looked at: first, whether the subjects perceived any danger in the use of amphetamines; second, the advantages gained from amphetamines, and third any ill-effects experienced.

Ten subjects admitted danger in amphetamine use, the remaining seventeen denied any danger. Of these ten, however, only three had given up amphetamines, but the remaining seven used them only occasionally. It is not justifiable to infer a causal relation between the perception of danger and the giving up of drugs, because not all subjects who stopped taking amphetamines realized the danger involved.

The advantages of using amphetamines related chiefly to their stimulant properties. These were described as 'producing rapid thought', 'increasing perception', 'keeping awake', 'relieving depression', 'increasing sociability'. Some advantages mentioned were odd ("I take them once a year to clear the poisons from my body through perspiration") and six subjects denied that any advantages or benefits accrued from the use of amphetamines. However, only one of these six had stopped using amphetamines.

The ill effects of the drug were specifically mentioned by seventeen subjects. These effects included depression, exhaustion, nausea, nervousness, and loss of appetite. Ten subjects experienced no ill effects, but again this does not differentiate those who have given up from those who still use amphetamines. The only interesting relationship concerns the three subjects who use amphetamines frequently—they experience no ill effects.

The question of source of supply was raised in a general way, without reference to any specific drugs. However, because the particular drug used seemed to depend largely on availability, and not on the user seeking out a specific type, the sources of supply should not change from one drug to the other. Most of the subjects obtained drugs through friends or their family, and most knew the supplier well. Only seven admitted getting drugs from a 'pusher', with whom they were not particularly friendly. There was no indication of the ultimate supplier—the person who gave the drugs to the friends. There were, however, frequent references to the non-availability of certain drugs at the time of the survey, and the general impression given is that when supplies are exhausted the user switches to another drug and not to alternative sources of supply.

The use of amphetamines in this drug using sample appears to be incidental to the general exploration of drugs. Most subjects take amphetamines rarely, and seem to use them specifically for their general stimulating properties which are incidental to other activities, e.g. in order to keep awake for studying, or for all night parties, or for weekend romps around the clubs. (Only five subjects suggested that amphetamines were taken for the experience itself, for the changes in thought and perceptual processes produced.) This is in sharp contrast to the reasons given for the use of marijuana and such drugs as LSD, mescaline and even heroin. For all these drugs the increase in self awareness and the alterations of cognitive functioning are cited as reasons for their use—a general intellectualizing of the drug taking process. The impression gained from this study is that the use of amphetamine in a population chiefly concerned with 'cult' drugs is a minor fringe exploration into the drug field, a brief experimental or initiating experience which ceases as the user becomes more committed to alternative experiences gained through marijuana or the psychedelic drugs on which the greatest emphasis is placed.

THE PHOENIX HOUSE THERAPEUTIC COMMUNITY: AN OVERVIEW

Mitchell S. Rosenthal

Addiction Services Agency, New York, N.Y.

Introduction

EXPERIENCE during the past ten years in different parts of the United States has demonstrated that addicts can be treated effectively. Occasionally individual psychotherapists have reported success. Successful treatment has occurred in therapeutic communities such as Synanon in California, Phoenix House and Daytop Village in New York, and the Addiction Research Center in Puerto Rico. What Boorstein has stated for the offender in general, I would re-emphasize for the addict population. "At the present time, the only approach to the problem which can possibly deal with the numbers involved and the ego defects present is the Therapeutic Community." To take it one step further, I believe the therapeutic community to be the treatment of choice in the vast majority of cases of addicts, regardless of the availability of other methods.

A therapeutic community provides the necessary setting for the addict or severe sociopathic personality disorder to become rehabilitated. Only in a small community setting where each member is committed to do away with antisocial and criminal behaviour, and emotional support of the 'patient' during the process and consistent positive reinforcement for modified constructive behaviour are provided, is real treatment possible.

This paper describes in detail the structure and process of an ongoing therapeutic community, Phoenix House (operated by the

Addiction Services Agency, New York City). Since the Phoenix project has only been in existence for twelve months, only preliminary data will be reported.

Therapeutic community: Phoenix House

The overall formal structure can be outlined briefly. There is a pyramidal power matrix. At the top is the facility director. Under him are two assistant directors and two coordinators. One each of the coordinators and assistant directors is a woman. There are seven section heads who work for the coordinators. Each has a crew of men and women with a particular area of responsibility. In this way, the problem of *underestimating* patients with the consequent stagnation and social breakdown (Schwartz & Schwartz, 1964) and institutional neurosis is avoided. (Fig. 1, p. 400.)

The residents in the more senior positions have earned them from the time they entered the community. Previous work and life experience does not entitle a man to any position in the status system. Any man entering the project can realistically envisage that he may eventually hold any key position. A new resident is interviewed by residents formerly in 'his shoes' and 'with his background', for example, a former addict from the same or similar neighbourhood rather than a doctor or professional with whom he cannot identify and thus at some level cannot believe. From the beginning, the new patient is confronted with an achievable status system.

Addictive or character disorders suffer from a lack of identity, which can be considered a deficiency syndrome. In such cases, replacement therapy is indicated (Hilgard, 1948; Lederer, 1964). This requires the therapist and/or the therapeutic model to be a *whole person** who offers himself to the patient as an example of experienced strength and firm moral purpose;

---

* Used to distinguish the 'therapist' or therapeutic model from the neutral analytic model of Freud where the analyst remains 'unknown'. Biographical and other personal information about the 'therapist' is readily available.

in doing so he establishes commitment and this kind of identity as possible and therefore mandatory.

Toward this end, society's rules are strictly enforced. The street culture taboo of no 'squealing' is removed. It is the duty of each man in the community to see that rules are observed, and if someone breaks them that he is brought to task. Justice is fair, but harsh. A man may literally be given a haircut and/or be required to wear a sign to help him pinpoint his deviance for both the group and the patient. Moral values are taught. Cummings & Cummings (1964) have pointed out how psychiatrists have been uncomfortable with the task of moral teaching; yet, the teaching of norms and values goes on at all times whether we acknowledge it or not. In a Phoenix House the teaching of socialization and its consequent morality is made both explicit and emphatic. In society there are generally one or more peers who subtly or openly reinforce antisocial behaviour. There is a feeling of rebellious hatred for those in authority. The tough guy or rebellious resident who enters the community is isolated. He may look for, but will find no support for his former value system.

A therapeutic milieu is one which aids the patient to minimize his distortions of reality, increases meaningful communications, reduces anxiety, provides insight into his illness and mobilizes his initiative for development (Satir, 1961). A therapeutic community is a fairly small group of patients (thirty to a hundred) living and working together, attempting to change the patients' faulty social functioning to a more satisfactory adjustment by means of various social techniques (Clark, 1964; Grinker, 1948; Lewin, 1948). The therapeutic community is organized so that adaptive ego functions can be developed and strengthened. The adaptiveness of particular behaviour can be tested by its consequences for the achievement of community goals as well by as the group's response to it (Edelson, 1964). The ego's operation may be observed in characterologic form as expressed in the patient's general behavioural response to the treatment situation, his mannerisms, dress, and attitudes and, in fact, the ego syntonic aspects of his way of life—described by Wilhelm Reich (1949); in the defence against external threats and in transformations undergone by affects—desribed by Anna Freud (1962); in the phenomenology of ego experience as outlined by Paul Federn (1964); in the ego's response to common group tensions and the structural and processed patterns of group life as investigated by Kurt Lewin.

Edelson points out that the ego's task is: (1) to cope with group tensions and group emotions that block work of the group in its attempt to explore and understand personal relations in the group; (2) to find a satisfactory place in the structure of the community and to participate in the struggle with the problems the community confronts as its goals are formulated and the tasks of achieving them arise.

In the therapeutic community, ego illness can be treated, ego functions maintained and enhanced, the integrity of the ego experience restored, and a sense of identity sought (Leland, 1964).

At least once each day the entire community holds a meeting, which usually follows the morning meal or noon meal. These are not 'free discussion groups'. There is a format so that information can be dispersed from above. Current events, national and local, are discussed. Community projects, plans, expected visitors, etc., are noted. There is also a formalized 'bitch session'. This is harnessed for the total community's use; personal and interpersonal difficulties are not handled at these meetings. It is the job of the moderator to see to this. Problems such as violation of rules, deportment, group activities may be discussed as necessary. There is, in this way, a train of communications and a temporary slackening of the authority pyramid. Special meetings may be called at any time. An example of a member's poor behaviour might be discussed at such a meeting.

Work programme

The underlying guidelines are that work should be productive and enhancing to the individual sense of self-esteem. Meaningless busy work is avoided. At the same time, a man may very well be assigned work, especially early in his treatment, that has nothing to do with his previous job experience. This is in order both to separate the man from his old pattern and also to enable him to see vividly how he takes his personality problems with him. Furthermore, because the new man has no status, regardless of his background, he must start at the bottom and work up.

The concept of self-reliance (Emerson) as it affects all work projects is vital. Wherever possible, outside professional shops are used minimally. Cooking, carpentry, gardening, painting and maintenance are done by the men themselves. The tie-in with the concept of ego-identity is important. The importance of ritualization of a man's work-life for his inner defences is well described by Erickson. "The adolescent process is complete only when an individual has subordinated his childhood identification to a new kind of identification, achieved in absorbing sociability and in competitive apprenticeship with and among his age mates." Erickson has further postulated a psychosocial moratorium in adolescence during which the individual through role experimentation finds his niche in society. In this process it is necessary for him that the community 'recognize' him; that he be responded to and given status as a person whose gradual growth and transformation make sense to those around him. A man who has formerly been passive, obstructive, dependent and hostile, at some level has also been helpless and like a child. Instilling a sense of identity is essential.

Every man has a job. He belongs to one of the various work sections: (1) service crew; (2) building crew; (3) kitchen-commissary; (4) supply; (5) administrative; (6) education, and (7) archives. It might seem paradoxical to establish this micro-bureaucracy in the midst of one of the world's great bureaucracies. In the larger bureaucracy these men have been unable to master their feelings of isolation, identity and helplessness. By narrowing the focus, the patient is able to see all the intricacies

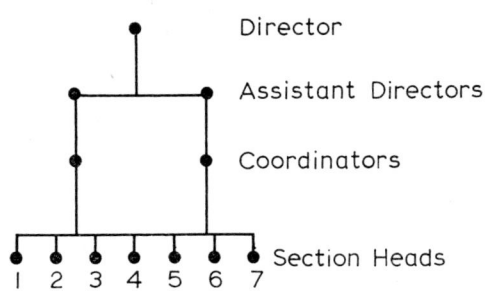

FIG. 1. Phoenix House Organization Chart.

1. Service
2. Building
3. Kitchen-commissary
4. Supply
5. Administrative
6. Education
7. Archives

of the community, contribute to the total effectiveness with favourable results and simultaneously unlearn his maladaptive coping patterns through the feedback provided by his peers. Job changes are frequent. Promotions, demotions, transfers are arranged by the section heads in order to separate certain individuals or bring others together so that personality clashes may be brought into sharper relief and resolved.

The encounter

The Phoenix encounter is a specialized form of group psychotherapy particularly designed to be effective with character disorders. All residents regularly participate in encounters at least three times a week and frequently more often. An encounter consists of eight to twelve people chosen and balanced according to pressures that may have developed between individuals, talkativeness, level of insight and experience. Most encounters do not have the same individuals twice in a row; participants are mixed so that a stagnant pecking order with its reciprocating contracts is not established. Within groups or communities, individuals tend to make 'mutual protection contracts'. For example, "You don't say anything about my habitual lateness, and I won't say anything about your incessant cursing". Most often these contracts are with several people—perhaps even a dozen. It becomes impossible to make contracts with the entire community. In analytic outpatient group psychotherapy patients only know one another within the context of the group and, therefore, the same group must meet regularly. In the framework of the Phoenix Community, everyone knows everyone else and has ample information to bring to the encounter. Within the community everyone has a 'personality jacket'. This is generally known by everyone else. For example, "He is a mama's boy" or "He doesn't like to take orders". There is no privileged or private communication. All is open to group scrutiny.

The only rules are honesty and non-violence; everything and anything else goes. There is nothing that can't be said—there is no social, religious, or personal area that is 'off limits'. The emphasis is generally on present behaviour rather than past. The encounter has been likened to a verbal street fight—screaming and yelling, and profanity are encouraged; the height of emotional intensity is incredible. "Cuss words express feelings, not an idea. Communicating thoughts is more difficult" (Schur, 1965). The use of profanity broadens the emotional spectrum and dramatically demonstrates that emotionally anything goes. In the theory of traditional group psychotherapy, the importance of venting hostility is stressed (Federn, 1964; Schmideberg, 1965), yet transcripts of patient interaction reveal bland, polite, social exchanges in what might be called 'Victorian style'. Interestingly, this is also true in the transcripts of Wilmer's (1964) San Quentin Prison group meetings. Laughter, tears, rages, compassion are all parts of the encounter. The very brutality of the verbal attack can be seen as an expression of love and concern. The patient soon learns various types of verbal attack and defence. No one has immunity, but no one can be forced to participate. The group will spare no verbal punches. The group pressure and emotional intensity can set off verbal catharsis. When this occurs, the individual is supported. The only real defence is honesty.

There are two types of encounters. The basic encounter is the 'floor encounter'. This is especially for newcomers. Emotional catharsis is the goal, and the accuracy of psychological confrontation or interpretation is not important. It is a sort of training ground where the newcomer can both loosen up and toughen up psychologically, learn that he can yell or be yelled at without anything happening to him or to anyone. There is no appointed leader. The more advanced encounter is the staff tutorial encounter. Here there is an appointed leader. He controls a group of experienced participants. He commands a powerful force. He can spearhead an attack and harness the energy, insight and experiences of the group, bringing them into focus in turn on each participant. The impact is tremendous. Participants are also instructed about the process of the group (Jones, 1952) and the individual defences used. One of the coordinators has the job of arranging encounters. He sees to it that requests to be in an encounter with someone are honoured. Encounters sometimes may be rigged, for example, by bringing all the targets of a particular resident's hostility together.

The encounter addresses itself to the problem of ignorance. This has nothing to do with intelligence or the lack of it. It has to do with failure to achieve social maturity to whatever problem may manifest itself (Dederich, quoted in Yablonsky, 1963). We regard antisocial, anti-military, amoral, and acting-out behaviour as 'stupid'.* This is brought up vividly in the

---

* This emotionally laden word is used to emphasize that the group takes a firm moral stand. Stupid in this sense has nothing to do with I.Q. or intelligence.

encounter. In fact, the encounter demands that the individual express himself. We direct ourselves against stupid behaviour, past and present, as well as against the camouflage of rationalization and denial that follow in the wake of such behaviour. It is amazing how quickly and easily facades of bravado, self-rightousness and rationalization crumble under the blistering scrutiny of the group. In the process, those who are attacking frequently gain greater insight and understanding than the attacked. Stripped of his stupid behaviour the individual is now open to learn new techniques of controlling his feelings. Frequently the group will give the patient a 'motion' or suggestion to follow. For example, a patient who has been generally sloppy in appearance will be told to 'try out' being exceptionally neat for a week, starting by shining his shoes, cutting his hair, and so forth. Or a resident who has been acting depressed will be told to act 'as if', to go 'through the motions' of acting pleasant, removing his sour face, engaging in extra activities and going away with a pass—without an attempt to interpret his behaviour. Motivational factors and dynamics are not license for bad behaviour. Frequently a man is told, "After you have been doing the right thing for a while, maybe you will understand why you used to 'screw up'".

There are clear and explicit rules so that residents do not take 'encounter license' into the environment when outside an encounter setting; that is, patients are expected to speak and act with politeness, and a heightened sense of social awareness is demanded.

Following an encounter, there is generally a social gathering, e.g., coffee and cake, sing-along, listening to music, etc. This accomplishes three ends. (1) A person troubled or wounded gets a chance for some 'human first aid'. He finds that people still relate to him as a person regardless of what might have been said a few moments before to emphasize a point. (2) It provides time to talk over some of the areas covered in the encounter again critically and aids in assimilating this material. (3) It demonstrates dramatically that what goes on in an encounter stays in an encounter and is not brought outside.

Once a week, after a resident has lived in the community for a few months, his family may visit. The advantages are obvious. It furthers our observations and knowledge of the resident's 'ego blue-print'. It gives an opportunity to correct behaviour in an area of a man's life that either might not be brought into sight, or in any event would not be in proper focus. By observing and learning to understand communication in the family, we can discover the rules that govern each individual's behaviour (Erikson, 1959; Rapaport, 1960).

Education

The Education Department is a subdivision in the structure of the Phoenix Community which is responsible for any activities pertaining to the acquisition of knowledge, skills, or the development of abilities of any members of that community. The central purpose of the Education Department is to reduce the general ignorance of the members, who tend to be severely limited in formal, vocational and social education. Based on the premise that ignorance and stupidity go hand in hand, this department seeks to eliminate ignorance and the complacency of ignorance by strengthening and stimulating the individual. The department seeks to demonstrate a need for a member to improve himself in a particular area and, subsequently, provides the opportunity for the achievement of that goal. The approach to learning is directed first toward the individual in the expectation that there will occur a reciprocal experience. The group will learn from the individual and, in turn, the individual will gain knowledge and perspective from the group. This idea of mutual enlightenment has produced a motive of interaction resulting in a high degree of motivation for learning. Rapaport (1960*a* & *b*) and Glueck (1959) have pointed out that analytic psychiatry has not had an ample learning theory. Of the three modes of learning—conditioning, insight and identification—the last has been most neglected by theorists. We attempt to capitalize on learning by identification, by harnessing the various skills of our patients as well as the use of the role model concept.

To produce this flexible learning experience, the department uses a number of programmed devices. The first, and basic beginning for all members of the community, is the personal interview and educational history chart. In this chart the abilities and weaknesses of an individual are assessed. Special testing such as general educational development may be used. This is recorded in detail. A projected study programme consisting of seminar topics and special courses is made. Upon an individual's completion of work in the programme, a final summary is compiled. The chart not only provides a course for a member to follow, but also enables the department to keep a graphic record of his development. A major section in educational activities is concerned with seminar programming. There are five general types of seminars utilized.

(1) *The department seminar.* In this type of seminar (lecture) the members of the Education Department present lectures on subjects of vital interest to all members of the project. These subjects may include topics such as personality growth and development, basic psychological principles, transactional analysis, proper English usage, etc. The members of the Education Department are responsible for the research and presentation of material in these lectures.

(2) *The individual seminar.* This type of lecture is one in which a selected member of the community gives a talk on a subject of his own interest. That member researches and presents his material. Those who are highly motivated or those who are in need of special assistance are given private and closely guided teaching aid in connection with their seminars. This type of seminar is a good example of individual-to-group relation.

(3) *The concept game.* This form of seminar is a free group discussion in which a concept is taken from literature, philosophy, religion, or psychology (purposefully out of context) and placed on a blackboard. The individuals of the group are then invited to voice their personal interpretations of the concept. Each man here has the opportunity to draw from the scope of his own experience and get practice in articulating and expressing his ideas. It is an exercise in abstract and conceptual thinking, as well as a vivid example of the reciprocal learning experience.

(4) *The impromptu speaking engagement.* This kind of seminar involves spontaneous and unrehearsed speaking in front of a group of people. A person is allotted a subject to present to the group and given a few minutes in which to collect his thoughts. The speech will last between five and ten minutes. After the speech, the group offers constructive criticism. Emphasis is placed on the development of the ability to organize thoughts quickly and present them to an audience in a comprehensive manner. A man is encouraged to draw upon his own life experiences.

(5) *Debate.* The central purpose of debating is to develop formal polemic skills with which a member may express himself in an analytic and critical manner. Members are grouped into teams of two each and are given a specific amount of time in which to prepare affirmative or negative case briefs on a predetermined resolution. Stress is placed upon objective or non-emotional thinking, on statistical evidence and rational analogy. Participating members also observe traditional collegiate rules of speech construction, argumentation and rebuttal.

Each Phoenix House maintains a library consisting of both fiction and non-fiction. Material is maintained by the members involved directly with education. These members are responsible for proper cataloguing of all books, and procurement of books. Community members are encouraged to use the library in order to familiarize themselves with this important academic skill.

Before residents are admitted to a Phoenix House, they have generally spent one to three months being prepared and motivated toward this commitment.

Following successful treatment, generally twelve to eighteen months later, the resident is transferred to a re-entry house, a more senior therapeutic community of peers, where the final phases of resocialization and vocational training take place. Depending on vocational choice, the candidate will remain in the re-entry house for three to twelve months.

Some preliminary results

To date, relatively few results are available for study. There are at present five Phoenix Houses in operation with a total of 450 patients, and with an average duration of stay of four months. Ten per cent of the residents have been in treatment for a year and have been transferred to the re-entry training programme. During the past twelve months, the drop-out rate has been 9%. Almost all of these drop-outs have left within ninety days after admission.

The average drug history of the 450 Phoenix residents is estimated at twelve years. There has been no evidence of any drug use within any Phoenix House. Considering the voluntary nature of the programme, these figures are of tremendous significance.

The method for uncovering relapse (drug use) consists of a random sample of 20 per cent of the population of each Phoenix House each week. Without going into details of the various difficulties in the use of urine sampling such as false positives and false negatives, thin-layer chromatography appears to be the best tool for the identification of covert drug use.

Summary

This paper reviews the structure and function of the Phoenix Therapeutic Community. The author emphasizes that a therapeutic community is the treatment of choice in addiction and severe character disorders.

REFERENCES

Ackerman, N. (1958). *The Psychodynamics of Family Life*. New York: Basic Books.
Aichorn, A. (1935). *Wayward Youth*. New York: Viking Press, Inc.
Aichorn, A. (1964). *Deliquency-Child Guidance*. New York: International University Press.
Casriel, B. (1963). *So Fair a House*. Englewood Cliffs, N.J.: Prentice-Hall.
Clark, D. H. (1964). *Doctor's Role in the Therapeutic Community*. London: Tavistock Publications.
Cummings, J. & Cummings, E. (1964). *The Value Problem in Psychiatry*. London: Sixth International Congress of Psychotherapy.
Edelson, M. (1964). *Ego Psychology, Group Dynamics and the Therapeutic Community*. London: Tavistock Publications.
Emerson, R. W. (1962). *Self Reliance*, from *Emerson's Essays*. New York: Thomas Y. Crowell.
Erikson, H. Identity and the life-cycle. *Psychological Issues*, Vol. 1, No. 1 (1959), p. 113.
Federn, P. (1964). *Ego Psychology, The Psychosis*. New York: Basic Books.
Fleck, S. (1964). *Some General and Specific Indications for Family Therapy*. London: Sixth International Congress of Psychotherapy.
Foulkes, S. H. (1964). *Therapeutic Group Analysis*. London: Penguin.
Freud, A. (1961). *Ego and Mechanisms of Defense*. London: Hogarth Press.
Glueck, E. (1959). *The Problem of Delinquency*. Boston: Houghton Mifflin Company.
Grinker, R. (1948). *Nervous and Mental Disorders*, **107**, 279–287.
Hilgard, E. (1948). *Theories of Learning*, 1st Ed. New York: Appleton-Century Croft.
Jones, M. (1952). *Therapeutic Community*. New York: Basic Books.
Lederer, W. (1964). *Dragons, Delinquents, Destiny*. Psychological Issues No. 15, IUP Vol. IV, No. 3.
Leland, P. B. (1964). *T-Group Theory and Laboratory Method*. New York: Wiley.
Lewin, Kurt (1948), *Resolving Social Conflicts*. 1st Ed. New York: Harper & Brothers.
Michaels, J. & Stiner, I. P. (1965). The impulsive psychopathic character according to the diagnostic profile, *Psychoanalytic Study of the Child*, Vol. XX. New York: International University Press.
Piers, G. & Piers, M. (1964). *Modes of Learning and the Analytic Process*. London: Sixth International Congress of Psychotherapy.
Rapaport, R. (1960*a*). *Community as Doctor: New Perspectives of Therapeutic Community*. Springfield, Illinois: C. C. Thomas.

Rapaport, D. (1960b). The structure of psychotherapy: a systemizing attempt, *Psychology Issues*, Mon. No. 6.
Reich, W. (1949). *Character Analysis*. New York: Noonday Press.
Satir, V. (1961). *Conjoint Family Therapy*. Palo Alto: Science & Behavior Books.
Schmideberg (1965). Reality therapy with offenders. *British Journal of Criminology*, Vol. 5, No. 2.
Schur, E. (1965). *Crimes Without Victims: Delinquent Behavior and Public Policy*. Englewood Cliffs, N.J.: Prentice Hall.
Schwartz, M. S. & Schwartz, S. G. (1964). *Social Approaches to Mental Patient Care*. New York: Columbia University Press.
Slavson, S. R. (1964). *A Textbook in Analytic Group Psychotherapy*. New York: International University Press.
Smith, A. Neuropsychologist commenting on Ernest Coe uttering curses first as he recovered from anesthesia following hemispherectomy. *Time*, Aug. 5, 1966.
Stanton, A. (1963). Milieu therapy: the development of insight. *Psychiatry*, Vol. 24, pp. 19–29.
Yablonsky, L. (1963). *The Tunnel Back: Synanon*. New York: Macmillan.
Wilmer, H. (1964). A living group experiment at San Quentin Prison, Corrective Psychiatry and Journal of Social Therapy, Vol. 10.

DISCUSSION

Oswald: Dr. Vaillant has emphasized that parole played a special therapeutic part. But one of his slides shows that those kept abstinent under supervision for more than twenty-one months made the best progress. Those in prison (with no parole) for more than nine months were next best, and progressed twice as well as those in prison for less than nine months. He has not told us the modal duration of stay in voluntary treatment—I suspect it was very brief. In short, could his results not be interpreted as indicating that the longer the period of enforced abstinence, the better the result, irrespective of parole?

I am interested in this because if one takes barbiturate dependence and looks merely at waking EEG abnormalities after withdrawal, they persist for perhaps six days. If one looks at the clinical features of tremor, fits, etc., they last for perhaps fourteen days. If one looks at more subtle but measurable neurophysiological abnormalities in sleep after withdrawal, as my colleagues and I have done, they last a couple of months. May it not be that in our present state of ignorance we do not have sufficiently sophisticated techniques to demonstrate physiological abnormalities in the heroin abstinence syndrome which may take a year or more to disappear?

Vaillant: I certainly feel that enforced abstinence in an institutional setting which lasts for four to twelve months is beneficial; after that, my evidence suggested that month-for-month compulsory supervision in the community was more effective than in an institutional setting.

Hill: This study of patients who had only recently started to take heroin raises the interesting question of whether any data is available on the rate at which tolerance to the drug becomes evident. Have the speakers any information about this?

de Alarcon: Sir Denis Hill has asked whether we (Dr. Rathod's paper) have found tolerance. Most of our patients started using heroin in the last quarter of 1966 and the first half of 1967. They are relatively new on the scene and still experience a 'lift' from the injection of heroin. Some of the patients whom we had seen in mid-1967, and who were then taking heroin just at week-ends and thought that they did not require treatment, came to us again recently and we found that they were now taking the drug daily. It may simply be a question of time. We did have several patients who had started two to three years ago and were now taking up to four grains of heroin a day.

Zacune: I should like to comment on Dr. de Alarcon's reply. In our study we did not find a definite relationship between tolerance and the lengths of time heroin has been used. Several of our subjects had taken heroin intermittently for up to two years and are not yet using it daily. The outcome of course remains to be seen.

Willis: Dr. de Alarcon's answer emphasizes the difficulties of estimating daily doses of heroin. It is very likely that 240 mg per day could be regarded as a high dose for English addicts, but there are a substantial number of Canadian addicts in this country who are taking even higher doses than this. For example, one patient under my care gets 720 mg of heroin a day—and this has been observed while he was in hospital.

Neal: I should like to ask Dr. Rosenthal to comment on the sending back of post-addicts into endemic drug areas. Does this not make their readdiction more likely?

Rosenthal: We have found that sending addicts back to endemic areas after enough rehabilitation work has been done enables them personally to master further a previous problem area. In addition, they are an essential link to the active addict with whom they can talk in a common language.

Vaillant: In my follow-up of New York addicts, although more than fifty achieved abstinence of one year or more, very few of these abstinence periods occurred in settings where drugs are unavailable. My suspicion is that abstinence achieved in endemic drug areas is more lasting.

Mullin: I take it from what he has said that Dr. Connell would advise that heroin should only be given to an 'unknown' addict if the urine test, taken at the time of the initial interview, proved positive for morphine.

If this is so, are sufficient facilities available in the United Kingdom to perform the tests? In Glasgow we were in the fortunate position of having contact with a research laboratory at the University of Strathclyde with a particular interest in the estimation of morphine and other drugs in biological materials. Estimation facilities were not available in most hospital laboratories. If it is suggested that routine estimations must be done, are there in fact enough special laboratory facilities to deal with the tests?

Connell: Ideally no heroin should be given to an addict unless a positive urine test for morphine had been obtained.

In my paper I indicated that 24 hours was really the minimum time before a result of a test could be expected. However, development of laboratory facilities in order to provide such a service is proceeding apace.

Richter: Dr. Connell has mentioned regulations which come into operation on April 16, 1968, prohibiting private doctors from prescribing heroin and cocaine to addicts. This is a step in the right direction, but I wonder if Dr. Connell feels that this is adequate, since it leaves private doctors still free to prescribe morphine and methedrine? It is true that addicts who register at the National Health Service Treatment Centres will be able to get drugs there, but many young addicts are unwilling to register, since they do not want their names known. It is rumoured that a mixture of powdered heroin and caffein has recently become available on the black market, and I wonder if this is a serious danger?

Connell: So far as I know there is no evidence to suggest that powdered heroin and caffeine was being distributed. A few months ago, before the new regulations came into effect, some doctors were prescribing powdered heroin and this may have given rise to the rumours.

There was, I think, an isolated case of heroin and caffeine powder, but Mr. Jeffery of the Home Office is here and can confirm this.

I also stated, I think, that morphine, if prescribed to addicts by private doctors, could easily be placed under the new arrangements by powers under the Dangerous Drugs Act 1967, but that methedrine could not and would require new legislation. I think I gave my view that amphetamines, and particularly methedrine ampoules, should be under much closer surveillance and control.

Wartburg: One important point should have been raised, too, with respect to factors of drug dependence: which are the sound legal approaches for dealing with drug abuse? What kind of features (control measures, availability on medical prescription only, unauthorized possession, special licensing for manufacturers, etc.) should be embodied in reasonable and efficient public health legislation concerned with drug dependence and drug abuse? Which should be the criteria for placing a given drug under a specific drug abuse control legislation clinically proven dependence liability *plus* relevant incidental figures of evidenced abuse situations?

In short, the establishing of scientific criteria for drug dependence should be paralleled by the propagation of sound principles for legislation.

AUTHOR INDEX

BECKETT, A. H., Distribution and metabolism in man of some narcotic analgesics and some 'amphetamines', 129

CHEIN, Isidor, Psychological functions of drug use, 13
COLLIER, H. O. J., Humoral transmitters, supersensitivity, receptors and dependence, 49
CONNELL, P. H., Drug dependence in Great Britain: a challenge to the practice of medicine, 291
COX, B. M. and GINSBURG, M., Is there a relationship between protein synthesis and tolerance to analgesic drugs?, 77

DAVIES, D. L., Stabilized addiction and normal drinking in recovered alcohol addicts, 363
DE ALARCON, R., RATHOD, N. H. and THOMSON, I. G., Observations on heroin abuse by young people in Crawley New Town, 331
DENEAU, Gerald A., Psychogenic dependence in monkeys, 199

EVANS, J. I. See OSWALD, Ian et al., 243

GEBER, Beryl A., Non-dependent drug use: some psychological aspects, 375
GINSBURG, M. See COX, B. M. et al., 77

HILL, Sir Denis, Chairman, Session IV, Social and clinical factors, 285

JAFFE, Jerome. See SHARPLESS, Seth et al., 67

JANSSEN, Paul A. J., Development of new potent analgesics, 149
JOYCE, C. R. B., Quantitative estimates of dependence on the symbolic function of drugs, 271

KOSVINER, A. See ZACUNE, J. et al., 323
KUMAR, R., STEINBERG, Hannah and STOLERMAN, I. P., How rats can become dependent on morphine in the course of relieving another need, 209

LEWIS, Aubrey, Introduction: definitions and perspectives, 5
LEWIS, S. A. See OSWALD, Ian et al., 243

McILWAIN, H., Chairman, Session II. Pharmacology and biochemistry, 94
McNAMEE, H. Brian. See MELLO, Nancy K. et al., 259
MADINAVEITIA, J., Search for addiction in a new analgesic, 155
MELLO, Nancy K., MENDELSON, Jack H. and McNAMEE, H. Brian, An experimental approach to the examination of drinking patterns of alcoholics, 259
MENDELSON, Jack H. See MELLO, Nancy K. et al., 259
MITCHESON, M. See ZACUNE, J. et al., 323
MULÉ, S. J., The relationship of the disposition and metabolism of morphine in the CNS to tolerance, 97

OGBORNE, A. See ZACUNE, J. et al., 323

OSWALD, Ian, EVANS, J. I. and LEWIS, S. A., Addictive drugs cause suppression of paradoxical sleep with withdrawal rebound, 243

PATON, W. D. M., *Chairman*, Session I, Definitions and approaches, 1

PATON, W. D. M., A pharmacological approach to drug dependence and drug tolerance, 31

PICKENS, Roy. *See* THOMPSON, Travis *et al.*, 177

RATHOD, N. H. *See* DE ALARCON, R. *et al.*, 331

REMMER, H. Tolerance to barbiturates by increased breakdown, 111

ROSENTHAL, Mitchell S., The Phoenix House therapeutic community: an overview, 395

SHARPLESS, Seth and JAFFE, Jerome, Withdrawal phenomena as manifestations of disuse supersensitivity, 67

STEINBERG, Hannah, *Chairman*, Session III, Laboratory studies of animal and human behaviour, 173

STEINBERG, Hannah. *See* KUMAR, R. *et al.*, 209

STIMSON, G. *See* ZACUNE, J. *et al.*, 323

STOLERMAN, I. P. *See* KUMAR, R. *et al.*, 209

THOMPSON, Travis and PICKENS, Roy, Drug self-administration and conditioning, 177

THOMSON, I. G. *See* DE ALARCON, R. *et al.*, 331

VAILLANT, George E., The natural history of urban narcotic drug addiction — some determinants, 341

WILLIS, J. H., The natural history of drug dependence: some comparative observations on United Kingdom and United States subjects, 301

WILSON, C. W. M., An analysis of the mechanisms involved in the taste for drink, 221

ZACUNE, J., STIMSON, G., OGBORNE, A., MITCHESON, M. and KOSVINER, A., The assessment of heroin usage in a provincial community, 323

SUBJECT INDEX

Abstinence, efficacy in elimination of dependence, 191–193
  following dependence, incidence of, 344
  induction and maintenance of, 355–359
  self-imposed, 313
  syndrome *See* Withdrawal symptoms
Acetylcholine,
  release, by nerves, effect of opiates on, 33–35
    depression of, effects of, 37
    possible induction of tolerance by, 38
  response of superior cervical ganglion to, effect of denervation on, 91
  supersensitivity to, 51
Acidity of urine,
  effect on excretion of amphetamine, 130–133
  effect on excretion of ephedrine, methylephedrine and norephedrine, 133–135
  effect on excretion of narcotic analgesics, 136–142
  role in individual variations in drug metabolism, 138–142
Actinomycin D,
  effect on narcotic analgesic tolerance, 77–82
  site of action of, 81
Addicts,
  admission to Phoenix House therapeutic community, 396
  categorization of, 319–320
  development of, 21–24
  environment of, 346–348
  narcotic, in Great Britain, 291
    life histories of, 343–345
    preference for specific drugs, 184
  reasons for heroin use, 304–307
  special clinics for, under D.D.A., 294–299
  treatment of, 287, 289
  W. H. O. definition of, 6
Addiction *See* Dependence
Adrenaline, antagonism of sensitivity by, 51
  effect on transmitter release, 36
  supersensitivity of salivary gland to, induction by atropine, 50
Aerobacter aerogenes, response to barbitone, development of tolerance and dependence indications, 87–88
Age, distribution of dependence by, 302, 327
  of first experience of heroin, 310–311
  of first exposure to heroin, 309–310
Ailments inducing symbolic drug dependence, 284
Alcohol, as precursor of heroin use, 315–316, 337
  as substitute for drugs, 359
  blood level of, correlation with work efficiency, in alcoholism, 283
  deleterious effects of, 238–241
  dependence, 7, 9
    elimination of, 288
  effect on sleep, 252, 254
  psychopharmacological effects of, 17
  self-administration of, effect of environment on, 181
  taste for, effect of metronidazole on, 230–232
    pharmacology of, 228–235
    relationship to effect on metabolism, 223
  toxicity of, 11
  use of, effect of drug use on, 383

SUBJECT INDEX

Alcoholics Anonymous, 363, 368
  implications of methods of, 372
Alcoholism, classification of, 221–222
  controlled drinking after recovery from, 363–372
  definition of, 221
  drinking patterns in, 225–227, 259, 262–269
  physiological study of, 261
  social factors in, 222–227, 261
Alkaloids, lack of enzyme-induction by, 120–121
Aminopyrine,
  oxidation of, relation to induction of enzymes by phenobarbitone, 117–119
  role in induction of barbiturate tolerance, 116
Amitriptyline, effect on sleep, 253
Amphetamine, buccal absorption of, 144
  dependence, 7, 9
  distribution and metabolism of, in man, 129–148
  effect on reward (euphoric) system of brain, 55
  effect on sleep, 253, 254
  effect on transmitter release, 36
  excretion of, effect of urine acidity on, 130–133
  interaction with adrenaline and noradrenaline, 55
  non-dependent use of, 390–393
  possible abuse of, 298
  prescribing of, under D.D.A., 412
  repeat prescriptions for, 277
  status in scientific investigation, 3
  use with heroin, 313, 337
Amylobarbitone, effect on sleep, 247
  self-administration of, effect of environment on, 181
Anaesthesia, surgical, induction of, 150
Analgesic activity, of carbolines, 162–163
  of opiates, 31
Analgesics, antipyretic, central activity of, 283
  biological assay of, 170
  development of new, 150
  effect of correlation with anaesthetics, 91
  inadequacies of available, 152–154
  induction of dependence on, diagnosis of, 155–171
  narcotic, distribution and metabolism of, in man, 129–148
  effect on protein synthesis, 85
  excretion of, effect of urine acidity on, 136–142
  tolerance to, relation to protein synthesis, 77–92
Angiotensin, immunogenic reaction to, 59
Anti-authority function of drugs, 25, 29
Antibiotics, response of enzyme systems to, effect on tolerance, 87
Antiemetic effect, of piritramide, 152
Antipyretic analgesics, central activity of, 283
Anxiety, effect of alcohol on, 262, 267
  effect of drug withdrawal on, 250
Appetite regulating centre, influence on alcohol consumption and metabolism, 227
Atropine, effect on response of anterior hypothalamic receptors to pilocarpine, 71
Authority, in therapy of dependence, 397–398
Aversive stimuli, in elimination of dependence, 193–194

Barbitone, response of bacterial cells to, and effect on tolerance, 86–88
Barbiturates, cross-tolerance with ethanol, 167
  dependence on, 7, 9
  effect on punishment discrimination in rats, 55
  effect on sleep, 247
  effect on transmitter release, 36
  induction of pethidine oxidation by, 121
  metabolism and elimination of, effect on anaesthetic response, 114

SUBJECT INDEX

Barbiturates (contd.)—
  response of cerebral cortex to, compared with response to surgical isolation, 73
  status in scientific investigation, 3
  tolerance to, induction by metabolism of drugs, 111
    induction by oxidation of other drugs, 114–116, 123
  and, dependence on, model for, 52
  use with heroin, 337
  withdrawal symptoms of, 165
Behaviour, deviant, relationship to heroin usage, 336
  patterns, in maintenance of dependence, 354
Behavioural mechanisms in drug self-administration, 178
  responses, relationship to drug self-administration, 189
Benzedrine, non-dependent use of, 390
Bezitramide, duration of analgesia induced by, 153–154
Blood, accumulation of phenobarbitone by, 123
  alcohol level, correlation with work efficiency, in alcoholism, 283
    in alcoholism, 260, 264
    relationship to work performance, 266
  platelets, 5-hydroxytryptamine receptors in, 59
  uptake and distribution of barbiturates in, and effect on induction of anaesthesia, 112–114
'Blues', non-dependent use of, 390
Bradykinin, supersensitivity to, 51
Brain, accumulation of phenobarbitone by, 123
  intracellular location of morphine in, 103, 106–107
  reward and punishment systems in, cross-inhibition of, 54
  uptake and distribution of morphine in, during tolerance and non-tolerance, 98–100, 105
  effect of nalorphine on, 100–102
Bretylium, effect on sympathetic transmission, and tolerance to, 40–41

Buccal absorption test, of kidney absorption of drugs, 142–147

CNS, effect of alcohol on, 221, 223
  morphine metabolites in, 102, 106
  uptake and distribution of morphine in, effect of nalorphine on, 100–102
Caffeine, psychogenic dependence on, in monkey, 205
Cannabis, deleterious effects of, 238–241
  dependence on, 7, 9
  pharmacological and therapeutic uses of, 237–238
  psychopharmacological effects of, 17
  use with heroin, 314, 328, 337
Carbolines, analgesic activity of, 162
Catecholamines, uptake by nerve endings of, loss of, 69
Centrally active drugs, repeat prescriptions for, 277–279
Chemical similarity, role in predicting dependence liability, 163
Chloral, dependence on, 9
Chloramphenicol, effect on morphine tolerance, 82
Chloroform, dependence on, 9
  effect on transmitter release, 36
  responses to, 91
Chlorpheniramine, buccal absorption of, 144
Chlorpromazine, effect on sleep, 253
  non-dependence inducing, 205
Cholinoceptive cells, central nervous system, response to scopolamine and pilocarpine, 72
Cholinomimetic agents, effect on anterior hypothalamic neurones, 71
Class distribution of dependence, 302, 327
Cocaine, dependence on, 7, 9
  effect on sensitivity to noradrenaline, 60
  mechanism of, 61
  effect on transmitter release, 36
  interaction with adrenaline and noradrenaline, 55

SUBJECT INDEX

Cocaine (contd.)—
  prescription of, under D.D.A., 292
  psychogenic dependence on, in monkey, 205
  self-administration of, relationship to dosage, 185
  status in scientific investigation, 3
  tolerance, comparison of physical with pyschological, 56
  use with heroin, 315, 337
Codeine, effect on response of defecation to dependence, 158
  potency ratio of, 36
  psychogenic dependence on, in monkey, 205
  use with heroin, 314
Coffee, dependence on, 10
Conditioned responses, drug-reinforced, 178
Conditioning, pairing of drugs and other stimuli in, 188
  reinforcers of, effect on abstinence, 357–358
  relationship to drug taking, 177–198
  role in maintenance of dependence, 352, 354
Cortex,
  cerebral, response to barbiturates, comparison with response to surgical isolation, 73
  surgically isolated, supersensitivity of, 72–73
Craving, for alcohol, 260
  in dependence, 318–319
Crawley New Town, heroin abuse in, 331–339
Cross-tolerance, 120–122, 123
  between ethanol and barbiturates, 167
Cyclazocine, dependence on and tolerance to, relation to agonist activity, 90
  effect of partial agonist activity on tolerance to, 41
Cycloheximide, effect on morphine tolerance, 82

Dangerous Drugs Act 1967, 292–293

Defecation, effect of dependence on, 157–158
index of dependence, 168
Delinquency, relationship with drug abuse, 287, 328–329, 347
Delirium tremens, effect of antiparadoxical sleep drugs on, 252
Denervation, effect on superior cervical ganglion, 91
  effect on transmitter release from neurones, 92
  pharmacological, effect on receptors, 57
  induction of supersensitivity by, effect on withdrawal symptoms, 50–52
  time course of, 38
  model of physical dependence, 52
  surgical, induction of supersensitivity to drugs by, 52
Dependence, acquisition of, effect of current circumstances on, 181, 183
  acquisition and maintenance of, 179
  age, class and sex distribution of, 302–327
  agents of, 9
  barbiturate, 52
    response of cerebral cortex to, comparison with response to surgical isolation, 73
  behavioural, 177
  cocaine-like, effect on noradrenaline receptors, 61
  definition of, 3, 5–11
  development of, 336, 345–350
  effect of subjective reactions on, 14
  drugs inducing, effect on transmitter release, 36
  effect of social factors in, 183, 217
  elimination of, 191
  emotional factors in recognition of, 10
  etiology and pathogenesis of, 288
  heroin, pattern of, 21–24
  typology of, 316–320, 329
  in U.K., 4, 291–299
  indicators of, 317
  induction by analgesics, diagnosis of, 155–171

SUBJECT INDEX

Dependence (*contd.*)—
  induction of, social factors in, 376
  influence on effect of drugs on sleep, 245, 249
  laboratory investigation of, 174
  liability to, 288, 375
    correlation with personality, 282
    maintenance of, 350–355
    methods for conducting surveys of, 290
  morphine, effect on psychological drives, 54
    induction during relief of other needs, in animals, 209–220
    procedure for, 211–212
  narcotic, induction of deterioration by, effect of environment on, 282
  natural history of, in U.K. and U.S. compared, 301–321, 328
    in urban environment, 341–360
  on symbolic drugs, 279
  patterns of, 345
  pharmacological factors in, 31–47, 89
  physical, 177
    association with drug-induced supersensitivity, 52
    Martin's theory of hypertrophy of redundant motor pathways in, 74–75
    relation to reduction of neural activity, 67–68
    and psychological, 7
    association with tolerance, role of transmitters in, 49
  physiological, detection by chronic administration experiments, 206
  physiological and sociological factors in, 4
  placebo prescribing in, 275
  psychogenic, in monkey, 199–207
  psychological, association with inhibition of punishment and reward systems of brain, 55
    association with tolerance, effect of site of action of drug on, 56
    drug-induced supersensitivity as model for, 53
  psychological factors in, 89
  quantitative estimates of, 271–280
  reacquisition of, 180
  relationship to biochemical pharmacology, role of various organs and substances, 95
  relationship to habituation, 247
  stabilized, 370
  total personal involvement in, 318
  treatment of, 287, 289, 292–293
    in Phoenix House community, 395–407
  treatment with other drugs of, 14
Depressant effect, of opiates, 31
Depressants, psychological dependence on, 54
Depression, alleviation of, cause of heroin use, 305
  effect of alcohol on, 262, 267
Detention, compulsory, of addicts, 288, 289, 293
Dexamphetamine, dependence on, effect on sleep, 245
  non-dependent use of, 390
  psychogenic dependence on, in monkey, 205
Diagnostic problems, of heroin dependence, 294–295
Diethylpropion, effect on sleep, 252, 253
Dosage, assessment of, 298
Dreaming, effect of drugs on, 244–254
Drinamyl, non-dependent use of, 390
Drinking, controlled, in recovered alcoholics, 363–372
  patterns, in alcoholism, 225–227, 259, 262–269
Drug abuse, susceptibility to, in monkey and man, 199, 205
Drug-receptor interaction, 49
Drugs, criteria for control of, 412
  dependence-inducing, effect on transmitter release, 36
  effects of, variates in, 14
  first experience of, 307–308, 336, 381
  misuse of, classification of, 15–29
  non-dependent use of, 375–393
    effect on alcohol and tobacco use, 383
    escalation of, 380–381, 386

SUBJECT INDEX

Drugs, non- dependent use of,
    frequency and classification of, 378
    relationship to personality, 384
    orally taken, delay in action of, 281
    partitioning of, effect on kidney absorption, 142–147
    psychopharmacological effects of, 16, 18
    special functions of use of, 25

ECT, effect on sleep, 253
Education, in Phoenix House therapeutic community, 404–407
Educational background of heroin users, 327
Emetic effect, of morphine, 152
Employment
    background of heroin users, 328
    in therapeutic community, 399–400
Environment, effect on acquisition of dependence, 181–182
    effect on alcoholism, 222
    effect on drinking pattern, in alcoholism, 283
    effect on drug experimentation, 90
    effect on heroin dependence, 287
    effect on induction of alcoholism, 369
    effect on narcotic dependence-induced deterioration, 282
    effect on re-addiction, 174, 280, 410–411
    effect on self-administration of drugs, 182
    provincial, assessment of heroin usage in, 323–330
    relationship to abstinence, 355–359
    relationship to drug use, 346–348, 382
Enzyme systems, inhibition by antibacterial agents, effect on tolerance, 87
Enzymes,
    induction of, by liver barbiturates of, 166
    importance of body acidity in assessment of, in man, 142
    role in oxidation of drugs, 116–120
    phenobarbitone-induced, effect on liver, 119

Ephedrine, excretion of, effect of urine acidity on, 133–135
    lipid solubility of, effect on acid-sensitivity, 135
    non-dependent use of, 390
Ethanol, cross-tolerance with barbiturates, 167
    oxidation of, induction of barbiturate tolerance by, 114–116, 123
    psychogenic dependence on, in monkey, 205
Ether, dependence on, 9
Etiology of dependence, 288
Etonitazine, effect on morphine-reinforced responses, 181
Etorphine tolerance, effect of actinomycin D on, 78
Eudystat, non-dependent drugs affecting, 56
    role in psychic dependence, 55
Euphoria, cause of heroin use, 306
Euphoric system, in brain, link with dysphoric system, role in genesis of psychic dependence, 55
Excitatory activity, drug-induced supersensitivity to, 51

Family, attitude towards drug use, 382, 386–387
Fenfluramine, effect on sleep, 253
Fentanyl, effect of, and similarity to morphine, 150–151
    potency ratio of, 36
Fluorouracil, effect on morphine tolerance, 82
Foetus, transport of pentazocine and pethidine into, 147

Gambling, relationship to alcoholism, 262
    relationship to blood alcohol levels, 267
    use in evaluating drinking patterns in alcoholism, 265
Gastric disease, relationship to alcoholism, 261
Gastrin, immunogenic reaction to, 59
Gland cells, release of transmitter from, 71

SUBJECT INDEX

Glutethimide, oxidation of, induction of barbiturate tolerance by, 114–116, 123
Guanethidine, effect on sympathetic transmission, 40

Halothane, effect on transmitter release, 36
Harmala alkaloids, analgesic activity of, 162
Heart, uptake and distribution of morphine in, effect of nalorphine on, 100–102
Heroin,
　abuse, in Crawley New Town, 331–339
　screening methods for assessing prevalence of, 332–335
　addicts' introduction to, 303–304, 336, 345–350
　age at first dose of, 310
　dependence, 14, 15, 20
　and treatment of, 338–339
　comparison between New York and London cases of, 286–287
　comparison between U.K. and U.S. cases of, 301–321
　diagnostic problems of, 294–295
　effect of over-prescribing on, 291
　elimination of, 288
　liability to, 183
　pattern of, 21, 22
　recent increase in, 323
　typology of, 316–320, 329
　duration of usage of and age of first exposure to, 309–312
　estimation in body of, 411
　first experience of, subjective evaluation of, 307–308, 336
　mode of administration of, 308
　prescribing of, under D.D.A., 292–298, 411
　psychopharmacological effects of, 17, 20–21
　reasons for use of, 304–307
　tolerance, effect of actinomycin D on, 78
　rate of onset, 410

usage, assessment in provincial community of, 323–339
　frequency of, 337
　other drugs accompanying, 313
　symptoms of, 332
Hexafluorobenzene, responses to, 91
Hexafluoroethyl, responses to, 91
Hexobarbitone,
　oxidation of, relation to induction of enzymes by phenobarbitone, 117–119
　role in induction of barbiturate tolerance, 116
　uptake and distribution in blood of, 112–113
Himmelsbach's homeostatic theory of dependence, 68
Histamine, supersensitivity to, 51
Homeostatic theory of dependence, 68
Hospitalization, compulsory, of addicts, 288, 289, 293
Hostility-expressing function of drugs, 25
Humoral transmitter, role in induction of dependence, 49
5-Hydroxytryptamine, blood platelet receptors of, 59
　receptors of, uptake of morphine by, induction of dependence by, 53
　supersensitivity to, 51
Hypnotic effect, of phenobarbitone, relationship to blood and brain concentration, 124
Hypnotics, effect on sleep, 247, 250
　iatrogenically-induced consumption of, 250
Hypotensive drugs, effect on sympathetic transmission, 40

ICI 49455 See Isopropyl tetrahydro-β-carboline
Immunogenic reaction, to drugs, 59
Imprisonment, effect on induction of abstinence, 349, 356–357
Inadequacy, factor in development of dependence, 23–24
Inhibitory activity, induction of, 51
Institutionalized addicts, 325, 349

SUBJECT INDEX

Intelligence, relationship to heroin usage, 336
Isopropyl tetrahydro-β-carboline, analgesic activity and low toxicity of, 162
  effect on respiration, 167–168
  non-dependence and non-tolerance of, 164, 168–169

Khat, dependence on, 9
Kidney
  function, effect of alcohol on, 261
  tubules, drug absorption by, effect of partitioning on, 142–147
  permeability to lipid soluble bases, effect on excretion of drugs, 135–136
  uptake and distribution of morphine in, effect of nalorphine on, 102

LSD, dependence on, 9
  effect on sleep, 253
  psychopharmacological effects of, 16
  use with heroin, 315, 337
Laboratory investigation of dependence, 174
Levallorphan, effect on response of defecation to dependence, 158
Licensing regulations, under D.D.A., 293
Lipid metabolism of drugs, effect on kidney absorption, 142–147
  solubility, of ephedrine, methylephedrine and norephedrine, effect on acid-sensitivity, 135
Liver
  function, effect of alcohol on, 261
  intracellular location of morphine in, 103, 106–107
  metabolism in, effect on response to barbiturates, 116
  response to phenobarbitone-induced enzymes, 119
  uptake and distribution of morphine in, effect of nalorphine on, 102
Lung, uptake and distribution of morphine in, effect of nalorphine on, 102

Magazine training, in conditioning, 179
Marijuana *See* Cannabis
Martin's theory, of hypertrophy of redundant motor pathways, in physical dependence, 74–75
Memory, effect of alcohol on, 261
Meprobamate, effect on punishment discrimination in rats, 55
  effect on sleep, 251
Mercaptopurine, effect on morphine tolerance, 82
Metabolism, effect of alcohol on, relationship to desire for alcohol, 223
  effect on drinking habits, in man, 222
  of drugs, individual variations in, role of urine acidity in, 138–142
Methadone, buccal absorption of, 144
  effect on self-administration of morphine, 218
  excretion of, effect of urine acidity on, 136
  in treatment of dependence, 14
  response to, in heroin addicts, 353
  substitution for opiates, in elimination of dependence, 193
Methedrine, non-dependent use of, 390
  prescribing of, under D.D.A., 142
Methscopolamine, effect on response of anterior hypothalamic receptors to pilocarpine, 71–72
Methylamphetamine, buccal absorption of, 144
  excretion of, effect of urine acidity on, 132
Methylephedrine, excretion of, effect of urine acidity on, 133
  lipid solubility of, effect on acid-sensitivity, 135
Methylpentynol, effect on transmitter release, 36
Methylphenidate, effect on sleep, 252
  induction of dependence on, 61
Metronidazole, effect on taste for alcohol, 230–232
Monoamine oxidase inhibitors, analgesic activity of, 162
  non-dependent character of, 57

SUBJECT INDEX

Moral values, in therapy of dependence, 397
Morphine
dependence, 7, 9
and tolerance, relation to agonist activity, 90
effect on psychological drives, 54
liability to, 183
role in diagnosing dependence on other analgesics, 156–158
voluntary, in monkeys and rats, 159–162, 169
deprivation of, effect on morphine-reinforced responses, and response to nalorphine, 180
effect on sleep, 252, 254
effect on transmitter release, 36
estimation in body of, 411
induction of dependence on, during relief of other needs, in rat, 209–220
procedure for, 201–212
induction of withdrawal symptoms by, effect of levallorphan on, 32
interactions with humoral mediators, 53
intracellular location in brain and liver, 103, 106–107
lack of enzyme-induction by, 121
local anaesthetic effect of, 35
localization in CNS, and relation of tolerance, antagonism and abstinence to metabolism of, 165
metabolites of, in CNS and urine, 102, 106
partial agonist activity of, effect on tolerance, 41
preference for, in rat, 212–215
effect of pre-treatment with morphine and withdrawal on, 215–216
prescribing of, under D.D.A., 411–412
psychogenic dependence on, in monkey, 205
re-addiction to, 174
reinforced responses, 188
effect of etonitazine on, 181
repeat prescriptions for, 277

role in surgical analgesia, 151
self-administration of, effect of environment on, 182
interaction with other reinforcement stimuli, 189
relationship to dosage, 185
self-reversal, 42–43
tolerance, effect of actinomycin D on, 77–82
effect of protein synthesis inhibition on, 82
inhibition by antibiotics, 60
possible induction by axonal acetylcholine accumulation, 38
relation to distribution and metabolism in CNS, 97
transfer to other subjects by brain extracts, 60
withdrawal symptoms during, effect of nalorphine on, 106
uptake by brain of, effect of tolerance on, 167
uptake and distribution
in brain and CNS, during tolerance and non-tolerance, 98–100, 105
effect of nalorphine on, 100–102, 105
in heart, lung, liver and kidney, effect of nalorphine on, 102
Motivational factors, in alcoholism, 260
in conditioning, 180
in response to treatment, 357
Motor pathways, effect of pharmacological blockade of, 69
redundant, Martin's theory of hypertrophy of, in physical dependence, 74–75
surgical blockade of, 72
Muscle, smooth, release of transmitter from, 71

Nalorphine, comparison with morphinomimetics in post-operative analgesia, and side-effects of, 151–152
dependence, and tolerance, relation to agonist activity, 90

Nalorphine dependence (contd.)—
 diagnosis by withdrawal symptoms, 155
 dysphoric effects of, 56
 effect of partial agonist activity on tolerance to, and morphine antagonism of, 41-42
 effect on distribution of morphine, in brain and CNS, 100-102
  in heart, lung, liver and kidney, 102
 effect on intracellular location of morphine in brain and liver, 104, 107
 effect on morphine-deprivation, 180
 effect on response of defecation to dependence, 158
 induction of withdrawal symptoms by, during morphine dependence, 353
  during morphine tolerance, 106
 morphine-like agonist and antagonist activity of, 36
 non-dependence inducing, 205
Narcotics
 dependence on, induction of deterioration by, effect on environment on, 282
  liability to, relationship to method of administration and magnitude of action, 186
  secondary to therapeutic action, 67
 distribution and metabolism of, in man, 129-148
 effect on protein synthesis, 85
 excretion of, effect of urine acidity on, 136-142
 relation between tachyphylaxis and tolerance to, 90
 tolerance to, relation to protein synthesis, 77-92
Nerve activity, reduction by drugs, as cause of dependence, 67
Nerves, postganglionic, response to electrical stimulation and to acetylcholine, effect of opiates on, 33
 release of acetylcholine by, effect of opiates on, 33-35
 responses to opiates, 32

Nervous system,
 central, effect of alcohol on, 221, 223
 effect of disuse supersensitivity on, 71
 response to drugs, correlation with response of peripheral nerves, 91
 role in tolerance, 122-126
 uptake, distribution and metabolism of morphine in, relation to tolerance, 97-100, 105
Neurones, anterior hypothalamic, effect of cholinomimetic agents on, 71
 disuse supersensitivity in, 70
 transmitter release from, effect of denervation on, 92
Nialamide, effect on sleep, 253
Nicotine, buccal absorption of, 144
 interaction with adrenaline and noradrenaline, 55
Nightmares *See* Dreaming
Nikethamide, oxidation of, induction of barbiturate tolerance by, 114-116, 123
Nitrazepam, effect on sleep, 249
Noradrenaline, effect on transmitter release, 36
 release, depression of, effects of, 37
 sensitivity, effect of cocaine on, 60
 mechanism of, 61
Norephedrine, buccal absorption of, 144
 excretion of, effect of urine acidity on, 135
 lipid solubility of, effect on acid-sensitivity, 135
Norpethidine, buccal absorption of, 144

Opiates,
 dependence on, 7, 9
  diagnosis by withdrawal symptoms, 155
  pharmacological factor in, 31

SUBJECT INDEX

Opiates (contd.)—
  effects on transmitter release and on nerve responses, 32
  partial agonist activity of, effect on tolerance, 41
  potency ratio of, comparison between man and isolated intestines, 36
  psychopharmacological effects of, 18
  specificity of, 43
  status in scientific investigation, 3
  tolerance to, effect of self-reversal on, 43
  time course of, 38
  use with heroin, 314–315
Opium, use in oriental countries, 11
Oxidation of drugs, effect on anaesthetic response to barbiturates, 114–116, 123

Pain
  mechanisms, basic, 149–150
  post-operative, analgesic control of, 151–152
Parasympathomimetic agents, effect on disuse supersensitivity, 69
Paregoric, use with heroin, 314
Parole, effect on abstinence, 349, 356–359
  effect on treatment of dependence, comparison with enforced abstinence, 409
Pathogenesis of dependence, 288
Pentazocine, comparison with morphinomimetics in post-operative analgesia, and side-effects of, 151–152
  effect of partial agonist activity on tolerance to, 41
  excretion of, effect of urine acidity on, 141
  transport across foetal membrane of, 147
Pentobarbitone, effect on sleep, 249
  psychogenic dependence on, in monkey, 205
  tolerance to, effect on anaesthesia, and relation to blood levels, 113–114

Peptide hormones, immunogenic reaction to, 59
Perceptual effects of drugs, 16
Personal relationships, stable, role in abstinence, 359
Personality, correlation with dependence liability, 282
  relationship to drug use, 384
Pethidine, buccal absorption of, 144
  effect on response of defecation to dependence, 158
  excretion of, effect of urine acidity on, 141
  lack of enzyme-induction by, and barbiturate-induced oxidation of, 121
  tolerance to, effect of actinomycin D on, 78
  transport across foetal membrane of, 147
  use with heroin, 315
Pharmacological factors, in dependence and tolerance, 31–47
Phenacetin, dependence on, 9
Phenmetrazine, dependence on, effect on sleep, 245, 253
Phenobarbitone,
  accumulation by blood and brain of, 123
  effect on hypnotic response, 124
  induction of enzymes by, 117–119
  induction of pethidine tolerance by, 121
  lack of induction of morphine tolerance by, 122
  oxidation of, induction of barbiturate tolerance by, 114–116, 123
  tolerance to, effect of dosage on, 126
  effect of response of CNS on, 124
Phenothiazine, effect on sleep, 253
  tolerance, 56
Phoenix House, therapeutic community, 395–407
Physical dependence, 7, 318
  association with drug-induced supersensitivity, 52
  Martin's theory of hypertrophy of redundant motor pathways in, 74, 75

Physiological
  dependence, detection by chronic administration experiments, 206
  relationship to drug abuse, 199
  factors, role in psychological dependence, 247
Pilocarpine, antagonism of sensitivity by, 51
  response of anterior hypothalamic receptors to, and effect of atropine and scopolamine on, 71
Piritramide, analgesia and antiemetic effects of, 152
Placebos, quantitative estimate of use of, 272–275
  reaction to, 271
'Polar Bears', group of Finnish recovered alcoholics, 363–372
Post-operative analgesia, requirements of, 151–152
Prescribing, of heroin, safeguards for, 296–298
  over-, role in induction of dependence, 286, 291
  practices, 274–279
  under D.D.A., 411
Protein synthesis, inhibition of, effect on narcotic analgesic tolerance, 82
  relation to narcotic analgesic tolerance, 77–92
  role in increase of receptors, 60
Psychedelic drugs, possible abuse of, 298
Psychogenic
  dependence, 281
  in monkey, 199–207
  inducing and non-inducing drugs, 205
  induction of, 203–204
  polydipsia, 9
Psychological
  dependence, 7
  drug-induced supersensitivity as model for, 53
  role of physiological factors in, 247
  factors, in alcoholism, 222, 233, 259
  functions of drug use, 13–30
Psychomotor disturbances, in alcoholism, 261, 267

Psychopharmacological effects of drugs, 16, 18
Psychotherapy, group, in Phoenix House therapeutic community, 400–404
Punishment, in elimination of dependence, 193–194
Puromycin, effect on morphine tolerance, 82
Purple hearts, non-dependent use of, 390

Quinalbarbitone, effect on sleep, 249
Quinine, in drinking water, reaction to, comparison with morphine, in rat, 214–215, 218

RNA polymerase, inhibition by actinomycin D, effect on narcotic analgesic tolerance, 80
  synthesis, response to actinomycin D, effect on narcotic analgesic tolerance, 82
Re-addiction, effect of environment on, 174, 280, 410–411
Receptors, anterior hypothalamic, effect of cholinomimetic agents on, 71
  mechanisms of, 57
  morphine, different for agonist and antagonist activity, 53
  number of, drug-induced changes in, 58
  effect on response to transmitter, 58
  mechanism of increase in, 60
  silent, 59
Reduction of drug reward, in elimination of dependence, 194
Reinforcement stimuli, effects of pairing of, 188–189
  in conditioning, 177–198
  variables of, 183–185
  reduction of effectiveness of, in elimination of dependence, 194
Repeat prescribing, 275–279
Reserpine, effect on sleep, 252
  effect on sympathetic transmission, 40
  pharmacological effects of, 56

Satiation, in elimination of dependence, 193
Scopolamine, effect on response of anterior hypothalamic receptors to pilocarpine, 71–72
Self-administration,
  of drugs, 174, 177–198
    chronic intravenous,
      in monkey, dependence or abstinence-induced, 204
      methods of, 200–201
      procedures for, 201–220
    effect of environment on, 181–183
    methods of, 186
    reinforcement stimuli for, 281
    relationship with other behaviour, 178, 189–191
  of morphine, in rat, 209–210
Senses, effect on taste for alcohol, 233
Sensitivity, to drugs, detection by chronic administration experiments, 206
Sensitization to drugs, of various tissues, 50–52
Sensory effects of drugs, 16
Sex distribution of dependence, 302, 327, 336
Sialagogic drugs, antagonism of sensitivity by, 51
Sleep, effect of drugs on, 243–254
  types of, 244–245
Social
  effects, of cannabis and alcohol, 238–241
  factors, in alcoholism, 222–223, 231–232
    in dependence, in man, 183, 217, 329
    in drug self-administration, in monkey, 191–192
    in induction of dependence, 376
    in non-dependent drug use, 379–380
Socio-cultural factors, differences in, role in dependence, 287
Splenic nerve, release of transmitter from, effect of disuse supersensitivity on, 70

Status-conferring function of drugs, 26–29
Stereochemical structure, role in predicting dependence liability, 163
Stimulant effect, of opiates, 31
Stimulants, interaction with adrenaline and noradrenaline, 55
  psychological dependence on, 54
Substitutes for drugs, 358–359
Substitution therapy, in elimination of dependence, 193
Sulphonal, dependence on, 9
Supersensitivity, antagonism by sialagogic drugs, 51
  denervation by, effect of receptor membrane hyperexcitability on, 85
  relation to withdrawal symptoms, 68
  disuse, characteristics of, 69
  surgically induced, 72
  induction by pharmacological denervation, effect on receptors, 57
  effect on withdrawal symptoms, 50–52
  non-specificity of, 51
  time course of, 38
Sympathin, release from splenic nerve, effect of disuse supersensitivity on, 70
  release of, effect of opiates on, 33
Sympathomimetic agents, effect on disuse supersensitivity, 69
Synapses, neurone discharge through, effect of tenotomy on, 71
Synaptic transmission, role of safety factor in, 44
Synthesis of analgesics, 150

Tachyphylaxis, to narcotics, relation to tolerance, 90
Tea, dependence on, 10
Temperature, body, response to cholinomimetic agents, 71–72
Tenotomy, effect on synaptic neurone discharge, 71
Tetrahydro-β-carbolines, analgesic activity and low toxicity of, 162

Therapy, of dependence, 287, 289, 292–293, 329
  of heroin dependence, 338–339
Tobacco, dependence on, 10
  psychological function of, 18–20
  use of, effect of drug use on, 383
Tolbutamide, metabolism and elimination of, effect on anaesthetic response to barbiturates, 114
  oxidation of, induction of barbiturate tolerance by, 114–116, 123
Tolerance, association with physical and psychological dependence, 49
  barbiturate, 52
  cross, 120–122, 123
    between ethanol and barbiturates, 167
    detection by chronic administration experiments, 206
    development in specific brain areas of, 170
  effect of partial agonist activity of opiates on, 41
  hypotensive drug, relation to transmitter surfeit theory, 41
  induction by metabolism of drugs, 111
    morphine, effect of actinomycin D on, 77–82
    induction by drinking of morphine solution, 219
    relation to distribution and metabolism in CNS, 97–100
  narcotic, relation to tachyphylaxis, 90
  opiate, 31
    effect of self-reversal on, 43
    time course of, 38
  pharmacological factors in, 31–47
  phenobarbitone, effect of dosage on, 125
    effect of response of CNS on, 124
  physiological, relationship to drug abuse, 199
  possible induction by axonal accumulation of acetylcholine, 38
Toxicity, somatic and behavioural, detection by chronic administration experiments, 206

Training, in Phoenix House therapeutic community, 404–407
Transmission, synaptic, role of safety factor in, 44
Transmitter, accumulation by nerves and brain, 40
  endogenous, role in induction of dependence, 49
  humoral, effect on receptors, 57–58
  interaction with receptors, 60, 62
  release depression of, effects of, 37
    effect of opiates on, 32
    from neurones, effect of denervation on, 92
    from receptor cells, 70
  surfeit theory, 38
    relation to tolerance to hypotensives, 41
Tranylcypromine, effect on sleep, 249
Treatment,
  of dependence, in Phoenix House community, 395–407
  by transfer to other drugs, 14
Tryptophan, effect on sleep, 249

Unemployment, relationship to dependence, 350
Urinary excretion, role in individual variation of drug metabolism, applicability of, 166
Urine acidity, effect on excretion of amphetamine, 130–133
  effect on excretion of ephedrine, methylephedrine and norephedrine, 133–135
  effect on excretion of narcotic analgesics, 136–142
  role in individual variations in drug metabolism, 138–142
  morphine metabolites in, 102, 106
Utopia-achieving function of drugs, 29

Withdrawal,
  influence on effect of drugs on sleep, 245
  symptoms, association with nonnarcotics, as conditioned responses, 352–353
    in alcoholism, 261
    control of, 264

Withdrawal symptoms (*contd.*)—
  in barbiturate dependence, 165
  in diagnosis of dependence, 4, 8, 89, 155–158
  in disuse supersensitivity, 67
  induction by depression of transmitter release, 37
  induction by drinking morphine solution, 219
  induction by nalorphine during morphine tolerance, 106
  lack of, in heroin dependence, 20
  morphine-induced, effect of levallorphan on, 32